PAINTING THE CITY RED

D1559069

ASIA-PACIFIC: CULTURE, POLITICS, AND SOCIETY

Editors: *Rey Chow, H. D. Harootunian,* and *Masao Miyoshi*

PAINTING THE CITY RED

Chinese Cinema and the Urban Contract

Yomi Braester

DUKE UNIVERSITY PRESS
Durham & London 2010

© 2010 Duke University Press
All rights reserved

Printed in the United States of
America on acid-free paper ∞
Designed by Jennifer Hill
Typeset in Scala
by Keystone Typesetting, Inc.

Library of Congress Cataloging-
in-Publication Data appear on the last
printed page of this book.

For my parents, Dana and Carol Braester

CONTENTS

FOR YEARS, whenever in Beijing, I would visit a hole-in-the-wall eatery that served my favorite cumin mutton. One summer day in 2003, the waiter handed me a freshly printed business card. The whole row of houses was about to be razed, and the card bore a map indicating the restaurant's future location. The card drove home for me that I, like many who live in China's rapidly changing cities, have been keeping a mental map of places that no longer exist and of new spaces that will soon appear. Navigating the city is also a journey across times. This is a study of such journeys, taken by residents, planners, and filmmakers. This book is dedicated to all those who strive to preserve the city's multiple temporalities.

Creating better cities is a joint effort, and the same is true of my book. Many people generously contributed to this project. I was encouraged by the willingness of prominent filmmakers, theater professionals, and artists to talk at length and provide materials: Cao Fei, Arthur Chu, Feng Jicai, Feng Mengbo, Feng Xiaogang, Gao Yiwei, Han Yuqi, Huang Jianxin, Jia Zhangke, Stan Lai, Li Longyun, Li Shaohong, Lin Cheng-sheng, Lou Ye, Ning Ying, Ou Ning, Peng Xiaolian, Ren Ming, Sheng Qi, Shu Yi, Song Dong, Su Shuyang, Tian Zhuang-zhuang, Wang Haowei, Wang Xiaoshuai, Wang Zheng, Wu Nien-jen, Wu Qiong, Wu Tianming, Xie Fei, Xu Dawei, Yang Lina, Yu Kanping, Zhang Ding, Zhang Yang, Zhang Yuan, Zhao Liang, Zheng Dongtian, and Zhou Xiaowen. Their insights, especially into how movies and stage plays are influenced by negotiation with decision makers, have changed my way of thinking about what it takes to visualize and envision the city.

I encountered an even steeper learning curve when inquiring into urban policy. My principal guides have been Dan Abramson and Wang Jun, for whom the city is never what it seems. I am also indebted to members of the Organization of Urban Re's (OURS) team in Taipei, who provided written and photographic materials and information: Guo Boxiu, Huang Liling, Huang Sun Chuan, Min Jay Kang, K. C. Liu, and Zhang Liben. Other urbanists who shared their experience and knowledge include Jeff Hou, Qiao Yanjun, Zhang Song, Zhang Yan, and Zhao Peng. I treasure the many hours I have spent in their company.

The connections necessary for this study were often facilitated by friends, whose passion for their work is matched by the size of their address books. I am especially grateful to Chang Tsong-zung, Claire Conceison, Luo Xueying, Gloria Wang, Zhang Xianmin, and Zhang Yaxuan. Zhong Dafeng, now a longtime collaborator, introduced me to his charming mother, the late director Gao Yiwei.

I have consulted the following libraries and archives: Beijing Municipal Archive; the archives of the Beijing People's Art Theater Museum; China Film Archive; Chinese Taipei Film Archive; East Asia Library at the University of Washington; Harvard-Yenching Library; National Central Library, Taipei; National Library of China; the archives of the National Museum of the Modern Chinese Literature; Shanghai Audiovisual Archives; Shanghai Municipal Archive; Starr East Asian Library at Columbia University; Sterling Library at Yale University; Taipei City Archive; and the archives of the Urban Development Department of the Taipei Municipal Government. I am grateful to Mimi Lin at the Cloud Gate Dance Theater; Dianna Xu, then at the University of Washington; Yu Wenping at the Beijing People's Art Theater; and Zhang Jingyue at the Shanghai Media Group for being so proactive in locating resources. Cui Yongyuan, Ed Lafranco, Stefan Landsberger, and Paola Voci also provided valuable materials. Special thanks are due to Wang Zhaohui, who as Li Shaohong's assistant secured the image from Li's *Baober in Love* for the book cover.

When the dreaded moment came to sit down and write in relative solitude, I found support from colleagues who listened to my ideas and commented on drafts. These include: Jennifer Bean, Chris Berry, Marshall Brown (time and again), Robert Chi, Peggy Chiao Hsiung-ping, Paul Clark, Charles Laughlin, Wenchi Lin, John M. Liu (my editor-in-law), Lü Xinyu, Carlos Rojas, Sun Bai, James Tweedie, Ban Wang, David Der-wei Wang, Zhuoyi Wang, Emilie Yueh-yu Yeh, Zhang Enhua, Yingjin Zhang, and

Zhang Zhen. The excellence of my colleagues at the Department of Comparative Literature, the Department of Asian Languages and Literature, and the China Studies Program at the University of Washington has been a constant source of inspiration.

I am indebted to Chen Pingyuan and David Der-wei Wang for organizing the conference "Beijing History and Memory" at Peking University, at which I first presented my thoughts on *Dragon Whisker Creek*, now elaborated in chapter 1; to Elizabeth Perry and Xudong Zhang, for the conference at New York University on Shanghai that set me on the path that resulted in chapter 2; to David Bordwell, Ru-Shou Robert Chen, Nicole Huang, Wenchi Lin, and James Tweedie for putting together the symposia at National Central University, National Taiwan University, the University of Wisconsin, and Yale University, during which I first aired my thoughts on Taiwan cinema, as developed in chapter 5; to Zhang Zhen for the "Urban Generation" conference at New York University, which allowed me to first consolidate the ideas that have evolved into chapter 6; and to Julia Strauss and Michel Hocks, initiators of the *China Quarterly* workshop at Harvard University, which led to chapter 7.

I have received many valuable comments from colleagues and students during public talks at Columbia University, CUNY–College of Staten Island, Duke University, Emory University, Fudan University, Haifa University, Hebrew University in Jerusalem, Pacific Lutheran University, Pratt Institute, Reed College, University of British Columbia, University of Florida, and Yale University. I have also learned much from my students in Seattle and at my summer seminars at the Beijing Film Academy.

Although my research has taken me in different directions since, I have introduced related ideas and materials in essays in *China Quarterly, Journal of Contemporary China, Modern China, Journal of Modern Literature in Chinese, Modern Languages Quarterly*, and *positions: east asia cultures critique* (see bibliography). Related chapters appeared also in the volumes *Beijing: Dushi xiangxiang yu wenhua jiyi* (Beijing: Urban Imagination and Cultural Memory), edited by Chen Pingyuan and Wang Dewei; *Chinese Films in Focus: Twenty-Five New Takes*, edited by Chris Berry; *Cinema Taiwan: State of the Art, States of the Mind*, edited by Darrel Davis and Robert Chen Hsiu-ru; *Contested Modernities in Chinese Literature*, edited by Charles Laughlin; *The New Chinese Movement: Documentary Film*, edited by Lisa Rofel, Chris Berry, and Lü Xinyu; and *The Urban Generation: Chinese Cinema and Society at the Turn of the Twenty-First Century*, edited by Zhen Zhang.

Essential support for my research was provided by the University of Washington—a course release through the Simpson Center for the Humanities and travel funding from the China Studies Program Fritz Foundation; the East Asia Center; the Institute for Transnational Studies; and the Royalty Research Fund. Madeleine Yue Dong, Kent Guy, Kristi Roundtree, and Kathleen Woodward deserve special mention for facilitating these grants.

From the project's inception, I thought of Duke University Press as the most suitable publisher. I am grateful to J. Reynolds Smith for his constant encouragement, while I was still writing the book and after I submitted the manuscript to him. The entire team at Duke University Press was a joy to work with. The two anonymous readers provided detailed comments that have much improved the manuscript.

Writing a book is also a family affair. It is impossible to imagine this study without the support of my parents and of my wife, Michelle Liu, who has been a fellow traveler throughout the project—even if it often meant that we would travel on different geographical paths. Her common sense, doubt of accepted academic wisdom, and precise formulations show on every page. This book will remind me of my love for her and our shared love for Talia and Lelia.

Film and the Urban Contract

THIS BOOK inquires into the relationship between city and film in the People's Republic of China (PRC) and Taiwan from 1949 to 2008—from the establishment of the People's Republic to the Beijing Olympics. China's cityscapes have transformed from drab rows of uniform housing to gentrified neighborhoods and glitzy malls—and from live museums of vernacular architecture to showcases for brand-name urban design. The urban change is the result of policies that abandoned Maoist economic planning in favor of capitalist globalization, yet the transformation is also part of a shift in visual practices. The cities' new looks, now made famous by broadcasts from the Olympics, result from novel observation practices, imaging technologies, and concepts of visualization. The visual media, and especially the stage and screen arts, have played a crucial role in shaping Chinese cities in the past sixty years.

Like many modern urbanists around the world, Chinese planners set out to build better cities to engineer better citizens. The task required complex networks and collaborations, forming what I call "the urban contract." This book details how this evolving contract resulted in redacting structure designs and city plans, redefining interior and public spaces, and reassessing the value of cultural heritage sites and contemporary political monuments. New visual practices have accompanied the material developments—stage plays and films display architectural models; filmmakers borrow imaging techniques from advertising; playwrights redefine the "fourth wall" and performance spaces; cameramen use photography as a form of preservation. Urban planning and the cinema have coalesced in creating new ways to represent lived space and imagine historical time.

The urban contract foregrounds the power structure underlying urbanist discourses and cinematic trends. This book, however, does not simply seek to present another account of art in the face of autocratic and ideological state control.[1] I devote much of this chapter to explaining the fraught relations between filmmakers and the government and to showing the limits of audiences' agency—there is no escaping the crass political aspects of power. Yet my fundamental concern in this book is the interplay of image, space, and temporality. I am interested in how the cinema has translated ideology into time capsules identified with specific sites, creating reified—indeed habitable—allegories of power.

The road I take is circuitous, weaving through analysis of urban history, urbanist debates, and government policy, following leads suggested by archival material and ethnographic research. These seeming diversions may baffle my fellow literary and film scholars—I, too, was surprised to find myself using the tools of disciplines in which I still consider myself a guest. However, such an approach is necessitated by the task of tracing a discourse that has redefined concepts such as public governance, planning professionalism, and cinematic vision—all at the same time.

As a historical study, the book offers a long-term perspective on urban cinema in China. From our present vantage point, it is tempting to focus on the post-Maoist reforms; yet it is important to trace the arc back to the early days of the People's Republic and the Republic of China (ROC) in Taiwan. Our story begins with a high-level meeting in 1950.

⚑ URBAN HISTORY REDUX

Films about the city are unlikely candidates for intrigue and clandestine dealings by heads of state. Yet a history of urban cinema in the People's Republic of China may start with an intimate meeting among some of the country's senior officials. On July 14, 1950, the premier and foreign minister, Zhou Enlai, hosted a dinner. Among the guests was Li Bozhao—one of the only women veterans of the Long March and the wife of Zhou's right-hand man Yang Shangkun, as well as the director of the newly established Beijing People's Art Theater (BPAT). The times were tense—that same day, the campaign to resist the U.S. invasion of Korea and Taiwan was formally launched, and Zhou would become increasingly busy securing Soviet support in the developing Korean crisis. Yet that evening he dedicated his attention to a seemingly trifling matter. The evening's guest of honor was the novelist and playwright Lao She, and the premier discussed with him a plan to write a drama for Li Bozhao's theater about Longxugou, or Dragon Whisker Creek.[2] The Longxugou area, at the heart of Beijing's southern section, was undergoing extensive changes as part of efforts to facilitate worker mobility and transform the city into an industrial hub. The resulting piece by Lao She, *Dragon Whisker Creek*, was staged at BPAT, and a special performance was arranged at Huairentang Hall, inside the party leadership's compound at Zhongnanhai. Mao Zedong bestowed words of approval in person.[3] Lao She was rewarded with an appointment to the Beijing Municipal Government Council in 1951.[4] In 1952 the play was adapted into what became a film classic.

Official accounts of the making of *Dragon Whisker Creek* do not mention the meeting with Zhou Enlai. Even Lao She wove a different tale, claiming that he visited the formerly disaster-plagued site and was moved to write a play about its miraculous transformation.[5] Only when we cross Lao She's version with Li Bozhao's part in instigating the play, as detailed over thirty years later in the memoirs of the playwright's aide, and only by combining the two reports with the record of the premier's dinner with Lao She that same evening, do the political connections surface. The scant details about the conversation at Zhou's dinner table, supplemented by declassified memos of the Public Works Bureau, indicate that the play was an important tool for promoting urban redevelopment, complementing municipal and national policies.

Insofar as a stage play or film is defined through the joint efforts of all who produce and promote it, its "art world" (to borrow Howard Becker's term)[6] includes not only scriptwriters, filmmakers, distributors, censors, and critics, but also municipal- and state-level policymakers, professional planners, and—when their voice is heard—residents and grassroots activists. In the case of *Dragon Whisker Creek*, we should take into account the input of officials as high ranking as Mayor Peng Zhen and Premier Zhou Enlai, and of planners including the prominent architect Liang Sicheng and the head of the Public Works Bureau, Cao Yanxing (both Peng and Liang became Lao She's personal friends). *Dragon Whisker Creek* owes its ideological message, literary form, and very existence to the institutional structure within which it was produced.

Another privileged glimpse into the close management of the production's intended message is offered by a surviving playbill of the film's premiere. The release drew audiences by screening the film simultaneously in three locations: the Workers' Club as well as the Youhao (Friendship) and Jiefang (Liberation) theaters. The playbill includes a synopsis to be copied onto community blackboards as well as questions for discussion, the last of which reads: "Talk about the connection between *Dragon Whisker Creek* and today's democratic governance and establishing of a municipal government. How can they solve the most urgent problems of the working people?" The playbill reveals how officials hoped the film would influence public perception of policy.

Knowing the background for the production modifies our understanding of the relation between the cinema and the city. Rather than reflecting the existing urban conditions, *Dragon Whisker Creek* fudges historical facts, aggrandizes the role of the new government, assuages citizens' potential fears, fashions social organization as based on the vernacular architecture of the courtyard house, and idealizes the socialist city as a site of production. As this case shows, the city and the cinema are more than complementary manifestations of material structure and artistic imagination. They are also more than parallel spectacles of modern life. Rather, they play an active role in the imposition of government power, the formation of communities, the establishment of cultural norms, and the struggle for civil society. They are traces of the ongoing battle over the image of China's cities since 1949, which culminated in the 2008 Beijing Olympics.

I hope that this study offers a timely intervention. In my first book, *Witness against History*, I presented an alternative narrative of twentieth-century Chinese literature and film while engaging the post-Tiananmen debates on the "Chinese enlightenment." In this book I aim to participate in the discussions on how China's cities should grow. Many observers have noted the astounding growth of China's megacities and have argued that it is a key indicator of the evolvement of civil society and the processes of globalization.[7] Following the "spatial turn" in the late twentieth century, studies of urban culture have integrated geographical, architectural, and sociological insights. Few, however, have remarked on the role of visual culture in effecting urban transformation. The opening salvos in every wave of urban reform since 1949 have been fired through stage plays and films, not only because they are effective media but also because urban design must include cultural restructuring. The cinema has redefined the relationship linking the viewer, the screen, and the city as one between citizen, ideology, and political and economic power. Much more than a vehicle for forming individual and collective identities, film has provided a discursive framework for urban policies. Inquiring into the urban contract allows us to study how film has helped shape the city.

The cinema is often described as exerting power over the audience, and film scholars have attempted to probe the minds of filmmakers and filmgoers to explain how that power unfolds. Studies describe the attraction of the spectacle, focusing on the moment of encounter between the screen and the viewer. The cinematic experience purportedly either divests the spectators of their judgment or awakens them as autonomous subjects; film is either overpowering or empowering. Such accounts give short shrift, however, to the larger social structure within which films are made, disseminated, interpreted, and acted on. The relationship between cinema and the city, as I explore it, stipulates that the spectator is not merely a gazing subject; nor is the city merely a given environment where films are shot and in which the cinema is present in the form of studios, theaters, boards, and screens. The city neither frames the viewer nor is itself framed by the cinematic gaze.

This study diverges from the prevalent emphasis on the apparatus of film exhibition and its manipulation of spectators' desires. The classical model assumes the conditions of a dark theater, an immobile spectator, and a single viewing. Anne Friedberg notes the limitations of these suppositions and argues that contemporary screen technology and culture extend spectatorship in time and space, yet Friedberg too defines the cinema primarily by the act of viewing.[8] For my purposes, imagining the cinema's impact through the viewer's ingenuous encounter with luminous images is inadequate. The behind-the-scenes details of *Dragon Whisker Creek* exemplify how spectatorship theory is belied by the exercise of power at every stage of production, distribution, and critical response. The filmic event is predicated on political, economic, and ideological forces that channel cinematic production and predispose the audience. The influence of the cinema derives not so much from any intrinsic force of the moving image as from mediating among these external sources of power.

Rather than probing into subjective experience, I look at how films help to forge a social contract for the city. Manuel Castells and Jordi Borja have used the term *urban contract* to call for "an integral policy" relying on the collaboration "between the government and the citizens, between the administration and companies, between public bodies and citizen associations."[9] Whereas Castells and Borja find in the urban contract a model for civil society, I use the term not to prescribe but rather to draw attention to a particular power structure. For good and ill, the authorities, nongovernmental institutions, and the media are all invested in constructing the city. Urban policy, in the broad sense used here, may be defined as measures for regulating the balance among three major players—the government (state and local), the developers (self-funded investors and hired contractors), and the residents (existing and potential). The tripartite relationship is subject to constant negotiation. Other agents mediate among these elements, within the constraints of their own power. The most visible intermediaries are professional planners, who may work for the government, act as consultants, or engage in independent activism. Other mediators include writers, journalists, scholars, advertisers—and filmmakers. This book primarily addresses the cinema's mediation between different visions of the city.

Film and drama occupy a position similar to that of urban planning, as go-betweens in a high-stakes game of political and economic power. Filmmakers and playwrights confront the same obstacles that architects know as "planning in the face of power," the need to think professionally and act politically at the same time.[10] Filmmaking in the face of power—or rather, in the midst of the power structure—is at the heart of Chinese urbanism.

✤ URBAN FILM IN A HISTORICAL PERSPECTIVE

As a historical study, this book traces the symbiosis between film, drama, and Chinese cities since 1949. Although I focus on cinema, theatrical performances have also taken part in the interaction, especially since plays were often staged (and then typically modified and restaged) in preparation for, or in lieu of, film productions more costly in time and money. To symbolize the New China, cities not only had to be physically remolded, but their new image also needed to be disseminated and interpreted through plays and movies. The cinema was part of a larger experiment by the socialist state, aimed at producing new spatial practices. Screen and stage productions rallied popular support for urbanization plans. Since the dominant ideology was communism, the productions may be said to have *painted the city red*. Later films have carved out a space for criticism but continue to contribute to the discourse on urban policy.

The inevitable ideological coloring notwithstanding, I am not interested in turning the urbanist debates into exemplars of state oppression and heroic dissent. Admittedly, vested interest, hubris, and folly resulted in less livable cities and less viable urban growth. Legislation decreeing demolition-and-relocation has favored powerful developers over low-income residents, and cultural amnesia over historic preservation. Yet even though these concerns are uniquely manifest in Chinese cities, they are not unique to China. Tom Campanella, although highly critical of post-Maoist hyperurbanization, shows similar cases of bias and misjudgment in urban planning around the world.[11] Arguably unparalleled in China are filmmakers' and playwrights' attention to and involvement in details of urban policy.

A historical perspective allows us to discern shifting nuances in the cinematic intervention in urbanism. Both the aims and the means of policy —often hard to distinguish from each other—have changed over the decades, from facilitating state power to establishing sustainable communities, from channeling industrial growth to creating viable financial centers, from promoting ideological strongholds to preserving cultural assets. Interacting with the intended and unintended effects of policy, films have touched on every element of urban design. They have depicted the laying of sewage pipes and presented citywide plans; shown how houses are assigned and encouraged the redistribution of industry; made the case for historic preservation and celebrated the real estate market.

To investigate both trends and particularities, I rely on close readings and general discourse analysis of about 150 films and plays. To trace tangible connections between the cultural productions, professional plans, and political decisions, I draw not only on the texts but also on archival documents, including correspondence among municipal planners and memos of consultations within Communist Party units. In addition, I interviewed more than forty playwrights, theater professionals, film directors, planners, residents, journalists, and public intellectuals especially for this book. These exchanges have provided behind-the-scenes details such as changes to scripts and stage sets, meetings at the censors' board, neighborhood committee dynamics, and unreported protests by residents.[12] The passion and generosity of all those involved in sharing their experiences attest to the importance if not urgency that they ascribe to China's urban vision.

The result is a corrective history of Chinese urban cinema, with emphasis on its historical roots. The popularity and critical acclaim of Sixth Generation filmmakers and the New Taiwan Cinema, deserved as they are, are also misguided in stressing the trends' novelty. After the demise of Maoism (and the concurrent dismantling of the Chiangs' rule in Taiwan), films have helped change official policy and reinterpret city space. Yet the challenge of post-Maoist and post-Chiang cinemas lies largely in their reaction to the established images of state productions, harking back to *Dragon Whisker Creek* and other works. Moreover, both early PRC drama and film and less cutting-edge contemporary works have their rewards. The appeal of experimental and adversarial forms has drawn scholarly attention away from the fine scriptwriting, acting, and camera work that can be found in conservative and even propagandistic plays and films. A historical perspective is rendered even more necessary by the recent groundbreaking scholarship on contemporary urban culture and film, in particular Zhang Zhen's *The Urban Generation: Chinese Cinema and Society at the Turn of the Twenty-First Century* and Robin Visser's *Cities Surround the Countryside: Urban Aesthetics in Post-socialist China*. Visser argues persuasively that a new urban consciousness arose in the 1990s, so that "the city became a subject in its own right." Urbanism became the object of display, the topic of public debate, and the subject matter of sociopolitical scholarship.[13] In 2008, China Film Press published two monographs on urban cinema. Chu Weihua focuses on the evolving role of the urban citizen in Chinese films and catalogues the thematic concerns throughout the twentieth century. Chen Xiaoyun notes the ideological implications of depicting everyday urban existence in recent movies on perceptions of space and the body.[14] The current surge of interest in Chinese urbanism and Urban Cinema might obfuscate their roots in earlier discourses.

Studies of contemporary urbanism symptomatically limit their inquiry to the construction of new "urban aesthetics," "urban consciousness," and "urban identity," distinguishing between "how the city *is imagined*" and "its materiality."[15] Attention to the Maoist period, when the state played a key role in both envisioning the city and constructing it, gives the lie to this distinction. In film in particular, urban subject matter has been a consistent

concern since 1949, even through the period dominated by Fifth Generation directors and their purported focus on the rural environment. To regard
urban films as breaking free from Maoist and Fifth Generation aesthetics—
and perhaps returning to the golden days of prewar Shanghai cinema—
ignores underlying continuities across periods and sites.[16] John Friedman
notes that "adopting globalization as the analytical framework for the study
of cities tends to privilege outside forces to the neglect of internal visions,
historical trajectories, and endogenous capabilities. It also places emphasis
on economics to the exclusion of sociocultural and political variables."[17] The
same observations are valid for the study of urban film.

⚶ BEYOND THE URBAN AND CINEMATIC SUBLIME
Coming to terms with film's role in the urban contract calls also for rethinking the function of the cinema in urban modernity. The scholar's instinct,
when dealing with these issues, is to reach for the arsenal derived from the
writings of Siegfried Kracauer and Walter Benjamin. Observing the bourgeoisie of the Weimar Republic, Kracauer concluded that the new urban
environment caused ennui, which younger people alleviated through escap-
ist entertainment, including the cinema.[18] Inspired in part by Kracauer's
criticism of the modern city, Benjamin developed a theory of urban experience. Benjamin (following Charles Baudelaire) identifies the modern experience in the contact with the city crowd. Benjamin's "experience" (*Erfah-
rung*), whether in relation to the city or to film, is predicated on a first-hand
encounter (*Erlebnis*). This reliance on subjective contact delimits and strains
institutional analysis.

In view of Benjamin's influence, and for readers interested in related
debates, it is worth noting in detail Benjamin's reliance on a Kantian notion
of the subject—an autonomous, self-aware participant who contributes to a
greater consciousness. Benjamin's focus on the subjective reaction to the
urban environment is motivated by his wish to update Kantian epistemology, an effort he began already with his 1918 essay, "The Program of the
Coming Philosophy."[19] He achieved this program two decades later in his
study of nineteenth-century Paris, which explores the effects of placing the
Kantian subject among the buildings and crowds of the city. Whereas Kant
finds the reaffirmation of the subject in the encounter with the sublime,
Benjamin locates a similar moment, grounded in historical materialism, in

the urban experience. The Kantian "respect" (*Achtung*)—the figure of fear that partially revokes judgment only to reassert the observer's subjectivity—is transmogrified into Benjamin's "series of shocks and collisions" while moving in traffic, which numbs individuals but can also enhance their consciousness. The experience of the street is described in terms reminiscent of the Kantian dynamic sublime: "Fear, revulsion, and horror were the emotions which the big-city crowd aroused in those who first observed it." A similar experience, according to Benjamin, occurs when watching moving pictures, an endless succession of shocks, twenty-four frames per second: "In a film, perception conditioned by shock was established as a formal principle." In resisting the instinctive urge to repress the shock, the subject avoids being "cheated out of his experience."[20] The city and the cinema are catalysts in Benjamin's Kantian experiment.

Even though Benjamin places Kantian epistemology within a materialist framework, his view of the city and the cinema is remarkably dependent on the individual psyche. Benjamin grounds his thesis in philosophical reasoning rather than in empirical observation, continuing the search for human transcendence over materiality that has obsessed Kantian philosophers. For Benjamin, subjects who recognize themselves in the crowd achieve nothing short of the awakening of their historical consciousness. Benjamin famously acknowledges the role of urban planning (notably through the figure of Georges-Eugène Haussmann, the designer of Paris's boulevards) and of visual renditions of the city (such as the photographs of Félix Nadar, who documented Haussmann's projects). Yet for Benjamin, the streets and moving images are ready-made stimuli, the prerequisites to a chain of events that starts with the encounter and results in the self-affirmation of the subject. The neo-Kantian project sees the city and the cinema as spectacles offered for the subject's sensibilities, impervious to the flows of power.

In the Chinese context, Benjamin's terms resurface in Yingjin Zhang's *The City in Modern Chinese Literature and Film*. Zhang regards "the city as a site of cultural production," which leads him to inquire into "how the city is perceived and imagined," "recollected," and "reconstructed."[21] The city, described in the passive voice, remains a given entity. Many subsequent readings, including some of my earlier essays, focus on subjective alienation and consumer culture, disregarding the ties between urban culture and policy.[22] "Urban culture" is widely used as shorthand for urban *commodity* culture, fetishizing the everyday and marginalizing urbanist discourse.

The impetus behind the inquiry into cinema and urban culture remains important in that it asks what spheres outside film production and reception help define the cinema. A growing number of studies acknowledge how other cultural fields border and interpenetrate filmmaking to the point of changing the social functions, latitude of action, and even physical media of what is understood as cinematic. Yet analysis of "urban culture" tends to stay at the level of the individual subject, a hero surviving in an alienating environment. Film studies too often glorify the individual who sublimates sensorial stimuli. Scholars such as Giuliana Bruno and Tom Gunning have compared the early filmgoer to the paragon of Benjaminian subjectivity, the flâneur.[23] Studies of many hues have focused on subjective reaction. Laura Mulvey investigates how the spectator is called on to identify with the film's dominating ideology. David Bordwell looks for the cognitive formula through which the spectator processes visual stimuli. Steven Shaviro asks whether it is an optical or more corporeal experience. And insofar as the spectator's reactions should be historicized, Miriam Hansen inquires what modes of perception are precipitated by the cinema as a modern technology of observation.[24] These questions look for answers in the human psyche rather than in systemic structures. The Kantian inquiry into the sublime has persisted in the repeated question of whether urban film culture overwhelms the subject and plays into the hands of an oppressive social system or resists and sublimates conforming structures.

The neo-Kantian emphasis on subjective experience leads to another problematic assertion, namely, that the cinema can create an alternative public sphere. Inspired by Oskar Negt's and Alexander Kluge's argument for multiple, potentially counterhegemonic public spheres, Miriam Hansen finds in early screening locations "an alternative . . . organization of experience" and argues that "early cinema . . . provided the formal conditions for an alternative public sphere, a structural possibility of articulating experience in a communicative, relatively autonomous form." Zhang Zhen makes a similar claim in the Chinese context, proposing that "the experience of film becomes deeply enmeshed in the metropolitan experience as a whole" and that cinema in early twentieth-century Shanghai "helped forge a new human sensorium . . . against the dehumanizing effects of industrial capitalism and colonialism."[25] Hansen's and Zhang's interest in "the cinematic experience" as the seed for subjective transformation dovetails with Benjamin's quest for emancipatory elements in modern culture. Yet in celebrating vernacular culture, the body, and affect as sites of alternative signification, scholars might slight the warnings of Michel Foucault and Antonio Gramsci that self-expression and resistance are co-opted into the hegemonic structure. As I have argued elsewhere, there is no reason to believe that the public sphere is transparent or committed to the common good.[26] Film studios, critics, and advocacy groups have been infamously reluctant to let the audience form its independent impressions. Audiences often go into the theater with clear knowledge of what they are going to think of the film, and opinions outside of the mainstream are stifled. Hollywood in particular has thrived on giving moviegoers the illusion that they patronize socially engaged films.[27] Not only is there a dearth of evidence that the cinema creates an alternative consciousness; existing data also point to the pervasive and effective manipulation of spectators by interested parties. Deliberate and sometimes forced policies may override individual perception.

The filmgoer is neither an autonomous subject nor an entrepreneurial agent. Spectators, rather, are regulated subjects, subsumed by the structure of the urban contract; they are Foucauldian "subjects of discourse" rather than autonomous entities.[28] The urban citizen does not discover identity through cinematic experience; on the contrary, films actively promote an ideological mold that forms the citizen. Insofar as the cinema provides a "horizon for the experience of modernization and modernity," as Miriam Hansen contends, it is a horizon that is often receding rather than expanding, and an experience that is at least as institutionally imposed as it is subjectively generated.

Even to the extent that Hansen and Zhang offer valid observations on early cinema, 1949 marks the emergence of new urban and cinematic discourses in China. City governance was identified with caring for the nation's well-being, and the cinema was subjected to heavy-handed political intervention. Film production and reception included directors conferencing with state ministers, scriptwriters working under Party fiat, and audiences primed by campaigns. The urban policies and cinematic practices in the PRC and Taiwan since 1949 cannot be contained within the dynamics of spectatorship.[29]

To move beyond questions of subjective experience—that is, beyond the urban and cinematic sublime—we must reconsider the relationship between the citizen, the city, and the cinema. Mark Shiel notes that to understand the cinema as an active agent we must resist the classical Marxist model of economic base and ideological superstructure, with its "reifying tendency to speak of cinema simply in terms of the text and its reflection of urban and social change 'on the ground.' " Shiel calls for "a sociology of the cinema . . . with specific focus on the role of cinema in the physical, social, cultural, and economic development of cities."[30] To this challenge we may add the need to acknowledge the importance of policy and planning. The city's social functions are prefigured by power relations, and film studies should also address the institutional context provided by the urban contract.

James Hay further interlinks the cinema and the city: "Film's role in maintaining and modifying social relations has to do both with how it becomes part of an environment and how it enables or constrains navigation of that landscape."[31] In other words, the cinema produces the social dimension of space, by dint of its mere presence and as an active force. Yet Hay makes a more provocative observation: film is "dispersed within an *environment* of sites that *defines* (in spatial terms) the meanings, uses and place of 'the cinematic.' "[32] To extrapolate from this statement, the cinema's distinct attributes include its existence in space and demarcation of space, and "the cinematic," often shrouded in the mystique of subjective feelings, arises in fact from discourses of power.

Key thinkers on urban modernity, from Kracauer and Benjamin to Michel de Certeau and David Harvey, have bequeathed the following questions: How does urban technology account for the formation of the modern subject? What is the role of visual culture in transforming modern identity? I suggest that these questions may be reversed: What ideological formations enable the new material environment? What institutional changes and social contracts privilege visual expression, and the cinema in particular? It is not the city that gives rise to movies; the cinema is not even merely the continuation of the city by other means, as David Clarke proposes.[33] It is rather films—in direct interaction with political decisions and architectural blueprints—that forge an urban contract and create the material city and its ideological constructs.

PROPAGANDA: FILM IN LONG DURATION

The epistemology of the cinema, defined by the encounter between spectator and ready-made artifact, presumes not only the autonomous subjectivity of the spectator but also the uniqueness of the projected image. Too much hinges on speculating about the moment of sitting in the film theater as a singular event, as if it were a temporal rupture that transforms the spectators' consciousness. It is useful to think of the films examined here not as events confined to the time and place of their screening but rather as long-duration historical processes. The encounter between the film and the audience is often prescribed, monitored in real time, and rewritten after the fact. In other words, films have been marketed and consumed as propaganda products.

Many critics have targeted propaganda films as anathema to the spectators' agency—an understandable view given formulations such as Sergei Eisenstein's call for the cinema to "plough [the audience's] psyche."[34] Propaganda is perceived as a menace to faithful representation and the robber of subjective experience—whether in André Bazin's discussion of Stalin films as mythmaking and a distortion of history, in Jacques Ellul's view of mass media as a technique that renders social manipulation imperceptible, or in Jean Baudrillard's mention, in the same breath, of the October Revolution and advertisement as related forms of marketing, be it of ideas or commodities.[35] After discarding the quest for mimesis and recognizing the inevitability of a mediatized world, propaganda has remained the last straw man to beat in defending reality from the simulacrum.

The political system in the PRC adds an unsavory dimension to propaganda, but the utility of film deserves more evenhanded scrutiny. Vying for the power to represent and shape the city has often resulted in the overwhelming influence of the government over the cinema and of the cinema over the citizen. Yet we should not dismiss the films at hand as mere tools of totalitarian control. Few filmmakers are blind followers of doctrine—or, for that matter, indomitable freedom fighters. Insofar as filmmaking is on a par with urban planning, as a form of negotiation with power, it needs to constantly redefine its relation to current politics. Fashioning films as either tools of oppression or vehicles for individual and collective awakening ignores the position of the cinema as an intermediary between centers of power.

Propaganda has acquired a bad name among critics for its resistance to systems of meaning that leave space for multiple interpretations. Cultural criticism has largely focused on eliciting concealed and repressed signs and values. Yet the joy of unearthing the collective desires in what Fredric Jameson calls "conspiratorial texts"[36] is thwarted by propaganda works that lay claim to total representation: all that should be expressed has already been expressed. I have analyzed elsewhere the Maoist insistence on the proper transmission of doctrine, to the point of foreclosing multiple decodings.[37] Postulating the existence of a "political unconscious" requires a better understanding of the abjective conscious that proscribes it.

In other words, the study of propaganda is not only necessitated by the subject matter of this book, it is also important for resituating film within the structure of the urban contract. Propaganda, like genre conventions, develops over time and in response to the producers' changing needs. Rick Altman observes that the discourse on genre evolves to suit the interests of studios, critics, and distributors.[38] Likewise, we must look at propaganda productions not only diachronically but also synchronically—that is, not as endless repetition of dogma but rather as context-sensitive iterations of contemporary policies.[39] Paradoxically, it is the time-sensitive nature of propaganda that requires its analysis as a long-duration process.

✥ FILMMAKING AND THE NEGOTIATION WITH POWER

In outlining the shifting relationship of the cinema to seats of power, this book may be divided schematically into two halves. The first (the first three and a half chapters) deals with plays and films instigated by the PRC government and demonstrates the immediate stakes for urban policy in state propaganda. The second half of the book is devoted to filmmaking outside the official PRC production system and in post-Chiang Taiwan and examines how film promotes alternative urban visions. This division does not amount to distinguishing between selling out and political dissidence. Rather, all filmmakers—whether in the service of policymakers or independent of the state—renegotiate the urban contract and their position in between the government, developers, and residents.

Urban policy in China may be characterized as aiming to facilitate the government's regulatory powers, augment its prestige, and increase its capital (typically in land value). These goals can be achieved by redistributing the government's resources, mostly land and built property (used for infrastructure, recreational grounds, housing, public buildings, state monuments, industry, and land reserves) and liquid funds (the government's, developers', and citizens'). As this book illustrates, films and plays have emphasized various aspects of shifting resources around—housing reassignment (see especially chapters 1, 3, 5, and 6); setting aside public spaces (see chapters 1, 2, 4, 5, and 7); the relocation of urban industry (chapters 1 and 2); and the mobilization of private capital (chapters 2, 3, and 7).

The Maoist control of production, distribution, and critical response—which continues in some forms even today—has severely restricted PRC theater and cinema (much more than its literature and visual arts). In certain cases, the brush with power was unmediated and brusque. I have already mentioned Zhou Enlai's and Mao Zedong's personal interest in *Dragon Whisker Creek*. *Sentinels under the Neon Lights*, as I show in chapter 2, involved not only the national leadership but also every echelon of the military and the Propaganda Bureau. Even in Deng Xiaoping's reform era and beyond, official supervision and the "concern" of leaders have required filmmakers to negotiate with the state to approve the productions. Censorship has played a major role—exercised during preproduction by film studios and during postproduction by the central government (formerly by the Ministry of Culture and since 1986 by the State Administration of Radio, Film, and Television—SARFT). For example, as I discuss in chapter 6, specific shots are excised from films to present a more favorable image of the city. Content can also be foisted on scriptwriters; I give notable illustrations of such situations in chapter 3, showing the influence of BPAT's party secretary in the choice of repertoire.

In other cases, the regulation does not take an adversarial form but relies on the prescriptive distribution of desired topics. During the Maoist period in particular, the "planning of subject matter" (*ticai guihua*) delineated a normative range and shaped popular taste. City life was symptomatically absent from the officially designated categories. Urban issues were addressed through the ideological prism of topics such as "the PLA protects and constructs the motherland" or "adaptations of literary masterpieces."

The cinema shares the plight of urban design, which is subjected to a double-tier centralized control—state-level "economic planning" (*jingji jihua*, handled after the Soviet model by the State Planning Commission) as well as municipal-level spatial planning (*chengshi guihua*, literally "urban planning," under the Ministry of Construction).[40] An exceptionally candid, albeit schematic, cinematic portrayal of architects' work in Maoist China is found in *The Footsteps of Youth* (1957). The film addresses the new charge of the Ministry of Construction and Engineering to plan new cities; the opening shots show a city in the process of accelerated construction. A couple of sweethearts, young architects working in the same planning office, partici-pate in a competition to design a workers' dormitory. The woman ends up on top after having an affair with the section chief. The woman's blueprint, based on the section chief's suggestions, excels in integrating the floor plan and the exterior design. The young man's draft, in contrast, is superior in considering the workers' practical needs. (The contrast reflects a debate on aesthetics and functionalism in architecture that raged in the 1950s.)[41] Once the woman's affair with the elder cadre is revealed, the betrayed young man volunteers for labor reform in Qinghai, while the remorseful woman stays behind. The film shows not only the battle between two different approaches to planning—the purely aesthetic and the class-conscious—but also the plan-ners' ulterior motives and self-interest as well as the superiors' intervention and bias. (Another description of urban planners' work is found in *Neighbors* [1981], which I discuss in detail in chapter 6). Moreover, *The Footsteps of Youth* presents the architects' work and interpersonal relations as expressions of the ideological challenges in the New China. This portrayal of architects as embroiled in complex political, economic, and social structures—akin to that in *The Fountainhead* (1949)—may also illustrate how playwrights and film-makers have been scrutinized when they mediate between the powerful elements involved in urban policy.

Within a few years after the demise of Chiang Kai-shek in 1975 and of Mao Zedong in 1976, independent film production in Taiwan and the PRC was thriving. Movies questioned the official discourse and fueled public debates over urban policy. In chapter 5 I detail the most overt of these interventions, made possible by the political atmosphere in Taiwan. Grassroots protest (including amateur filmmaking) has destabilized political power in Taiwan, to the point that academics at the Institute of Building and Planning were in a position to negotiate with Taipei's mayor, Ma Ying-jeou, against the evacua-tion of the slum at Baozangyan. I include Taiwan, although it has been separated from the mainland for most of the period since 1895 and governed by a different system, to show how Taipei films also are deeply imbricated in policy issues. Just as enthusiasm for Urban Cinema in the PRC since the late 1980s has obscured the concrete considerations of politicians, developers, and residents, so did the critical reception of New Taiwan Cinema ignore institutional dynamics. Directors such as Tsai Ming-liang, Edward Yang, and Lin Cheng-sheng not only pay tribute to Taipei locations but also participate in a dialogue with policymakers, planners, and activists.

The power balance in post-Maoist PRC has been more subtle. Since the mid-1980s, and especially since the rise of independent, so-called Sixth Generation filmmakers in the mid-1990s, urban subject matter has been associated with a critical view of social change. Yet post-Maoist cinema is more reluctant to address the systemic reasons for city trouble. Moreover, as Yingjin Zhang remarks, Sixth Generation directors have enjoyed an "institutionally imposed but self-glorified status of marginality."[42] Urban Cinema was lionized as a form of dissidence, even after it had become part of the commercial mainstream. The rise of New Urban Cinema, a genre of wide appeal, in the late 1990s signaled a shift to more commercial production, in the phrase of Paul Pickowicz and Yingjin Zhang, "from underground to independent."[43] In fact, New Urban Cinema is a good test case for the collusion of state capitalism and the new culture of commodified leisure. Filmmaking in the face of power has always entailed compromise, minding the powerful participants in the urban contract.

SITES OF IDEOLOGY: CHAPTER OUTLINE

To foreground the shifting power relations in the urban contract, I have arranged this book around particular locations and architectural forms that promoted tailored accounts of the city. Ideological constructs, and especially historical narratives, were reified through geographical sites. I refer to the coupling of specific locations and temporal perceptions as *chronotopes*, a term coined by Mikhail Bakhtin for the imaginary place and time frames that forge fictional realms.[44] Bakhtin was concerned with hermetic fictional worlds unrelated to any concrete location or period, yet the cases before us depict real places, forcing the spectators to interpret the films in the factual and symbolic registers at the same time.[45] The chapter layout follows these sites.

Chapter 1 looks at Longxugou, a Beijing slum, and its redevelopment into a more prosperous neighborhood in the early 1950s. Unlike the following chapters, chapter 1 looks at a single work, albeit in two forms: the play and film versions of *Dragon Whisker Creek* (1951 and 1952, respectively). *Dragon Whisker Creek* has given special significance to Beijing's Outer City (*waicheng*), also known as the city's southern quarters (*chengnan*). The Outer City was walled in 1564 and designated for those who serviced the imperial court and its retinues in the Inner City. As a proletarian district, the Outer City was touted by the Communist government as embodying the true spirit of Beijing. *Dragon Whisker Creek* focuses on a courtyard compound (*za-yuan'r*) as a microcosm of society and of class struggle in particular. The most important contribution of *Dragon Whisker Creek* to urban discourse is what I call its *prescriptive chronotope*. Written and performed even before the completion of the public works it describes, the play projects onto the present an ideal version of the future. All existence is defined as either spent in anticipation of communism or already enjoying the bliss of socialist urbanization. Communist utopia is manifested in developing the Outer City and integrating the intimate compound into the large public spaces of the state.

In chapter 2 we turn to the Shanghai landmark of Nanjing Road. Nanjing Road was the city's commercial center since Shanghai's colonial occupation in 1842. It stretched between two other symbols of colonial power, namely, the waterfront Bund and the Horse Race Club. The Communist takeover in 1949 resulted not only in the physical transformation of the site—most noticeably in turning the Horse Race Club into People's Park, People's Avenue, and People's Square—but also in redistributing the city's economic power from the center to new satellite towns and from the service sector to heavy industry. The policy—expressed blatantly in the 1963 campaign to "emulate the Good Eighth Company of Nanjing Road"—was accompanied by portrayals of the city as a shelter for counterrevolutionaries. Films such as *A Married Couple* (1951) and *Sentinels under the Neon Lights* (1964) present Nanjing Road as the location of a *recidivist chronotope*. Communist cadres and soldiers settling on the road become entangled in revisionist heresy, and it is the task of the Party to save them and the city. The portrayal of Nanjing Road as a site of decadence and corruption amplified the stereotypes, established before 1949, to change the image of postliberation Shanghai. The films discussed in chapter 2 illustrate the cinema's involvement in urban policy at the apex of the Maoist period.

Chapter 3 surveys more than a dozen plays staged since 1980, mostly set in Beijing's traditional courtyard houses (*siheyuan'r*), dilapidated and designated for demolition. The distinct architecture of the courtyard houses, together with the narrow alleys (*hutong*) along which they were built, has increasingly given way to wide roads and apartment buildings. The plays, sponsored by state theaters on the occasion of launching new policies, invariably side with the developers, show the need to tear down the old houses, and argue for ways of preserving Beijing's cultural heritage that focus on external appearance. The plays often refer explicitly to *Dragon Whisker Creek* and further develop the prescriptive chronotope already found in Lao She's play, anticipating a better future in modern housing. In addition, the theater productions present redevelopment as an overnight transformation that skirts the social problems arising from the intermediate phase of evacuation and relocation. The courtyard plays subscribe to a *chronotope of instantaneity*, which telescopes historical processes and presents a ready-made new city poised to take part in the global economy.

Although this lengthy chapter deals exclusively with stage plays, its argument is also relevant for discussing cinema. The theater pieces can be produced more quickly than films and are tightly controlled by the Propaganda Department of the Central Committee of the Communist Party. (This Party organization and SARFT, which supervises film production, are the strictest and most conservative censoring bodies, making drama and cinema most indicative of government policy.) In their capacity as testing ground for the mass media, the stage plays are the first to establish tropes and visual symbols that find their ways into films. Practically every Maoist film mentioned in this book was preceded by a theatrical version. Even in recent years, many screen actors, playwrights, and directors started their careers at the Central Academy of Drama and on the stage. The courtyard plays in particular evidence the crossover between the genres.

Chapter 4 examines Tiananmen Square, the most ostentatious of the public spaces identified with the Chinese state. Whereas the previous chapters depict a fragile partnership between state power and artistic creativity, Tiananmen casts the authorities and the filmmakers in sharp contrast. Ironically, this architectural emblem of the state has been more easily reappropriated for alternative visions of the city than the intimate residential spaces discussed in chapters 1 and 3, precisely because Tiananmen has been established as a public space. Formerly a vestibule to the emperor's seat in the Forbidden City, the square was redesigned in the 1950s as a gathering place for rallies as well as the center of government. The cinema adds to the site's symbolic significance by referring back to the images recorded at the founding ceremony of the PRC and distributed in the documentary *The Birth of New China* (1949). As the distilled expression of the Communist revolution, the founding ceremony was reenacted in the docudrama *The Founding Ceremony* (*kaiguo dadian*, 1989). The purported immutability of the square is borne out in what I call the *chronotope of perpetual revolution*, which locks the site in time, covering up for the many changes that have in fact taken place in the square itself and in its relation to the urban layout. Planners in the service of the national and municipal governments fashioned the new Tiananmen as a symbolic break with the imperial city plan but at the same time reintegrated the square into old monumental spaces, suggesting that the site was impervious to historic change. In the post-Maoist period, however, movies challenged the square's self-contained design as a symbol of the state, separated from the surrounding urban context. Instead, films showed the square as part of city life. The most salient example is the documentary *The Square* (1994), which presents the place as a site of leisure, akin to New York's Central Park. Against the chronotope of perpetual revolution, recent films have foregrounded alternative spatial and temporal matrices of interpreting Tiananmen's place in the city.

Chapter 5 evidences how urban cinema can give the lie to official accounts of urban development. I focus on films depicting Taipei's veterans' villages (*juancun*), architectural residues of Taiwan's de facto secession from mainland China in 1949. The villages, in actuality large communities embedded in the urban fabric since the early 1950s, housed military personnel, retirees, and their families. As part of Taipei's gentrification since the early 1980s, the veterans' villages were demolished, often replaced with public parks. The inhabitants of those villages built on military property were peacefully relocated; the residents of other villages, overgrown slums of makeshift houses, had no means to sustain themselves outside their original abodes and mounted violent protests. Films such as *Moonlight* (1983) and *My Whispering Plan* (2002) linger on the collapse of familial structures as a result of demolition. Other works, such as *Vive l'Amour* (1994) and *Robinson's Crusoe* (2002), present the city as a palimpsest of coexisting temporalities. The *chronotope of simultaneity* in Taipei cinema collapses the city's history and makes past, present, and future visible at the same time through the camera lens.

Different circumstances notwithstanding, there are common roots to urban policy issues and present challenges in Taiwan and the PRC. In both cases, urban housing projects in the early 1950s were part of a national agenda to take care of the new government's support base, just as films were mobilized for nation building. On both sides of the Taiwan Strait, planners inherited the problems created by those short-term housing solutions and were drawn to authoritarian interpretations of land-use laws. Rapid rezoning, confiscation, and construction were enabled by state and municipal agencies' ownership of developed land; at the same time, concern for historic conservation and the cities' symbolic significance presented particular challenges. As both the PRC and Taiwan experienced a spectacular surge in urbanization in the aftermath of political changes in the late 1970s, demolition-and-relocation became prevalent. In the 1980s, Taiwanese activists and film-makers protested against erasing the city's past, in voices emulated in the PRC since the mid-1990s.

The cinematic treatment of demolition-and-relocation is also the subject of chapter 6, which deals with PRC films since 1980. I discuss the rise of Urban Cinema in the 1980s and New Urban Cinema since the 1990s. Exponents such as *Black Snow* (1990), *Weekend Lover* (1993), and *Good Morning, Beijing* (2000) show how urban films withdrew to an intense concern for the individual subject, divorced from the context of urban policy. The chapter focuses, however, on films that resonate and engage with the growing professional and public interest in protecting the urban environment, at least by preserving its image on film. Demolition sites are seen as architectural open wounds and as evidence of a traumatized urban fabric. By recording these sites, films become repositories of the city's memory. To match the planners' attention to preservation, films chronicle the vanishing city. As markers of disappearance, demolition sites as shooting locations mark a *preservational chronotope*—acknowledging a sense of loss and recognizing the need for keeping a record of the expired architecture. The preservational chronotope is manifested in a documentary impulse to grab the moment in visual form. To varying degrees of explicitness, the filmmaker becomes the protagonist of the cinematic attempt to keep snapshots of the city in its present condition.

The documentary impulse is found in films from before and after 1989, in various genres, and spread over many cities and locations. The films may be overtly nostalgic, like *Sunset Street* (1983) and *Farewell My Concubine* (1992); they can expose personal traumas, as in *No Regret about Youth* (1992) and *Baober in Love* (2004); they sometimes experiment with new forms of realism, like *Neighbors* (1981) and Ning Ying's Beijing trilogy (1992–2000); they are likely to foreground the presence of the amateur camera, like *Shower* (1999) and *Suzhou River* (2000). The plot may follow the evacuation of a traditional courtyard house, as in *Love in the Internet Age* (1999); dorms at a communal corridor building (*tongzilou*), as in *Strangers in Beijing* (1996); a modified courtyard house, as in *A Tree in House* (2000); or a market stall, as in

Life Show (2000). In these and other cases, the cinema may be unable to change the course of urban development, but it can fill in for the absence of open debate by presenting the results of policy in relatively candid terms.

Chapter 7 concludes the book by considering Beijing's booming real estate market as the city joined the global economy and geared up for the 2008 Olympics. Two films I discuss stretch the limits of what may be put up for sale—in *Big Shot's Funeral* (2001), the Forbidden City is fashioned as advertising space; in *The World* (2004), one can buy access to the entire planet, at least in the form of amusement park replicas. With the subjugation of architectural heritage to market economy and the compromising of urban planning to the whims of transnational capital, space ceases to reference concrete places. The cinema presents a *postspatial chronotope*—a virtual time/space framework that challenges the very possibility of constructing the city, except in the cinematic imagination and in postcinematic technologies of virtual reality.

⚡ SITES OF CINEMA

The sites introduced in this book can hardly represent all aspects of Chinese urbanization, or even all major locations. I focus on Beijing, Shanghai, and Taipei due to the prodigious number of films made in these cities and because the large cinematic oeuvre reflects their prominence as political centers and cultural hubs. These three cities provide poignant examples of planning and filmmaking in the face of power. Even though the recent astounding growth of inland metropolises (notably, Chongqing Municipality, now at about 34 million inhabitants) has captured the headlines, the three cities examined here, with their rich architectural heritage, vibrant art scenes, and political clout, provide the testing grounds for integrating national, cultural, and urban policies. In the PRC, Beijing and Shanghai serve as models for other municipalities. The transformation of Beijing's *hutong* and Shanghai's *longtang* into modern commercial centers is arguably no more dramatic or important than the destruction of, say, Kashgar's old streets, but the gentrification of all Chinese cities mimics projects such as Beijing's Oriental Plaza and Shanghai's Xintiandi (*xintiandi* is now also used as a verb, in the sense of creating a hip commercial center with an architectural heritage flavor). That urban policy has been portrayed in films only concerning a small number of cities, with Beijing at the top and even

Shanghai a distant second, points to the privileged place of Beijing and Shanghai in the PRC, and of Taipei in the ROC. In chapter 6 I briefly mention a few films addressing urban development in places such as Guangzhou, Chongqing, Tianjin, and Xi'an, yet closer analysis of cinema and policy in these cities, which awaits another occasion, is likely to yield different views, precisely due to their peripheral status.

In mapping Chinese responses to urbanization, this book skirts Hong Kong cinema, for a while the most prolific film industry in East Asia. Hong Kong films have been persistently concerned with urban growth, from the didactic *In the Face of Demolition* (1953), through the comedy *House of Seventy-Two Tenants* (1973), to the experimental *Chungking Express* (1994). The reasons for excluding Hong Kong are both practical and methodological. Scholars such as Ackbar Abbas, Leung Ping-kwan, and Helen Hok-Sze Leung have skillfully explored questions of urbanism in Hong Kong films.[46] Moreover, urban policy in Hong Kong follows a different logic from that of other Chinese cities, responding to British colonialism, migration from the mainland and Southeast Asia, and the tension between local initiatives and directives from Beijing. A prominent example is found in the site of Kowloon City (Gao Lung Sing), the evacuation and demolition of which has been portrayed critically on screen, notably in *Cageman* (1992), *Hollywood, Hong Kong* (2001), and *Re-cycle* (2006). The gentrification of Kowloon City, one of the first joint endeavors by the British colonial authorities and the PRC government, may provide an entry point to a future study of the complex dynamics in a city whose urban policy has been as blurry and fragmented as its identity.

My focus on seats of political power and cultural hegemony, at the expense of marginalized locations of a hybrid ethos—from the sweatshops of Shenzhen to the pidgin idioms of Kuala Lumpur—leaves it for future studies to address other meeting points between film and the city. James Tweedie and I have argued for the importance of looking at "the city's edge"—the location where the cinema challenges existing conceptions of urbanism and ultimately encounters its own limitations.[47] My book awaits being complemented by studies of urban cinema with emphases on what lies beyond the cities—the suburbs, intra-Asian links, and global contexts.

Any definition of "the Chinese city" is bound to reveal ideological bias and neglect important aspects of urbanism and film. Insofar as this study weaves a history out of the disparate locations, as if they were islands linked by submerged ridges, it also foregrounds the unique dynamics of each place. Rather than what Gilles Deleuze calls "any-space-whatevers" (*espaces quelconques*),[48] which seem universal and suspended outside any power structure, the sites at hand literally reterritorialize ideological abstractions. These concrete spaces bridge through symbolically pregnant chronotopes, between the material city and its imaginary constructions. From the Longxugou project promoted by *Dragon Whisker Creek* to the image overhaul occasioned by the Olympics and spoofed in *Big Shot's Funeral*, films have taken an active part in forging the city.

ONE

New China, New Beijing

Staging the Socialist City of the Future

AMONG THE EVENTS that have come to stand for liberated Beijing is the drying up of Longxugou, or Dragon Whisker Creek. The engineering feat was made famous in Lao She's play *Dragon Whisker Creek*, performed in 1951 by the Beijing People's Art Theater (Beijing Renmin Yishu Jutuan, henceforth BPAT) and filmed the following year by Beijing Film Studio, in collaboration with BPAT and the Beijing Youth Art Theater. In fact, the popular movie has come to stand as a reference for urban restructuring in the early years of the PRC, quoted in histories of urban planning and integrated into documentary films, as if it were historical footage.[1]

In this chapter I explore the facts behind the public works at Longxugou and analyze the stage and screen productions to inquire into what made possible the interdependence between urban development and fictional accounts. I ask how *Dragon Whisker Creek* bridged the material city and its allegorical visualization, and argue that the stage play and film went beyond serving planners and decision makers: they retooled the audiences' vision. *Dragon Whisker Creek* draws much of its power from striking a balance between faithful representation and turning the city into a parable.

It is no coincidence that Longxugou was the site of one of the first public works projects in liberated Beijing, and that *Dragon Whisker Creek* was the first original play staged by the newly established BPAT.[2] The convergence of city planning, drama, and film to make one of their earliest contributions to the New China is emblematic of their symbiosis. The engineering project, the play, and the movie supported a shift to a socialist conception of the city. Moreover, finding a visual vocabulary for presenting the city entailed novel staging and filming aesthetics, as well as challenging the hierarchy that privileges built environment over its visual representation. Stage plays and films not only recorded and propagated the new urban vision but also reified the new planning concepts and redirected the citizens' gaze. The theater and cinema became necessary for imagining and imaging the city.

Dragon Whisker Creek turned to the city in an effort to envision Maoist ideology not only through rural production and international strife but also through urban identity. Other productions of the same period emphasized military themes, preeminently in the context of the contemporary campaign to "resist America and support North Korea" (*kang Mei yuan Chao*), or addressed industrial and agricultural reform. *Dragon Whisker Creek* offered yet another site of building socialism by focusing on Beijing's poor and the slums in which they lived. Revolutionary ideology and collective identity were expressed by city life no less than through struggles at the national level. "New China, new Beijing," a key phrase in the film version, draws an analogy between the city and the nation. The Communist Party's hold over China relied on the claim not only that it was reinvigorating the nation-state but also that it was making over the capital.

Dragon Whisker Creek set an important precedent in distilling a temporal and spatial form to represent the socialist city. The workers' city is constructed through the residential courtyard (the formal *siheyuan'r* or the less regular *zayuan'r*), viewed at eye level yet penetrable by the authorities' gaze. The play defines the revolutionary regime of vision in the new Chinese city through the dialectic between two forms of urban space: residential quarters, on the one hand, and open squares and wide roads, on the other. *Dragon Whisker Creek* signals the emergence of the courtyard as the central location of social drama and primary site of governance, only to trump the enclosed vernacular architecture of the courtyard in favor of new public squares. In another important contribution, the play depicts the new construction as if the plans have already materialized. The reference to the future socialist city as an accomplished fact is an extreme case of the modernist conceit that promises a radically new world built on ruins of the old one. The projection of the future onto the present—what may be called the *prescriptive chronotope* of *Dragon Whisker Creek*—as well as the focus on the courtyard as a microcosm of class struggle, would become key devices in later stagings of urban policy.

The prescient vision of *Dragon Whisker Creek* is part of a complex structure for conveying urban policy. The play's strong rhetoric may be read as crass propaganda, marking it as a lesser work by Lao She, whose *Teahouse* (1958) has been ushered into the canon of twentieth-century Chinese drama. I argue, however, that *Dragon Whisker Creek* (which inspired *Teahouse*) was pathbreaking in both theme and form.[3] In establishing the relation between urban space and revolutionary time, the play laid the grounds for dramatic and filmic discourse on urban development and renewal in the PRC. Beijing's image in literature, film, and the collective imagination at large cannot be fully appreciated without understanding the role played by *Dragon Whisker Creek*.

I look at the material and ideological construction of Longxugou by examining the policymakers' considerations as well as by analyzing the theatrical and cinematic works based on Lao She's play. In the following discussion, I use the title *Dragon Whisker Creek* to refer to all versions of the play, staged dialogue, and film script. Yet I will also distinguish among the various scripts and stagings, since their evolution evidences shifting emphases.[4] The texts, stage sets, and cinematic images refashioned and gave new meanings to urban spaces, and Beijing's in particular, in the formative first years of the PRC.

❦ URBAN GEOPOLITICS:
PUBLIC WORKS AT DRAGON WHISKER CREEK

Lao She describes how, on returning to Beijing at the end of 1949 after fourteen years' absence, he found the city changed. Sewers had been mended, streets cleaned, and fresh water and electricity supplied. He was especially impressed by the Longxugou project. The playwright explains that despite its picturesque name, the creek was no more than a stinking ditch. The municipal government built a covered sewer and filled the open canal. Lao She praises the authorities: "I know that after more than a decade of anti-Japanese resistance and civil war, at a time when countless flaws await mending, the government's financial situation is not easy. Yet the government has shouldered the heavy burden for the sake of people's welfare." Lao She explains that he wrote the play "to express . . . gratitude and admiration for the government."[5] The playwright's description evidences the high stakes involved in public works. As internal memos of the municipal council also show, the Longxugou project was a major endeavor, carried out by a government fully aware of its implications for the urban structure, national economy, and ideological representation of the New China.

The project should be viewed in the context of the economic retooling implemented in the early 1950s. The new government was eager to improve urban conditions, for practical and ideological reasons. Political stability depended on high productivity; Mao Zedong decreed that "the consumerist city should be turned into a productive city."[6] In fact, the new authorities revived the efforts that had begun already in 1914, when comprehensive urban planning was introduced in an effort to turn the old capital into a modern metropolis. Madeleine Yue Dong argues that in the 1930s Beijing became a "city of planners," and the Municipal Council implemented "a new, more open spatial order conducive to increased mobility of people and goods."[7] In addition, the Communist government implemented a Soviet-style central economic policy that stressed urban industry, further increasing the need for workers' housing and transportation.[8] A long-term policy was eventually laid out in September 1952, when the Central Finance Committee held the first National Conference on Urban Construction, resulting in the creation of the Bureau of Urban Development in the Ministry of Construction. Until that point, the new government had focused on rebuilding the urban infrastructure, such as the sewage system at Longxugou.

The task of improving workers' quarters and facilitating mobility in and out of the working-class districts was compounded by hygiene hazards. One of the most urgent problems was that garbage was heaped along the roads, while rainwater and sewage drained through filthy open canals. Municipal governments mobilized the residents to repair pipes and clean up garbage. The situation in Beijing was especially severe, and by March 1951, more than sixty tons of garbage were hauled away from around the city walls and moats. The water system was improved by dredging Beihai and Zhongnanhai lakes, followed by mending pipes and ditches and building a new network. Once the conditions permitted, streets were widened and new roads constructed.[9]

Longxugou was an important component in the urban development scheme. The creek, a remnant of the natural topography, became part of a scenic system of rivulets and ponds during the Ming dynasty. The ponds, deepened and used for fish and shrimp farming, drew many visitors, though the area was not as highly regarded as other scenic districts strewn with graceful temples and villas. During the eighteenth and nineteenth centuries (the Qing period), the area lost its elegant allure but remained a popular place for strolling.[10] Comporting with the typical plan for a Chinese capital, the center of which is the seat of the emperor, associated with the dragon, the corridor south of the imperial palace was imagined as a dragon's snout, and so the stream to the east and west of the meridian road was compared to the dragon's whiskers.[11] The stream ran through a large portion of the southern walled city (known as *waicheng*, or Outer City), and districts were named after the aquatic landmarks along its path: spanning Dragon Whisker Creek west of the Altar of Heaven was the Heavenly Bridge (Tianqiao); north of the altar lay the Goldfish Ponds (Jinyuchi); on the Altar's northeastern corner the creek was crossed by the Red Bridge (Hongqiao). Even though the creek is now gone, these names are still useful landmarks for orienting oneself in modern Beijing. At the Red Bridge, the stream shifted from an eastbound course to the south, passing through the Sun Temple (Taiyanggong) area before flowing into the southern moat (map 1). Since Beijing slopes toward the southeast at a rate of 1.2–1.3 percent, a large part of the southern quarters' rainwater and sewage flowed into the creek.[12] The population growth in the Outer City during the Qing strained the creek's capacity. Passing through the poorest areas of town, the waterway filled with garbage, clogged, and often overflowed, inundating neighboring residences and causing severe hygiene problems.[13] Even though it was often dredged in late winter, when the water froze, the creek by the turn of the twentieth century had acquired the reputation of "a stinking ditch." As part of rehabilitating the districts essential for small urban industry, and before any construction could take place, the Communist government needed to deal with the creek's ecological system.

Soon after Beijing's liberation, the provisional council commissioned works at Longxugou "to improve the environmental hygiene of the workers residing in the area." A survey conducted starting in March 1950 confirmed the immense obstacles facing the project and the huge scope required. Along the creek, firm soil was covered by five meters of trash; dirty water flowed as close as two feet to the surface. The creek's low-lying, 1.35-square-mile basin had to drain 10,567 gallons of water per second. Any attempt to replace the creek with a single modern sewer system would be nearly impossible with current technology. A pipe eight to ten feet in diameter would have to be put in place, inside a trench sixteen to twenty feet wide. A corridor of the same width would have to be evacuated and the houses demolished. Moreover, the creek's course would have to be lowered, necessitating in turn

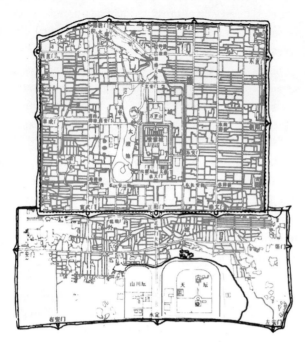

Map 1 Beijing in 1949. Highlighted: the city walls, moat, and Dragon Whisker Creek, including Goldfish Ponds.

the rebuilding of the railroad bridge and wall gates in its path. Finally, the southern city moat would have to be deepened by twenty to twenty-three meters. The impracticality of such measures led the government to seek a different solution.

By the end of April, the new plan was ready. The water flow would be divided between two parallel pipes on both sides of the original creek. To the north, a four-foot pipe would be laid down along Dongxiaoshi Avenue; to the south, a 2.6-foot pipe would stretch along Jinyuchi Avenue. East of the Dongxiaoshi Avenue section (that is, east of the Altar of Heaven), the creek passed through a sparsely populated area, and would therefore be dredged but not rebuilt. Later, additional conduits would drain the flow from the northern side of the creek basin. Despite the weather and hard terrain, the workers proceeded to execute the plan; by the end of July 1950, they finished constructing some four miles of pipeline, thereby doing away once and for all with the problem of flooding. The works continued until 1952, by which time running water and electricity were supplied and tramway tracks installed.[14] The hygiene and transportation problems were finally resolved.

Although the completion of the intricate project could be declared a success, authorities were also worried that their efforts might be misconstrued. In an internal memo, Cao Yanxing, head of the Public Works Bureau, mentions the unsavory prospect of demolishing a swath six meters wide along the canal. He also details concerns about problems that were not made public.[15] Some setbacks, such as the crumbling of a supporting wall and the theft of construction wood, resulted from lack of experience or oversight. Such waste of work and materials, he explained, made a negative impression on those who witnessed the incidents. Other issues revealed the inadequacy of the first stage of the project and, more worrisome, caused miscommunication with the working-class residents on whom the authorities were counting as a power base.

Cao's memo cites specifically the residential courtyards in Beitangen, along the northern side of the Altar of Heaven. Since they were located too low for the water to be drained, rainfall was still causing lasting inundations. A citizen asked an engineer about the contingency plans, only to be told, "Mending the ditch is for the benefit of the majority of the residents, and we cannot take care of each single household." Another person inquired, "When the water can't be drained and the house falls down, what then?" The engineer retorted, "These houses are going to collapse no matter what. The government will build new ones for you." The incidents exacerbated the unrest among the already-dissatisfied residents, or, in the memo's cautious parlance, it "had unfavorable influence" on them. Bureau Head Cao issued directives to fix the remaining problems. The internal document evidences the municipal government's touchiness about criticism. To balance the impression left by the insensitive engineers, to ensure that the hard work and self-sacrifice of those involved would be acknowledged, to avoid alienating the working class, and to gain credit for improving urban infrastructure and workers' living conditions, the government had to employ more savvy public relations tactics. In this context, Lao She's play would become instrumental.

To complement the engineering efforts and put them in the right light, the government propaganda apparatus availed itself of Lao She's play. The stage play, and especially the film, could reach a large audience and were enlisted for documenting and propagating the importance and success of the project.[16] Li Bozhao, the director of BPAT, wrote: "Lao She's play presents a good lesson for those who had little opportunity to understand and gain intimate knowledge of Beijing's indigent working people."[17]

At first, BPAT may have simply stumbled on the chance to contribute to urban policy. In 1950, the theater troupe, many of whose members were newcomers to the capital, was searching for a revolutionary repertoire that would connect the newly established institution with Beijing culture. As Li Bozhao reported at the time, BPAT gave priority to original native productions over Soviet and other imported texts: "We want to represent workers, that is—Chinese workers."[18] It was a natural choice for BPAT to collaborate with Lao She, who was completing for the China Youth Art Theater the play *Fang Zhenzhu*, about the liberation of Beijing, told through the travails of Beijing singsong performers. Lao She had returned to Beijing from a four-year stay in the United States in December 1949 and was welcomed by the cultural and political establishment. In May 1950, he was elected acting chair of the Beijing Municipality Literature and Art Workers Representative Assembly, and in July, he became a member of the Central People's Government Ministry of Culture's Steering Committee on Cinema and the Committee on Theater Reform.[19] Lao She's prestige and his Beijing-centered plays allowed BPAT to establish itself—especially in its new form since 1952[20]—as the mouthpiece not only of the Communist government but also of Beijing's new spirit as a socialist capital.

Dragon Whisker Creek was not, however, simply the result of a fortuitous collaboration. (Nor, for that matter, was it the only literary piece to extol the Longxugou project—1951 saw the publication of Gao Shen's *The Transformation of Dragon Whisker Creek*.)[21] Lao She fashions writing *Dragon Whisker Creek* as his initiative and tells how a visit to the creek area prompted him to write about the project, to express his gratitude to the government. Lao She's description comports with the requirement set by Mao's Yan'an talks, that a revolutionary writer should "go among the masses" to observe and experience their living conditions.[22] Another source complements the playwright's account by telling how Lao She, at a dinner with Zhou Enlai, told the premier of his intention to write about the change in Beijing, and Zhou approved and encouraged the playwright.[23] Yet the firsthand testimony of Pu Siwen, Lao She's assistant, shows that *Dragon Whisker Creek* was part of the government's calculated move to propagate its urban policy. Earlier in the day on which Lao She was invited to Zhou's residence, BPAT Director Li Bozhao assigned Pu to work with Lao She on the play. She told Pu that following the Beijing Municipal Council's decision to mend Longxugou, Lao She was asked to write a play about it for the second anniversary of Beijing's liberation, on January 31, 1951. The formal dinner with Zhou Enlai placed BPAT's endeavor in the context of the government's efforts and added the seal of authority. As Lao She's son, the literary historian Shu Yi, confirms,[24] Li Bozhao came up with the idea of the play and presented the task to Lao She as his service for the people. Lao She's first and only visit to Longxugou took place on July 15, 1950, the day after his meeting with Zhou (the playwright continued to get reports from Pu Siwen).[25] Ten days later Lao She made public his intention to write on Longxugou. The playwright produced the text within a month, and the premiere took place on February 2, 1951.[26]

The play was welcomed with political support and critical acclaim. A special performance was staged at the leaders' compound at Zhongnanhai, in the presence of Mao (for whom it was the first play he had attended since the liberation) and Zhou Enlai (who also viewed the play on a number of other occasions).[27] At the end of 1951, the playwright was honored as "Artist of the People" in recognition of *Dragon Whisker Creek*, which, according to the award letter, "movingly represents the municipal government's policy of constructing in the service of the entire people, and especially the workers, and its deep concern for the workers' life conditions."[28] The tailored play met all of the government's expectations.

Dragon Whisker Creek was placed at the center of an educational campaign. Multiple newspapers republished Lao She's essays on the play, as well as a variety of articles praising it.[29] The print workers' meeting to evaluate *Dragon Whisker Creek* and supplement it with firsthand testimonies, as reported on May 18 in the Party's organ, the *People's Daily*,[30] was likely one of many.[31] Many articles were published in the *People's Daily*. In one such piece, Zhou Yang, deputy minister of culture and cultural policy czar, held up the play as a paragon of realism and a model of writers' attitude: "We can learn many things from *Dragon Whisker Creek*, yet the cardinal thing is to emulate Lao She's genuinely warmhearted attitude to politics and his truly realistic approach to writing."[32] The play, staged by troupes all around the country, as well as the following film version, became linchpins in the government's effort to shape the image of the new Chinese city. The seemingly spontaneous expression of a new Beijing spirit—supported by the playwright's own testimony—was in fact a production commissioned to showcase the Longxugou project at the anniversary celebrations.

☙ IN THE NAME OF THE PEOPLE

Lao She's play proved useful for propagating the municipal agenda in multiple ways. The fictional play and the film provided an overview of the project more engaging than any factual survey.[33] Large-scale urban reconstruction is hard to document, especially since the material evidence of the preexisting conditions is destroyed in the process. Furthermore, the Longxugou project involved no photogenic landmarks. (The film's credits do roll over the image of the nearby Altar of Heaven.) *Dragon Whisker Creek* provided a compact and easily digestible narrative.

The play puts human faces on the policy. It focuses on a small group of people who share a courtyard: the Wangs—a widow and her daughter, who make a living by sewing and soldering mirror frames; the Chengs—a popular performer gone mad and his wife, who sells cigarettes at the local market; the Dings—the rickshaw puller Ding Si, his wife Sisao, who helps the family finances by sewing, and their two children, Little Niu and Gazi; and Old Zhao, a sixty-year-old single bricklayer. The film in particular provides memorable images and a catchy theme song, chanted by the workers: "We all join hands / In filling Longxugou . . . / Old society must be overthrown / Longxugou will soon be mended." The dramatization of the project made it into a household name.[34] The play has shaped collective memory, and even nowadays the word *Longxugou* is a synonym for heavily polluted waterways.

The strong connection between the new government's urban policy and the propaganda objectives of *Dragon Whisker Creek* is evident from the echos of the internal documents in the literary script. Bureau Head Cao quotes in his memo a woman from the Eighteenth Precinct, preserving her simple speech: "I used to walk out the door into a muddy road. Stinking water was running down the street. Big-tail maggots got to be the local specialty. But who cared? Today the people's government is spending a few million catties' worth of rice to build for us a canal inside the earth. They really care for us."[35] Lao She places similar words in the mouths of his characters through-out the play. Old Zhao, for example, says: "The stinking water flows into the houses and fills them with long-tailed maggots. The government knows it and is looking for a solution for you, me and all the people of Longxugou, so that we no longer suffer illness, death, stench, filth, or hunger. You and I are the people; the government loves the people and will mend the creek for the people."[36] One wonders if official documents on Longxugou were made available to Lao She.

As Old Zhao's speech shows, the official rhetoric is amplified by the claim to represent the people and speak in their voice. The *People's Daily* tells of Longxu-gou residents' excitement at watching the play,[37] thereby implying that the play functions as the citizens' vicarious testimony. By speaking in the name of the residents, the government can take credit for its actions and at the same time construe its decisions as a response to the citizens' wishes. Public policy is promoted in terms that tone down the government's role in initiating it.

The play pretends to give voice to the residents, but it abrogates their judgment. *Dragon Whisker Creek*—like the project itself—betrays a paternal-ism that would also be promoted in later theater productions. The play replicates to a large extent the official rhetoric, which leaves the residents no active role. Such was not the situation on the ground—before 1949, as the Nationalist government's power declined, grassroots initiatives took over. In 1939, under Japanese occupation, the residents petitioned to dredge the canal using their own resources.[38] The large-scale works after liberation and the municipality's good intentions notwithstanding, Lao She's piece mis-represents history by reducing the citizens' role to reiterating their gratitude to the government. In citing residents who enthuse over how the govern-ment "really cares for us," the municipal documents and *Dragon Whisker Creek* sidestep thorny issues. Dwellers' consent to the demolition project is taken for granted. There is no questioning of the heavy-handed state inter-vention in urban reconstruction, which would grow even more pronounced during the coming decades.

At the end of *Dragon Whisker Creek*, the courtyard comes under the control of Old Zhao, who offers information, provides jobs, and points to the correct ideological line. The play celebrates the spaces inhabited by the people, observed by the people, and surveilled by the people. Speaking in the name of the people defines the theater and cinema in the service of policymakers.

Dragon Whisker Creek establishes rhetorical devices that would reappear in later urban propaganda productions. In addition to speaking in the name of the people, the play claims to recover suppressed voices, tells in public the bitterness of oppression, identifies the people's enemies, dramatizes a dialectic between doubters and enthusiasts of the Revolution, and projects a future in which socialism will have fully materialized.

The suppressed and recovered voice is conveyed especially through the character of Madman Cheng, who is bullied out of his work as a singsong artist and loses all interest in public performance. After liberation, he regains his coherent speech and takes the stage again. Like the protagonists in Lao She's previous play *Fang Zhenzhu*, who in the aftermath of liberation become "art workers in the service of the people," Cheng finds his true vocation in praising the new government. Cheng's progression, from reclusive, incoherent rant to eloquent public performance, points to the stage and film productions as extensions of the emancipated urban space. The liberated voice is further foregrounded in the later versions of the play and in the film, which climax in Madman Cheng's singsong praise of the new government.

Parenthetically, self-reflexive references point at Lao She's play itself as embodying the recovery of the revolutionary spirit. Madman Cheng's concluding singsong is titled "Mending Longxugou,"[39] or in the film, "Praise Song for the People's Government"; Lao She described his *Dragon Whisker Creek* as "a praise song for the people's government."[40] Madman Cheng's newfound ability to speak up, so that he may express his gratitude to the government, is paralleled by Lao She's postliberation vocation as a propaganda writer. In 1952 Lao She described his reaction to the Maoist doctrine in terms of a conversion: "Before studying Chairman Mao's "Yan'an Talks," I could not have written anything like what I composed in the last two years. What I wrote in this couple of years isn't that good, but compared to my works before liberation, it's of a different quality altogether."[41]

The return of the repressed voice in *Dragon Whisker Creek* is complemented by the residents' testimony to being the victims of class struggle and proclamation of the public works as a heroic comeuppance. Lao She follows here the practice of "telling bitterness" (*suku*), already in wide use in the Liberated Areas. As Ann Anagnost notes, this practice allowed the Party to claim legitimacy by showing that the subaltern class subject could now speak.[42] Lao She follows to a large extent the approach of Bureau Head Cao, who describes the selfless sacrifice of the engineers, working long hours and endangering their health. A contemporary *People's Daily* article reports that a worker praised the play, saying: "Who knew of this bitterness and filth before?! Now Mr. Lao She has put it down in writing."[43] The Party's most prominent newspaper commends *Dragon Whisker Creek*, through the words of "the people," for producing an onstage spectacle of "telling bitterness."

The play also anthropomorphizes the creek and likens it to an enemy of the people, as in the following dialogue:

MADMAN CHENG: Old Zhao, now you get yourself busy fighting
tyrants, how come you don't struggle against that
terrible tyrant?
OLD ZHAO: Which terrible tyrant? Black Whirlwind?
MADMAN CHENG: No! That Longxugou that drowned Little Niu!
Who's more terrible than it?[44]

Madman Cheng, the mouthpiece of the downtrodden, is deeming Longxugou worse than the gangster Black Whirlwind, modeled after antirevolutionary villain characters and associated with Chiang Kai-shek.[45] Later, the struggle is fashioned by Sisao as a dramatic interchange: "It's as if the creek has always sat there and said, 'I'm stinking, but what do you dare to do about it? I drowned your child, but what do you dare to do about it?' Once the government started mending the creek, it's as if Ding Si talked back and said, 'You're stinking, and you drowned my child, huh? I'm going to level you, bastard!' "[46] The Longxugou project—and by extension, the urban policy—are justified as an ideological battle.

The battle against Longxugou is sanctified by a martyr. Any sacrifice required of the residents and laborers pales in comparison to the drowning of the innocent Little Niu in the creek. Ding Si, the rickshaw-puller who stands for the exploited working class (in the play, he sinks into lassitude and alcoholism), joins the laborers to avenge the death of his daughter. He explains: "This creek drowned our Little Niu. I have an account to settle with it!"[47] The project redeems past wrongs and gives Ding Si a purpose to live for. *Dragon Whisker Creek* reaffirms the moral imperative and material benefits of urban redevelopment, in the voice of its potential victims—people like Ding Si, who might be evacuated in the process.

The play's propagandistic function is aided by the plot structure, aimed at dispelling the audience's doubts. In a format that would be imitated in future productions (as I will discuss in chapter 3), Lao She's play presents possible reservations, voiced by ideologically weaker characters, only to refute them later. Question-and-response routines frequently stave off potential objections to the reconstruction. The elder women in particular represent conservative forces that need to adjust to the recent changes. Mother Wang is a skeptic whose doubts must be put to rest. In the film, another elderly woman resists emergency evacuation, only to witness her shack collapse under a torrent. Much can be learned from the suspicions voiced by the characters, which likely correspond to actual uncertainties. Sisao expresses her fear of being evacuated: "If the government goes on in this way, Longxugou will soon become a big garden—but one thing should be clear: once it's a garden, they should still let us live here!" The younger and more progressive Erchun responds: "Don't worry—when it was a stinking ditch it was for us to live in, and when it's fragrant, it will still be for us to live in!"[48] That the exchange was excised from the final stage version may evidence a lingering apprehension among residents.

Dragon Whisker Creek describes a city in the throes of mass-scale restructuring. According to a survey of conditions in 1950, 5 percent of all residential buildings were "structurally unsafe"—the official parlance for houses designated for demolition.[49] Ideally, the play would allay not only the fears of Longxugou residents but also a more widespread anxiety about future urban development. By anticipating the counterarguments, *Dragon Whisker Creek* forestalls the residents' potential dissatisfaction with the mass demolition and the tension with the engineers and construction workers. Never acknowledging these setbacks, the play presents the official plans as the only and ideal answer to the situation at hand. The propaganda aesthetic aims to iron out the creases in urban policy by expressing advantageous views and placing the public works in an expedient temporal frame of reference.

⚘ THE REVOLUTIONARY TIME-SPACE

One of *Dragon Whisker Creek*'s key contributions to urban discourse lies in creating an enclosed time frame, based not on the events taking place during the depicted period—roughly contemporaneous with Lao She's writing —but rather on anticipated future actions. The characters are revolutionary subjects-to-be, and the public works are depicted as if they had already been accomplished. In fact, the text was written months ahead of the depicted events and years before the construction at Longxugou was completed. Testimonies by actors who visited the area while rehearsing the play describe the creek and its environs in terms similar to the portrayal of the stinking open canal and run-down neighborhood portrayed in act 1.[50] In presenting a prescriptive chronotope—that is, making the site into a symbol of the coming socialist utopia—the play not only sacrifices historical accuracy but also reduces the characters to a life suspended in waiting for a better future. The prescriptive rather than descriptive plot is part of the play's function as not only documenting the public works but also creating a normative image of urban redevelopment. What is at stake in describing the Longxugou project is not so much recording the past as laying out a future program for the popular perception of urban policy.

By portraying the project when it will have been completed and its effects will have become clear, the play avoids describing current snags and emphasizes instead the bright future. In addition to showing the triumphal conclusion of the public works, *Dragon Whisker Creek* mentions even more distant plans: the scenic Jinyuchi area, to which Old Zhao refers as a future park,[51] was redesigned into a recreational lake area only in the mid-1950s. Meanwhile, the play leaves offstage designs of a more controversial nature. The improvement of infrastructure was followed by massive construction in the 1950s and '60s, as the area was rebuilt as a commercial and residential district for the working class (see chapter 3).[52] The prescriptive chronotope implies that all present shortcomings are temporary and short-lived.

The time frame contrasts the "feudal" past with the revolutionary future, thereby underscoring the merits of the new government. To represent the Communist liberation and its consequences, Lao She hit on the idea of a tripartite structure—act 1 takes place under Kuomintang rule, act 2 immediately after the Communist takeover, and act 3 while the project is already underway. Beijing's liberation and the establishment of the PRC serve as a sharp dividing line. Viewers of the theater production even suggested enhancing the spectacle by lighting firecrackers onstage, between acts 1 and 2,[53] and the film marks the liberation by inserting documentary footage of the October 1 fireworks at Tiananmen (on the celebrations at Tiananmen, see chapter 4). The entire play takes place in the same courtyard, but the courtyard's appearance gradually improves as the Party's hold over the neighborhood strengthens. The visual clues complement the social, economic, and political transformation of the place. By the last act, garbage is swept away, windows and doors are repaired, a sign reading "The Workers' Cooperative" is put up, and the sun—an allusion to Mao—shines bright. Lao She depicts life in Communist China in a strongly favorable light, or as the practice was called at the time, he "adds a red thread" (*jia hong xian*) to the plot. The audience is informed that education, health services, labor conditions, and women's rights have all been improved, and that racketeers, gangsters, and government corruption have been curbed. The villains are arrested, the doubters are won over, and Ding Si, Erchun, and Madman Cheng are employed in building the New China. The process through which Madman Cheng regains his voice as a performer is part of an overall rejuvenation, marking a decisive break from preliberation conditions.

To enhance the contrast between pre- and postliberation Beijing, Lao She presents selective historical information. Old Zhao refers to Longxugou as "this stinking ditch that has never been cared for" and draws an analogy between the creek and the political situation: "Only when the officials are clean will the water be pure."[54] He details how previous governments promised to mend the ditch and collected money yet did nothing, and he squarely blames the disrepair of Longxugou on the imperial dynasties and Chiang Kai-shek. Lao She also noted: "The [Communist] government doesn't act like past reactionary rulers, who only cared for building roads and mansions for officials and nobility. Neither does it care only about mending the large arterial roads and presenting a false picture of peace and prosperity. Instead, it looks for the most urgent matters. Although Longxugou is in a godforsaken place, the government does not neglect it just because it is out of sight."[55] Lao She's account of Longxugou's history is at best partial.

The playwright conveniently fails to mention that the creek had constantly been on administrators' minds. In fact, the officials did not think of the place as out of sight but rather described their concern precisely with the area's appearance, which they linked to its prospects of commercial vitality. In a report presented to the mayor on May 31, 1935, Fang Yiji, head of the Hygiene Bureau of the Beiping municipal government, explains the need to mend Longxugou: "The Tianqiao area, with its antique market, regularly draws outside visitors who like walking around. A way must be found out to put the district's appearance in good order. The adjacent southeastern section of Longxugou . . . has been in disrepair for years. Filth has heaped up and obstructed the flow of water. The stench is unbearable. It affects substantially the city's mien and hygiene."[56] The part west of Tianqiao had been covered during the Republican period, and the eastern part—the one mended under the Communist government—could not be completed earlier due to shortage of funds.[57] Various ideas had been floated to improve the remaining stretch—notably, in 1935 a plan was devised to employ four hundred convicts imprisoned on drug charges to dredge the entire two-mile-long open canal.[58] During the Second World War, the Japanese-controlled "special municipality" had even fewer resources and could only oversee a residents' initiative to dredge the creek.[59] Urban planners of the socialist Beijing inherited rather than invented a concern for Longxugou's appearance as a reflection of the quality of city governance.

Dragon Whisker Creek engages in a creative chronology—depicting the project before its completion, ignoring the roots of the Outer City's commercial revitalization in the Republican period, and dating all works at Longxugou to the postliberation period. Giving the new government more credit than it merited, *Dragon Whisker Creek* rewrites history in a socialist key. Paralleling Lao She's self-portrayal as a writer who, like Madman Cheng, has regained his voice, the playwright describes his transformation by the Communist liberation. According to the playwright's account, only with Mao's guidance did he find his voice and write *Dragon Whisker Creek*: "Now I'm even more proud, since Beijing is Chairman Mao's; Beijing's people and Beijing city have stood up and progressed under Chairman Mao's grace; how could I not write of my and Beijing's people's gratitude to Chairman Mao?!"[60] The ideological transformation (*fanshen*), constitutes a turning point. Just as Beijing has been changed by liberation, Lao She fashions himself as having been made a different kind of writer. Ultimately, staging historic change documents and sets an agenda not only for urban renewal but also for the artist as part of the propaganda machine. The author draws a clear line to disavow his past and stress his conversion to Maoist ideology.

In fact, even the play's prescriptive chronotope may owe something to the temporal perceptions established during the earlier twentieth century. Madeleine Yue Dong argues that in the 1930s Beijing was viewed through "nostalgia for the present and an active effort to preserve it for the future."[61] Lao She's piece straddles the preliberation attachment to old Beijing and the revolutionary urge to cross the great threshold to future utopia and leave the past behind. *Dragon Whisker Creek* celebrates Beijing's vernacular architecture of the courtyard and its attendant social structure of a cohesive local community, yet it also yearns for change. It distinguishes between preliberation and postliberation Beijing to signal the need to let go of the past. The play exhibits what may be called *nostalgia for the future*—a yearning to make the future present, to have already experienced socialist bliss.

⤇ THE BIRTH OF THE COURTYARD PLAY

Dragon Whisker Creek constructs not only a temporal but also a spatial frame of reference for the revolution. The play singles out the Beijing courtyard and invests it with a particular significance. The courtyard stands for the everyday life of the proletariat; it provides the urban equivalent to other revolutionary locations, such as the rural areas or the Korean battlefront. The courtyard establishes a spectacle of the city that is intimate and enclosed within the small architectural unit and that at the same time serves as a preamble to larger vistas and the monumental spaces reserved for government functions.

Representing onstage a large-scale and long-term project such as that at Longxugou called for innovative solutions. Lao She refers to the challenge: "But how should I write? I have no way to move the stinking creek onto the stage, and even if I could, that wouldn't be a ticket-seller. . . . I decided that . . . [the play] would not necessarily have a storyline, that it was good enough if I'd jot down a few vignettes. . . . If I could write in a few characters linked to the creek, they would be like tributaries branching off. Through their words and actions I would be able to outline the creek."[62] Lao She's novel approach would impact PRC drama for years to come. Since the introduction of Western-style "spoken drama" (*huaju*) in China in the first years of the twentieth century, the major influence was Ibsenian theater. Plays revolved around a linear plot in inner quarters. Lao She introduces the idea of replicating a piece of life with minimal narrative intervention, leaving the drama to the changing urban setting itself. Accordingly, the set is not designed to enhance a domestic drama but instead to exhibit a larger portion of the urban landscape, namely, a courtyard.

Lao She developed conventions set by earlier texts and productions. The author had already described Beijing—or, as it was called between 1928 and 1949, Beiping—in his prose, most notably *Camel Xiangzi* (1936) and *Four Generations under a Single Roof* (1946–51). By Lao She's admission, he used his skills as a novelist to write *Dragon Whisker Creek*,[63] which addresses a topic of geographical breadth similar to his earlier novels. The courtyard where the plot takes place lies halfway between the intimate setting used hitherto for domestic drama, on the one hand, and Lao She's previous novels, encompassing the entire city, on the other.

Dragon Whisker Creek is among the first dramas to be situated in the vernacular architecture of the courtyard. Even Cao Yu's play *Peking Man* (1940), situated in a courtyard, is exclusively set indoors, aiming to create a claustrophobic atmosphere. Most films made in Shanghai were limited to interiors, conceiving of cinema as an extension of stage drama, in the manner that later scholars have identified as "shadow play" (*ying xi*) aesthetics.[64] Some films made soon after the end of the Second World War looked at entire housing units in Shanghai—notably *A Myriad Lights* (1948) and *Crows and Sparrows* (1949)—yet the apartment-building structure dictates very different aesthetics. Of the few films set in Beijing, only *The Reunion* (1948) is largely set in a courtyard; *Fate in Tears and Laughter* (1932) and *Opera Heroes* (1949) both share with *Dragon Whisker Creek* the focus on popular performers but show no special interest in the residential quarters. The focus of *Dragon Whisker Creek* on a courtyard called for a new approach to stage and film production.

It may well be that Lao She drew inspiration for the stage play from a film, namely the screen adaptation of his own *This Life of Mine* (1950). The director Shi Hui (who also played the lead role of a Beijing patrol policeman) wrote the script based on Lao She's 1937 novel of the same title. Shi, a Beijinger working for Wenhua Studio in Shanghai, stylized the film in a way radically different from those set in Shanghai interiors. He located the action in the streets, integrated documentary footage, and insisted on a genuine Beijing accent.[65] *Dragon Whisker Creek*, written soon after the success of Shi Hui's film, takes a similar approach and targets city life at the basic urban building block—the courtyard and the small community inside it.

More specifically, the play is set in a *zayuan'r*, or mixed courtyard, which clues the spectators to the low socioeconomic background of its inhabitants. Unlike the more upscale *siheyuan'r*—enclosed courtyards designed for a single extended household—the mixed courtyard housed a number of families and provided inexpensive residences. The mixed courtyard became common after the 1911 revolution, when impoverished Manchu families resorted to renting out parts of their residences.[66] This architectural type was associated with the destitute population of Beijing's outskirts. Lao She,

1 Stage design for the 1951 premiere of *Dragon Whisker Creek*.
Source: Lao She, *Dragon Beard Ditch: A Play in Three Acts*, trans. Liao Hung-ying
(Beijing: Foreign Languages, 1956).

who expressed his concern for preserving Beijing's traditional alleys as a
vital framework for social interaction and mutual help,[67] uses the play as a
vehicle for documenting courtyard life and foregrounding its significance.

The social, economic, and historical context of the mixed courtyard is
conveyed in the stage design. The curtain opens onto a courtyard in a state
of disrepair. The ramshackle buildings are home to four households. The
walls, windows, and props are broken and falling apart. The dialogue constantly refers to the condition of the courtyard and its environs.

Key to shaping the stage sets was the director, Jiao Juyin. Jiao had studied
Konstantin Stanislavsky's method and used the play, the first he directed for
BPAT, to promote his idea of a theater true to life, which relies on meticulous
sets.[68] Chen Yongxiang, the set designer for *Dragon Whisker Creek*, tells that
Jiao "repeatedly talked about the relationship between life and the creation
of progressive art . . . and about using realistic technique to establish a new
stage art."[69] The stage designer paid meticulous attention to the brick walls,
windowpanes, doors, and electricity lines (fig. 1). Jiao's realism firmly linked
the stage and urban spaces. The director required the actors, set designers,
and others involved in the production to visit Longxugou (troupe members
frequented the site for two months) to acquire an unmediated impression of
the place and its inhabitants.[70] In accordance with Lao She's description of

the play as focusing on the site as much as on the characters, Jiao Juyin required that the sets convey a strong sense of the location: "Stage design, lighting, and effects are all like actors—they need to be alive in the play. The comrades in set design must get the feel for the wriggling long-tailed maggots and the filth and clamminess at Longxugou. Only then will they be able to represent that filth and clamminess on the stage." The result, writes Chen, was "a vivid stage imagery."[71] The sets became not simply a backdrop for the play but rather staged the city as a protagonist. Jiao's Stanislavskian approach not only impacted the acting, it also framed the representation of the city through vernacular architecture. *Dragon Whisker Creek* paved the way for later stage plays and films that have addressed urban development through the portrayal of a single courtyard (as I will discuss in chapter 3).

✦ THE SPECTACLE OF EVERYDAY LIFE

The focus on courtyard life in Beijing's receded alleys provides a particular kind of spectacle. The stage play replicates and amplifies the linguistic elements of courtyard life, namely, local idiom and vernacular storytelling. Lao She identifies Beijing with street performances and singles them out as a quintessential element of urban experience. The script of *Dragon Whisker Creek* specifies the cries of street peddlers advertising greens, turnips, and donkey meat; Chen Yongxiang describes the stage as filled with sounds.[72] The quasi-ethnographic aesthetics and the feel for the locale are supported by the use of the Beijing dialect, and the rehearsal script even includes phonetic notations for idiosyncratic words.[73] The dialogue is spiced with down-to-earth aphorisms, such as Old Zhao's claim that "mending the ditch isn't like mixing together three units of oil and two of vinegar."[74] These sounds and phrases complement the architecture on the set.

Lao She translates onto the modern stage the urban scene that developed in Beijing's Outer City during the Qing and the Republican period and became identified with the Tianqiao district. Madeleine Yue Dong details how Tianqiao, an alternative market to those in the Inner City, became in the early twentieth century a major attraction. The original plan was to make Tianqiao into a model commercial district surrounded by parks, sporting the equivalent of Paris's Eiffel Tower and leading to Yongdingmen Gate to its south, which would become Beijing's Arc de Triomphe. The open sewers in this area, including the western "whisker" of Longxugou, were covered in the late 1910s. Although the gentrification project partially failed as the district's claim to elite entertainment fell apart in the early 1920s, Tianqiao retained its allure as a place to visit and enjoy for its many sights. The busy commerce, abundance of theaters, and free circuslike street shows all contributed to making *guang Tianqiao*, or "wandering around Tianqiao," a popular pastime.[75] Beijing's streets became a spectacle in their own right, replicated in literary works, most notably in novels by Zhang Henshui and Lao She.[76]

Dragon Whisker Creek turns local flavor into a spectacle through the character of Madman Cheng, as a performer specializing in *shulaibao*, or Beijing-style rhythmic singsong. The use of singsong, accompanied by a castanet, to mobilize revolutionary audiences harks back to Zhao Shuli's "Rhymes of Li Youcai" ("Li Youcai banhua," 1943), written in the Communist base area before liberation,[77] but Lao She interweaves local flavor. The vernacular performance also adds to the play's geographical emphasis—the singsong artists of Tianqiao often lived in the adjacent Longxugou. In fact, Yu Shizhi, who played Madman Cheng in the BPAT premiere and in the movie (a role that established Yu as one of China's leading actors), modeled the character after Wu Jinkui, a well-known performer who resided in the vicinity of Longxugou.[78] The film version explicitly locates Cheng's performance hall in Tianqiao. Lao She translates the street spectacles into the medium of modern drama.

The dramatic focus on the Outer City and its street performances introduces also a specific mode of looking at the city. The stage and screen productions of *Dragon Whisker Creek* do not provide the expansive vistas of the city's parks and avenues—in contrast, for example, to the repeated views of the Summer Palace and Beihai Park in the film version of *Fang Zhenzhu*. Unlike such scenic spots, the congested Tianqiao and Longxugou allow only eye-level sight to short distances. *Dragon Whisker Creek* continues where the film adaptation of *This Life of Mine* left off. The earlier film starts with a wide pan across Beijing's old city, followed by a survey of palatial architecture at the Forbidden City, the Summer Palace, the Altar of Heaven, and the White Dagoba at Beihai, only to lament the squandering of the state's funds during the Qing dynasty and to turn to the suffering of the common people. The following sequence in *This Life of Mine* turns to the slums of the Outer City, from the point of view of the narrator, a rickshaw puller turned patrol policeman. *This Life of Mine* dwells on the squalor of the Outer City; it ends with Beijing's liberation and does not develop an iconology for the new socialist city. *Dragon Whisker Creek* takes the same eye-level view and transforms it into an implicit statement on the new order of the socialist city.

Through Lao She's script, Jiao Juyin's staging, and Xian Qun's camera, the audience occupies the point of view of a citizen who dwells on detail up close. The view at street level is associated with the working class—it is not that of the high imperial palaces, or (as students of Benjamin and de Certeau might assume) of the leisurely tourist, but rather of the manual laborer. According to Lao She, "officials resided in palatial quarters with beautiful gardens, whereas the poor lived in filthy courtyards. . . . places where the sedans or cars [of the emperors or Chiang Kai-shek] did not pass, never saw a broom or water bucket."[79] *Dragon Whisker Creek*, in contrast, stages the neglected point of view and architectural idiom of Outer City alleys by stressing eye-level images of the city. The inversion of the class structure is accompanied by a new aesthetic sensibility.

The spectacle of the everyday may be contrasted with the imperial vision of Beijing, which was based on privileged viewpoints. Reproducing a perception of the capital as a manifestation of a cosmological order, the city was plotted in the thirteenth century in a geometrical pattern with the imperial palace compound at its center. To appreciate the significance of Beijing's layout, one had to gain access to elevated observation points, most notably the Pavilion of Myriad Springs on Coal Hill, exactly at the center of the Inner City—or better yet, view a map, on which one could also discern patterns such as Longxugou's whiskerlike shape.[80] The abstracting approach to urban space continued into the Republican period. Madeleine Yue Dong argues that in the 1930s "space . . . was systematically organized and rationalized. . . . perceived from the perspective of looking down at a map, rather than from the vantage of an individual narrating what was noticed while walking in the streets."[81] *Dragon Whisker Creek*—together with *This Life of Mine*—signals a shift to imaging the city one alley and one courtyard at a time.

Peng Zhen, the secretary of the Communist City Council—that is, Beijing's first postliberation mayor—initiated in 1950 a new urban plan to turn away from the emphasis on the more affluent Inner City. Peng explained: "In establishing a city government for the capital, we must have in mind the viewpoint of the masses and the paths taken by the masses [*qunzhong guandian, qunzhong luxian*]."[82] Peng's words can be taken literally, as encouraging the clearing of new vistas that comport with vernacular architecture and transportation routes for the city's workers. The project at Longxugou took into account the citizens' "viewpoints" and "paths." Lao She's focus on the courtyard further visualized the residents' lines of sight and created a stage aesthetics to match the new urbanist vision.

◆ BEIJING, OPEN CITY

The shift of emphasis to vernacular residential architecture and the concomitant street-level sightline notwithstanding, *Dragon Whisker Creek* establishes a dialectic between the enclosed residential units and open gathering spaces. Although the courtyard is fashioned as a vital part of the cityscape, the play implies that the new Beijing must also be defined by wide avenues and public squares.

The play highlights the contrast between the courtyard and the city around it. In the first act, the courtyard provides relative security, a shelter from interferences that menace the residents' social stability, livelihood, and personal safety. The courtyard is Madman Cheng's refuge from the gangsters who have bullied him out of work in Tianqiao, and when a gangster intrudes and threatens the madman, the neighbors protect him. The residents help one another in the face of social adversity, poverty, and the elements of nature. The outside, on the other hand, is portrayed in act 1 as the realm of the gangster Black Whirlwind and the treacherous creek. The cigarette-seller Sisao and the rickshaw-puller Ding Si are intimidated and exploited whenever they venture out. Likewise, from the play's beginning, the ditch is singled out as dangerous. Little Niu is warned to stay indoors: "It's all muddy and slippery outside. What if you fell into the ditch?!"[83] In Jiao Juyin's version, Sisao complains: "Once you're out of the lane, not more than two steps, you fall into the ditch."[84] The topographic obstacle stands also for socioeconomic barriers. Lao She mentions that Erchun's character came to his mind when he considered the plight of women, who were not given in marriage to men outside Longxugou, since the residents could not afford losing a worker.[85] The topographical isolation of the district represents the residents' lack of social mobility.

The pattern of confinement melts away in acts 2 and 3, which take place after Beijing's liberation. The city ceases to be menacing, and gradually the courtyard opens to the public spaces. Madman Cheng is eager to go and sing at the People's Education Hall, and Erchun goes to settle accounts with

50   CHAPTER ONE

Black Whirlwind. Sisao backs her up: "Now women are respected and can go wherever they want."[86] (Sisao's phrasing, *zou nan chuang bei*, literally "go south and rush north," emphasizes Erchun's freedom in geographical terms). In Jiao Juyin's stage version, Erchun even goes out to work in a factory.[87] The workers achieve liberation when they gain access to the city's cultural and industrial spaces.

Lao She's characters formulate their vision of Longxugou's future place in the urban matrix through analogies to other districts. When some residents doubt that any good will come out of the new government, Old Zhao, who serves throughout the play as the voice of the proletariat, responds: "Dongdan, Dongsi, Gulouqian—what place doesn't need mending? Why should they come and mend our Longxugou? Yet the government isn't planning to make the city look pretty, but rather takes care of us first."[88] Old Zhao brings up landmarks of the imperial city, known also as commercial centers. Through this comparison, Old Zhao acknowledges the shift away from the imperial city planning based on visual grandeur and toward mending the urban infrastructure.

Old Zhao's reference also alludes to the growing integration of Longxugou into the city's social fabric. Dongdan was known primarily for the bazaars that had dominated the city's commerce since the early twentieth century.[89] Since the 1920s, the municipal government was paying attention to Longxugou largely because the neighboring Tianqiao had become an alternative to the upscale markets of the Inner City. Erchun's enthusiastic vision of the future captures that process when she compares her place of residence to the Dong'an Market next to Dongdan: "With this [mended] canal, aren't we soon going to become [like] Dong'an Market?"[90] Dong'an Market, established in 1902, introduced a Western-style glass-and-steel arcade. It was located at the center of Wangfujing, a shopping area that catered mostly to foreigners and was an exotic attraction for locals.[91] Through such geographical references, *Dragon Whisker Creek* shows how the courtyards in the Outer City's poor neighborhoods would be freed from their isolation, gain economic power, and become part of the modernizing Beijing.

An even more open model for the neighborhood is envisioned in Erchun's remarks, as rewritten by Jiao Juyin. In the staged version, she says, "Once they've mended the canal and paved a street, wouldn't this place soon become [like] Tiananmen?"[92] (In the film, Erchun invokes the imperial Summer Palace instead.) The remark diverges from the focus on the spectacle of the everyday and envisions Longxugou as a grand showcase of urban rehabilitation. Tiananmen—shorthand for the gate leading to the Forbidden City and the square to the gate's south—became an emblem of the New China when Mao declared the People's Republic at that spot on October 1, 1949. Beginning in 1950, the square was gradually widened to accommodate parades and rallies. The widening of Tiananmen underscored an aspect of the city that differed from *Dragon Whisker Creek*'s emphasis on the working-class quarters and vernacular performance at Tianqiao. Tiananmen—a large, empty public square, flanked by landmarks of imperial architecture—took over a popular marketplace to make room for a state-orchestrated spectacle best observed looking down from the gate's balcony (see chapter 4). The claim that Longxugou would equal Tiananmen implies not only a thorough makeover of the formerly neglected area in the Outer City but also points to the desire to make the residential district more akin to the square in the city's center, fit for ostentatious gatherings.

⚡ FROM COURTYARD CITY TO A CITY OF THE MASSES

The attention to Outer City courtyards is undercut by the references to Inner City symbols of commerce and the state. The double-edged message of *Dragon Whisker Creek* is evident in its concluding scene. The play's ending insinuates that the creek's transformation is complete only when it also accommodates an open arena for public rallies. The last scene shows the courtyard residents preparing for a meeting in celebration of the finished drain. One dons a ribbon, another a red silk badge; the child Gazi waves a red flag. Waist drums and a military band play in the background. They are expecting the mayor and the secretary of the City Council. Just before the curtain falls, one hears offstage "The March of Youth" and the cheers "Long live Chairman Mao!" All these elements were typical props and practices in the parades that became common rituals after liberation, street spectacles staged by the Communist Party to support its claim to authority and show its control over public space.

The concluding scene in *Dragon Whisker Creek* resonates with the "Sprout Song shows" (*yanggeju*) integrated into liberation parades and contemporary stage productions.[93] The street spectacle is foregrounded in the later stage versions and the film, which conclude with a gathering where Madman Cheng recites a *shulaibao*. The lyrics praise the government for attending to the poor residential area rather than to the more prominent landmarks, temples, and palaces, and envision joyful workers, a pacified country, and a revitalized city. In the words of the film script: "New China, new Beijing / The country prosperous, the people secure and enjoying peace" (Xin Zhongguo, xin Beijing / Guo tai, min an, xiang taiping).[94] The staged scene invokes the image of a large crowd enjoying the show;[95] it was reworked in the film adaptation into a mass rally. The film uses location shots to present the meeting in detail. The crowd convenes in a spacious area and faces the stand, where the speakers sit under a large portrait of Mao. The program includes speeches by dignitaries and model workers, congratulatory remarks, and performances. The list ends with Cheng's "Praise Song for the People's Government." The spectacle culminates when the officials cut the ribbon to the new street paved over the leveled creek.

The next shot, the film's last, is key to the message of Dragon Whisker Creek. It is one of a few scenes added to make use of outdoor locations and the versatility of the film camera. Lao She's script already exhibits a proto-cinematic sensibility, evident in the expansive mise-en-scène rather than interior tableaux. In various places, the film adds a depth of field left implicit in the stage play. In one scene, portraying the digging works, the camera tracks the workers past house fronts, and the sequence ends with a look down the open pipeline pit, extending as far as the eye can see (fig. 2). In the film's last shot, following the cutting of the ribbon, the camera captures the same location, now turned into a street. The screen is filled by the wide and straight new road (shot on a different location in the Outer City, the scene probably represents what is now Tiantan Road). The street is neat, flanked by saplings, and elegantly lined with electricity poles. The crowd cheers as youth, wearing young pioneer scarves and mounted on bicycles—the new mode of transportation for the working class—storm toward the camera (fig. 3). The dynamic movement into the offscreen city expresses the energy of the new Beijing. The deep focus and the mise-en-scène guide the viewer toward the back, where a smokestack rises in the rear center. The scenery accords with Mao's dream of erecting in Beijing "a forest of chimneys."[96] The shot drives home the point that the new Beijing creates a new urban spectacle. The progression from the secluded courtyard to mass rallies in the open draws a parallel between freeing city spaces, emancipating the urban spectacle, and liberating China.

Dragon Whisker Creek invents a revolutionary iconology for the new Bei-

2 *Dragon Whisker Creek* (1952): Digging a pipeline pit.

3 *Dragon Whisker Creek* (1952): Young pioneers ride their bicycles at the renewed Dragon Whisker Creek.

jing. The chimney, an earlier emblem of oppressive capitalism in woodcut art such as Jiang Feng's *Workers on the Wharf* (1932) and films such as *Goddess* (1934), turns in *Dragon Whisker Creek* to an icon of liberating industrialization.[97] The shift of emphasis from intimate courtyards to open spaces spans, in a single film, the ground that Soviet cinema covered from the early 1920s to the late 1930s. Emma Widdis discusses how Soviet films of the 1920s appropriated "the dynamism of the city . . . as the dynamism of revolution" and portrayed "new Moscow"—especially by foregrounding new transportation methods—as "a city in transition." Yet the 1935 master plan for Moscow focused on constructing boulevards and parade routes, turning "the lived city of the 1920s" into a city "on display."[98] *Dragon Whisker Creek* establishes the socialist Beijing as a lived and more livable city and, at the same time, a city of grand vistas and great ambitions. The cityscape in the last shot of *Dragon Whisker Creek* celebrates the dream of planners, inspired by Soviet experts, for the capital as a center for culture, science, and arts, as well as heavy industry.[99]

In hindsight, *Dragon Whisker Creek* marks an emerging tension between empowering the residents and growing government involvement. The rehabilitation of the Outer City did not result in the emancipation of the spectacle of the everyday but rather drew the district into the fold of regulated city spaces. The reconstruction of Longxugou did not change the leaders' logic that privileged wider streets and larger places of assembly. Even though the material courtyards survived mostly intact in the early 1950s, the boundaries of these inner spaces became transparent to the eyes of the authorities, and their social architecture as a self-sustained unit was compromised. The new urban dynamics are better understood when one compares *Dragon Whisker Creek* with the recent stage plays about the Dragon Whisker Creek area, detailed in chapter 3, and with the portrayal of Tiananmen, discussed in chapter 4. Perhaps the most significant and lasting contribution of *Dragon Whisker Creek* was its exhibition of the city on a one-to-one scale. The attempt to approximate the creek as closely as possible, using stage and filming sets of unprecedented complexity, indicated the increasing privilege of the image, viewed on a par with the city it represents. Inasmuch as the film was a reflection of the city, urban environment began turning into a copy of the cinematic image.

TWO

A Big Dyeing Vat

The Rise of Proletarian Shanghai and the Fall of Nanjing Road

ON NATIONAL DAY, October 1, 1952, the grounds of Shanghai's Horse Race Club, a colonial mainstay, were converted into People's Park, People's Avenue, and People's Square. The following year, Nanjing Road, the one-mile-long commercial thoroughfare to the east of People's Park, underwent a similar symbolic transformation. The road's distinctive wood brick paving was replaced with concrete.[1] It was renamed Nanjing East Road, while the adjacent Bubbling Well Road became Nanjing West Road. These material and nominal changes signaled the erasure of Shanghai's grandeur as "Paris of the East" and its new identity as a socialist city. Yet ten years later, it seemed that the battle for Shanghai was not over. On May 8, 1963, *People's Daily*, the Communist Party's mouthpiece, found it relevant to publish an editorial about the menaces that Shanghai posed at the time of its liberation in 1949. According to the editorial, the enemy was claiming, "Shanghai is a big dyeing vat. The Communist Party will enter red and emerge black."[2] The authorities complemented urban planning with a conceptual makeover. If Shanghai was threatening to dye the Party black, the cinema would counter by painting the city red. The war of images focused on the reform of Nanjing Road, an emblem of Shanghai's architectural uniqueness, commercial power, and urban vitality. Film singled out the road as the geographical epicenter of Shanghai's recalcitrance and promoted its subjugation to the state's socialist ideology.

In this chapter I trace the contribution of the cinema to the policy of transforming Shanghai from a city relying on commerce and services to an industrial base. The change was part of a nationwide policy, implemented in the early 1950s, to shift the country's industrial base to new centers (*zhongdian chengshi*, literally "cities of emphasis").[3]

Shanghai, with its large port and developed infrastructure, would continue to play an important role in the socialist economy, but it was stripped of its unique status as a hub of international commerce. I argue that the policy depended not only on reallocating resources and redesigning the city's layout but also on film's manipulation of the image of preliberation Shanghai. The city had been portrayed as an ideological bastion—the birthplace of the Chinese Communist Party (CCP) and the model for organizing the urban proletariat. The shift of emphasis reinforced Shanghai's reputation as a metropolis where unchecked economic growth followed colonial depravity sustained by prostitution, gambling, and cinematic illusion. The popular view of Shanghai, to a large extent prevalent even today, as a decadent city that offers an alternative modernity, a nation-within-a-nation that has resisted communism, owes as much to the campaigns of the 1960s as to factual conditions or preliberation descriptions.

The new vision for the liberated Shanghai accounts for the transformation of the city's image during the Maoist period in Party propaganda and in films in particular. Shanghai had already been declared *modeng*, or modern, before 1949. The Communist government had to show a yet newer Shanghai, in which technological advancement went hand in hand with ideological progress. The result was an ambivalent attitude toward the city. Films such as the documentary *A Million Heroes Descend on Jiangnan* (1949) and the fiction films *An Orphan on the Streets* (1949) and *The Battle for Shanghai* (1959) show the citizens welcoming the People's Liberation Army (PLA) as liberators. In addition, *City without Night* (1957) depicts the city's bourgeoisie as patriotic and corrigible; *Women of the Great Leap Forward* (1959) shows the successful collectivization of an urban community. Other films, less approving of Shanghai, focus on ideologically defiant elements, whether the renegade Party cadre in *A Married Couple* (1951) or the planted saboteur in *On the Docks* (1972). The two faces of Shanghai—the cradle of revolution and a revisionist base—reflected the vacillating policy toward the coastal areas and especially toward the vestiges of private enterprise. It was only in the mid-1960s that a political campaign was devised to outright vilify the city as a den of corruption.

Key to understanding Shanghai's change of reputation is the campaign to "emulate the Good Eighth Company of Nanjing Road" (*xiang Nanjing lu shang hao balian xuexi*), alluding to an army unit that participated in Shanghai's liberation. Much of this chapter is dedicated to the story of the Good Eighth Company (GEC), which lay at the foundation of an intensive political effort that peaked in 1963. In its later phases, the campaign changed Shanghai's image from that of a revolutionary stronghold to a reactionary base that had to be put right before it could join in building socialism. The campaign was supported by various art forms, preeminently by the stage play *Sentinels under the Neon Lights* of 1963, adapted into film the next year. As films took over the battle for Shanghai, the cinema became the continuation of war by other means.

The films culminating in *Sentinels* identified Nanjing Road as an emblem of counterrevolutionary revisionism and constructed around it a *recidivist chronotope*. The road was not only bundled with stereotypes of debauchery, from jazz music to sexual promiscuity, but also linked to the danger of returning to preliberation mores, even within Party ranks. The threat of revisionism was more than a slogan; it represented a challenge to the revolutionary narrative of progress and raised the question of whether nonrevolutionaries, backsliders, and repentant renegades could be forgiven and accommodated without menacing the Communist view of history. The movies present these weighty issues of doctrine through the icon of Nanjing Road.

The treatment of stray elements inside the Communist Party, the focus of national debate throughout the 1950s and 1960s, had direct impact on Shanghai's status. Once the city was declared a breeding ground for counterrevolutionary elements, its development as an urban center could be stemmed based on economic reasons as well as ideological principles. The revolutionary credentials of Nanjing Road not only determined Shanghai's place in collective memory but also influenced the city's future urban design and identity.

Tracing the campaign opens a unique vista on the use of film in conjunction with Maoist urban policy. The films I examine single out the architectural landmarks built on, and official parades held on, Nanjing Road to reshape Shanghai's symbolic layout and ideological makeup. The road was physically modified to suit a more encompassing change, as film and other media made it the centerpiece of the urban makeover. The road became a metonymy for Shanghai. Whereas *Dragon Whisker Creek* redefined Beijing after 1949 as a proletarian stronghold by foregrounding the Outer City slums (see chapter 1), *Sentinels* presents Shanghai's well-known landmarks around Nanjing Road to drive home the degeneracy of the city (and, for good measure, of the cinema itself).

The films of the Maoist period, and *Sentinels* in particular, played up iconic images of the city, to the point of determining our contemporary perception of Shanghai in the first half of the twentieth century. Just as the discourse on Shanghai's "colonial modernity" has bought into the self-congratulatory rhetoric of the colonizing Shanghailanders,[4] so our imagination of Shanghai's "jazz age" in the early twentieth century may be tinted by later movies. Scholars have focused on the preliberation period to call for "Nanjing Road studies" and to inquire into "inventing Nanjing Road,"[5] yet the road's fate since 1949 is equally essential to a historical understanding of Shanghai.

⚘ THE FIRST TEN YEARS OF SOCIALISM

Throughout the decade following Shanghai's liberation in 1949, Party leaders were seeking apt policies and rhetoric for Shanghai's future development. Political winds were changing from year to year, and the Shanghai film industry in particular stood at the center of a fierce rivalry among Party factions.[6] Movies during this period established an iconology based on the street parades and struggled to visualize the distinction between socialist sympathizers and bourgeois counterrevolutionaries. By the tenth anniversary of the liberation, cinema celebrated a city made over.

RESTRUCTURING THE CITY, REDEFINING THE URBAN SPECTACLE

As in other cities, the PLA's entry into Shanghai was made into a street spectacle and filmed for further dissemination of the images. The parades celebrating the Communist capture of the city established new spatial symbolism and cinematic tropes, which in turn precipitated material changes in the urban layout.

Immediately after entering Shanghai on May 25, 1949, the PLA marked the event by staging parades and recording them. The takeover was followed by military and civilian marches through the city's main streets, stressing the warm welcome extended to the liberators. First came a pageant on May 28, as Chen Yi, commander of the Shanghai battle arena, was declared mayor of Shanghai and chairman of the Shanghai Military Directive Committee. On July 6, 1949, Chen reviewed a military parade. Tanks decorated with red stars and trolleys with festive ornaments rolled into Nanjing Road. More ideological color was added by making the parade a commemoration of the Marco Polo Bridge Incident of July 7, 1937. A second military parade followed on October 8 to celebrate the founding of the PRC a week earlier. The first military parade was reported to have been attended by 1.5 million people, the latter by a million. The route included again the Bund, Nanjing Road, and other major thoroughfares. The staples of liberation parades were evident in abundance—national flags, five-pointed stars, and portraits of Zhu De and Mao Zedong. Big drums beat the rhythm. The banners on display conveyed China's role in promoting world revolution, as in a sign carried by women dressed to resemble the U.S. Statue of Liberty, stating, "Unite, Women of the World!" Some banners bore references to Shanghai's early revolutionary history, such as "Here the Chinese Started Rising!" The floats included mock-ups of industrial machinery, an airplane, and a locomotive. The production of the floats, the organization of crowds, and the coordination of the marching teams must have involved intensive preparation and guidance, evidencing the importance that Party cadres attributed to the spectacle as a means for generating enthusiasm and demonstrating widespread support for the PLA. The processions ended at the horse racetrack, where a rostrum was erected and dancing troupes and drummers played for the large audience.[7] Shanghai's major landmarks were enlisted in the service of the city's new masters and their visual vocabulary.

PLA film crews were enlisted to shoot the parades. Throughout the war, a camera team was placed on the front lines to capture the PLA's advance; in addition, a special team was sent to Shanghai from Beijing to supervise the filming of the liberation parades.[8] The resulting footage, together with material filmed before by the cinematography team of the Shanghai Film and Drama Association, was integrated into a documentary, *A Million Heroes Descend on Jiangnan*. The film was distributed all over the country and screened to large audiences.[9] *A Million Heroes* changed Shanghai's image in the same manner that *The Birth of New China* transformed Beijing (see chapter 4)—the city's surrender became part of the narrative of revolutionary victory, and the urban environment turned into a stage for the spectacles of liberation.

Military pageants had been mounted in the city before, but the liberation parades introduced a new focus. Shanghai had been known for its indoor and outdoor attractions. Teahouses offered variety shows, later joined by numerous nightclubs and movie theaters. A common thread runs through the illustrated newspapers (introduced in 1875), pictorials (used widely since 1912), kaleidoscope shows on the streets, and film shows for which Shanghai became famous.[10] These amusements were largely seen as exotic, identified with the foreign presence in the city. The extraterritorial jurisprudence of Great Britain, France, the United States, and Japan in the foreign concessions also brought European couture, window dressing, and avenue design, so that walking the elegant streets of Nanking Road and the Avenue Joffre (as Nanjing Road and Huaihai Road were known at the time) became a pastime in its own right, dedicated to watching and being watched.

A prime space for making the city into a spectacle was the Horse Race Club, known in the local idiom as *Paomating*, located at the western end of Nanjing Road since 1862. The club stood for a colonial spatial order. What started in Ascot, England, as the use of the countryside for weekend recreation grounds for townspeople became in the semicolonial context a showcase for British domination over Shanghai's spaces.[11] Originally the racetrack's location was chosen for its remoteness from the city center—in fact, the club had been moved twice, increasingly far from Shanghai's Old City. As Nanjing Road became a commercial hub, the fenced seventy-two-acre turf on prime real estate, including an imposing clubhouse with a fifty-three-meter-high clock tower (built in 1932), became an extravagant display of wealth and power.[12] As I have detailed elsewhere, the Horse Race Club created a fourfold illusion, of the availability of money, sex, space, and time.[13] In view of later changes in urban design, one should note two principles on which the spectacle at the races was based. First, it underlined class, by segregating between the Grand Stand—technically open only to members, all male Westerners—and the seats mockingly called the "Little Grand," accessible to anyone willing to place his money in the inexpensive parimutuel betting system.[14] Second, the club romanticized a sense of flight from the city into the countryside.[15]

The liberation parades through Nanjing Road and on the Horse Race Club grounds countered the logic of Shanghai's earlier spectacles. As I will discuss later, the films documenting the military parades presented them as the manifestation of a new society that would literally take over the streets to celebrate the rise of a collective identity. Fiction films would target all the colonial symbols—foreign movies, pictorial magazines, shop windows, fashionable attire, jazz clubs, and the races. Yet at a more fundamental level, the pageants challenged the urban design that enabled and privileged those spectacles. The case of the horse racetrack is especially enlightening. The frequent parading necessitated large gathering grounds at the city center, similar to Beijing's remodeled Tiananmen Square. In choosing to convert the Horse Race Club into People's Park and People's Square, which could accommodate crowds of up to two hundred thousand people, the municipal government solved the logistical problem and at the same time removed an emblem of colonial presence. The new layout preserved the facilities for leisure in the form of People's Park—perhaps the memory of the Horse Race Club lawn inspired a more nature-friendly plan than the barren squares constructed in other major cities. At the same time, People's Square, designed for mass political rallies, did away with the club's class-segregated spaces.

Between the park to the north and the square to the south lay the new People's Avenue. In 1953, the Soviet planner Mozhin, who was overseeing the new urban plan, suggested placing the city hall on the avenue's western end and extending the avenue all the way to the Huangpu River on the east and to the city's outskirts on the west. The plan would have created an axis reminiscent of Chang'an Avenue in Beijing, with a visible connection between the city center and Shanghai's new industrial zone to the west.[16] The plan would have in effect made Nanjing Road a side service street. Mozhin's proposal was never carried out, and People's Avenue remained a boulevard to nowhere. Nevertheless, until its restructuring in the early 1990s, People's Square constituted a monument to Shanghai's embrace of socialism. The new Shanghai was a city defined by mass rallies and street parades.

RETAKING THE STREETS

The new iconology that identified the street parades and new gathering grounds with the triumph of socialism was emphasized in films that juxtaposed the conditions before and after liberation. The first movie to address the new spectacle was released within months of Shanghai's takeover. The 1949 production *An Orphan on the Streets* follows Sanmao, a homeless boy, through the streets of Shanghai. Sanmao, a victim of both the city's affluent society and the criminal underground, remains resourceful as ever, always bouncing back from adversity. One of the more poignant moments occurs when Sanmao observes the Children's Day celebrations. Unable to enjoy candy with the richer children, he locates a seemingly more egalitarian space on the streets. When a children's band parade marches in, he joins the scouts. He learns the motions and steps in unison. Yet he is barefoot and dressed in rags, whereas the others wear shoes and smart paramilitary uniforms. While the loudspeakers blare slogans for children's welfare ("Children are the masters of the state's future! We must cherish the children and respect them!"), a gendarme throws Sanmao out of the ranks. After Sanmao organizes his own marching troupe of street urchins, the police beat them and chase them away. Sanmao's experience in the pre-liberation parade, limited to being an onlooker from the sidelines, stresses the spatial demarcations of class.

The Children's Day parade is contrasted with the concluding sequence, which takes place after Shanghai's liberation. As luck would have it, the film was planned for release in 1948 but was banned for screening by Kuomintang (KMT, or Nationalist Party) censors. After the PLA takeover, the film was cleared and the left-leaning Kunlun Studio added a new scene, in which Sanmao experiences a turn of fortune concurrent with the political change.[17] Sanmao's friends drag him to the liberation parade and push him in. Welcomed into the dancing crowds, even when he cannot follow the coordinated steps of the Sprout Song Dance, Sanmao beams with joy. The film ends with a view of the actual parade, accompanied by a song in praise of the PLA. The spectacle is a reflection of the social system at large. After liberation, the downtrodden classes are welcomed and encouraged to reclaim the streets and their right to power.

The last scene in *An Orphan on the Streets* also signals a shift in cinematic sensibilities, from cartoonlike vignettes to unscripted documentary footage. The film was based on a 1947 comic strip of the same title by Zhang Leping.[18] The director stayed close to the comic strip, often carrying a copy of the book version with him to the set. The film relied on the popularity of Zhang's three-haired cartoon figure and was conceived as a Chaplinesque comedy.[19] The added ending sequence sounds a more realistic and solemn tone by reconstructing the liberation parade of July 6, blending in documentary footage also included in *A Million Heroes Descend on Jiangnan*. The film cuts back and forth from the studio shots of Sanmao and his friends to images from the actual parade, presented as if from Sanmao's point of view. In projecting the documentary film in the background of the studio shots, *Orphan* blurs the line between historical records and filmic fiction. More specifically, the scene points to the parades as an indispensable part of Shanghai's urban spectacle and cinematic representation.

Signaling the new social order through reference to the parades draws on cinematic conventions established in the 1930s and lays the grounds for the films of the 1950s. *Street Angel* (1937) famously starts with a wedding procession that combines traditional paraphernalia and a brass-and-percussion band. The pomp is undercut, however, by the interactions of a trumpet player (played by Zhao Dan), who falls out of step and literally stands out as he motions to his girlfriend (Zhou Xuan), who watches the procession from her window. *An Orphan on the Streets* takes after *Street Angel* in using the parade to foreground the single protagonist. Yet *An Orphan on the Streets* adds a pre- and postliberation comparison central to the message of the film and of future productions. Notably, *Unity for Tomorrow* (1950), by *Orphan*'s director Zhao Ming, and *For Peace* (1956) both feature the struggle against the KMT through students' and workers' mass demonstrations along the Bund, and juxtapose them with the victory celebrations, shown through a montage of documentary and directed footage. The iconology of Shanghai films of the 1930s, which show the city as a sophisticated urban center full of elegant boulevards, extravagant dance halls, dazzling neon lights, and imposing high-rises—notably in the quick montage in *Cityscape* (1935)—gave way to imagining the city through political assemblies and ideologically motivated parades.

The parade films follow the example of preliberation Shanghai movies in replicating onscreen the city as spectacle. The parade films present the city through recognizable landmarks rather than through the vernacular flavor that anchors the portrayal of Beijing in *Dragon Whisker Creek*. Shanghai's idiosyncratic urban environment hardly shows through—which is not surprising, since such similar pageants took place all over China. The parade films construct a deterritorialized spectacle, a purely cinematic image that relates to the city only as an ideological abstraction.

SHANGHAI AS AN IDEOLOGICAL THREAT

In the early 1950s, planners at the national level formed a policy to redirect Shanghai's growth. Traditionally reliant on a large services sector, Shanghai was reinvented as an industrial center of sound ideology. The first postliberation urban plan was submitted in October 1951 and aimed to make the city into a center for light industry, commerce, and education. The five-year plan of 1953, following the Soviet model, did not make major modifications to the city center but called for added housing, factories, railroads, and warehouses in the suburbs.[20] Yet Shanghai had a distinct and different legacy of modern urban design. The semicolonial culture, powerful industrialist and merchant population, and consumerist habits continued to be essential for the city's growth, at least for an interim period. The cadres in charge were also at a loss, since they knew little about the place—most of them came with the Shandong-based forces that occupied Shanghai. A line had to be drawn between condoned norms and behavior worthy of criticism under the new policy.

The film *A Married Couple* (1951) was made in this context. Based on Su Yemu's short story of the same title, it tells of a cadre, Li Ken (played by Zhao Dan), and his wife, Zhang Ying (Jiang Tianliu), who experience marital difficulties after being assigned to Shanghai to oversee its postliberation textile production. Li, who grew up in the city, is tempted by its bourgeois lifestyle, while Zhang, of peasant background, retains her ideological uprightness. Eventually Li admits his wrongdoing; after the staple shots of the National Day Parade on Nanjing Road and the Horse Race Club grounds, the film ends as it began, with the happy couple walking with their child down a Shanghai street.

A Married Couple is the first film to point out the ideological dangers posed by city life and by Shanghai in particular. Zhang Ying tells Li Ken, "Once you moved to the city you forgot the large peasant population!" The originary short story takes place in Beijing, yet the screen version (taken up by Kunlun Studio at the instigation of *Guangming Daily*) associates urban luxury with Shanghai. In Su's story, Li Ke uses his earnings to buy a pair of leather shoes and a pack of cigarettes, go to a movie, and eat ice cream.[21] The same details acquire a more insidious undertone when set in Shanghai, where signs of foreign presence are still visible—the ice cream is Hazelwood, a popular preliberation brand; an oppressive capitalist is dressed in a Western suit, wears white leather shoes, and smokes a cigarette pipe. Zhang Ying remarks, with a blend of self-assurance and rural simplicity, "Shanghai . . . was ruled by imperialism for many years, so there are sure to be many unreasonable phenomena." Zhang's effort to "reform" (*gaizao*) her husband is also a mission to set straight, on a larger scale, the relationship between cadres and the city.

A Married Couple continues in the vein of left-wing cinema criticism of Shanghai's social ills, but it shifts the focus to the internal struggle within the Party. The director, Zheng Junli, had already portrayed Shanghai's downtrodden in *The Spring River Flows East* (1947) and *Crows and Sparrows* (1949). In *A Married Couple*, however, the future prosperity of Shanghai's poor is secured through the presence of the Communist forces. The dramatic tension lies between the old Shanghai way of life and Party ideology, which is identified with the rural hinterland. Zhang Ying, speaking in a heavy Shandong accent and unashamed of her country looks, provides a positive model. Li Ke, who cannot wait to get back to Shanghai as soon as it is liberated, quickly reverts to old habits. He looks on "the peasant problem" with alienation; he rebukes his wife for making her own shoes rather than buying them; eventually, he starts wearing urban clothes and orders around his adoptive daughter as if she were a servant. As he later admits, his knowledge of old Shanghai has impaired his judgment—he does not "know black for black and white for white." Although he blithely shoots down figurines of revisionists at an amusement park stall, he is in danger of becoming a revisionist himself. Shanghai poses the threat of nurturing the enemy within oneself—and inside the Party.

A Married Couple is probably the first film that redeploys Shanghai's iconology to signal its counterrevolutionary character. The city offers more colonial commodities and unwholesome pleasures. Just before sending off his adoptive daughter to polish his shoes, Li opens the window onto Shanghai's night with a view of the neon-decorated Park Hotel (Guoji Fandian), and jazz music wafts in. When Zhang Ying later chastises him, Li sits slumped in his chair in front of the same scenery, as if weighed down by the Park Hotel and the reactionary ideology it represents (fig. 4). (The hotel was the tallest building in town when built in 1931 by a joint venture of four banks.)[22] The view of the Park Hotel gives away the shooting location as the clubhouse of the Horse Race Club. The film eschews the club's history—in fact, the building is identified as a regular office building and is introduced through the façade of another structure. Locations seem to be chosen for aesthetic value, regardless of actual topography and with an eye to foregrounding the city's symbolism. In the film's final sequence, the reconciled couple envisions the bright future of the New China as they look at the Shanghai skyline from the rooftop of the Horse Race Club. The cityscape—actual and imaginary—acquires new meanings as the urban cadres reaffirm their socialist conviction.

As would often be the case with PRC propaganda productions, the criticism of stray cadres in A Married Couple hit home but in doing so scared Party leaders from touching raw nerves. Mao's statement, "[the CCP] should make a great effort to learn how to take care of the cities and how to build the

4 *A Married Couple* (1951): Zhang Ying chastises Li Ken.

cities" was easier said than done.[23] Cadres often felt awkward in the urban environment, and couples of different class background experienced growing tensions. Shanghai culture did not change overnight—as late as 1953, officials from Beijing were astonished to find out that Shanghai showed few visual marks of a socialist city. People were wearing the same clothing as before liberation—women sported high-collared cheongsams and woolen sweaters, men leather shoes; no one donned Lenin jackets or Mao suits.[24] Even though *A Married Couple* ends with the protagonists owing up to their past errors, the Party would not admit that its cadres could be easily swayed. Su Yemu's short story and Zheng Junli's film came under attack. The movie was bundled with another Kunlun production starring Zhao Dan, *The Life of Wu Xun* (1950), which was the target of harsh political criticism. *A Married Couple* was condemned for "sullying the reputation of the Party leadership and tainting the image of worker and peasant cadres."[25] After *A Married Couple* was shelved, the fraught relationship between the Shanghai way of life and the Communist ideology was left offscreen for over a decade.

SHANGHAI AT TEN: CELEBRATING THE SOCIALIST CITY
By 1959, the tenth anniversary of the PRC and of Shanghai's liberation, the city had been transformed under the five-year plan of 1958, also known as the Great Leap Forward. Property was collectivized, private enterprise was eliminated, and urban communes were established. Films during this pe-

riod abandoned the attack on Shanghai's colonial vestiges in the vein of *A Married Couple* and presented the city as developing hand in hand with the socialist state. In view of the virulent denunciation of Shanghai in the later campaign to emulate the GEC, it is especially important to note the continued use of a cinematic iconology that depicted Shanghai as a willing participant in implementing the new policies.

The problems in fitting films to the changing winds of Party policies are evident in the fate of *City without Night* (1957). The plot first follows the rise of Zhang Bohan (played by Sun Daolin) as he becomes owner of a successful Shanghai textile factory before liberation. A patriot, he nevertheless opposes workers' rights. After 1949 he collaborates with the new government and is classified as a "benevolent capitalist." During the movement to reform capitalism (*zigai*) of 1956, Zhang voluntarily strikes a partnership with the government and cedes control to a joint state- and privately run enterprise. Originally conceived as a propaganda piece that would showcase the peaceful collectivization of factories, the film fell victim to the antirightist campaign of 1957–58. Already during postproduction, the favorable portrayal of an industrialist was targeted for betraying the dictatorship of the proletariat. The film was put in storage and never screened until 1965, and even then only in internal Party circles as a negative example. The people involved in the production were labeled rightists, and leading intellectuals were told to write denunciations of the movie that they could not even see. In 1967, the film was singled out as one of the six major "poisonous weed films." A mass rally 100,000 strong was organized to repudiate the piece and a documentary film was produced, *Strong Criticism against the Revisionist Film "City without Night"* (1967). The movie was rehabilitated and released for public screening only in 1980.[26]

City without Night evidences the possibility, however brief, of envisioning Shanghai's capitalist sector as a willing partner in constructing the New China. In fact, even the critical *A Married Couple* takes care to show how a capitalist, brought in by the cadre couple to a police station for abusing a child, is treated in a friendly manner and let go after being fined. *City without Night* ends with the conventional sequence of a parade passing through Nanjing Road and the Bund. The neon signs that formerly advertised consumer goods now celebrate the merger of state and private enterprises (fig. 5). A sign of change, both at the ideological and architectural levels, is seen in that Zhang Bohan goes to celebrate at the Sino-Soviet

5 *City without Night* (1957): Neon signs celebrate the merger
of state and private enterprises.

Friendship Hall—a socialist landmark built in 1955 on the former grounds
of Silas Hardoon's Aili Garden. Shanghai's new economy is literally integrated into the urban fabric.

Safer subject matter is explored in *Women of the Great Leap Forward*
(1959). The plot follows a neighborhood committee as it organizes women
to set up workshops to contribute to the country's economy. Some of their
men initially object but are eventually drawn into pitching in. The film
reflects the drive to establish urban communes in residential areas, a concept introduced during the Great Leap Forward to convert urban divisions
into production units, resulting by 1960 in 2,300 committees in Shanghai.[27] The film does not feature Shanghai's iconic locales, nor does it focus
on the newly built industrial satellites. To emphasize the mobilization of
residential neighborhoods, *Women of the Great Leap Forward* is set in Shanghai's old city dwellings, the stone-gated lanes (*shikumen*). The rallies take
place within the compound, which is regulated by the neighborhood committee (*juweihui*). Unlike the parade films—and like *Dragon Whisker Creek*,
which portrayed the penetration of urban reorganization in Beijing down to
the level of the courtyard house—*Women of the Great Leap Forward* shows the
transformation of Shanghai into a socialist city lane by lane.

The showpiece of Shanghai films in the 1950s was *The Battle for Shanghai* (1959), produced by the PLA's August First Studio and based on a stage

play (*Shanghai's Battle Song* [1959]),[28] in celebration of the tenth anniversary. *The Battle for Shanghai* dramatizes material presented in the 1949 documentary *A Million Heroes Descend on Jiangnan*, with a dose of fiction thrown in to contrast the KMT's cowardice and ruthlessness with the PLA's bravery and compassion.

The film's importance lies in emphasizing that the liberation of Shanghai was not a trial for the occupying forces, as *A Married Couple* would have it, but rather a reunion of revolutionary forces, some advancing on the city and others working inside it to ensure military success. The takeover is literally a homecoming, since many of the PLA soldiers are originally from Shanghai, including Commander Fang, a former Shanghai underground activist. When a soldier mentions that he has no home, his commanders reply: "Shanghai is the home of our Party; it is also the home of the revolution—isn't it also home for all of us folks?" A soldier looks at Shanghai through binoculars and exclaims: "What a wonderful city! Our party was born here!" The fact that Shanghai was the location of the founding session of the Communist Party of China in 1921 and of the anti-Communist purge of 1927, in which many Communists were martyred, serves as the city's untarnished revolutionary pedigree.

In the context of the battle over Shanghai's ideological image, it is significant that the film presents the concluding parade as the culmination of the joint vision of the liberating soldiers and the citizens, who stand shoulder to shoulder in the film's final scene. The parades—as portrayed in the documentary *A Million Heroes Descend on Jiangnan* and the fiction films *An Orphan on the Streets, Unity for Tomorrow, For Peace,* and *City without Night*—not only introduce a new focus for the urban spectacle but also underline that the people of Shanghai welcome the PLA with joy. The characterization of the coastal city as willingly joining the revolution was cultivated already in newspaper reports at the time of the liberation parades. One article tells how soldiers and citizens shook hands and encouraged each other, the locals shouting, "Long live the PLA! Long live the Communist Party of China! Long live Chairman Mao!" and the soldiers replying, "Hurray to the people of Shanghai! Defeat Taiwan, liberate the entire country!"[29] Another article, titled "Shanghai's People Welcome the PLA with Unparalleled Enthusiasm and Warmth," depicts workers welcoming the soldiers and saying, "We have united! We have united!"[30] *A Million Heroes Descend on Jiangnan* draws to a climax with images of citizens singing and dancing, throwing confetti on the rolling tanks and touching them with admiration. The documentary also shows workers, soldiers, and intellectuals working side by side to mend war damage. Offering a similar portrayal of the parades, *The Battle for Shanghai* also reflects on Shanghai in 1959 and presents the city in a favorable light.

Even more than previous portrayals of the liberation parade, *The Battle for Shanghai* shows the pageant as a symbolic closure. Taking over Shanghai stands for the final defeat of the KMT and its U.S. backers, and vindicates the Communist martyrs of 1927. While the battle is still raging, the army prepares itself for the parade. Under enemy fire, a fighter approaches the commanders, shows them his medaled shirt, and asks, "Walking down Shanghai's streets like this I'll look like a real PLA soldier, won't I?" Parading through the city streets is presented as the final goal that will reaffirm the PLA's heroism in the eyes of Shanghai's residents. Finally, the PLA marches through Shanghai to calls from the sidelines, "Welcome the PLA! Long Live!" and Commander Fang (in Ding Ni's stentorian voice) provides the film's last words: "We have triumphed. In the last one hundred years, the people of this heroic city have much suffered and been humiliated. Today we have finally thrown off the shackles of slavery and stood up! Shanghai's liberation marks the ultimate annihilation of imperialism's expansionist power in China. It shows that the Chinese people has achieved independence and liberation forever." The speech presents Shanghai's fall as the final victory in an anti-imperialist struggle that began, according to Maoist historiography, a hundred years earlier, with the First Opium War in 1839.

The Battle for Shanghai further underscores the ideological significance of the parade by juxtaposing it with previous ones. The film features a pageant staged by the KMT on the eve of the PLA offensive. The scene is based on an actual incident—on May 24, one day before the PLA entered the city, the KMT set up a "victory parade" on the Bund. Bands marched, children sang patriotic songs, and red and blue streamers flew down. This last-ditch attempt to boost morale was seen by contemporary observers as a charade and a smoke screen for the evacuation that had begun on May 21.[31] *The Battle for Shanghai* ridicules the event, the announcers' vacuous phrases accompanying the progress of the clownish KMT general to off-key band music. A bystander urges his friend to leave, only to be told: "You don't get to watch a farce like this every day for free!" The parade is turned against the organizers.

The scene also highlights that the parades were battlegrounds for political propaganda. While the cars roll through the streets and distribute flyers, other flyers shower on the spectators. Released from the rooftops by the Communist underground, they announce that the battle over Shanghai has already begun and that the KMT forces have been decimated. The crowd soon disperses. While the ground troops wage war in the fields outside Shanghai, the ideological battle is fought on the city streets. Even though *The Battle for Shanghai* includes elaborate scenes of urban warfare, it impresses on viewers that an equally important fight is waged through the staged spectacles. Student demonstrations in preliberation Shanghai provided a street theater that challenged the KMT pageants and prepared the ground for the Communist takeover.[32] The liberation parade in *The Battle for Shanghai* shows that the fight for control and legitimacy has been won. *The Battle for Shanghai* amplifies the approach of the parade films and presents the city as a cinematic spectacle, seen through binoculars and staged in parades.

With some foresight, *The Battle for Shanghai* invokes the city's future in the film's first sequence. The PLA soldier who looks forward to the parade also envisions his role: "We will go up the tallest building and see all of Shanghai, and then I'll stand on top of that building every day and guard Shanghai." The image of the soldier standing guard on Shanghai's rooftops would be taken up as the icon of *Sentinels under the Neon Lights*, the centerpiece of the GEC campaign.

THE GOOD EIGHTH COMPANY CAMPAIGN

The Good Eighth Company campaign was initiated to repudiate the threat of ideological backsliding in the heat of the Cold War. It grew, however, into the single most influential movement on urban development. The stage play and the films associated with the campaign demonstrate the close relation among state politics, urban policy, and cinema.

THE GOOD EIGHTH COMPANY: BIRTH OF A SYMBOL

In 1959 China celebrated the realization of Shanghai's revolutionary potential and its successful makeover into a socialist city, in films as well as in editorials by prominent leaders,[33] yet the late 1950s also marked the intensified change in Shanghai's urban layout and the beginning of the city's fall out of political favor.

Shanghai's economic power, based on international trade and domestic consumption, declined with the imposition of a U.S.-led international embargo on the PRC and the CCP's clampdown on the bourgeoisie. On February 27, 1957, Mao gave his seminal speech "On the Correct Handling of Contradictions among the People," which targeted joint state-private ventures, industrialists, and businessmen.[34] The backbone of urban economy, extolled only months earlier in *City without Night*, came under attack. (In fact, Mao's speech "On the Ten Major Relationships," given in April 1956, already had shifted the emphasis of industrial development to inland cities.) Consequent plans, and the Great Leap Forward in particular, transformed Shanghai into a hub for heavy industry, located in accordance with the first five-year plan in an increasing number of satellite towns.[35]

With the accelerated urbanization, the city became known as Greater Shanghai (*da Shanghai*). Greater Shanghai, like the so-called New Beijing, expanded at the expense of the old city center's identity.[36] The construction of industrial suburbs and the consolidation of an ideological vision for the Greater Shanghai had the added benefit, from the CCP's point of view, of marginalizing the memory of preliberation urban culture. *The Battle for Shanghai* opens with Commander Fang shouting the order, "Comrades, toward Greater Shanghai, forward march!" The reference signals the rise of a new urban vision.[37]

"Greater Shanghai" comported with Great Leap Forward policies, but in the early 1960s a new strategy sought to stem Shanghai's industrialization. In 1961 Defense Minister Lin Biao, fearing that Shanghai was vulnerable to naval attack, initiated a plan for moving factories from the coastal cities to the hinterland, known as "the great rear" (*da houfang*) or "the great third front" (*da san xian*). The effort to dismantle factories in Shanghai, Beijing-Tianjin, and Shenyang sought to decentralize what amounted to more than half of the country's industrial capacity.[38] The practical considerations were also accompanied by an ideological suspicion of Shanghai's urbanism. The second phase of the campaign to "emulate the Good Eighth Company of Nanjing Road" vilified Shanghai and enlisted the cinema for that cause.

The first signs of the campaign seemed innocuous. As part of the tenth anniversary celebrations, the municipal council's newspaper, *Liberation Daily*, published on July 23, 1959, an essay titled "The Good Eighth Company of Nanjing Road." It singled out the exemplary behavior of a PLA company that had guarded the city since its liberation. The company formed in Shandong in August 1947 and was later reassigned as the Eighth Company of the Third Battalion of the Shanghai Garrison Regiment.[39] Although initially based in the Pudong area, the company was transferred to patrolling duties in the vicinity of Nanjing Road in 1956, thereby earning its name. The article cites the GEC as a paragon of proletarian thought, and vignettes extol the soldiers' frugality, hard work, honesty, and diligent political study.[40]

At first, the story of the GEC was one of many reports on model workers, peasants, and soldiers. According to Zhang Zheming, at the time a young propaganda officer in Shanghai, a soldier approached him and asked permission to write a story about his company. The idea was approved by the Shanghai Military Command, resulting in the July 23 publication. Soon after, political leaders encouraged Zhang to write more articles on the same company, and he penned essays such as "Red Flag Bearer on the Political Battlefront—on Liu Renfu, the Political Commissar of the Eighth Company," "The New Men and New Events of the Good Eighth Company," and "The Stories of the Good Eighth Company Are Inexhaustible."[41] During 1959, articles on the GEC were also printed in *Literature and Arts*, *Xinmin Evening News*, and *Labor Daily*, and featured on the Shanghai radio station.[42]

At this point, the story became the center of a political campaign. Such campaigns, or "mass movements" (*qunzhongxing yundong*), were initiated to mobilize support for ad hoc causes and peaked during the collectivization and privatization campaigns of the late 1950s.[43] As the GEC campaign shows, the planning of campaigns took advantage of fortuitous material— such as the first *Liberation Daily* article—and proceeded through trial and error at the local level before being adopted on a national scale.

The first phase of the campaign included a documentary film, *The Good Eighth Company of Nanjing Road*, produced by August First Studio and completed in July 1960. The film records the daily life of the company in staged tableaux typical of contemporary propaganda. The commentary details the soldiers' thriftiness—instead of spending their money on the merchandise on Nanjing Road, they donate part of their earnings and send the rest to their families. They mend their own belongings and help civilians. In a dramatic scene, a commune presents the GEC with a banner expressing its gratitude. The man in charge says: "The Good Eighth Company has always been our model for emulation. Your spirit of hard struggle will always be the backbone of our progressive forces!" The newspaper articles and the documentary film associated Shanghai's liberation with an identifiable icon in the form of the GEC.

The content of the 1959 campaign does not differ significantly from earlier accounts of Shanghai's liberation. It recycles reports from 1949, which cite the troops' courtesy toward Shanghai's citizens, such as the fact that the soldiers slept on the streets, refusing even offers to help dry their soaked clothes,[44] and reflects the need to economize as the disastrous consequences of the Great Leap Forward began to be felt. Even though the consumerism of Nanjing Road is sometimes mentioned as a temptation to avoid, the city is mostly lauded for its past and present virtues. A children's book on the GEC published in 1961 and again in 1963 opens by expressing pride over the commercial city center: "Shanghai is the big city of our country; it is also a world-famous metropolis. . . . The bustling Nanjing Road is in Shanghai."[45] The documentary's introductory words unequivocally praise the metropolis: "Shanghai is a city with a glorious revolutionary tradition. It is also a city resplendent with the beauty of the blossom of the Great Leap Forward in the midst of our country's socialist construction." Yet descriptions of the GEC included elements that appealed to a different agenda, and the company would soon be reintroduced as the focus of a more aggressive campaign.

The campaign was stepped up gradually. In September 1960, the Youth League's Shanghai Council organized small-scale activities around the legacy of the GEC.[46] The following month, a meeting of the Military Commission adopted an emphasis on "four-goods companies" (sihao liandui).[47] The GEC would become the paragon of such model military units. On March 30, 1963, PLA Magazine published long articles and an accompanying editorial on the GEC. The essays elaborate and embellish the anecdotes told in the 1959 articles about the company's frugality and helpfulness.[48] The interest in the GEC received the public stamp of approval on April 12, when the company's political commissar, Captain Liu Renfu, was summoned to a meeting with Zhou Enlai at the Party headquarters in Zhongnanhai. Subsequently Liu and other GEC commissars were promoted—Liu himself was made deputy head of the Cadre Bureau of the Nanjing Military Command.[49] On April 25, the company was officially renamed "the Good Eighth Company."[50]

ANATOMY OF A CAMPAIGN

The renewed interest in the company at the national level was part of an orchestrated campaign directed at Shanghai's image. Internal documents reveal the makings of a campaign stage by stage. Since such glimpses are rare, it is instructive to dwell on the full process.

In mid-April 1963, soon after the editorial on the GEC appeared in print, the Propaganda Team of the Chinese Communist Youth League Shanghai Council organized meetings to check potential responses to the campaign.[51] The team's report on elements that should be emphasized or dropped is reminiscent of current advertising practices that use focus groups, and the activities of early 1963 may be regarded as a pilot launch, looking for feedback and input from local cadres. The propaganda team of the Shanghai Workers Association, for example, convened a meeting on April 19, 1963, "to strengthen the socialist education of the working masses, and to study from the 'Good Eighth Company of Nanjing Road' how to further improve progressive thought and ways to conduct hard struggle."[52] A circular of the Chinese Communist Youth League Shanghai Council, composed on the same date, outlines the campaign's goals:

1 To emulate [GEC] in raising the red flag of Mao Zedong thought, persisting in the fighting spirit to promote proletarian thought and annihilate capitalist thought, maintaining throughout a high level of class alertness and staunch proletarian stance. Although [GEC soldiers] were physically located in the bustling city, they came out spotless, repelled the onslaught of the "sugar-coated bullets" of the capitalist class and remained forever the revolutionary fighters of the proletarian class.

2 To emulate their lofty thought of selfless determination, putting others before themselves, placing the collective as primary, and seeing to others first. Competing in how much one contributes, not in how much one can benefit. Regarding building socialism stone upon stone as one's utmost happiness.

3 To emulate their good manners of hard struggle, diligence, and thriftiness. To see glory in hardship and simplicity, to see shame in extravagance and waste.

4 To emulate their diligent study, modesty and sincerity, without arrogance or rashness, cautious and conscientious in their relentless advancing of the revolutionary spirit.[53]

Other internal memoranda followed, using similar phrasing. While the wording largely comports with earlier descriptions of the company, it is important to note that the first item emphasizes class struggle and identifies capitalists not only as the enemy within but more specifically as exerting their influence in the metropolitan environment. The company's revolutionary values are juxtaposed with those of Shanghai, a place that requires "high class alertness" against becoming tainted.

The document not only formulates the propaganda goals months before the campaign would be launched publicly but also explicitly outlines the campaign's scale and means. The memorandum calls for publishing material on the GEC in newspapers, organizing reading sessions of the material, holding conferences on questions such as "How to Emulate the Good Eighth Company?" and using stories, drama, blackboard bulletins, broadcast stations, and exhibitions. The directive summarizes that "every front-line Youth League branch, every team and youth group, should study the political thought and working experience of the Good Eighth Company, to become . . . 'a revolutionary crucible' and 'a fighting collective' like the Good Eighth Company."[54]

The campaign picked up speed within a few weeks. On May 8, the *People's Daily* published an editorial extolling the GEC; on the next day, the political commissar of the PLA published a detailed paper laying out the importance of the campaign.[55] The document draws on the internal memos cited above, often repeating the phrasing word for word. The drafting of all Workers Association and Youth League units, the mobilization of diverse art forms, and the use of eminent Party mouthpieces evidence the campaign's central place in contemporary policy.

In response to the directive to use various forms for disseminating the message, the campaign produced a multimedia extravaganza. Among the visual artifacts were an illustrated children's book and a comic book, drawn under supervision of the famous painter He Youzhi, with a first print of two hundred thousand copies.[56] I have found a GEC Mao badge, a woodcut included in a painting manual to be retraced by amateur painters on propaganda billboards, and a set of scrolls in the New Year's painting (*nianhua*) style, which participated in the Third PLA Art Exhibition (fig. 6). A set of twenty-two large posters was produced to provide an instant exhibition when hung on the walls of a large room (fig. 7).[57] The set includes high-quality reproductions of photos, oil and brush paintings, military documents, statistical tables, and calligraphic slogans. The posters show the soldiers as avid students of Mao Zedong thought, frugal, caring, and incorruptible. The images in all these artifacts establish an iconology of the company. Most prominent are the repeated portrayals of a soldier mending his straw sandals against the Bund skyline and of a sentinel guarding the

6 A soldier guarding Nanjing Road and soldiers frugally carrying out everyday chores. Gao Shan and You Chongren, *The Good Eighth Company of Nanjing Road.* Two scrolls of a four-scroll set, watercolor in the New Year's painting (*nianhua*) style, dated June 1964. Source: *Zhongguo renmin Jiefangjun disanjie meishu zuopin zhanlanhui xuanji* [Selected works from the Third PLA Art Exhibition] (Beijing: Renmin Meishu Chubanshe, 1965), plate 104.

high-rises of Nanjing Road with a rifle in hand—the very image described verbally in *The Battle for Shanghai.*

The staging of the GEC campaign is reminiscent of the tactics used for promoting the spirit of Lei Feng, and the two campaigns were explicitly linked. The soldier Lei Feng was held up as an emblem for the self-sacrificial attitude required of all citizens, and the campaign to emulate him established the PLA as a model of selfless patriotism. The campaign outline cited above, dated April 19, 1963, states that the company is a "collective Lei Feng"

7 Soldier guarding Nanjing Road. A rifle in his right hand, he rejects a loose woman with his left. Anonymous painting reproduced in a poster titled "Staying in the Bustling City, yet Not a Single Fleck of Dust Has Stuck" (*Shen ju naoshi, yi chen bu ran*), no. 12 in a twenty-two-sheet set titled "Posters on the Deeds of the Good Eighth Company of Nanjing Road" (*Nanjing lu shang hao balian shiji guatu*), each 77 x 53 cm (N.p: Zhongguo Renmin Geming Junshi Bowuguan, ca. 1963).

and that "emulating the Good Eighth Company is the in-depth development of the activities to 'emulate comrade Lei Feng.' "[58] Indoctrination activities on Lei Feng and the GEC were conducted hand in hand. A progress report dated July 3 explains, in hyperbole typical of campaign rhetoric, that "formerly many workers would talk, eat, and drink, pay little attention to politics, and be reluctant to study. Yet after the great influence of the progressive thought of Lei Feng and the GEC, the phenomenon has been reversed at once, so that they now show a new willingness to seek study and progress."[59] Through 1964, the two campaigns proceeded simultaneously, using similar propaganda strategies. On May 5, 1963, Mao appeared in public to write the slogan, "emulate Lei Feng"; on August 1, in celebration of PLA Day, the Great Helmsman composed a ditty titled "In Praise of the Eighth Company" ("Balian song"). Its first lines read: "The Good Eighth Company is a legend throughout the world / Why? For its strong will / It has served the people for decades / Repelled corruption, forever unsullied."[60] The poem equates self-sacrifice with vigorous resistance to capitalist corruption, a theme central to the campaign.

Like the drive to emulate Lei Feng, the GEC campaign in its 1963 form is better understood in the context of the Socialist Education Movement (SEM) of 1962–65, which identified the most immediate danger in a Soviet-style "revisionism," and in conjunction with the "five antis" campaign, which singled out urban corruption.[61] As in other campaigns, after the main message had been set by the SEM, smaller movements including the GEC campaign conveyed more specific ideas.[62] The focus on the GEC emphasized that the PLA, rather than the Party, was the guardian of revolutionary ideology. Furthermore, the stress on the GEC focused on fighting the enemy from within, using the Maoist metaphor of "sugar-coated bullets" that also drew attention to the suspect nature of urban intellectuals.[63] The campaign targeted especially the recidivist tendencies within the forces seemingly loyal to the Party, a theme of added relevance since the ouster of Peng Dehuai in 1959 and throughout the Cultural Revolution (1966–76). The *People's Daily* editorial of March 8, 1963, dubs the counterrevolutionary elements "cow demons and snake spirits," a phrase that would reappear in Chen Boda's *People's Daily* editorial of June 1, 1966, and become synonymous with persecuting "enemies of the people" during the Cultural Revolution. In ideological agenda, rhetoric, and organizational structure, the GEC campaign helped set the stage for the later upheaval.

Even as the GEC campaign targeted national-level politics, it stands out in addressing urban policy and shaping Shanghai's symbolic imagery. Unlike most movements of that time, the campaign focused on a specific city and on particular locales within it. (The site-specific campaign about the model farm at Dazhai is an exception, but even in that case the site was previously unknown.) In singling out Shanghai, the propaganda had to wrestle with established impressions of the coastal metropolis. The movement shifted the delicate balance in the perception of Shanghai as either a revolutionary bastion or reactionary stronghold, representing the city as a menace to socialism and as the PLA's nemesis. The GEC campaign came close to condemning Shanghai as a whole. Even though the immediate target was backsliding cadres and dormant spies, the rhetoric against "the dregs of the old society," "the bustling city," and Nanjing Road associated the entire city with the enemies of socialism. It is impossible to pinpoint the objective of the slogans—indeed, they were intentionally vague—but the phrasing suggests animosity toward Shanghai for its capitalist past and its continued importance. Perhaps most significant, the *People's Daily* editorial quotes the enemy, calling Shanghai "a big dyeing vat."[64]

The catchy name of the campaign exemplifies the rhetorical slippage that conflated class issues with Shanghai locales. The company was originally stationed across the Huangpu River, and even when the soldiers were temporarily lodged in two locations in the downtown area—the Horse Race Club stables and the Liu family compound on Qinghai Road—neither place bore a Nanjing Road address.[65] Yet the campaign invoked Shanghai's main commercial street, and the company was portrayed as garrisoned on Nanjing Road proper. Iconic images showed soldiers on Nanjing Road and on the Bund.

The focus on Nanjing Road modified Shanghai's revolutionary history and foreshadowed the imminent change in the city's ideological status. The campaign increasingly showed Nanjing Road as teeming with unrepentant capitalists, counterrevolutionary elements, and outright spies. Nanjing Road was fashioned as an emblem of capitalist enterprise and extravagant luxury and as a place that had already corrupted many armies. A sheet in the educational poster set, captioned "living in the bustling city, not sullied by a single fleck of dust," tells how soldiers had to contend with the residual "dregs of old society and lurking enemies." The illustrated scenes specify Nanjing Road as the location where soldiers on patrol sternly rebuffed attempted bribes and sexual seduction.[66] The soldiers' achievement resides in resisting the temptations located on and represented by Nanjing Road.

THE VILIFICATION OF SHANGHAI IN *SENTINELS UNDER THE NEON LIGHTS*

The full extent to which the campaign targeted Shanghai as a whole, and Nanjing Road in particular, is evident in the stage play and film adaptation extolling the GEC, titled *Sentinels under the Neon Lights*. In fact, the *People's*

Daily adopted the description of Shanghai as "a big dyeing vat" from the play. As part of the GEC campaign, *Sentinels* redefines Shanghai's place in the revolution, targets the city as a source of decadence and vice, and extends the PLA's mission to eradicating the city's evil. Even more than other elements in the campaign, the play and film focus on Nanjing Road as a metonym of Shanghai's depravity.

The stage play and film were part of the PLA's contribution to the campaign. The script was authored by Shen Ximeng, the deputy political commissar of the Shanghai Military Command—the same unit that in 1959 cleared for publication the first article on the GEC (Shen collaborated in writing it with the director Mo Yan and the reporter Lü Xingchen, who had written previous accounts of the GEC). The play, first conceived in 1960, went by the various tentative titles *The March of Nanjing Road* (*Nanjing lujinxingqu*), *Engaging in Battle under the Neon Lights* (*Nihong deng xia zaoyu zhan*), and *Marvelous Soldiers under the Neon Lights* (*Nihong deng xia de qibing*);[67] it was eventually performed as *Sentinels under the Neon Lights* by the Nanjing Military Command's Frontier Theater Troupe. Like the appellation "the Good Eighth Company of Nanjing Road," the final title juxtaposes the PLA's correct ideology and Shanghai's counterrevolutionary spaces.

At first, the play seemed likely to share the fate of *A Married Couple*—since *Sentinels* portrays a cadre who wavers in his ideological stance as well as a private who falls in love with a capitalist's daughter, many wanted to declare the play a "poisonous weed." Zhang Ying, the editor of *Juben*, the leading publication of dramatic scripts, brought the matter to the attention of her Yan'an-days commander, now the premier, Zhou Enlai. Zhou believed in showing the human aspect of cadres, and he investigated the case during a trip to Shanghai. The play was subsequently cleared by the Shanghai censors. To ensure the play's success, Zhou attended its staging during a Beijing tour on February 20, 1963, walked up the stage and declared his approval in public, saying, "The entire military and the entire country must emulate the Good Eighth Company." Zhou also organized a forum, during which he praised the play.[68] In April, Youth League documents mentioned *Sentinels* as an example of propaganda activities that should be attended by the masses.[69] The play was also endorsed by the top leaders Zhu De, Deng Xiaoping, Chen Yun, and Chen Yi.[70] On November 29, 1963, during the troupe's second tour to Beijing, the play was shown in Huairentang Hall at Zhongnanhai. Mao praised it: "This is a good play, moving, well written, and well acted. It should be viewed by more people." The play was staged by more than one hundred troupes around the country, as well as in North Korea, Vietnam, and Albania, and won the 1964 Ministry of Culture award, presented by Mao Dun.[71] The initial difficulties encountered by the play indicate the high stakes in its production and the investment of the highest levels of Party leadership in using drama and film for promoting urban policy.

Following Mao Zedong's endorsement, exposure to the play was widened by adapting it to the screen.[72] Zhou Enlai oversaw the production in person, allotting it exceptional resources, including Eastman-Kodak film purchased especially for the shoot. Two units vied for the prestigious production; the choice reveals the leaders' vision. Shanghai Film Studio claimed its right to produce the film based on its location. August First Film Studio in Beijing saw itself as the appropriate venue for a story involving the PLA. The matter was referred to Zhou, who decided to award the production to August First Studio while commissioning the cinematography to Tianma Film Studio, a branch of Shanghai Film Studio. Zhou also named specifically the director Wang Ping, of the August First Film Studio. Wang was a member of the Shanghai Amateur Dramatists' Association (Shanghai Yeyu Juren Xiehui) during the war and an actor in Kunlun Studios in the late 1940s. She became China's first woman director in 1952 and won the Hundred Flowers Best Director Award for 1963.[73] Wang's revolutionary credentials and Shanghai background had already earned her the privilege of directing *The Undying Transmission* (1958), which portrays the Communist underground in Shanghai. Wang Ping involved Shanghai filmmakers in the production, asking for guidance from Sun Daolin (the lead actor in *City without Night*) and Zheng Junli (who had directed *A Married Couple*).[74] Yet the choice of studio and director may signal Zhou Enlai's reservations about Shanghai's propaganda apparatus.

Sentinels' story line follows the exploits of the GEC after Shanghai's liberation. In line with the later phase of the campaign, the film centers not on the soldiers' frugality but on their struggle against counterrevolutionary activists. The soldiers are entrusted with guarding Nanjing Road; the street teems with danger that might catch them unawares, weaken their revolutionary resolve, and enfeeble the PLA as a whole. The plot foregrounds the metaphor of the "big dyeing vat." A citizen driving a luxurious car observes the soldiers enter the city and remarks: "Within three months, the Communists will lie face down in Nanjing Road, decay, mold, and rot away!" At first the company does not seem to rise to the challenge. Two soldiers almost succumb to the allure of Nanjing Road. One, a Shanghai native by the name of A'nan, cannot stand the military discipline and runs away. The other, Platoon Commander Chen Xi, is tempted by the city's luxurious lifestyle, dismisses his wife (also a comrade-in-arms and Party member), associates with other women, and indulges in the vice of filmgoing. Chen's wife remarks that he "wasn't taken down by the enemy's gunfire, but fell amid the splendor of Nanjing Road!" Only after the soldiers realize the threat posed by Shanghai's lifestyle do they revert to the true revolutionary spirit. Reinforced in their ideological conviction, they depart for the Korean front.

Significantly, *Sentinels* was released just as two earlier films on Shanghai, *City without Night* and *The Battle for Shanghai*, were coming under direct attack.[75] Reviews promoting *Sentinels* were printed practically alongside denunciations of *City without Night*, which was accused of "distorting history" in favor of Shanghai's capitalist class and promoting "capitulationism."[76] *City without Night*, like the popular novel *Shanghai Morning* (1958) by Zhou Erfu, was repudiated for its leniency toward "red capitalists."[77] Unlike the works of the late 1950s, which emphasize Shanghai's contribution to the Communist victory and the benefit rendered by repentant capitalists, *Sentinels* stresses the city's subversive power. *Sentinels* resonates with *The Battle for Shanghai* in that both films begin with the offensive on the city's outskirts and follow the PLA regiment as it takes over Shanghai, but *Sentinels* does not declare the city liberated once the PLA enters the city.

The play reflects the Cold War politics of the time. The Soviet Union's policy since 1956 was considered a dangerous example of ideological backsliding, or "revisionism." U.S. Secretary of State John Foster Dulles predicted that socialist countries would undergo a "peaceful evolution" into capitalism within a few generations.[78] In response, Mao warned in "On the Correct Handling of Contradictions among the People" (1957) that one should not relax one's vigilance after the coming of socialist society; *Sentinels* warns of becoming complacent while class enemies are still at large. Appropriately, the film starts with a scene in which the head saboteur disguises himself in a PLA uniform. The enemy, it is implied, is capable of appearing in any guise and infiltrating the revolutionary ranks. In his preface to the play, the scriptwriter Shen Ximeng describes the situation: "A struggle without the smoke of explosions developed surreptitiously."[79]

The anxiety about ideological corruption from within can be detected in the mushrooming of counterespionage films. *Sentinels* follows the classical antiespionage movie formula, resolving the conflict among "positive characters," "grey characters," "problematic characters," and "negative characters."[80] The counterespionage theme had been explored in many earlier films (such as *National Day at Ten o'clock* [1959]), yet *Sentinels* diverges from the formula in describing the danger as stemming not only from underground saboteurs but also from the manifest and accepted norms of Shanghai.

Sentinels employs a rhetoric more vehement than contemporary productions. Another drama was staged in 1964, one supported by the top political leaders and adapted to film, namely *The Young Generation* (film version 1965).[81] The film presents ideological objections to Shanghai, but only insofar as the city's urban identity repudiates rural areas. The film revolves around the differences between two Shanghai youths sent to the remote province of Qinghai. Lin Yusheng succumbs to the difficulties and returns home, while Su Jiye remains steadfast. The conflict between the two is highly symbolic—Yusheng's name literally means "apprentice in training," whereas Jiye stands for "continuing the task." Yusheng is interested in fashion and popular music and rejects Jiye's passionate speech on the need to benefit the collective by going to Qinghai. Jiye responds: "Without our country's wide ravines and the backing of the rural areas, our big cities and industries would have lost their livelihood!" Curiously lacking any visual reference to Shanghai's landmarks, *The Young Generation* simply links city and countryside in the vein of Mao's "ten major relationships" and refrains from attacking Shanghai. The film ends on a reconciliatory note as Yusheng boards the train back to Qinghai. The characters in *Sentinels*, however, present much starker dilemmas. The renegade Chen Xi, who fails to heed his wife's ideological remonstrations, is a veteran cadre. In this respect, *Sentinels* seems inspired by *A Married Couple*. Schematically, Li Ken's character in the earlier film is split in *Sentinels* between Chen Xi and the Shanghai-born A'nan. Yet whereas *A Married Couple* and *The Young Generation* are content to reform cadres and local youth, *Sentinels* calls for the city itself to change.

Sentinels identifies Shanghai's streets as an ideological battleground. When the regiment regroups inside the city, the soldiers are informed that they have been given a new mission. "Is it Taiwan?" they ask. No, they are told instead, "it's Nanjing Road!" Nanjing Road is equated with the renegade province, a hornet's nest to be subdued and reformed. Earlier conceptions of semicolonial Shanghai as exotic and decadent feed the imagina-

8 *Sentinels under the Neon Lights* (1964): Soldiers guarding Nanjing Road.

tion of the city, even when under PLA control, as an extraterritorial space that must be brought into the fold of the PRC—not simply by occupying it, but also by remolding its culture. The idea is enforced toward the film's end, when the task on Nanjing Road is equated with the Long March and the Korean War: "In Korea as on Nanjing Road, we have the same single goal— to see the Revolution through!"

The film identifies the foreign-scented consumerism of Nanjing Road with the subversion of revolutionary ideals. The PLA regiment commander walks along the road's shop windows displaying Max Factor beauty products and says, "If this kind of thinking isn't corrected, we will be unable to stay on Nanjing Road!" His subordinate replies: "The conservative flavor of Shanghai is indeed detestable, but even more troubling is the perfume that assails the nostrils." In a scene that recalls the imagery in *A Married Couple*, a soldier is almost driven mad by the Duke Ellington tunes and neon light penetrating his lodging (in order to pit the soldiers and the city against each other, the film diverges from historical fact and moves the company's quarters to Nanjing Road). The movie's title comes to represent a fundamental conflict, as if the sentinels are physically under attack by the neon lights. The set for the earlier stage version had already foregrounded the visual effect of the neon lights to symbolize the changing mood in various acts.[82] In the film, the ideological victory is marked by a shot in which a soldier overlooks the city, figuratively subduing the lights under his gun and resolute gaze, in a posture that replicates the iconology in other artifacts of the campaign (fig. 8). Toward the film's ending, blinking neon lights on top of the Park Hotel spell the slogans: "Long live Chairman Mao, long live the Communist Party of China, long live the PRC!" *Sentinels* presents itself as the antithesis of the 1930s Shanghai films, in which the city is identified with—if not outright celebrated through—neon signs. The city lights, as well as Shanghai's spaces, are remolded to comport with the New China, not only overcome but also incorporated into the PLA's display of power.

RESTAGING THE REVOLUTION, REMAPPING SHANGHAI

Sentinels rewrites revolutionary history by remapping Nanjing Road onto a new symbolic scheme. At a key moment, an underground Communist leader spells out the need to redefine the road's association, from a capitalist bastion to a battlefield sanctified by martyrs' blood. The leader, Zhou Degui (played by Ding Ni, who also portrayed in his baritone voice Commander Fang in *The Battle for Shanghai*), declaims, "This Nanjing Road, from the Horse Race Club to the Bund, has the blood of our martyrs splattered on each of its bricks. Some capitalists say that Nanjing Road was built by foreigners heaping pound sterling upon pound sterling. I say, No! It was opened with the hands of our working masses, it was paved by the blood of our martyrs!" The speech recalls two historical moments: the paving of Nanjing Road with wooden bricks in 1908, financed with six hundred thousand silver dollars donated by the British merchant Silas Hardoon,[83] has become a symbol of Western intervention. Nanjing Road was also the site of the large antiforeign protest in 1925, which ended with the shooting of thirteen labor demonstrators by British police, at the corner of Yunnan Road.[84] Moreover, the reference to the road's location, between the Horse Race Club and the Bund, literally brackets Nanjing Road with two emblems of colonialist privilege. The Horse Race Club won the enmity of the Communist government; it would later be dubbed as "the great gambling den of imperialism in the Far East."[85] Its conversion to People's Park came to symbolize the erasure of "old society" and foreign extraterritorial rights. In response to the speech, the recidivist soldier A'nan, nearly lured away by Shanghai's corruption, reaffirms his revolutionary mission. These topographic allusions spell out the vying visions of Shanghai's urban design. The underground leader's speech redefines the meaning of Nanjing Road's location, rewriting Shanghai's symbolic landscape in parallel with the concrete restructuring of the city's layout.

Sentinels also uses a factual incident, in which Shanghai's spaces were contested by foreigners and reclaimed by the PLA. The event occurred during the July 6 parade, when a jeep driving the former U.S. vice-consul William Olive disregarded the temporary special traffic arrangements. Olive was detained for violating traffic regulations, damaging public security equipment, and causing physical injury to a man on duty. The case ended three days later, when Olive was released from jail after writing a public letter of apology.[86] The incident was given wide newspaper coverage to underscore the PLA's control over the liberated areas and its unbending attitude toward foreign powers. Sentinels embellishes on the Olive incident, in a scene first excised from the film script due to time considerations, then shot and added back for political reasons.[87] The parade is disrupted when an unnamed American from the consulate drives his jeep into the pageant. The use of the streets is literally contested and by two mutually exclusive power structures. The jeep continues unhindered until it is stopped by a soldier who strikes a heroic and uncompromising pose. The American orders the crowd to scram and confronts the soldier: "What right do you have to stand in my car's way? Don't you know? Anywhere in the world, we Americans go through without hindrance!" Diverging from the factual incident, the film shows the American as unrepentant, claiming, "We Americans have never had the habit of admitting guilt!" Drawing on the anti-American sentiments during the Korean War, the film doctors the events of 1949 to fit the political atmosphere of 1964. The crowd cheers as the American is whisked away under PLA armed escort, and the parade resumes. The American conveniently becomes the negative focus of the revolutionary street spectacle, which not only stages the Communist takeover but also signals the city's reconfiguration to eradicate imperialist influence.

Equally important, the parade scene introduces the conflict between the PLA's control and Shanghai's subversive influence. Mandarin and the

Shanghai dialect are portrayed as vehicles of two competing ideologies. When the American is stopped by the PLA, a local merchant (identified in the script as "a capitalist") steps forth and tries to protect the foreigner in the name of Shanghai business interests. He speaks in Shanghainese and addresses a local worker arrogantly: "Little brother, you're too young to know that when things come to an impasse you must apologize!" A soldier replies: "Hey, aren't you Chinese?" To which the capitalist answers nonchalantly, "What kind of talk is this?" The local resistance leader intervenes: "'What kind of talk?' Chinese talk!" He then switches the dialogue, conducted until this point in Shanghainese, to Mandarin and rebukes the capitalist: "Chinese people should speak in Chinese! We're all Chinese, aren't we?" By implication, the Shanghai dialect is condemned as marking separatist tendencies and as incompatible with pan-Chinese patriotism. The Chinese promoted by the revolutionary commander, even though he is a local Shanghainese, is Mandarin in a standard Northern accent.

A similar conflict takes place when a PLA soldier runs into a hoodlum, who aptly wears a flowery shirt and sells copies of *Life* magazine. The hoodlum helps a spy get away by slowing the soldier down. When the soldier asks (in Mandarin) which way the spy has gone, the hoodlum answers (in Shanghainese), "I don't know." The Shanghai dialect is construed as an ideological affront and a form of sabotage. The linguistic twist associates Shanghai localism with hypocrisy, political subversion, and resistance to the PLA.

It should be noted that until not long before *Sentinels*, Mandarin had not enjoyed ideological privilege. Even though the Communist Party promoted Mandarin as the national language, local idioms, and Shanghainese in particular, had been tolerated and even promoted by some filmmakers since the left-wing cinema of the 1930s.[88] One may note the Shandong accent of the upright woman cadre in *A Married Couple*. Dialects other than Mandarin were marginalized rather than vilified. The years preceding the production of *Sentinels* witnessed a revival of silver-screen comedy in local dialects, including *Sanmao Studies Business* (1958), an adaptation of a Shanghai *huaji* comedy. The film did not come under attack until the Cultural Revolution.[89] Other productions featured the Suzhou dialect and Sichuanese.[90] The comedies present characters that fit the stereotypes associated with provincial dialects, unsophisticated but sincere and resourceful. Moreover, reports of Shanghai's liberation record dialogue in the local idiom to stress citizens' friendliness to the PLA. A rickshaw driver offers his help to a soldier: "Com-

9 Set design for the 1963 stage production of *Sentinels under the Neon Lights*. Source: *Nihong deng xia de shaobing* (*Sentinels under the Neon Lights*). Beijing: Zhongguo Xiju Chubanshe, 1964.

rade, where are you going? Sit in *ala*'s [Shanghainese for "my"] rickshaw."[91] Whereas in this earlier account the dialect demonstrates the camaraderie between citizens and soldiers, in *Sentinels* Shanghai local identity is stigmatized as a marker of treachery and separatism in every respect, class notwithstanding, and as producing ideologically unsound, even intentionally harmful practices.

In parallel with ascribing counterrevolutionary undertones to Shanghai's architectural landmarks and local idiom, *Sentinels* is antagonistic even toward the city's portrayal on screen. *Sentinels* distances itself from the city's earlier cinematic grandeur to the point of effacing preliberation and even early Maoist filmic practices. Unlike previous productions about Shanghai's liberation, *Sentinels* does not integrate any documentary footage. *Sentinels* preserves the originary play's simple stage aesthetics of a nearly empty proscenium (fig. 9). Even though the film was partly shot on location, the cinematography uses shallow focus, centering on the actors (following Zhou Enlai's directive, the cast was based on that of the original stage play, leading—despite Wang Ping's efforts—to stilted onscreen performance).[92] The images are static, confined to an invisible stage. The abstraction of space and erasure of the city's local identity, initiated by the parade films, reaches its zenith in *Sentinels*, which creates a spectacle that is neither urban nor distinctly cinematic. Repudiating old Shanghai entails also banishing it from the screen. *Sentinels* reverts to operatic gestures and stage aesthetics; in this respect, too, the GEC campaign turned its back on Shanghai's legacy and foreshadowed the Cultural Revolution.

It bears repeating that even though accounts of Shanghai since the late nineteenth century had established the coastal metropolis as an icon of decadence, moral degeneration, colonial extravagance, and oppression of workers, the GEC campaign promoted a more radical condemnation. It has been argued that the left-wing films of the 1930s portrayed Shanghai as evil, providing the progressive forces with a clearly outlined adversary.[93] The contrast between immoral city and wholesome countryside is drawn in films such as *Humanity* (1932), about a country bumpkin corrupted by the city.[94] Yet left-wing films do not denounce the entire city; in fact, Shanghai is often seen as a crossroads, offering protagonists the chance to either join the revolutionary forces or betray their ideals. Moreover, films such as *Daybreak* (1932), *New Woman* (1934), and *Crows and Sparrows* (1949) describe the oppressed heroes as native Shanghainese. The line is drawn at class allegiance rather than local identity. In contrast, the GEC campaign, and *Sentinels under the Neon Lights* in particular, remolded existing stereotypes to fit the political agenda of the 1960s and implied a wholesale condemnation of the city. *Sentinels* took up earlier descriptions of Shanghai icons such as jazz and neon lights and played up their role in the city's depravity.[95] No other production during the first seventeen years of the PRC took policy against the coastal urban centers to such an extreme rejection of the city.

THE CULTURAL REVOLUTION AND BEYOND

In portraying Shanghai as a hideout for counterrevolutionaries and a menace to the true bearers of socialist ideology, the GEC campaign foreshadowed the Cultural Revolution. For reasons yet to be fully investigated, the campaign nearly died out during the Cultural Revolution. The propaganda units were also likely to notice the association of Shanghai's underground with Liu Shaoqi and of Shanghai's liberating forces with Chen Yi, both of whom came under attack. The forgiving attitude toward backsliding, which had caused the play to be classified at first as a "poisonous weed," did not suit the new, inclement atmosphere. The film version of *Sentinels* also suffered from the association with director Wang Ping. Wang came under attack for initially excluding the anti-American scene, an incident that also implicated her mentor Xia Yan. For a while, *Sentinels* was shelved; nothing materialized of Shen Ximeng's plan to write two more plays that would follow the protagonists through the revolutionary reconstruction of Shanghai.[96]

Some of the imagery and messages of the campaign were incorporated into the modern revolutionary opera *On the Docks*. Like *Sentinels*, it is set in postliberation Shanghai (the year is 1963), and the plot revolves around apprehending a spy who intends to sabotage China's aid to Africa. Shanghai is portrayed as an industrial city; in a possible paraphrase of Shanghai's earlier reputation as a "city without night," the team leader Gao praises "the Shanghai docks, where loading and unloading never ends!" The city is no longer described through the old downtown landmarks but rather through the visually nondescript but ideologically sound, productive harbor and its proletarian workers.

The connection between Shanghai's changing fortunes and the role of the cinema in promoting the city also became clear during the corrective efforts made immediately after Deng Xiaoping's rise to power. In 1981 the newly reopened Shanghai Film Studio adapted the play *Mayor Chen Yi*, directed by Huang Zuolin, a Shanghai celebrity also responsible for the films *For Peace* and *Sanmao Studies Business*. The play was first staged in Shanghai on May 15, 1980, in belated celebration of the PRC's thirtieth anniversary, and toured Beijing in August, including a show for the leaders at Zhongnanhai. The film rehabilitates Chen, who is portrayed as an able, warm-hearted, incorruptible, and ideologically upright commander.

On the one hand, *Mayor Chen Yi* repeats the familiar tropes of the GEC campaign. Chen thinks out loud: "Shanghai is a big dyeing vat, you go in red and come out black. I'll show them—is it Shanghai that will paint us black, or will we paint Shanghai red?" On the other hand, the bourgeoisie is embraced again—clearly not only to signal a repudiation of earlier policies in Shanghai but also to promote Deng's economic reforms. Chen Yi addresses the citizens and explains that the CCP will protect the bourgeois and welcome them back. He is not afraid of befriending Mr. Fu, a powerful entrepreneur, and even appoints a former KMT official to help carry out a professional city plan. Although Chen is uninterested in jazz, he shows knowledge of classical music. His support of a penicillin production line shows how independent ventures are necessary to solve shortages—yet another allusion to Deng's policy of introducing a market economy. At the end, as in the film's beginning, Chen views the city from the top of Broadway Mansion (later known as Shanghai Dasha). He looks down at the Bund, bedecked in festive lights, invoking the iconic image of *Sentinels*. Chen's last words defend him—and by extension, Deng: "Some people whisper behind my back and say that my work in Shanghai has been too rightist, that I have betrayed the basic interests of the proletariat. What is the final verdict? The free people will judge my merits and faults." *Mayor Chen Yi* adapts the iconology of Shanghai films to post-Maoist policies.

The GEC continued to be evoked intermittently—like other movements, the GEC campaign was never declared over but rather was allowed to dissipate and revived for convenient occasions. The company was mobilized, for example, in a 1971 comic book titled *The Good Eighth Company: A New Tune Continuing the Revolutionary Songbook* that showed the GEC leading a Cultural Revolution rally in Shanghai's streets, raising Little Red Books and carrying a slogan saying, "Down with Liu Shaoqi!"[97] *Sentinels* was rehabilitated as soon as the Gang of Four was overthrown. The reorganized Guangzhou Drama Troupe staged the play in 1976; a restaging in 2001 was accompanied by a video CD; and a TV series of twenty-eight episodes was produced in 2007 (and made available on DVD).[98] In the post-Maoist period, the line in Mao's poem on the GEC, "Resist corrosion and be untainted for ever" (*ju fushi, yong bu zhan*), became a slogan for internal purges of the Party. Deng paraphrased it in 1989, in the wake of June Fourth, and Jiang Zemin evoked it in his attacks on greedy cadres in 1992 and again in April 1996, when the stage play was revived to underline the message.[99]

Moreover, the GEC campaign left a legacy of using filmic representation of Shanghai's liberation to reassess the city's ideological values. *Once upon a Time in Shanghai* (1998) and *The Great Combat: The Big Battle over Ningbo, Shanghai, and Hangzhou* (1999)—two state-sponsored propaganda films— attest to the ongoing effort to rewrite the city's history. Although Shanghai was fashioned as "a big dyeing vat," it is in fact the cinema that continues to paint over the city's image.

Commercial movies since the 1990s have abandoned the recidivist chronotope. As I will discuss in the next chapters, the 1990s introduced a new temporal perception, which saw new construction as a miraculous leap over current urban troubles. Shanghai at the turn of the twenty-first century is forward-looking, in accordance with the policy, launched in 1993, of developing a global center in Pudong New Area under the slogan "Developing a new Shanghai." Films now paint Shanghai with new ideological colors. The new urban dream, as portrayed in films such as *Shanghai Fever* (1994) and *A Beautiful New World* (1999), is to escape the cramped living conditions and join the free economy. *Shanghai Fever* ends with the image of a family moving out of their stone-gated lane apartment, passing a construction site displaying the slogan "Developing a new Shanghai," and crossing the Nanpu Bridge to Pudong (Pudong housing conditions are also portrayed in *Shanghai Bride* [1997]). In *A Beautiful New World*, a country bumpkin is lured to Shanghai and finds hope in not socialism but the new housing market.

As the new policy changes Shanghai, even Nanjing Road is no longer physically the same. In 1999, in conjunction with the PRC's fiftieth anniversary, Nanjing East Road was paved over yet again, to create a pedestrian mall one kilometer long. Nanjing Road, associated through the GEC campaign with ideological backsliding, now evokes the unbridled growth of Chinese cities at the expense of erasing its older identities, a topic I will take up in the next chapters.

THREE

Mansions of Uneven Rhyme

Beijing Courtyards and the Instant City

MR. ZHANG was visibly moved as he pointed out to me the exact place where Longxugou (Dragon Whisker Creek) had run until it was covered in the early 1950s. He had grown up here and seen the dramatic transformation of the creek from a dirty ditch to a symbol of the new Beijing. In this particular location, where the public toilets stood now, it took little effort to imagine the filthy creek and its stench. Now, as a retired man, Zhang lived in the newly built Jinyuchi (Goldfish Ponds) compound, on the former grounds of Longxugou. He was proud to have witnessed as a child the celebrated Longxugou public works project, immortalized in the play and film *Dragon Whisker Creek*. Zhang was more ambivalent about the present reconstruction of the neighborhood, even though it too was being glorified onstage.

The Jinyuchi construction project imparts a sense of déjà vu. When the play *Goldfish Ponds* was staged in 2001, it was hailed as the sequel to *Dragon Whisker Creek*. Like Lao She's play, it depicts the transformation of a residential district from a nearly uninhabitable slum to a modern housing compound. Jinyuchi, which largely overlaps Longxugou, was chosen as dramatic material for its resonance with the earlier piece. Both *Dragon Whisker Creek* and *Goldfish Ponds* stand for key changes in urban policy—in the case of the latter play, the policy of bringing together housing reform and market economy. Like *Dragon Whisker Creek*, the construction was accompanied by a closely monitored theatrical production by the Beijing People's Art Theater (BPAT). The later policy change gave rise, in fact, to two plays—BPAT replaced *Goldfish Ponds* with another version, deemed more representative—*A Myriad Lights* (2002). For the production of *Dragon Whisker Creek* the state mobilized Lao She, a writer famous for describing Beijing's common folk and local customs; similarly, *A Myriad Lights* involved Li Longyun, known for his plays set in Beijing courtyards.

Invoking the spirit of *Dragon Whisker Creek* in stage plays since 1979, culminating in *A Myriad Lights*, might seem at first to be a nostalgic return to the themes and aesthetics of the 1950 play. In fact, the new courtyard plays were carefully staged to coincide with shifting urban policies. To a large extent, they sought to erase time—bridging over the ravages of the Cultural Revolution, and especially ignoring the painful transition to a market economy and the attendant hardships of large-scale demolition-and-relocation.

In this chapter I trace post-Maoist theater's involvement in the transformation of Beijing's vernacular architecture of the courtyard house to accommodate the growing demand for commercial-use structures. The courtyard house (*siheyuan'r*)—the residential building block of imperial Beijing, a walled compound constructed around multiple internal courts—is identified with the old city, contrasted with the high-rises and shopping malls that have become Beijing's new symbols. Since 1979, the courtyard plays have become a prolific genre, establishing iconic stylistic conventions and ideological constructs. Even earlier plays are being reread in light of the new genre—notably, Cao Yu's *Peking Man* (1940), in its 2006 run at BPAT, used a courtyard stage set rather than interiors. The courtyard plays have to a large extent formed and sustained the public image of courtyard houses, as both the essence of Beijing's way of life and an outdated form that must yield to modernization.

The courtyard plays further contributed to urbanist debates by incorporating maquettes to visualize the future city. To present entire buildings, courtyards, and even alleys onstage, and to refer to other constructions beyond, art designers made innovative use of rotating stages, downscaled sets, and various props borrowed from architectural modeling, such as floor plans and maquettes. These devices provided natural solutions for overcoming theatrical limitations, yet their use went beyond stage design. Film also appropriated architectural visual aids, signaling an integrated vision for urban planning and the stage and screen arts. As I will show, featuring blueprints and miniatures promoted the official agenda for transforming the city.

The theater is particularly well suited for promoting policy, since plays can be put together quickly (in the case of *Goldfish Ponds*, it took three months to write, rehearse, and stage the play), modified, and even fully rewritten at short notice (as the case of *A Myriad Lights* exemplifies), and with skillful marketing can reach a large urban audience (*A Myriad Lights* is claimed to have had revenue equivalent to almost 1 million U.S. dollars).[1] Elements such as sets, acting, and distribution on video are under strict control. Like all state-run theaters, BPAT (the flagship venue) is subject to a double vetting mechanism, artistic and political. To find new scripts—BPAT is committed to staging four new plays every year—more than fifty scripts a year are read by the Creative Office (*chuangzuo shi*), an internal department. The best scripts are turned over to a joint party-and-artist committee (*dangyiwei*) comprised of Communist Party cadres and BPAT drama professionals. The final decision is made in a meeting between the secretary of the BPAT's Party Committee (who also holds the position of first vice-director) and the theater's director in chief. Modifications can be introduced at each stage. (This occurred with *Sentinels under the Neon Lights*, as we saw in chapter 2). In view of the tight control of spoken drama, the plays in their final version may be taken to indicate the messages intended by policymakers.

The ideological message of post-Maoist drama picks up where *Dragon Whisker Creek* left off in the early years of the PRC—that is, describing urban development and also prescribing its desired image. The courtyard plays stress the common people's aspirations for a better future, but they gloss over the birth pangs of the new Beijing. Onstage, the transforming city is shown through ramshackle structures ready for demolition or for selective preservation, justifying the destruction of the existing architecture. The old buildings are often contrasted with new construction, in the form of blueprints and downscaled models, as if the demolition-and-relocation process could take place overnight and painlessly. The courtyard plays subscribe to what may be called the *chronotope of instantaneity*—the moment of planning and narration becomes, presto, also the moment of the task's accomplishment.

The chapter is divided into two parts, reflecting the dual problem facing recent policy. The first part traces the development of the courtyard plays from *Next-Door Neighbors* (staged in 1980) and *Small Well Lane* (first staged in 1983) to *Beijing Pretenders* (1995) and *We're All Beijingers* (1997). These plays take place in courtyard houses about to be demolished and present a false dilemma in which one must choose between preserving the structures' cultural value and the need for modernization. Dovetailing with the evolving official discourse, the plays present various justifications for the eventual demolition. The second part, covering mainly *Forsaken Alley* (1993),

Goldfish Ponds, and *A Myriad Lights,* deals with the even more sensitive topic of relocation in the aftermath of demolition. The plays put a benign face on relocation, fashioned as placing the residents in a better environment. The plays give credit to planners for working for the good of the community and cover up negligence and wrongdoing by the decision makers. My intention, however, is not simply to expose inaccuracy and bias in the plays. Rather, I wish to explore the role of drama in post-Maoist policy and visual culture and the theater's place in the urban contract.

⚡ IN THE FACE OF DEMOLITION

The umbilical connection between PRC drama and urban policy, established in *Dragon Whisker Creek,* reappeared in the late 1970s. During most of the Maoist period, the emphasis on heavy industry and on the countryside shifted the ideological focus away from urban issues. During the Cultural Revolution, spoken drama *(huaju)* was taken offstage altogether in favor of revolutionary opera. When BPAT began performing again in 1979, it made a symbolic gesture in restaging Lao She's *Teahouse* (a film was adapted from the play in 1982). *Teahouse* had come to represent Lao She's bond with Beijing and his work for BPAT. Yet the play had been criticized repeatedly as a "poisonous weed" ever since its premiere in 1957,[2] leading to the brutal assault that resulted in the playwright's death in 1966. Like *Dragon Whisker Creek, Teahouse* presents the city's transformation in three acts, spanning in this case the period from 1898 to the mid-1940s. The play's 1979 revival signaled not only the return to earlier BPAT repertoire but also the BPAT's renewed commitment to plays that capture Beijing's everyday life. Soon after, new productions were added to the repertoire to reflect the new urbanist concerns.

REVIVAL OF THE COURTYARD PLAY:
NEXT-DOOR NEIGHBORS AND *SMALL WELL LANE*

Two BPAT plays in particular signaled the new trend, namely, Su Shuyang's *Next-Door Neighbors* and Li Longyun's *Small Well Lane.* The two plays share the structure, aesthetics, and ideological agenda of *Dragon Whisker Creek* and *Teahouse*—and they have been acknowledged as heirs to Lao She's dramatic vision.[3] Each play is set from beginning to end in the same courtyard, and each act depicts the residents' changing lives. The courtyard houses function as microcosms of China, and the events represent the transformations experienced by society as a whole. The plays subscribe to a Chekhovian realism in relatively mannerless acting and in sets that reflect Beijing's vernacular residential architecture. The plots reaffirm the current urban policy and end on an optimistic note. The two plays look forward in hope after the bleak days of the Cultural Revolution.

Next-Door Neighbors, first staged at the Central Academy of Drama in 1980, is comprised of three acts, set on National Day (October 1) in 1976, 1977, and 1978 respectively.[4] The plot follows the fall of reactionary elements associated with the Gang of Four and the rehabilitation of people persecuted during the Cultural Revolution. The structure, according to the playwright Su Shuyang, reflects Lao She's *Teahouse*, which (in the words of the dramatist Ying Ruocheng) ends every act with an absurd yet also perfectly reasonable situation.[5] Even more than Lao She's plays, *Next-Door Neighbors* revolves around multiple characters of equal interest. The format was a breath of fresh air after the prominent, heroic protagonists in Cultural Revolution productions, and the play was praised for its innovation.[6] *Next-Door Neighbors* emphasizes the justice of Deng Xiaoping's measures and their success. Most important, the Communist Party is vindicated, despite the ten-year-long aberration of the Cultural Revolution. As the critic Huang Weijun writes, "Whoever sees this play . . . will not give his hand to the recurrence of those days."[7] As the play concludes, a mother just freed from jail comes back to the courtyard and exclaims: "Our Party was bound to triumph eventually!" Her husband admonishes the children: "remember Mother's words!"[8] For those looking for political allegory, the play was an indirect criticism of Deng's predecessor, Hua Guofeng. The playwright himself would later explain that he wanted to convey the "awakening" of the people during the years 1976–79.[9]

Even as the play foregrounds national politics, Beijing's development remains a central concern. *Next-Door Neighbors* reflects the policy of forcing subletters on existing households, especially during the Cultural Revolution. The selfish cadre Hong Renjie has taken over the main building in the courtyard from the Li family, provoking rancor among the compound's residents. The Cultural Revolution is also portrayed as the cause of the city's material destruction. Grandpa Li is preoccupied with the erasure of landmarks of old Beijing. He makes miniature models of a memorial arch (*pailou*) and a pavilion, explaining, "These are our architectural national treasures. This memorial arch was demolished—to facilitate traffic, that's what some of them said. But this pavilion—whom did it bother? It's called one of the Four Olds, and then—snip-snap, demolished! The fine city of Beijing, with its ornamented buildings and carved stones—smashed, destroyed! Bang! Like a peacock plucked of its feathers. Now Beijing has become a bald-tailed quail, and they call it revolution!" The demolition is associated with the evils of the Cultural Revolution, whereas the subsequent political relaxation is linked, in act 2, to renovating the Altar of Heaven and the Summer Palace. *Next-Door Neighbors* contrasts Maoist policies and Dengist reforms by recalling the demolished structures in miniature effigy and reaffirming the courtyard house as the primary social frame of reference.

Small Well Lane, first written in 1980 as *Next-Door Neighbors* was being staged, is even more ambitious in its scope. The play's five acts mark milestones in PRC history: 1949, 1958, 1966, 1976, and 1980. The plot shows the transformation of the courtyard house from the backyard of a wealthy mansion in preliberation days into a productive space in its own right, and from the space of class struggle during the Cultural Revolution into a place where wrongdoings are aired and perpetrators apprehended after Deng's ascent to power. The courtyard becomes the stage of history. At the same time, the courtyard house is also portrayed as the subject of history, through the changing stage set. During the Great Leap Forward, the buildings are in danger of demolition, as the residents search zealously for smelting iron and are lured by the rumor of a buried cannon. Act 2 ends with cries of "Tear down the house! The government will build us a new high-rise!" and "Right! Eat at the dining hall and live in high-rises. Communism lies ahead!"[10] Housing conditions become a metonym for the annals of the PRC.

Li Longyun had been in fact the first to use the courtyard house to stage the changes in post-Maoist China. His first script, *There Is a Small Courtyard* (1979), pays tribute to earlier plays set in Beijing and especially to *Dragon Whisker Creek*.[11] The play bridges vernacular architecture and the mass spectacles at Tiananmen Square. *There Is a Small Courtyard* takes place in a courtyard house in the Nanchizi neighborhood, just northeast of the square. The play describes the antigovernment demonstrations of May 1976 through reports given from eyewitnesses returning from Tiananmen. The events are seen and heard onstage, in the form of banners hanging from helium balloons flown on the square and the offstage singing of "The Internationale."[12] Even though the script focuses on the national events and pays no attention to courtyard life, *There Is a Small Courtyard* is important in establishing the courtyard house as the place of narration. Political change is conveyed through the intimate space of the courtyard house, a device that the playwright Li Longyun takes up in *Small Well Lane*.

Even though *Small Well Lane* would later be targeted by the campaign against spiritual pollution of 1983–84, the play is a mainstream production, emphasizing Maoist "revolutionary realism" and justifying current policies.[13] *Small Well Lane*, written after Li's assignment to BPAT, imparts the official line and contrasts the Cultural Revolution with the current benign situation. The 1980 version ends with a lantern made by a victim of the Cultural Revolution handed over to a young woman—a clear allusion to the model play *The Red Lantern* (filmed in 1970), in which a railroad lantern becomes the symbol of revolutionary succession. Yet in Li's play it is the light of the Cultural Revolution's martyrs that is carried forth, and the wrongdoings of the "ten years of chaos" are repudiated in an encomium to the new policies. *Small Well Lane* has been described as an oral history,[14] a claim supported by the play's concluding words in the 1983 version, "It would be great if our Small Well Lane had a storyteller!"[15] Li's mentor, Chen Baichen, explains that history as seen through life in a small alley is an alternative to official history.[16] Yet rather than going against the grain of official accounts, the play presents the residents' viewpoint only to endorse the government's urban policy.

Small Well Lane should be understood in the context of Deng Xiaoping's reversal of Cultural Revolution policies, including a rapid urbanization based on the 1978 Ladder-Step Doctrine (*tidu lilun*), which prioritized resources for the coastal provinces and their large cities. The play's support for Deng's economic reforms is especially evident in the description of housing problems in different periods. During the Great Leap Forward, a military unit is given shelter in the courtyard; when the Cultural Revolution is in full swing, Red Guards are put up at the expense of those residents tagged as counterrevolutionaries. Like *Next-Door Neighbors* before it, the play touches on the policies that encroached on house owners' rights since the late 1950s by forcing them to give up part of their property, at times by outright confiscation and more often through accepting tenants at an "economic rent" (*jingfang*), controlled rent that the landlords in effect subsidized. *Small Well Lane* sides with the reversal of these conditions in line with the contemporary policy, adopted by the National Construction Committee in August

1980, to move away from socialist urban planning,[17] and endorses the transition to local government that would be implemented in the early 1980s. The play ends with the democratic election of a new neighborhood committee. Such committees were created when the National People's Congress issued the "Rules on the Organization of Residents' Committees" in 1954 and lent the guise of grassroots participation in government.[18] *Small Well Lane* applauds the return to such committees, legitimating the Dengist reforms as a genuine response to the residents' interests.

Even more pertinent to the shifting urban discourse is the treatment of demolition-and-relocation. A more controversial version, written in 1983, replaces act 5 and ends in 1980, as the residents rejoice over the news that they will be moved to new apartment buildings. Li was criticized for the possible implication that the first thirty years of Communist government had brought no benefit to residents.[19] The relocation—and the implied concomitant demolition of the alley—comport with the policy, starting in the late 1970s, of tearing down whole neighborhoods and moving out their residents. The play portrays the move to new housing as a positive development for which the tenants had been waiting ever since 1957. The text also hints, however, at adverse effects. The loss is symbolized by the Small Well Lane street sign, which the residents intend to take with them, since "our Beijing can't exist without the sign of Small Well Lane."[20] The 1983 version ends as four men hang up the now-dislocated street sign. The unmistakable resonance with the somber conclusion of Lao She's *Teahouse* darkens the otherwise celebratory tone and foreshadows the difficult issues that later plays would have to address.

Next-Door Neighbors and *Small Well Lane* contain the elements that would stand at the center of staged contributions to urban discourse in the following two decades. The "economic rent" system persisted, and the grandfathered tenants (sometimes the same party officials who had ousted the original residents to the courtyard wings) continued to crowd the compounds and present legal challenges to renovating old neighborhoods and to getting compensation for demolished houses. Demolition-and-relocation would go through several stages, each represented in stage plays. The theater would become a major arena through which the government shaped urban identity.

Small Well Lane was instrumental in establishing not only the courtyard genre but also the emphasis on local dialect and customs. The next decade witnessed a flurry of plays that foregrounded the history of specific locales and portrayed an idealized traditional Beijing way of life. BPAT in particular promoted the courtyard plays and other Beijing-flavored pieces (although such plays were also produced by the China Youth Art Theater and the Central Experimental Drama Theater). As the mouthpiece of the Beijing municipal government, BPAT used the courtyard plays to endorse current urban policies. The plays became highly popular; they defined BPAT, re-established its prestige after the Cultural Revolution, and won the troupe a loyal audience.

Some plays eluded politics altogether. The plays of the early 1980s were still preoccupied with the national collective, evident in the focus on the scars of the Cultural Revolution and use of normative Mandarin. In the late 1980s, however, less political plays emerged—especially after June 1989, when playwrights were barred from making sensitive references. *The World's Top Restaurant* (1988) relates the rise and fall of a Beijing duck establishment. As Xiaomei Chen notes, the play was both praised and criticized for lacking direct relevance to contemporary politics by dint of being set between 1917 and 1928. The playwright, He Jiping, stressed her desire to present the daily habits of the city's unrefined workers.[21] The most voluminous and popular contribution to the genre of Beijing plays was made by Guo Shixing, through his "loafer trilogy"—including *Fish Men* (1989; performed 1997), *Bird Men* (1991; performed 1993), and *Chess Men* (1994; performed 1996)—as well as his later *Toilet* (2003). *Bird Men* portrays a group of bird lovers in contemporary Beijing. A foreign psychoanalyst regards the local custom of keeping birds and strolling with them in the neighborhood park as pathological. The play thus distinguishes between the Beijing way of life—involving connoisseurship of birds and opera—and foreign ideas that misunderstand traditional practices and favor forcible intervention. *Bird Men* celebrates local customs, even though, as Xiaomei Chen notes, Beijing as staged in this play has lost some of its old charm and atmosphere.[22] *Bird Men* takes place in a modern, characterless park; the only sign of the old city is the silhouette of a tower. One may find a veiled reference to Beijing's present state in the opera lines quoted twice: "Your stronghold's fall and ruin—do you recall? . . . And how I built you a mansion with high walls . . . ?"[23] Rejecting the playwright's experimental vision, the BPAT production followed conservative realism in staging and set design.[24] The potential for criticism gave way to risk-free reference to a romanticized Beijing spirit.

These characteristics are accentuated in Guo's *Toilet*, which was described by the playwright as *"Teahouse* [acted] in a crouching position."[25] Like Lao She's play, *Toilet* spans in its three acts a long period, in this case the early 1970s to the 1990s, through a specific locale—a public toilet. Daily life in a Beijing alley is captured through witty repartee, and the social and political changes are reflected in the gradual improvement of the toilets. The drama set new standards of representing quotidian activities onstage, including even the most intimate ones. It is emblematic that *Toilet*, like Guo's *Chess Men* and *Street of Foul Talk* (1998), was not staged at BPAT: the latter two ran at the Central Experimental Theater, and *Toilet* was produced independently by the director Lin Zhaohua and premiered at Tianqiao Theater. While BPAT has relied on the classical repertoire and served as a venue for "main melody" (*zhuxuanlü*) plays—propaganda productions tailored to the changing political winds—Guo's plays aspire primarily to entertain.

Plays like those of Guo Shixing have diverged from the politicized tradition of Lao She and post–Cultural Revolution courtyard plays. They have contributed to an emerging urban identity, neither through mobilizing the audience for an ideological agenda nor by alluding to urban redevelopment, but rather by bolstering local pride in the everyday practices of Beijing residents. This emphasis harks back to Lao She's and Jiao Juyin's politicized realism, yet it also caters to a nascent middle class that regards theater as an innocuous night on the town. The accumulation of wealth among city dwellers was accompanied by an official policy that encouraged consumption and, since 1994, had explicitly promoted "leisure culture" (*xiuxian wenhua*).[26] Insofar as going to the theater has become part of urban identity, it is by creating a community of spectators who can celebrate at the same time their interest in Beijing life and their ability to spend time and money.[27] The new drama colludes with the electronic media for wider distribution—*Small Well Lane* was turned into a popular TV series—yet the high price of theater tickets (*Toilet* tickets sold for the equivalent of thirty U.S. dollars) enhances the cultural prestige of theatergoing. The Beijing loafers onstage reflected the leisure-oriented members of the audience.

While nonpolitical plays were celebrating Beijing customs and idioms for their own sake, policy-oriented drama faced a dilemma. As the 1983 version of *Small Well Lane* already had intimated, redevelopment threatened the very fabric of traditional life and the vernacular architecture that the government had chosen to represent the city. The urban renewal of the 1990s targeted the heart of Beijing, where many traditional courtyards were to be found. The courtyard houses were considered a national treasure, protected by major cultural figures and promoted by literary works. In fact, the identification of Beijing with the courtyard house—a common feature of northern Chinese architecture in general—was partly a product of the novels, plays, and films of the 1980s. Now that plays on urban redevelopment needed to address the demolition of courtyard houses, they had to abandon the simple formula of extolling the juggernaut of modernization, which destroys all that stands in its way, and show instead that cultural preservation and rapid urbanization could advance hand in hand.

These contradictory forces are especially evident in the 1995 BPAT production *Beijing Pretenders*. Set in a contemporary Beijing courtyard house through all four acts, the play follows a strict unity of time and place absent in its predecessors. De Rengui, a sixty-six-year-old retired firefighter of Manchu descent, lives with his wife and three children in a fourteen-room courtyard house that has passed down intact through generations for more than one hundred years. The plot centers on the household's downfall, as De's eldest son is hit by a scam that leaves him in deep debt and the youngest son is pursued by his gambling creditors. For all three children, there is only one solution: to sell the courtyard house or at least part of it. Due to the courtyard's central location, two companies are vying for this piece of real estate, yet the old man does not budge. Even though the remuneration would be extremely generous by contemporary standards—he is offered 200,000 RMB to rent out a single wing or 800,000 RMB to sell it—De Rengui turns away all seekers. The play ends with De's moving pledge to keep the old house.

At first glance, the drama seems to continue in the vein of earlier courtyard plays, nostalgically celebrating old Beijing. In fact, much of the script is devoted to presenting the arguments for and against tearing down the old neighborhoods and building a modernized, consumer-oriented city instead.

In the tested formula used in *Dragon Whisker Creek* and other propaganda pieces, the objections are refuted one at a time, promoting in this case the courtyard's partial demolition. By the play's end, De Rengui is portrayed as irrational, or at best a tragic hero who defends the worthy cultural values embodied in the courtyard house against inevitable and unyielding historic forces, ranging from physical decay to economic necessity.

De Rengui, who as a firefighter protected the city's buildings, speaks for the value of preserving Beijing's cultural heritage. In arguing for keeping the courtyard house intact, he evokes the continuity of the family's hold over the house even through political tribulations. Against the demand to split the courtyard so that each child could control his or her own fate, De retorts: "We have never separated households in our family."[28] The statement, together with De's later description of the Cultural Revolution, not only emphasizes the ideal of familial cohesion but also De's success in keeping the property united despite the "economic rent" policy.

The conflict between De Rengui and those who favor tearing down the courtyard is couched in different views of history. De appreciates continuity: "I was born here, I grew up here, spent my old days here . . . no matter which period, neither the Japs nor the Red Guards destroyed my house. Could it be destroyed by my own hands?! Could I tear out a piece of my own flesh?" De invokes landmarks of national disaster; by implication, he is the guardian against a new crisis of historic proportions. He also speaks as an eyewitness to the city's destruction, having fought fires at "Wangfujing by Dong'an Market and Dashalan'r by Qianmen Avenue." The reference to the city's old economic centers pits modernization against the survival of the old alleys and courtyards located beyond the hustle and bustle of trade.

Finally, De Rengui stands for unwavering morality (his name literally means "morality and humanity are precious"). Just as he refrained from looting the burning commercial centers, he is unwilling to dig up a family treasure hidden in the courtyard, and he expresses his responsibility to the family line. After he learns that one of his sons is pursued by loan sharks and the other faces jail, De falls to his knees and cries out: "Ancestors, I am unworthy of you! Your offspring does not resemble you, the family finances are in ruin, we have to mend the house, return debts, save a man [from jail], earn a living. . . . I'm at tether's end, I'm at tether's end!" (fig. 10). The scene constitutes the play's emotional apex. The passage is reminiscent of the climax of *Uncle Doggie's Nirvana* (1986), where the eponymous antihero

10 *Beijing Pretenders* (1995): De Rengui kneels and begs forgiveness from his ancestors.

realizes that a memorial arch is going to be pulled down to make way for a factory (both De Rengui and Uncle Doggie were played by BPAT star actor Lin Liankun, an association that would not escape theater aficionados). Immediately following the kneeling scene, De Rengui hears a fire alarm and runs around, striking heroic poses. His bravery, moving as it may be, seems to suit better the dated revolutionary spirit and Maoist rhetoric. The critic Tong Daoming sees in De Rengui the same weaknesses as those attributed to Madman Cheng, the protagonist of *Dragon Whisker Creek*: self-deprecation and at the same time self-importance; impracticality; inability to see the future coming, and obsession with the past.[29] De Rengui is admirable but ultimately outdated.

De's arguments are rebuffed by Ou Rihua, a Guangdong entrepreneur in his twenties who tries to take over the courtyard. Ou never refutes De's values but speaks rather in the name of realistic calculation. Not only would the family's financial difficulties be resolved, he points out, but the courtyard in its present condition is unsustainable: "The building . . . is in danger of collapsing at any moment. . . . I looked carefully at your house. Many of the pillars and beams have rotted; the foundations are sinking unevenly; the inner parts of the wall have been seriously corroded by rain. This way, the beams' connecting tenons and mortises loosen, and once they are subject to strong external force they quickly become unable to support the building's frame." Ou Rihua's technical language is clearly meant to stump his lay listeners (tenons and mortises—in Chinese, *sun*—are used to connect wooden pieces without nails). To further establish his authority, Ou explains that he majored in urban planning and worked in the Construction Bureau.

Ou replicates the Beijing Construction Bureau's official reason for demolishing old residences, namely, that the old buildings are uninhabitable and beyond repair. In the ensuing dialogue with De Rengui, Ou Rihua explains that although the structural weaknesses do not show, they are in fact critical. Even though the compound has been renovated every few years, the workmen simply used paint and plaster, covering the rotting insides. Ou's proposal fits in the government's development scheme, which would preserve specific buildings but give commercial interests a foothold in the city's old quarters. He offers to finance a full restoration and pay an additional sum of money in return for taking over the wing facing the street. Although it is never spelled out, one may presume that he would demolish the wing to make room for a modern building.

Ou counters De's accusation that he is dishonest and money-grubbing by explaining that he is thinking of the good of both parties. De's and Ou's arguments seem equally valid. Ou sounds sincere, while De makes the point that Ou suggests that any building is for sale—after all, De says, Tiananmen and Zhongnanhai (historic landmarks and symbols of the state) cannot be bought with money.[30] Yet whereas De Rengui ignores monetary value, Ou Rihua represents the Dengist reforms and speaks in the name of modern commerce and the market economy. The balance between the two viewpoints is tipped by De's daughter, Wenzhu. She is her own woman and manages a successful business—unlike her younger brother, who steals the family's antiques to pay his gambling debts, and unlike her older brother, who puts down the house as collateral in a deal that goes sour. Even though she is loyal to the family and has no urgent need for money, she too sees that the house is on its last legs. She blames her father for thinking "that the older the house the more solid it is, that what was made by our ancestors is made of iron and can never collapse." She admonishes De Rengui: "Haven't you seen they're demolishing houses all over Beijing? Even if you keep [the house] today, you won't be able to keep it tomorrow!" Her disinterested judgment underscores the fact that De Rengui errs on the side of idealism and fails to see things realistically.

Eventually, the father loses his moral authority. Insofar as De Rengui is the eponymous hero of the play, the title of which literally translates as "Beijing uncle," he is not only the undisputed patriarch but also the ultimate target of criticism. The play's title—*Beijing daye*—is also slang for a good-for-nothing (hence the English title *Beijing Pretenders*). More precisely, the phrase refers to an old Beijinger who, though kind and loyal, sticks to vacuous rites, is full of empty talk, and does little to earn a living.[31] In light of the title, De Rengui symbolizes those Beijingers who do not keep pace with the present and cling to self-pride.

In the play's final scene, Ou and an associate appear at the door, wearing formal business attire. Wenzhu addresses her father: "Dad, this house . . ." The lights fade out for the last time, implying that the courtyard will be sold. Even though the play does not spell out the outcome, it makes clear that time is on Ou's side. Ou tells De's daughter: "Wait for an opportunity! Look at both sides of this avenue—they've already been converted into shop fronts. Only the wall of the small De family courtyard stands there pitifully. It's like a small islet in the ocean. Sun Yat-sen said it well: 'The tide of world events is mighty. Those who follow it prosper, whereas those who resist it perish.' In my opinion, Beijingers are simply returning to the Peking Man caves." Ou's words point to the inevitable course of urban development, invoking the historical determinism through which revolutionaries from Sun Yat-sen to Mao Zedong have justified their efforts to modernize the country. Whereas De Rengui venerates an unchanging tradition, Ou sees the future in change, even at the expense of demolishing Beijing's courtyard houses. The play ends with the same sound with which it begins: a clock chime to the tune of the revolutionary song "The East Is Red." Time requires unceasing transformation and its bell tolls for old Beijing.

THE COURTYARD HOUSE IN THE ERA OF ECONOMIC REFORMS

Beijing Pretenders was staged at an opportune moment for urban policy. The argument over the future of the De family courtyard bears a striking resemblance to the various viewpoints in the public debate over urban renewal in the 1990s—at least as these views were represented by the government. A number of concurrent processes have colluded to create the new urban discourse. Rapid urbanization put real estate at a premium, catapulted developers to power, redefined the relationship between planners and residents, and enhanced the stakes in the debate over preservation.

In the 1980s and '90s, policies were implemented to attract overseas investors.[32] These forces are represented in *Beijing Pretenders* by Ou Rihua, whose name literally means "Europe, Japan, and Chinese [diaspora]" and who is backed by Hong Kong investors. At the time, investors were drawn to the large, unexploited, and poorly regulated market. Some real estate companies specialized in scouting courtyard houses whose residents could be easily relocated and reselling the refurbished premises on the luxury market.[33] Land reform and housing privatization brought many new potential buyers to the market and resulted in a scurry for construction funds. Old buildings were demolished, original residents relocated, and new houses built. In common parlance, this form of redevelopment became known as *weigai* (short for the euphemistic *wei jiu fang gaizao*, "reconstruction of hazardous and old houses") and relied on putting together the resources of the government, work units, and individual citizens. Weigai originated in the late 1970s—the relocation in the last act of *Small Well Lane* represents such a project—yet only in the late 1980s did redevelopment become a major market force. In April 1991, the municipal government formulated the official policy, which opened the way for aggressive intervention by developers.[34] In an economic system transitioning from socialism to a market economy, where the municipal government was embarking on large projects with relatively low income to finance them, the scales were tipped in favor of the developers, who became active participants in shaping urban policy.[35] De Rengui's battle should be seen in the context of the encroaching entrepreneurs.

The government's rhetoric has been protective of the residents. For example, a key document—the Urban Real Estate Management Act of 1994, Article 4—states: "In keeping with the state of development of society and the economy, the state shall support housing construction for residents and progressively improve living conditions."[36] Yet couched in the language about citizens' welfare, the act upholds a paternalistic attitude whereby the state maintains full control over housing conditions, including the authority to decide which structures need "improvement" and which residents must find alternative housing. Moreover, the new legislation provided only partial and eroding protection from the private entrepreneurs. Developers often put themselves above the law; some cases of corruption have since become infamous. The Hong Kong mogul Li Ka Shing is rumored to have bribed Beijing's mayor, Chen Xitong (later removed from office on other charges), to gain access to the prime lot on which he erected the Oriental Plaza office and apartment towers; Chau Ching-ngai secured a site along Shanghai's Nanjing Road practically for free before being arrested in an unrelated fraud case.[37] For the majority of Chinese city dwellers, urbanization by the mid-1990s had come to mean graft-ridden gentrification that benefited mostly government officials and real estate tycoons.

Through the intricate character of Ou Rihua, *Beijing Pretenders* offers a roundabout defense of the need to develop Beijing at the expense of the city's old neighborhoods. Whereas De Rengui enacts an unrealistic attempt to preserve the courtyard, Ou conveys that urban redevelopment is undertaken with sincere and benevolent intentions. As a state-employed urban planner turned independent entrepreneur, Ou embodies the collaboration between government agencies and private developers. He is a mouthpiece for economic reform and modernization, repeating the official line that the old buildings constitute a danger to their residents and cannot be saved in their present form. Yet Ou never acts unscrupulously. Even though he first gains access to the De courtyard by pretending to be a simple worker, he is honest and law-abiding. If throughout the negotiation with De Rengui Ou conducts himself with confidence, this is not the result of arrogance but simply because the law is on his side. He may bring unwelcome news, but he is not unjust. The play presents the developers as earnestly shouldering the task of rebuilding the city.

Beijing Pretenders offers a public explication of the new urban policy and a direct response to brewing social unrest. As a state-sponsored and state-acclaimed production (on the occasion of the fiftieth anniversary of the PRC, it received the Beijing Art Award), the play presents the government's viewpoint on subjecting Beijing's cultural heritage to the market economy and putting it in the hands of real estate developers.

DEVELOPMENT AND PRESERVATION: THE LITERARY DEBATE

The doctored version of weigai in *Beijing Pretenders* stirred a public debate that drew planners and intellectuals to advocate preservation of the old courtyards. Contrary to the picture painted by *Beijing Pretenders*, the need to keep courtyard culture intact was not only expressed by obsessed eccentrics like De Rengui. Preservation had become a major concern among planning professionals and was defended by prominent public intellectuals.

Preservation had, in fact, been integrated into official discourse as soon as Deng's reforms were launched. The 1978 plan for Beijing, drafted in response to a resolution passed by the Third Party Plenum, no longer refers to Beijing, along Soviet principles of urban planning, as an economic or industrial center. The new plan acknowledges the capital as first and foremost a political, technological, and cultural hub. The 1978 plan was also the first to mention environmental concerns, the need for "a gradual reconstruction of the old city," and Beijing's status as a historic city whose unique character must be preserved. Subsequent plans elaborated on these concerns. In 1983, a plan targeted specifically the preservation of Beijing's cultural relics, the first policy of its kind in China.[38] The impact, however, was mostly topical—the Municipal Planning Institute drew up in 1987 "construction control zones" (*jianshe kongzhi didai*) that stipulated protective greenbelts around specific sites.[39] Even as an official survey in 1989 identified 805 well-preserved courtyards in Beijing's Old City, this low estimate, based on very strict standards, was in fact used to justify the demolition of other structures and entire areas.[40] The terms of debate were tilted toward restoring landmarks rather than conserving vernacular architecture in its larger context.

Such biases notwithstanding, the emerging preservation policy was made possible by the rise of professional urban planning.[41] In the early 1990s planning was restructured as a profession with specific vocational concerns. The Urban Planning Act (approved by the People's Congress in 1989 and implemented in 1991) provided for the first time legal foundation for zoning, land use, and the preservation of historic relics.[42] As I will argue later, professional practices were also mobilized to legitimize political decisions, yet planners should be credited for working within the establishment to mediate between political decisions and professional considerations. These considerations included the adjustment of urban infrastructure, the effect on the social fabric, and the need for historic preservation. Of these mediators, the most prominent was Wu Liangyong, a veteran planner and scholar. Wu's advocacy of weigai has earned him criticism, however, from more confrontational preservation activists.

Professional planners have found it difficult to contend with the powerful interest groups backing development. A second line of defense is offered by intellectuals who enlist public support and negotiate with the authorities. Even though scholars, writers, and artists were marginalized in the 1990s by the collapse of the state apparatus that ensured their livelihood and prestige and by the rise of the market economy that privileged mass entertainment, public intellectuals nevertheless continued to have wide connections and access to the media. They were in an influential position to counter the collusion of political decision makers and private developers. Special mention should be made of Feng Jicai, an outspoken writer who used the electronic media to challenge Tianjin's municipal government (see chapter 6),[43] and the "four iron pillars" (si da tiegan'r) of Beijing preservation—Shu Yi, Liang Congjie, Yang Dongping, and Li Yan. Shu Yi, the son of Lao She, enjoys particular political and literary influence as a member of the Chinese People's Political Constructive Conference and the director of the National Museum of Modern Chinese Literature. For his efforts, he has earned the nickname "the patriotic troublemaker" (aiguozhe daodan). As Shu explains, preservation is hindered not by the high-level decision makers but rather by district heads who compete to be the most "modern," residents who simply look for comfort, and international corporations carried by the winds of globalization. Under these circumstances, preservation is possible only through gentrification.[44]

The preservationists' uphill battle has been made even more difficult by plays such as Beijing Pretenders. The playwright, Zhong Jieying, would soon make his position explicit and public. In 2000, Zhong appeared on the popular TV talk show Tell It as It Is and debated the wisdom of altering the course of a proposed highway to keep alive a tree one thousand years old. Zhong's opponent on the show was Liang Congjie, China's foremost environmental activist. One of the "iron pillars," Liang also champions preservation of Beijing's old city, a cause made prominent by his father, the architect Liang Sicheng. During the debate, the old tree quickly turned into a symbol of China's architectural heritage. Against Liang's lament over the destruction of Beijing's old wall, Zhong advocated "replacing the old with the new." Zhong proudly evoked his personal experience as a planner who for twenty years "demolished a good number of houses and felled quite a few trees," including a sixteenth-century house. He explained that the residents welcomed the demolition, since it allowed them to improve their living conditions. In Zhong's opinion, activists such as Liang Congjie are overprotective.[45] Beijing Pretenders comports with Zhong's position, as does the government's aggressive promotion of urban redevelopment through demolition-and-relocation.

The play signals the shift in mid-1990s drama to basing Beijing's local identity not only on traditional customs and daily habits but also on the market economy.

Critics recognized the high stakes in *Beijing Pretenders*. The play initiated a lively debate between the "developmentalists" (*kaifa pai*) and "preservationists" (*baohu pai*). Leading newspapers contrasted Zhong Jieying's views with those of critics and scholars, and in July 1995 a symposium brought together advocates of both sides.[46] Tong Daoming praised the play as one of the major cultural events of 1995; others stated that in the play one "hears the footsteps of history."[47] The courtyard's fate was readily identified as a metaphor for the future of Beijing, which can be viewed as a blown-up courtyard, architecturally and socially.[48] Zhao Ming, a leading historian of Beijing, stressed the play's function as a parable, bringing into focus the question, "Should modernization destroy completely our way of life?"[49]

One of the prominent preservationists, "iron pillar" Yang Dongping, avoided in his essays direct criticism of *Beijing Pretenders*. Instead, he leveraged the play to talk of De Rengui as "the last guard" in a city that needs to preserve its historic relics and cultural heritage. Yang drew attention to the fact that places such as the former residence of the painter Qi Baishi were condemned for demolition and that some would not even object to razing the Forbidden City. Yang concluded with a snide observation at BPAT's expense: *Teahouse* was produced after Beijing's teahouses had disappeared; now a courtyard is placed on the stage just as Beijing's courtyards are dying out.[50]

Much of the discussion focused on the double-entendre in the play's title. Zhong Jieying admitted that he had had both interpretations of *daye* in mind—as an honorific for the patriarchal De Rengui and as a disparaging reference to his self-importance.[51] Zhong's position was countered by the prominent "iron pillar" Shu Yi. As the son of Lao She, author of the foundational Beijing plays *Dragon Whisker Creek* and *Teahouse*, Shu spoke with authority on the relation between drama and the city. Shu took umbrage at Zhong's description of Beijingers as self-centered good-for-nothing dayes. Shu Yi admitted that to a large extent Beijingers have become reliant on others (were the out-of-town street vendors and nannies to leave the capital, there would be no one to sell food or look after the children). In so doing, maintains Shu, Beijingers are no different from others who have taken advantage of the reform-era economy, but Beijingers' love of culture and leisure stands out in a commercially minded environment. Shu Yi concludes with a jab at the play: "The main note in writing a play about these people, caught in the maelstrom of commerce, is to criticize them. Yet it makes an attractive play because they have their own act to play out."[52] Shu Yi retaliates for Zhong Jieying's pun on *daye* with his own word plays. Even when Beijingers are written, in Zhong's "main note," into a "main melody" (propaganda) play, they can fend for themselves. They "have their own act to play out," writes Shu Yi, using the colloquial expression *you xi*, which indicates that the residents' prospects are looking up. But in a more literal translation, the phrase gives Beijingers control over the stage. They are not daye slackers but rather resourceful enough to turn the circumstances to their advantage.

Shu Yi places the play in a larger context and claims that *Beijing Pretenders* is "the latest attempt to use artistic form to criticize Beijingers." Indeed, the responses in support of the play can be read as a smear campaign against local customs. Zhong Jieying characterizes Beijingers as arrogant, self-fashioned aristocrats known for being "vacuous, insipid, aloof, and unkind" (*qingxian, qingdan, qinggao, qingku*).[53] Another essay elaborates: Beijingers promote a vain Manchu bannermen culture that revolves around local snacks and opera.[54] Not only do residents of the capital regard themselves as second to none, but Beijingers and Beijing culture also suffer from systemic isolation and smugness. Townspeople regard the city as a country within a country, exclude out-of-town people, and never leave its boundaries. According to the critic, BPAT had so far based its repertoire on the Beijing-centric works of Lao She, Guo Moruo, and Cao Yu, and *Beijing Pretenders* was a welcome corrective.[55]

The attempt to paint a whole city in one ideological color is reminiscent of the Good Eighth Company campaign of the early 1960s, which characterized Shanghai's residents as bourgeois and counterrevolutionary. Yet unlike the earlier campaign, there was no concerted attempt to discourage local Beijing identity in the mid-1990s. The courtyard house remained Beijing's hallmark—at least as long as it comported with the national policy of promoting a market economy, development through real estate privatization, and urban planning focused on ease of transportation and commerce rather than on preservation.

The dispute over *Beijing Pretenders* lays bare the process of constructing city identity and promoting urban policy. Insignificant idiosyncrasies and everyday activities are magnified into stereotypes. Shu Yi, for example, lists the following traits: "Beijingers . . . are good at growing flowers and trees, raising cats and dogs, keeping crickets and caterpillars, listening to opera and singing it, drinking tea and wine, cooking, climbing mountains, swimming, painting and stele appreciation, polite talk, caring for the old and young, humor . . ."[56] Many critics mention Zhong Jieying's Guangdong extraction, setting up a contrast between the traits of the northern capital, on the one hand, and the southern commercial centers of Shanghai and Guangzhou, on the other. The debate over urban redevelopment may be seen as a reincarnation of the literary rivalry between the "Beijing clique" (*jingpai*) and "Shanghai clique" (*haipai*) of the early twentieth century. Admittedly, some critics saw the debate as a chance to find common traits in residents of Beijing and Shanghai, or even assert (as did Qian Guangpei of the Academy of Sciences) that daye characteristics are not a "local specialty" of Beijing but rather a malady shared by all contemporary urban societies.[57] Yet many others offered observations on the unique nature of Beijing. A cottage industry emerged to support the city's claims to cultural grandeur. Books waxed nostalgic about Beijing customs and compiled descriptions of the city by famous literary figures; other anthologies put side by side Beijing and Shanghai, establishing their historic and contemporary identities.[58] Photo albums dwelled on old Beijing sites, such as Tianqiao market of the Republican era and the now-demolished city gates.[59] An entire genre offered photos of the city's *hutong* (the alleys leading to the courtyards) and explained "hutong culture"; in 1993, the prominent essayist Wang Zengqi wrote the introduction to one of these books, *The Disappearance of the Hutong*, and concluded with the words: "Goodbye, hutong!"[60] Such coffee-table books, which are in themselves a symptom of the commodification of culture for the burgeoning middle class, established the traits associated with Beijing and canonized the city's representative writers.

Beijing Pretenders is among the prominent test cases for the Beijing courtyard plays' function as a tool to shape public opinion in the era of economic reforms. As the literary debate evidences, the play only partially convinced the audience. Filmmakers were starting to use similar materials to offer alternative views (see chapter 6). The importance of the BPAT productions lies in their defining the terms of debate, identifying the demolition of the courtyards as the result of modernization, economic mobility, and resistance to ossified tradition. While the tactics used by real estate developers continued to be disputed, no article covering *Beijing Pretenders* questioned the assumption that De Rengui exemplifies dated thinking, nor did any writer suggest practical ways to preserve the courtyards. Instead, the issue as defined by the play was how the market economy would make best use of Beijing's spaces. Culture was deemed viable only insofar as it could be transformed into capital, in what came to be known as cultural economy.

CULTURAL HERITAGE AND CULTURAL ECONOMY:
WE'RE ALL BEIJINGERS

Beijing Pretenders skirts not only alternative views of preservation but also the awkward fact that courtyard houses are coveted not only for their location but also for their cultural cachet, which can be redeemed for cash. De Rengui's defense in the name of cultural heritage, as hardheaded as it may be, ironically contributes to the place's monetary value. De makes the mistake of believing that in arguing for the courtyard's antiquity he can save it; in fact, the price of the real estate rises in developers' eyes since gentrifying the courtyard house fits the paradigms of the new cultural economy.

Since 1994, the Beijing municipal government had advanced the policy of cultural economy (*wenhua jingji*), aimed at converting cultural capital into economic capital. The March 1996 plenary of the Eighth Assembly of Beijing's Municipal Political Consultative Committee decided to "found the capital city on culture" (*wenhua lidu*). Even as the committee was following the examples of Shanghai and Guangzhou in turning to a service-based economy, its members noted Beijing's edge over the southern metropolises in having a cultural heritage on which to capitalize.[61] This policy not only helped redefine culture in terms of its marketability; equally important, the privatization of culture used the market economy to redefine the city. The primary agents of cultural economy were the city government and the district committees, which packaged specific sites for tourism.

The redefinition of culture in terms of its market value resulted in conflict between older conceptions of cultural heritage and the novel marketable culture. The gentrification of old Beijing was accompanied by contradictory messages about the intrinsic value of the courtyard houses and the need to convert them into cash. Propaganda units had to step in to resolve the cognitive dissonance and ensure the success of the new policy. It is in this context that one should read the China Youth Art Theater production *We're All Beijingers* (1997).

As the title suggests, *We're All Beijingers* tones down the anti-Beijinger implications of Zhong Jieying's *Beijing Pretenders*—at one point, a returning emigrant says: "I too am a Beijinger. I bow in respect to you old Beijingers."[62] In many other aspects, however, the play is modeled on Zhong's work. The plot centers on the Di family, of Manchu origin, who inhabit a well-preserved courtyard. A conflict arises between the patriarch, steeped in Beijing culture and stubbornly upright, and his children, who run large businesses and subscribe to a market-oriented view. Financial trouble arises when the son, who runs his own enterprise, sells fake merchandise to a state-owned company, implicating his sister, who works for that company. Unless they can come up with an amount equal to the damage—a hefty 300,000 RMB—the sister will lose her job or the brother will go to jail. In a surprising move, the father solves the problem by deciding abruptly, as the play draws to a close, to sell the courtyard. Compared to *Beijing Pretenders*, whose drama stems from the father's unwillingness to part with the courtyard house, *We're All Beijingers* concludes less tragically, though still uneasily.

To cast the decision to give up the courtyard house as relatively unproblematic, the play distinguishes between two forms of inherited property. On the one hand, the courtyard house is presented as an asset of little sentimental value, which can be sold off without any discussion; on the other hand, certain personal mobile artifacts are deemed worth keeping at all cost. The priceless artifact featured in the play is a sandalwood walking staff that had belonged to the Di family for generations. It disappeared during the Cultural Revolution, when the house was ransacked. When the family treasure miraculously finds its way back—the son buys it for its collectible value—the father recognizes it and lectures the family on the nature of "a cultural artifact" (*wenwu*), which he defines as "a cultural object bequeathed by history." It is provenance rather than any material attribute that gives an object its value. The father can sell the courtyard because tradition and heredity are better embodied in the staff. Although the father is spared the dilemma of choosing between the staff and the courtyard house, since the staff's value (even at a whopping 130,000 RMB) would not be enough to save his children, the play also implies that keeping the staff is the better alternative.

We're All Beijingers stresses the message already spelled out in *Beijing Pretenders*, namely, that the courtyard house is doomed and that its upkeep is unsustainable as the rest of Beijing fills with high-rises. The play also visualizes the message by erecting scaffolds onstage, behind the courtyard and in front of a backdrop featuring a silhouette of the Forbidden City wall towers

11 *We're All Beijingers* (1997): The courtyard house is dwarfed and hemmed in by scaffolding.

(fig. 11). The courtyard is visually set apart from Beijing's core architectural heritage, and modern buildings are about to take its place. Between the acts, men with hardhats stomp on the scaffolding, accompanied by construction noises. The new buildings are already intruding into courtyard life, the perishing of which is imminent. The set design reproduces the courtyard house on a smaller-than-life scale, perhaps to indicate the dwarfing of the cramped quarters by new structures. The father's decision to sell the house only seals the place's inevitable fate.

It is not that the play sets no value in traditional architecture. The father holds in high regard structures such as the Altar of Heaven, and he launches into a diatribe against modern buildings. In his view, the latter look like matchboxes, and those that feature a rotating restaurant on top resemble "a fat man with a wok on his head" (such restaurants became fashionable with the construction of the Great Wall Sheraton in 1983 and the Kunlun Hotel in 1986). Yet the solution to the architectural crisis, according to *We're All Beijingers*, is not to hold onto the courtyard house but rather to sell it to those who can take better care of it. At one point the daughter suggests to bring in tourists; one may surmise that the site may avoid demolition by being gentrified and mummified into a museum-like site. Yet the other daughter mentions that "now they're demolishing courtyards everywhere," which, in conjunction with the loud construction noises at the end of the play, casts doubt on the place's chances of survival.

The distinction between the courtyard and the sandalwood staff, as that between an obsolete vestige and a valuable relic, foregrounds the logic of cultural economy. At the very beginning, the play presents the son, Di Yu, as the general manager of a "cultural development company." A high school dropout with coarse manners and a harsh laugh, he admits readily that he is in the cultural development business "because I have no culture." "I do whatever makes money!" he admits, implying that he owes his success to being impervious to the mystique of high art. Yet when it comes to the sandalwood staff, Yu reveals a tender heart. He is hurt by his father's comment that the offspring's ignorance leaves him as good as childless, and the son starts learning about ancient architecture. He shows his morality by his willingness to go to jail to protect the family. Participating in the market economy and in the art trade does not mar his upright character. The cultural economy facilitates the moral choices between the different components of Beijing's heritage.

The play so eagerly defends cultural economy—toward the end, one family member asks rhetorically, "If there were no cultural economy, where would there be hope?"—that the plot glosses over two contentious issues. The daughter's suggestion that they turn the courtyard into a tourist destination and charge foreigners for visiting is not unusual in today's Beijing. Indeed, such enterprises have become commonplace, to the point of disrupting better-preserved districts with hordes of guides and tourists, often racing through the narrow alleys on garish tricycles that bear the sign "touring the hutong." Neither does the play problematize the latest provenance of the walking staff, the Panjiayuan antique market. Panjiayuan has become the venue of choice for selling looted relics. As the prominent preservationist Feng Jicai has remarked, the antique market is full of windows with carved latticework for sale, evidencing the speed with which houses are being torn down. When no more such artifacts are sold at Panjiayuan, comments Feng, it will be either because people have finally realized the importance of cultural relics and started preserving them or, more likely, because all relics have been sold off.[63] The Di family heirloom is retrieved through the same process that encourages trading in cultural relics and dismantling China's heritage in accordance with market dynamics. The sandalwood staff suggests that "priceless" items, too, can be had for the right price.

We're All Beijingers marks the degradation of urban discourse to the point where even the voices speaking ostensibly in favor of preservation express a reductive position, treating architectural relics as no more than economic assets. The playwright, Liu Jinyuan, was asked to speak at a conference held in October 2001 on housing development in Beijing. Liu mentions preserving the courtyards, laments the fake façades on newly gentrified streets such as the Ping'an arterial, and deplores the incongruent architecture of the rebuilt Longfusi Temple. Yet the model he draws for Beijing is equally problematic. Liu focuses on an approach that "takes tradition as the starting point and uses both modern and traditional sensibilities, both development and continuity."[64] His example—the old city of Lijiang, Yunnan—is telling: Lijiang was rebuilt after a devastating earthquake in 1996 and made into a tourist attraction that has destroyed its previous way of life. Liu may be simply stating the unsavory truth, yet his words and his play evince the conclusion that Beijing's renewal cannot be achieved without catering to tourism and viewing the city's heritage primarily through its economic value.

RELOCATING TO NEW HOUSING

Next-Door Neighbors, Beijing Pretenders, and *We're All Beijingers* trace the evolving conflict between development and preservation, yet they leave unaddressed a central element: the relocation of residents. The debate over development often revolves around the modified land use and designation of buildings, yet an equally thorny issue is the fate of the dwellers of the renovated or demolished houses. It is no coincidence that the final version of *Small Well Lane* omits the original reference to relocation, which was and still is among the most sensitive topics in urban discourse.

Relocation is especially disruptive for the residents of the old city. Demolition-and-relocation projects are usually implemented in old city districts, where the old houses are an eyesore to visitors and the land is of great value to developers. The tenants, typically of low income and with little clout, derive intangible and easily ignored benefits from the original housing, such as an established and cohesive community and proximity to services. Moreover, the relocation process itself is often disorienting and traumatic.

The remuneration formula does not reflect the intangible factors; instead, policymakers set much store by visible material changes, such as the modern utilities in the new locations. Since the government initiates the projects and determines the level of compensation, dissatisfaction can turn into political unrest. The plays surveyed so far focus on the fate of old buildings and touch only fleetingly on the human factor of urban renewal. The residents' inconvenience during the relocation and their uncertain future remain offstage. The combination of demolition and relocation—two inseparable aspects of the same process—seems too explosive for any play to take on at the same time. By the mid-1990s, however, relocation became a pressing issue, addressed in major productions.

FROM PRESERVATION TO DEMOLITION: *FORSAKEN ALLEY*

The 1993 BPAT play *Forsaken Alley* was the linchpin of the government's efforts to promote onstage its demolition-and-relocation policy. Already in 1988, as soon as weigai policy started to be widely implemented, municipal government officials approached BPAT's vice-director, Yu Shizhi, and requested that the theater produce a play on the subject, which "has immediate implications for the benefit of the larger public." The task of portraying the process of demolition-and-relocation, involving the sensitive relation between the government and the residents, met with apprehension. In 1990, Yu approached Li Longyun, the author of *Small Well Lane*, "to write a new *Dragon Whisker Creek*" based on the Ju'er Hutong project (1989–93, designed by the weigai advocate Wu Liangyong). Li replied diplomatically that he was not the right person to describe contemporary material.[65] Eventually the secretary of BPAT's Party Committee, Liu Jinyun, circumvented the professional vetting process at BPAT and exhorted the veteran Lan Yinhai, who had written a number of TV series on courtyard life (and served as head of the BPAT Creative Office from 1986 to 1993), to pen the play.[66] In April 1993, Liu revised Lan's first draft, and the script was further modified at the instigation of Beijing's mayor, Chen Xitong. After the premiere on August 10, 1993, the play was scheduled for one hundred performances, all the way to the end of May 1994. On March 15, 1994, the country's leaders, Jiang Zemin and Li Peng, watched the play and commended it. The play received many awards from official units such as the Beijing municipal government and the National Propaganda Bureau.[67] It is telling that urban housing reform was deemed a topic deserving of a high-level commission, more reminiscent of the 1960s and 1970s.

The play was fashioned as the torchbearer of Lao She's *Dragon Whisker Creek* and the successor to *Next-Door Neighbors* and *Small Well Lane*, in terms of both subject matter and style. Reviews presented the play in propagandistic terms, as promoting awareness for the " 'Two Services' policy" (*"er wei" fangzhen*), that is, working in the service of the people and in the service of socialism. *Forsaken Alley* was applauded as theater at its best—not abstract, plotless, or introverted, but rather closely connected to people's lives.[68] Another review praises the play's message: "Weigai . . . reflects the urgent needs of the masses and the true concern of the people's government for the people. Weigai, the reconstruction of hazardous houses, is in fact also the reform of people's thinking."[69] Such passionate and at the same time stilted rhetoric was a rare reminder of the Maoist period.

Forsaken Alley stands out as the first courtyard play to show the process of demolition-and-relocation. Rather than look at a single courtyard house, it presents a microcosm of society by looking at an entire alley, in the tradition of *Small Well Lane*. A revolving stage allows the audience to glimpse into each house, in the manner explored earlier by the China Youth Art Theater production *A Courtyard with a Backyard* (1985). The device presents the entire gamut of responses to the government's decision to raze the alley.

Forsaken Alley sees no problem in the disappearance of significant landmarks and even glosses over the pending demolition of a recently refurbished courtyard, yet it acknowledges the difficulties involved in relocation. The play starts by depicting the cramped and unhygienic living conditions in the alley and gains momentum after the announcement of the demolition-and-relocation project. The redevelopment plan is introduced through the disembodied voice of the (district) Bureau Chief. He addresses the residents: "Comrades, as I stand among the derelict buildings of Forsaken Alley and see the people crammed four generations under a single roof, I am rendered speechless."[70] He proclaims that the demolition-and-relocation project will be overseen by a development company. A clock strikes to the portentous tune of "The East Is Red," and the Bureau Chief warns a resident about the plan: "Once this opera goes onstage, it won't be an easy one to sing!"

As predicted, the project exacerbates underlying social tensions, and verbal exchanges at the Relocation Bureau often end in shouts and even in violence, when a resident draws out a cleaver. The plot moves from one family to another, showing how each reacts to the new regulations. Problems arise because the residents are compensated according to the "demolish one, give one" policy—that is, one room in a city center apartment for each demolished room. Only by relocating to the outlying suburbs can residents be allocated more space, according to family size. The regulations work in favor of a divorced couple, which currently has no choice but to continue sharing a single room. They welcome the change, since now they will each get a single-room apartment. Others find themselves in a bind: a wealthy entrepreneur has invested 300,000 RMB in a traditional courtyard house; an intellectual couple would like to get additional space and avoid living in the same room with their son and his nanny, yet they face a long commute from the new apartment; one man is too greedy to accept the apartment for which he qualifies and plans to become a "stuck-nail tenant" (*dingzi hu*) who refuses relocation; an old woman is unwilling to part with the last mementos of her son, who died in the Sino-Vietnamese war. The Bureau Chief offers financial help to the intellectual couple; the entrepreneur receives ample compensation; the greedy man is handed an evacuation order by the police; and the old woman agrees to move when the Bureau Chief appears in person, shows that her house is beyond repair, and asks her to regard him as her son. The message is clear: the party leaders take care of the financially strapped and treat investors fairly; troublemakers are dealt with mercilessly, using the full force of the state; yet the authorities do not lose their humanity when attending to the families of those who have sacrificed their lives for the country. By covering almost the entire demolition-and-relocation process, *Forsaken Alley* presents both the problems and their solutions, foregrounding the success of current policies.

Forsaken Alley is a heavy-handed propaganda play. As in *Dragon Whisker Creek*, the characters are at first incredulous. After a resident hangs up the upbeat sign, "Welcome to the Asian Games / We'll Spark a New Spirit," his neighbor jeers cynically that the sign should also read, "Build New Houses!" In another conversation, a resident retorts: "It's already been forty years since liberation; how come I'm still here? Sure they've built a good many high-rises, but where's the one for you? Where's the one for me?" The dissatisfaction is neutralized in two stages. First, a fellow dweller explains that the government cannot build new houses for Beijing's 10 million citizens all at once, and that one should be thankful to have a roof over one's head. At this point, the defender of official policies is still ridiculed: "How come you sound like a [Maoist] model play?" Yet the government is vindicated when the alley is soon designated for reconstruction. An inebriated resident goes as far as to challenge the Bureau Chief himself: "Housing department, *housing* department—it should be taking care of *housing!*" In response, the Bureau Chief puts the complaining resident in charge of the entire relocation project. An old woman—calling to mind the last scene in *Dragon Whisker Creek*—literally sings the authorities' praise to a TV reporter: "Redevelopment!—I really didn't think it would happen / There's joy in my heart, my worries are gone / There is only one way to say my thanks: The government's achievements are higher than Heaven." The plot not only vindicates the official policy but also shows that the citizens accept the government's wisdom. The propaganda strategy of *Forsaken Alley* notably diverges, however, from that of *Dragon Whisker Creek*. Unlike Lao She's play, which stresses the common class background of the residents and their shared purpose, *Forsaken Alley* dwells on each resident's problems and thereby acknowledges the social diversity that belies collective aspirations. Whereas *Dragon Whisker Creek* ends in open vistas that privilege a common vision, the rotating stage in the later play signals the privatization of space. Even as *Forsaken Alley* stresses the municipal government's ultimate authority, it does so by recognizing each individual resident's claim to a space of his or her own and to a custom-tailored solution to housing problems.

Arguably the most significant gesture in *Forsaken Alley* to deflect criticism is the show of concern for the fate of the native trees. The play follows the sensibilities of the Ju'er Hutong project, which it was designed to propagate.[71] In Ju'er Hutong, houses were built around existing trees.[72] *Forsaken Alley* imbues this fact with new symbolism, fashioning the saving of trees as proof of the planners' consideration for social and cultural values. Granny Hé, who in her dementia keeps waiting for her fallen son to come back, refuses to leave the courtyard. She is especially attached to a locust tree by which her son used to find his way home (her living son's name, Shude, may be translated as "establishing virtue" as well as "tree virtue"). The choice of tree built on existing symbolism. Beijing is distinguished by the many ancient locust trees, and in 1986 "the national locust tree" (*guohuai*) also was chosen as Beijing's "city tree."[73] Many of the 141,796 trees counted in 1980 did not survive the large-scale demolition of the 1990s. In the play's emotional climax, the Bureau Chief promises to keep all the trees in the

12 *Forsaken Alley* (1993): The Bureau Chief places a miniature tree in a maquette of the planned redevelopment.

demolished zone (ironically, the imposing tree on the stage was felled especially for the play by the Parks Bureau, courtesy of Mayor Chen Xitong).[74]

When the Bureau Chief takes a step back, looks up at the tree, and exclaims: "The national locust tree!" he recognizes the tree's importance as an emblem of local identity and historical continuity and implies that preserving the trees makes up for the demolition of the houses. As the play ends, the Bureau Chief reinforces his promise by placing a miniature tree inside a maquette of the new neighborhood (fig. 12) and proclaiming: "There are some locust trees in Forsaken Alley that are more than two hundred years old. These trees must be preserved. Were we to cut them down, we would be cutting down two hundred years of history. Construction where hazardous buildings stand now is a good thing—we are repaying a debt to the people. Yet we cannot erase an old debt by incurring a new one. If we didn't preserve these trees, we would be wronging our ancestors and our descendants!" The trees, as the only living things that cannot be relocated, present a challenge to the image of demolition-and-relocation as a progressive process, and it is in this context that one should understand the heated debate, seven years later, over the playwright Zhong Jieying's televised support for cutting down an old tree. The promise in *Forsaken Alley* to protect the trees conveys the message that relocation does not neglect human feelings and does not absolutely erase the past.

For eight years after the staging of *Forsaken Alley*, courtyard plays did not return to address the problems of demolition-and-relocation, and focused instead on preserving cultural heritage. The association between reconstruction and the fate of the residents resurfaced in the production of *Goldfish Ponds*, which premiered on June 28, 2001, in time for the eightieth anniversary of the Chinese Communist Party. The play's director, Ren Ming, who had made his name directing *Beijing Pretenders* and identified with the earlier production, would acknowledge that *Goldfish Ponds* was a heavy-handed "main melody" play.[75] The plot follows the known formula: a neighborhood is in dire need of reconstruction—the houses are nearly uninhabitable, the outside toilets stinking and dangerous, the electrical wires old and unreliable. Social problems arise: an apartment is under contested ownership since the Cultural Revolution; a young tenant loses his fiancée because she is unwilling to move into the derelict building. The situation seems hopeless as entrepreneurs see no profit in redevelopment, and the tenants—low-income blue-collar workers, some of them unemployed—are unable to raise funds. Eventually, the government steps in and erects new buildings, allowing the residents to move into modern housing.

The theatrical revival of the demolition-and-relocation theme in 2001 coincided with important developments in urban policy. In the 1990s, the housing market rode a roller coaster—first a speculation-driven real estate boom that started in 1990 and peaked by 1995 (in both 1994 and 1995, 26,000 families were relocated each year and 750,000m² were demolished); later, government initiatives for redevelopment, which waned by 1998; and finally, a rebound of demand by an emerging middle class and overseas investors, now allowed access to the property market. To draw residents into investing, the municipal government issued the Management of Demolition-and-Relocation in Beijing Act (Document 16, December 1998) and the Management of Accelerated Reconstruction of Hazardous and Old Houses in Beijing Act (Document 19, March 2000). These directives outlined a new policy, known as "redevelopment by housing reform" (*fanggai daidong weigai*, or in short *weigai + fanggai*), aimed at involving residents in redevelopment by giving them three options. In addition to the familiar weigai-style demolition-and-relocation, citizens could take advantage of the free market. If a family decided to return to the original site, it could buy fifteen square meters per household member at cost value, and the rest at market value, with a small government subsidy. Were the family to move out, a formula was established for subsidizing basic-level "economic apartments" (*jingji shiyong fang*). At the same time, the Urban Housing Demolition Ordinance of 1991 was rewritten in 2001 to legislate the compensation and resettlement options. The policy led to large-scale projects. Five areas in the Chongwen, Xuanwu, and Fengtai districts were immediately redeveloped. A total of 13,233 families were relocated, and 375,900 square meters were demolished. The plan was expanded in 2001, and in that year alone 67,000 families were relocated, and 814,000 square meters were demolished. The government hoped to complete all redevelopment in Beijing's old city by 2005.[76]

The staging of *Goldfish Ponds* in 2001 came in time to celebrate and promote the new policy and to stem nascent criticism. "Redevelopment by housing reform" introduced an entrepreneurial model of citizenship and urban governance. The new model in effect shortchanged existing residents. Moreover, in a transitional economy and immature housing market, the policy left large loopholes for graft and encouraged forced evacuation. So-called stuck-nail tenants who chose to stay in place were evicted forcefully on the basis of ungenerous compensation formulas. In their new apartments, residents would often find unfinished infrastructure and expensive utilities. The living quarters in a "vertical courtyard" (*liti xiaoyuan'r*), as the multistory apartment houses are called, often derogatorily, no longer include a common open space that can double as a living room and kitchen. Ma Qiang, an activist writing for the Asia Democracy Foundation, writes bluntly: "Beijing's so-called reconstruction of hazardous buildings is nothing but a disguised process of robbing citizens' basic livelihood."[77] The authorities have turned a blind eye to violations of law by developers, but public knowledge of wrongdoing is widespread. The most meticulous documentation of the abuses of redevelopment policies was presented in Fang Ke's *Contemporary Renewal of Beijing's Old City*, published in June 2000.[78] An image face-lift was needed to show the advantages of redevelopment.

Summer 2001 was an especially sensitive time for crafting Beijing's public image. On July 13, two weeks after the premiere of *Goldfish Ponds*, the International Olympic Committee announced it had chosen Beijing to host the 2008 games. Winning the bid was the culmination of a campaign for "New Beijing, Great Olympics" and the beginning of an intensified effort to present by 2008 a picture-perfect capital. Images associated with the Olympics promoted easily digestible, postcard versions of the city, subjecting local identity to a vision promoting both nationalism and globalization (see chapter 7). Just as *Forsaken Alley* links the Asian Games and the demolition-and-relocation project, *Goldfish Ponds* resonates with the construction and public relations drive around the Olympic bid.

Goldfish Ponds was instrumental for municipal officials and especially Chongwen District administrators, who wanted to make their management of "redevelopment by housing reform" visible to large audiences, and perhaps especially to the state leaders.[79] As I detail later in this chapter, the construction was publicized in various art forms. The BPAT production was an ideal venue for reaching the various target audiences—the Beijing residents it sought to inform of the new demolition-and-relocation regulations, the Chinese at large to whom it wanted to promote Beijing's modernized image, and the national policymakers to whom it wanted to showcase the successful redevelopment.

FROM DRAGON WHISKER CREEK TO GOLDFISH PONDS

By depicting an existing project, *Goldfish Ponds*, more than any previous courtyard play, links the staged drama and the material conditions on the ground. Ever since *Dragon Whisker Creek*, the courtyard plays had offered a metaphorical representation, giving the locations onstage symbolic names such as Small Well Lane and Forsaken Alley. Jinyuchi (Goldfish Ponds), however, is a genuine geographical designation, referring to the neighborhood bordering the northern wall of the Altar of Heaven. Moreover, Jinyuchi is part of the former Longxugou (Dragon Whisker Creek) area. In stressing the continuity between one of the earliest public works in the PRC and the current housing project, the play implies that the contemporary demolition-and-relocation is part of the government's unrelenting effort to create a sustainable urban infrastructure and equitable housing.

As the curtain rises, Grandpa Cheng relates the history of the area: after the works conducted in the 1950s and immortalized in Lao She's play, a second stage of reconstruction in the 1960s erected fifty-three apartment blocks. Since that time, however, two more generations had joined the original tenants and crammed into the same spaces; some had added improvised constructions. The buildings had become ugly, foul smelling, and dangerous to live in, and the residents started looking forward to the day the blocks would be demolished. Grandpa Cheng's account is true to fact: the construction depicted in Lao She's play largely targeted the creek; it left in place the ponds and integrated them into a park. In 1966 the ponds were leveled and apartment blocks (*jianyilou*) were built on the grounds.[80] The simple brick constructions were sturdy but bare, lacked heating facilities, and the elementary sanitation and electricity infrastructure deteriorated over the years. Moreover, dwellers' needs rose, leading to helter-skelter extensions and additions. Apartment blocks like these became an eyesore to visitors and a source of dissatisfaction to residents who were comparing their conditions with the new apartments built during the real estate boom. It is no coincidence that a character in *Goldfish Ponds* wishes to move away to an apartment at Yayuncun, the Asian Games Village area whose construction launched the housing market frenzy in 1990.

Having described the two previous reconstructions, *Goldfish Ponds* proceeds to stage the third phase, namely, the contemporary redevelopment. The play describes how the area, one of the five first neighborhoods slated for renewal under the "redevelopment by housing reform" policy, is transformed within a year. The apartment buildings are torn down, and the residents express their enthusiasm for a technologically advanced, green, and modernized neighborhood. A more detailed account of the project is given by Wang Guangtao, who served at the time as Beijing's vice-mayor. The reconstruction was put in motion as part of the policy stated in Document 19 (the Management of Accelerated Reconstruction of Hazardous and Old Houses in Beijing Act). In an area of 10.27 hectares, 55 apartment buildings and 492 single-story houses, totaling 103,000 square meters, were demolished. The project forced the relocation of 3,055 families, or 7,828 people, and 19 work units.[81] Jinyuchi was made into a model district. Its construction was overseen by the Beijing Sixth Development and Construction Company (Beijing Zhuzong Diliu Kaifa Jianshe Youxian Gongsi), a state-run enterprise that had participated in building the Great Hall of the People, the Mao Memorial, and other prestigious monuments. Since 1997, when it adopted the motto "Builders who always have the residents in mind," the company has prospered as a contractor for housing compounds, with Jinyuchi as its flagship.[82] The neighborhood keeps high sanitation standards, with a team of twenty-seven members dedicated to sweeping the entire neighborhood every day and enforcing a ban on posting advertisements.[83] The new buildings were designed around common spaces, in a manner reminiscent of traditional courtyard houses. The central open space includes a rivulet and a small pond, an allusion to the scenic ponds of yore.

The project is adorned with public art designed by a team from the Beijing Parks Design Institute. A computerized information kiosk and a huge outdoor LCD screen were set up near the main gate, part of a short-lived drive in 2003 to create a web-based information network in Beijing. (The kiosk has since been dismantled.) The Jinyuchi redevelopment has been promoted through various means, including a video CD (produced by the Chongwen District Propaganda Bureau in September 2002) and the BPAT plays. Placing a showcase project next to the Altar of Heaven, a major tourism destination, and linking it to Lao She's famous play ensured a steady stream of visitors, such as high school students bused in to witness the efforts of the district government.

The Jinyuchi project, as depicted in the play and by official sources, was a successful implementation of the new policy, balancing real estate development and management of the related human concerns. Yet residents of Jinyuchi disagree with the official narrative. The project took exactly one year—demolition began in April 2001 and the keys to the new apartments were handed over on April 18, 2002 (to ensure an unmarred image, few journalists were invited to the ceremony). The haste to comply with the twelve-month schedule resulted in inferior construction. Residents returning to claim their new apartments were angered to find unaligned supporting platforms and walls leaning at five to ten degrees. The apartments were not wired for telephones, and cell phone reception was bad.[84] Roofs started leaking as soon as the residents moved in. A man in his seventies, born and raised in the area, told me he preferred the old apartment blocks, which "were given to us by Chairman Mao."[85] The residents also compared the construction plans in their area, in the Chongwen District, with those in the adjacent Xuanwu District, and found the latter to be superior. Even if the grass is not greener elsewhere, the perception among the residents shows an untold and unflattering aspect of the demolition-and-relocation project.

More thorny problems were raised by methods of compensating the residents for their old living quarters, and these, too, are reflected in the stage play. As in *Forsaken Alley* before it, the characters in *Goldfish Ponds* have to choose between moving away and adding money to purchase an apartment in the new compound. A dialogue elaborates the dilemma: even though an apartment at the original site is more desirable and is a good real estate investment, the residents are afraid that they will not have enough money to buy it. They are willing to resist the relocation and become "stuck-nail tenants." Whereas *Forsaken Alley* skirts the issue of government sub-sidy, *Goldfish Ponds* spells out the importance of public investment. Only when the government steps in and takes over the project, which entrepre-neurs have deemed unprofitable, do the new apartments become affordable. An unidentified "Director Liu," representing the municipal-level decision makers, meets with the residents and enumerates the options available to households that earn less than 1,000 RMB a month: those who wish to move back to Jinyuchi will be awarded a government loan; those who move out will receive property rights to a new apartment; those who choose neither will get money for their relinquished apartment and will rent a place on their own. The meeting is one of the play's highlights—the scene breaks the theatrical "fourth wall" and places the residents among the audience. While the theatergoers can better identify with the residents, the stage is literally handed over to the authorities to explain the new policy.

The play presents in detail the measures stipulated by Document 19, but it glosses over some wrinkles. In actuality, the sums for reacquiring Jinyuchi property were forbiddingly high. The arrangements accorded with "redevel-opment by housing reform": each household received a subsidy based on the number of years it had lived in the area and the condition of the old apartment. Usually this amounted to around 15,000 RMB, up to 20,000 RMB for the most long-standing residents. In addition, for each family member one could buy fifteen square meters at 1,485 RMB (touted as cost value) per square meter. Beyond that, all supplementary space had to be purchased at the market rate of 4,500 RMB per square meter. Yet these numbers were fudged—parking space, for example, was now available only in underground lots at additional cost.[86] The head of one household com-plained that he had to pay 100,000 RMB up front and more than 600 RMB a month spread over the next twenty-two years, a total of 260,000 RMB. For a family in which each member earned about 400 RMB a month, this entailed giving up one's life savings—a far cry from the affordability portrayed in *Goldfish Ponds*.[87]

The residents' dismay may be better understood in the context of what Jonathan Unger and Anita Chan call the "moral economy." With the dis-solution of the socialist safety net and the newfound wealth of some work units, senior workers expected to be compensated for their contribution during the socialist period.[88] The same may be said for the residents of older neighborhoods, who considered the local government beholden to them for

suffering without complaint through the Maoist era. The residents of Jinyuchi vociferously protested the pricing and number of rooms allotted per
family. In February 2001, dwellers demonstrated by walking slowly on the
adjacent Tiantan Road and causing traffic jams. The timing was chosen to
coincide with the visit of the International Olympic Committee assessment
team (the idea is uncannily similar to the troublemaker's plan in *Forsaken
Alley* to protest in front of Zhongnanhai during the 1990 Asian Games).
Jinyuchi residents leveraged the international attention drawn to Beijing—
ironically, the same tool that the government was using to promote its
modernization plans—to force a quick settlement. Such details, which contradict the portrait of Jinyuchi in the BPAT production, have not become
public knowledge. Instead, *Goldfish Ponds* presents a utopian Beijing, a
garden city with open vistas.

BEIJING, GARDEN CITY

At the beginning of *Goldfish Ponds*, one character exclaims in dismay,
"Jinyuchi has become a second Longxugou!"[89] As the plot progresses and
the problems are addressed, the return to the location of Lao She's foundational play foregrounds Beijing's new image. Whereas the Longxugou project solved sanitation and housing issues for a limited period, the Jinyuchi
redevelopment purportedly offers an integrated vision, combining quality
construction and community-oriented planning. The old neighborhood becomes a modern version of the "garden city"—creating self-contained communities that emphasize green areas. In conjunction with wooing foreign
investment and preparing for the Olympics, a conceptual shift takes place in
urban planning, from housing reform to city image overhaul.

The play extols Jinyuchi as a paragon of urban renewal. When the curtain
rises, a singsong is heard in the background: "Jinyuchi is Longxugou, where
apartment blocks were built. In the blink of the eye thirty years have passed,
and the capital has changed its looks. The water is clear, the skies blue, the
roads wide; everywhere new vistas have appeared. Jinyuchi is awaiting redevelopment, to give a new face to the beautified capital." Resonating with
the Olympic bid rhetoric, the prelude presents a "new Beijing." In claiming
that the redevelopment opens "new vistas" (*xin jingguan*), the text calls to
mind the open views presented in *Dragon Whisker Creek*. Insofar as the
public works of the 1950s promoted an eye-level view of the city, the current
construction further prioritizes an urban spectacle of expansive panoramas.

As Beijing geared up for the 2008 Olympic Games, the city and Jinyuchi in particular were promoted through the iconic image of the Altar of Heaven. To make the Hall of Annual Prayer—the tower that dominates the site—into a visible landmark, a new urban north-south corridor, Tiantan Beidajie (Altar of Heaven North Avenue), was opened up, leading directly to the Altar's northern gate, on the southeastern corner of Jinyuchi. Of questionable transportation value, the avenue functions as part of a network of roads that exhibit the city's grandeur, such as the adjacent avenue that leads to the newly rebuilt Yongdingmen Gate. The Altar of Heaven has become an emblem of Beijing's and Chongwen District's revamped visual matrix. An anthology of essays on the coming Olympics, for example, displayed on its cover a montage of a bicycle racer and the Hall of Annual Prayer.[90] A flier, distributed in summer 2003, offered apartments in the adjacent Jiayuan housing compound; next to a large photograph of the Hall of Annual Prayer, the advertisement promotes "a home neighboring the Altar of Heaven" starting at 5,160 RMB per square meter. A complimentary photo calendar issued by the Chongwen District authorities to celebrate the Jinyuchi project bears the familiar tower's image and the slogan "Expanding the Altar of Heaven's Spirit, Constructing a Common Home." The monument also figures prominently in *Goldfish Ponds*. Residents mention the neighborhood's location on "the capital's historical and cultural artery," between Zhengyangmen [Qianmen] Gate to the north and the Altar of Heaven to the south. An entrepreneur exclaims: "If Jinyuchi is redeveloped, as soon as this building is torn down, we will be able to see the Altar of Heaven." The redevelopment is understood in terms of the new urban aesthetics, based on open vistas.

The project at Jinyuchi fits into a trend that has taken root in China since the 1990s: adding prestige and monetary worth to real estate through landscape design. Gardens and public art have been integrated into construction. In 2000, an estimated twenty thousand professionals were involved in commercial landscape design in China.[91] Special value was placed on assimilating culturally significant sites into the new developments, leading to the gentrification of historic sites, whether retaining a large part of the original structures (as in Shanghai's Xintiandi, completed in 2001), token remnants (as in Beijing's Imperial Wall Ruins Park, 2002), or newly built reconstructions (as in Beijing's Ming Dynasty City Wall Historic Landscape Park, 2002). Glossy advertisements of architectural projects were commodified for their own sake, entered for award competitions and reproduced in coffee

13 Billboard at the Goldfish Ponds construction site, July 2001:
"Builders who always have the residents in mind." Photograph by author.

table books.[92] The Jinyuchi redevelopment is in fact modest in comparison
to high-end projects, although it contains a rivulet and a pond, water fountains, and other decorative elements. The billboards that the contractor put
up around the site at the time of construction showed a wider waterway with
grassy banks and a promenade (fig. 13). The exaggerated details, in line with
the new practices of architectural advertising, emphasized the open lines
of sight.

The shift in visual regimes is also visible in the elaborate stage sets
designed for *Goldfish Ponds* by Wu Qiong. Wu tells that he often took a
twenty-minute walk from his home to Jinyuchi, familiarizing himself with
the place, but he also admits that the set design idealizes the site. Both the
old street and the rebuilt compound were elaborated on, borrowing typical
architectural elements from other neighborhoods in the Outer City. Notably,
Wu shortened the distance between Jinyuchi and the Altar of Heaven. The
last act shows the Hall of Annual Prayer looming large, centered behind the
new buildings, since Wu "wanted to meld together the cultural spirit of the
Altar of Heaven and that of the neighborhood."[93] To fully capture the visual
impact of the redevelopment, Wu designed an exceptionally intricate set,
which included an old apartment building 7.8 meters high and 14 meters
wide. Newspaper reports marveled at the realism of the fully functional
three-story structure, replete with stairs and clogged toilets, which ends up

being torn down in the last scene.[94] An elaborate set for the last act shows the site after development; this was probably the first onstage representation of a new compound—*Forsaken Alley* only brought onstage a maquette. (Originally, Wu's sets for *Goldfish Ponds* included also the building in its demolished state, but the act in which the demolished building appeared was excised from the play's final version.) The stage becomes not only a life-size replica of the cityscape but also an extension of the spectacle provided by the new redevelopment.

The play's final act drives home that new planning practices seek to make the city into a spectacle. A young woman, Jingjing, places a goldfish in the pond at the center of the housing project. The gloomy apartment blocks give way to a bright compound; a large open space at center stage allows a clear view of the Altar of Heaven, behind a wall of verdant trees against azure skies. At the front, a playground wreathed with flowerbeds closes on a small pond. Jingjing, dressed in glowing red, stands under the silhouette of the Altar of Heaven and releases goldfish from a red basin into the pond (fig. 14). Celebrating the return of the goldfish via a flag-red basin, by a young woman dressed in red and whose name identifies her with Beijing, to their place of origin, now remade into a clean and beautified environment able to sustain them, is crass iconography for the "new Beijing."

Parenthetically, PRC bureaucrats' love of ritual has topped even the heavy-handed theatrical symbolism. At the inauguration ceremony of the Jinyuchi project, politicos took large red and blue buckets and poured goldfish into the pond, choreographing the act for the cameras (fig. 15). The political spectacle, ten months after *Goldfish Ponds* was staged, took over the theatrical imagery to make government officials the conduit through which past glory returned.

The concluding tableau of *Goldfish Ponds* shows the distance of the current urban vision from that during the first years of the PRC. The differences become manifest when the scene is placed side by side with the last shot in the movie *Dragon Whisker Creek* (see fig. 3). In the film based on Lao She's play, the young pioneers ride bicycles out of the frame and into the city. The new neighborhood is dominated by a wide road, and the city looms in the background in the form of a smokestack. In *Goldfish Ponds*, in contrast, the future generation is symbolized by an elegantly dressed young woman; the self-contained compound is green and beautified; the city is represented by the Altar of Heaven—a cultural relic and a tourist destination. The stark

14 *Goldfish Ponds* (2001), act 3: Jingjing releases goldfish into the pond. Photograph by author.

15 Goldfish Ponds inauguration ceremony, April 18, 2002:
Politicians and administrators release goldfish into the pond.
Source: www.cwi.gov.cn/main/zhuanti/jyc/images/pic/a4_00.jpg.

contrast between the two cityscapes underlines the gap between the socialist and neoliberal ideals.

The return of the goldfish in the last scene of *Goldfish Ponds* also endows urban planning with the power to affect a historical closure. The gestures of integrating a small pond into the architecture of Jinyuchi and foregrounding the pond's significance through the play are steeped in nostalgia for an ineffable "old Beijing." The past is reified in the form of a metonymical icon. Like the street sign carried over to the new location in *Small Well Lane*, the sandalwood staff kept in the family in *We're All Beijingers*, and the locust tree left to grow in the new compound in *Forsaken Alley*, the pond in *Goldfish Ponds* pays homage to local cultural heritage—if only to enhance the project's value within the cultural economy. The historical closure vindicates the new economic structure.

The justification of the Jinyuchi project in historical terms is underlined in the play's homage to Lao She's *Dragon Whisker Creek*. *Goldfish Ponds* exploits in full its geographical affinity with Lao She's play and reveals in the process the strong ties between urban planning and the stage. The later play construes its redevelopment project as continuing the plot of *Dragon Whisker Creek*—in fact, the play was first titled *Dragon Whisker Creek: The Sequel*.[95] As the curtain rises, Grandpa Cheng pushes a cart with goldfish for sale. He is no other than Madman Cheng from *Dragon Whisker Creek*, now ninety-three years old. Grandpa Cheng does not play a major role in the new play, yet the character functions as a historical link. Paradoxically, to support urban modernization, *Goldfish Ponds* enlists the audience's yearning for the past, and in particular for the 1950s, when the Longxugou project was carried out. Grandpa Cheng stands as a reminder of the urban renewal initiated by the earlier project as well as of the government's continued concern for its citizens' welfare.

Jingjing's act of returning the goldfish harks back to *Dragon Whisker Creek*, in which the nine-year-old Little Niu finds comfort in slum misery in a goldfish bowl before drowning in the creek. Grandpa Cheng, who now raises fish, is "a living cultural relic" of the old ponds. The reappearance of the nonagenarian Cheng and his pledge to return his fish to the new pond once completed signal the return to the revolutionary utopia promised by the PRC's founding generation.

Yet Grandpa Cheng does not return the fish with his own hands; instead, he delegates the task to the young Jingjing. A college student, she has been assigned a senior thesis on "the history and future of Beijing's central axis" and has chosen to write on "the history and future of Jinyuchi." Her studies identify her as a guardian of local history, and as her name's allusion to Beijing suggests, she stands for the new Beijinger, in touch with the past yet looking to the future. She exclaims enthusiastically that if Little Niu were alive she could be her classmate. In the play's final act, Jingjing places Grandpa Cheng's fish into the pond. The gesture makes Jingjing Little Niu's proxy and successor. Urban redevelopment is portrayed as an ongoing undertaking, to which residents of all generations are committed.

In referring back to Little Niu, *Goldfish Ponds* also endows the project—and by extension, the demolition-and-relocation policy as a whole—with ideological legitimacy. As I discussed in chapter 1, Little Niu as a martyr figure motivates the Communist government's actions. *Goldfish Ponds* enlists Little Niu again, this time to justify the project carried out by the Chongwen District government. The dramatic allusion was also used off-stage: next to the decorative pond of the Jinyuchi compound, the planners placed a larger-than-life bronze statue of Little Niu, by the sculptor Yu Hua-xiang. The statue celebrated the second anniversary of the project, on April 18, 2004. For the ceremony, young pioneers brought goldfish bowls to the bronze Little Niu.[96] The cultural cachet of *Dragon Whisker Creek* directs the public interest in, and lends prestige to, the current urban renewal project.

Little Niu's statue demonstrates how stage productions exert influence beyond the theater, and even intrude into the city in material form. Whereas most plays simply allude to public policy, elements from *Dragon Whisker Creek* have been physically integrated into the plans for Jinyuchi. Little Niu's statue is one of many bronze sculptures erected at the site. First planned as a "culture alley," a one-mile-long corridor with twenty-eight statue groups, the public art project now comprises nine locations.[97] The gateway to the neighborhood sports a three-meter-tall sculpture of three books, Lao She's three works on the Outer City (*Dragon Whisker Creek*, *Camel Xiangzi*, and *Teahouse*), with the author's image on the front cover. Another book-like monument is engraved with the history of the area since 1949. In addition, eight tableaux from *Dragon Whisker Creek* are placed along the two south-to-north streets flanking the central compound. Each tableau depicts a scene in Lao She's play in relief on a massive slab, about fifteen feet wide and four feet tall, mounted on the roadside fence. An accompanying plaque reproduces lines from the play. The two most elaborate sets also include life-size sculptures, placed on the sidewalk in front of the reliefs. The composite installations depict Madman Cheng singing at a teahouse and at a mass rally after liberation (fig. 16). (The sculptures resonate with a resident's promise to Grandpa Cheng in *Goldfish Ponds*: "We should raise a monument for you by the pond!") Since the sculptures reconstitute scenes that purportedly took

16 Public art at the Jinyuchi compound (2002). Photograph by the author.

place in the vicinity, the historic site melds with the present location, and the neighborhood's literary heritage becomes part of its spatial configuration.

The Jinyuchi project also exemplifies the contribution of the cinema, and specifically the film version of *Dragon Whisker Creek* (1952), to promoting Beijing's changing cityscape. The video CD on Jinyuchi, produced by the Chongwen District government, portrays the site's early transformation through a sequence of iconic images, starting with Little Niu's goldfish in the film *Dragon Whisker Creek*, followed by Mao Zedong's declaration of the founding of the PRC—a shot taken from the documentary *The Birth of New China* (see chapter 4), and ending with Madman Cheng's inauguration of the mended Longxugou as shown in the 1952 film. The collective memory of Longxugou, which provides the ideological foundation for the Jinyuchi project, is mediated through Lao She's play and its film adaptation.

Goldfish Ponds uses the groundwork laid by earlier films, which privileged the cinema as an access point for imagining the city. In the first scene, Grandpa Cheng presents the area, saying: "Fifty years have passed in an instant. . . . [past events] often flash by my eyes, as if in a movie." The cliché is represented literally. While Cheng utters his lines, images are projected on the stage—the old Longxugou, the PLA's entry into the city, parades, and scenes from *Dragon Whisker Creek*. The clips from documentary and fiction films blend together cityscape, historical records, and filmic representation. Later in the play, when the residents imagine the redeveloped Jinyuchi as a tourist attraction, they suggest that the film *Dragon Whisker Creek* be screened for visitors. The road to cultural economy passes through the cinema.

The Jinyuchi project overflowed into a plethora of visualizations, including a temporary sidewalk display of the area's history put up in 2002, a permanent exhibition at the Jinyuchi activity center (located underground, just below the pond), an elaborate website,[98] the aforementioned video CD, and the two BPAT productions. The architectural project and the multimedia presentations alike place the city within a new visual regime.

ANTICIPATING THE OLYMPIC GAMES: *A MYRIAD LIGHTS*

Unlike *Dragon Whisker Creek*, *Goldfish Ponds* did not become an iconic piece; instead, it was shelved and replaced by yet another BPAT production on the redevelopment of Jinyuchi, *A Myriad Lights*. The new play premiered on October 15, 2002, just over a year after *Goldfish Ponds*, and was declared one of the "main melody plays" celebrating the sixteenth plenum of the Chinese Communist Party. BPAT made sure that the new version would be a hit. The theater commissioned the playwright Li Longyun, of *Small Well Lane* fame, and the PRC's leading mainstream director, Lin Zhaohua, who had also worked on Guo Shixing's plays. The cast included the charismatic male actor Pu Cunxin and the comic star Song Dandan, in her first stage performance in twelve years. During its fifty-one performances, box office revenues—a number often manipulated by the authorities—were reported to have set an all-time record at 7,680,000 RMB. The play enjoyed wide release in a special DVD series produced by the Ministry of Culture, introducing "the essence of national stage art." Such heavy-handed doctoring of the repertoire has become rare by the twenty-first century. *A Myriad Lights* set a new standard for courtyard plays as propaganda.

Continuing the tradition of Lao She's *Teahouse* and Li Longyun's *Small Well Lane*, *A Myriad Lights* follows a small community through a longer period, in this case starting in 1990 and ending in 2002, the time of the play's staging. The elaborate sets emphasize the striking change from the old neighborhood to the new apartment buildings. The play details the problems in several households. The place suffers from the problems already enumerated in *Goldfish Ponds*, such as frequent power outages caused by outdated electricity infrastructure. Outsiders look down on the area for its primitive living conditions, and the residents scheme ways to earn fast money and buy an apartment elsewhere. "Better be crushed to death in an earthquake than live in such run-down houses!" they complain.[99] The Hé family courtyard is singled out as rapidly dilapidating, as its roof leaks and its walls slant. The son calls it "Mansion of Uneven Rhyme" (Zeyunlou), punning on the double meaning of ze as "using uneven rhyme" and "cramped"; later he proposes that the name be given to Jinyuchi in its entirety. The elegant name mocks the crowded living conditions. Eventually, the house collapses and the Hé son's marriage falls apart, the divorce precipitated by the uninhabitable structure. Housing shortage results in social disharmony.

Discord is an opportunity to demonstrate the government's good intentions and successful management, making residents mouthpieces for the official policy. At first, the residents are impatient: "They demolish and relocate over there, then over there, but there's no word of Jinyuchi!" In particular, the incredulous Granny Hé echoes Mother Wang in *Dragon Whisker Creek* in her persistent doubts. Granny Hé questions the government's promises, only to ask for forgiveness from the head of the residents' committee in the final act. Another tenant expresses his preference for one-storied buildings, but a fellow resident counters that three floors would be needed to accommodate all the present inhabitants. The explanation presents the contentious practice of multistory construction in the old city as aimed at the citizens' comfort rather than as adding to developers' profits. In the end—after the project has been completed—emigrants return from abroad to live in the new compound, and a family that has broken up comes back together. The residents launch into an orgy of gratitude, and "Mansion of Uneven Rhyme" is renamed "Mansion of Felicitous Destiny" (Xingyunlou). The new epithet, coined by the previously disgruntled citizens, declares their travails over.

The local government is given a convincing and authoritative voice in Old Tian, a retired policeman and the head of the residents' committee. Old Tian embodies the harmonious confluence of the citizens' wishes and the authorities' will. Whereas in *Forsaken Alley* the Bureau Chief registers his empathy for the residents from a distanced position of power, in *A Myriad Lights* the government and the residents are one. Old Tian's part was extensively rewritten and doctored during preproduction to fit the Party line. In the final version he enunciates the government's caring approach: "Demolition-and-relocation is bound to happen in our place. . . . we will surely demolish what should be demolished, but we will definitely keep what should not be demolished!" Old Tian also relays to the residents the district head's considerate attitude. Old Tian tells how in a meeting with investors, the district head roared with bulging eyes at other participants: "I'm telling you, if you want to make money, don't bother with Jinyuchi! But if you want to gain prestige, please come to Jinyuchi! . . . Investment is going to be made according to weigai [policy], but listen carefully! I want construction by commercial housing standards, so that the buildings don't look dated by 2008." As the play explains later, city leaders were taking special interest in the Jinyuchi project during Beijing's bid for the 2008 Olympics and saw its successful completion as "a historic responsibility." Like earlier plays, A Myriad Lights depicts residents as won over by the officials' benevolence (patronizing as it may be).

The play provides an even more authoritative voice in the form of factual broadcasts by Beijing Radio. A broadcast report precedes each act, detailing the progress of public works and housing redevelopment in various parts of the city to the citizens' joy. The report introducing the last act, which takes place after the completion of the Jinyuchi project in 2002, addresses that neighborhood. The lengthy report—over two minutes of dead stage time—tells how the city government pushed for accelerated development in Jinyuchi, resulting in the largest demolition-and-relocation ever of 1960s apartment blocks. The radio report itemizes the benefits of the new compound: private toilets, parking spaces, a community center, a scenic pond, and more. Statistics are provided, though the numbers are somewhat fudged—the residents, it is told, bought the apartments at two thousand RMB per square meter (in fact, as I have detailed previously, that price was only applicable to the first fifteen square meters). The propagandistic tone culminates in the play's last words, a soliloquy by Old Tian, who asks with ostensible humility: "I did some good deeds, but wasn't that my duty? Whom does the national emblem over our heads represent?" The play upholds an unmarred, glowing image of the government and its concern for the residents, to match the most propagandistic productions in the BPAT's repertoire.

PROPAGANDA AND NOSTALGIA

As a heavy-handed "main melody" play, on a par with Forsaken Alley, A Myriad Lights is evidence of continued political intervention in theatrical production. Like other propaganda pieces, the play was commissioned by the Party apparatus, circumventing the professional vetting process. The Municipal Council and the heads of the Propaganda Bureau turned to the secretary of BPAT's Party Committee, Ma Xin. The party organs had decided in advance on the theme, approach, and artists: the play should describe the redevelopment at Jinyuchi; it should reflect the changes in material conditions and mental makeup of Beijing's citizens in recent years; it should involve Li Longyun as playwright, Lin Zhaohua as director, and Pu Cunxin as lead actor; and it should be ready within three months, for the October 2002 celebrations.[100] The party directive was handed down, cut through red tape, and ignored institutional divisions.

The CCP quickly enlisted the reluctant artists. The playwright Li Longyun was put in an especially awkward position. Li was by now an established and popular author, who had written since *Small Well Lane* a few successful plays at BPAT. He had, however, declined to write the propaganda piece that would turn into Lan Yinhai's *Forsaken Alley* and left the theater because of undisclosed differences of opinion. For the production of *A Myriad Lights*, Li had, against his will, to return temporarily to BPAT after only three months at the National Theater Company of China. Nor was Li given latitude to write a script to his liking, which had to be ready within a month.[101] We can read Li's concern and apologetics between the lines of his published diary. Unlike the playwright Zhong Jieying, who defended *Beijing Pretenders* publicly, and unlike the director Ren Ming, who gave many interviews about *Goldfish Ponds*, Li Longyun and Lin Zhaohua—otherwise friendly and talkative—dismiss *A Myriad Lights* as a "main melody" production put on in a hurry that does not compare to their other works.[102]

Yet *A Myriad Lights* also shows the limitations of propaganda during times of growing public concern and doubts over the objectives of redevelopment. The choice of leading artists with established styles signaled policymakers' willingness to relinquish some control. Wang Zhi'an, the playwright of *Goldfish Ponds*, toed the Party line to a fault, but his piece proved to be box office poison. Li Longyun took some artistic liberties: even though the explicit subject is the redevelopment of apartment blocks, he fashioned the piece as a courtyard play and added the Hé family compound.[103] The drama diverges from the somber tone of *Goldfish Ponds*—Song Dandan as Granny Hé provides humorous interludes, and even the more reserved Pu Cunxin as the self-important sociologist Ding Yifu gives a comic performance, resonating with his role as Ding Baoluo in *Bird Men*. In comparison with *Goldfish Ponds*, which includes reams of dry numbers on the economics behind demolition-and-relocation, *A Myriad Lights* is a lighthearted play, comprised of loosely strung vignettes from daily life. Rather than concluding on a dogmatic note, Old Tian admits in the concluding soliloquy that even though the residents have moved to new apartments, "there is a lingering ineffable feeling in our hearts." Old Tian explains that with the redevelopment completed, the alleys of his childhood and the mellifluous cries of street peddlers are gone. Here the play echoes Li Longyun's earlier *Small Well Lane*, in which a resident laments, "Before relocation we were looking forward to it. Now that we're just about to move, it's hard to let go."[104] In allowing a nostalgic tone similar to the one excised from the staged version of *Small Well Lane*, the text gains in dramatic energy—instead of hammering in the message, the play establishes its credibility and addresses the spectators on their terms.

Those who commissioned *A Myriad Lights* faced a dilemma common to all propaganda productions: the need to stay convincingly truthful while presenting a closely trimmed version of truth. The play must address the implementation of policy in a specific neighborhood yet skirt the concomitant real-world problems without losing credibility. To bolster the claim to factual representation, the acts are prefaced by ostensible reports from Beijing Radio, and at curtain call the actors were joined onstage by eighteen actual residents of Jinyuchi. The device breaks down the "fourth wall" and facilitates the spectators' identification with the model citizens onstage. The residents' presence in the theater also shows a perceived need to validate the play's veracity and moral authority. Ever since Jiao Juyin exhorted that *Dragon Whisker Creek* should bring onto the stage "the feel for the wriggling maggots," courtyard plays have been haunted by the need for a convincing theatrical rendition.

A Myriad Lights employs yet another strategy for gaining authority, shared with other contemporary "main melody" productions: it turns to nostalgia, only to repudiate the past and justify present policy. Unlike earlier courtyard plays, *Goldfish Ponds* and *A Myriad Lights* do not address the demolition of structures of historic value. Nevertheless, the two plays turn into celebrations of old Beijing. *Goldfish Ponds* stresses that the essence of Jinyuchi gains from the architectural makeover. A character in *A Myriad Lights* distances himself from "this place crowded with blocks like skin boils" only to exclaim later, "Jinyuchi, you are my father!" The fictional residents declare allegiance to an abstract sense of place, which can conveniently be given varying meanings as policies change. By celebrating the lost way of life, the authorities become self-appointed custodians of the city's heritage—or rather of the little they deem to be salvageable.

Waxing nostalgic establishes the characters' credentials as local patriots, after which they can proceed to endorse the redevelopment spree that has, as one resident describes it in the play, "almost razed Beijing to the ground." Old Tian holds onto his longing for old Beijing, only to marvel at the new pedestrian street on Wangfujing and the development of Xidan, even though they mark the disappearance of the places of his childhood memories and the larger process of what Anne-Marie Broudehoux calls "the malling of Beijing." The Propaganda Bureau may have learned a negative lesson from Zhong Jieying's intransigent and unappealing wholesale defense of demolition. The best advocates of redevelopment are those who openly if cautiously speak of its losses as well as its gains.

The nostalgia onstage mirrors the official rhetoric. Duan Muqi, head of the Beijing Parks Design Institute, explained in an address on real estate landscape design that placing the sculptures at Jinyuchi observed the principle that real estate development should take into consideration the cultural uniqueness of each site. According to Duan, the Jinyuchi project combines two historical elements: the neighborhood's connection to Lao She's play and the former use of the streets for goldfish stalls. To foreground these aspects, the institute's team drew up a small brook, with tiles depicting goldfish peddlers. In addition, the designers included allusions to traditional architecture. "When the returning residents see these [allusions]," Duan says, "they can feel a sense of return. When they touch these objects, they can feel a sense of belonging and homecoming. By these means we emphasize how this residential area is different from others, what we can call its uniqueness and irreplaceable nature. This is the only way to create landscape design for residential neighborhoods in China that would be different and special."[105] The rhetoric of homecoming assumes that redevelopment entails moving back to the place of origin—an overly optimistic view of the "redevelopment by housing reform" policy. Moreover, the talk of "a sense of return," combined with stylized visual signs of purportedly local character, implies that the new project allows the city itself to regain its former symbolic geography. The gentrified city is supposedly even more truthful to Beijing's history than what has been demolished.

Government publications further exploit nostalgia. The video CD produced by the Chongwen District Propaganda Bureau includes a theme song of little subtlety: "It's still the same place, which has now changed its appearance; Decrepit tenements have become tall houses, stalls have become a shopping mall; Dirt mounds turned into greens, sewers into a fish pond; Yesterday we sowed our aspirations, today we reap hope; Rickshaw pullers are driving taxis, overseas students have returned home; Ah, Jinyuchi, my homestead! You tower majestically by the Altar of Heaven, writing a new chapter in history." As in *A Myriad Lights*, "home" is defined not by particular structures but by its symbolic value. The recent past is not cherished; rather, what is celebrated is the capability to transform it—dirt becomes grass, rickshaws become taxis, stalls become malls. The present recalls the past and repudiates it at the same time. The campaign to reinvent Beijing's image in anticipation of the Olympics put nostalgia in the service of wholesale demolition. As playwrights placed nostalgia and progress as mirror images of each other, city leaders celebrated the old Beijing and in the same breath issued orders to erase many of its landmarks.

THE MODEL PROJECT AND THE PROJECT MODEL

The coupling of nostalgia and progress in the Jinyuchi plays reaffirms the time-space configuration advanced by earlier courtyard plays, which envision the making of an instant city. The plays discussed in this chapter tend to present urban history in line with the planners' ideal—development without the dust of construction, the sweat of laborers, or the broken dreams of residents. The illusion of instantaneous housing reform finds visual expression onstage in the form of architectural miniatures (*Next-Door Neighbors*), maquettes (*Forsaken Alley*), apartment distribution diagrams (*Goldfish Ponds*), and stage sets representing entire new compounds (*A Myriad Lights*). BPAT has often used extravagant stage décor. The courtyard plays are no different, presenting realistic and elaborate architectural sets, yet the representation of projects still unbuilt, whether in minute mock-ups or meticulous backdrops, deserves special attention. The detailed reference to the accomplished project, materialized at stage center, signals impatience with the process of redevelopment. The future promise is fulfilled already during the staged production; utopia is here and now. The post-Maoist plays follow the prescriptive chronotope I discerned in *Dragon Whisker Creek*, which projects an ideal image of the future onto the present. The more recent plays stand out, however, in that they convey the dream of instantaneity in terms borrowed from professional architectural discourse.

The neighborhoods portrayed in the courtyard plays resonate with contemporary model projects, notably Ju'er Hutong and Jinyuchi. The idea of using specific structures and compounds as real-life laboratories to verify and demonstrate new theories, in the spirit of modernist experimentation, suited the socialist ideals and centralist planning practices of the PRC. The shift to dense construction that would give rise to a new sense of community may also be regarded as part of a worldwide reaction after World War II against the individualism of the garden city. In the PRC, wholesale reconstruction of entire divisions—often called "village" (cun) or "community" (xiaoqu, modeled after the Soviet mikrorayon)—was implemented already in the early 1950s and integrated into the first five-year plans. The trend gained momentum during the construction boom of the 1990s, especially in so-called pilot communities (shidian xiaoqu), which emphasized the integration of buildings, existing topology, and designed environment; innovative styling; modern amenities such as parking; and planning for rising property values.[106] These characteristics were key elements in the Jinyuchi project. In foregrounding the innovative traits of pilot communities, plays such as Forsaken Alley and A Myriad Lights not only promote the current housing policy but also support the architectural vision of using model developments as ready-made molds for new construction. The models transcend the specific architectural circumstances and propose prototypical spatial patterns and structural principles to be reproduced and disseminated with minor modification. (The "cookie-cutter approach to policymaking" does not, of course, preclude innovation in urban design, as Michael Keane has pointed out.)[107] The instantaneous transformation of Chinese cityscapes relies on the adoption of molds for mass reproduction. Declaring the success of a single project is tantamount to pronouncing the mission of building the new Beijing accomplished, if only in theory.

The Jinyuchi plays inherit the recent official attitude toward pilot communities. On the one hand, judging the projects by the standards of experimentation, uniqueness, and excellence prioritizes the professional architects' viewpoint and recognizes urban planners as responsible not only for construction but also for social engineering, a role previously monopolized by Party ideologues. On the other hand, the pilot communities become a tool for setting normative values and prescribing the expected relations between the residents and the state. In this capacity, model projects use the architectural discourse to enhance the government's regulatory power and legitimize urban policy.

The courtyard plays also take after other visual presentations of urban change in using maquettes as props. The Jinyuchi project, for instance, has been presented through various models, from the billboards around the construction site to computerized projections of the project in Wang Guang-tao's book on "preservation and development" in Beijing, which provides the view of a high-level official, including a 3-D map that is also shown at the underground exhibition hall at Jinyuchi. Such public display of architectural models has become common; even more elaborate examples have been displayed at the Beijing Urban Planning Exhibition Hall, opened in September 2005. The exhibit includes, among others, a miniature model of the entire city, a bronze cast of the capital in 1949, a model projecting the future layout of the central business district, and wide-screen film simulations of the city's past and future plans. Commercial enterprises have also flooded the public realm with architectural models. Bookstores sell glossy books such as yearbooks of real estate advertisement and surveys of urban design, which include maps and charts, newspaper ads, artistic imaging of construction projects, and computer-generated images of restored sites.[108] Large models are also at the center of media events (see, e.g., my description of the SOHO Shang Du press launch in chapter 7); slick artistic renderings of landmark projects such as the National Opera House, the CCTV Tower, and the Olympic Village venues have been widely reproduced during the bids and various construction phases, further contributing to the dissemination of international architectural practices. Chinese architects have long used models, but since the late 1990s such visual aids have gained in sophistication and in visibility beyond the professional planning circles. The elaborate models not only promote the projects but also enhance the prestige of the designers and entrepreneurs—or in the case of government-sponsored construction such as that depicted in the BPAT plays, of the sponsoring agencies.

By enlisting professional planning practices and putting the diagrams and models onstage, the plays privilege the government's point of view, illustrate its mastery over the constructed space, and present the projects as a done deal. Miniature models, like sand tables for military battle planning, give the presenter a sense of spatial control. The Bureau Chief's gesture in the last scene in *Forsaken Alley*, placing a miniature tree in the maquette, claims to bridge the historical rupture and presents the future in the form of manageable building blocks, ready for human engineering. Moreover, like the theme parks I will discuss in chapter 7, the models draw the onlookers into experiencing themselves in a fantasy world. The miniature accentuates the real estate as a commodity and at the same time endows the project with a dreamy aura. The promise of the future is literally tangible.

The veteran architect Wu Liangyong (of Ju'er Hutong fame) envisions the role of urban planners as disinterested mediators between government, developers, and community.[109] Yet the use of professional lingo in courtyard plays (notably by Ou Rihua in *Beijing Pretenders*) and the staging of maquettes show how the government tilts the urban contract in its favor by enlisting the discourse of planning. The professionalization of Chinese urban planning goes hand in hand with its mobilization by state propaganda. The close ties between planning and the theater facilitate the presentation of the instant city, covering up the messy demolition, relocation of residents, and integration of sustainable preservation into redevelopment. It took a different institutional and personal dynamics, by more independent filmmakers, to address these issues, a matter that I take up in chapter 6.

FOUR

The First Precinct under Heaven

State Symbolism and Unplanned Urbanism
at Tiananmen Square

A SQUADRON of naked identical men, arms spread like jet wings, hovers serenely in V formation over a festively bedecked Tiananmen Square (fig. 17). This striking image ends Zhao Liang's video art piece *Jerks Don't Say Fuck* (2000), a four-and-a-half-minute, MTV-style montage that includes also armed forces marching through Chang'an Avenue, an ecstatic rock music fan, and a demolition worker in action. The juxtaposition of these scenes, the repetition and distortion of shots, and the surreal concluding image strike a derisive note, which is better understood in light of the official images of parades at Tiananmen Square since 1949. Zhao's irreverent digital manipulation of material from the 1999 National Day parade TV broadcast spoofs an icon of the state; equally important, the video art piece places the square in the context of Beijing, and especially the rapid demolition of its urban texture. Can Tiananmen Square and the city coexist? Can the cinema intervene in the delicate balance between heavy-handed state symbolism and organic urbanism?

This chapter explores the cinematic portrayal of Tiananmen from 1949 to the present. It might seem questionable to discuss Tiananmen—a mostly empty space designed exclusively for state functions—in the context of urban policy. Yet it took a concerted government effort, buttressed by the cinema, to exclude the square from the fabric of daily life and fashion it as an autonomous area impervious to the very city whose center it occupies.

In fact, in the early days of the PRC leaders suggested rethinking the square as part of the city. A report on urban planning in Beijing drafted in the late 1950s proposes that a huge swath comprising Tian-

17 *Jerks Don't Say Fuck* (2000): A squadron of half-naked men hovers over Tiananmen Square. Courtesy of Zhao Liang.

anmen Square, the Forbidden City, Beihai Park, and the areas lying farther north—Shichahai and Jishuitan—be partly demolished to make room for "one large flower bed" at the city center.[1] "The Forbidden City was built by the old emperors," noted PRC Chairman Liu Shaoqi and Beijing Mayor Peng Zhen, asking, "couldn't we just reconstruct it to make room for government office buildings?"[2] Their question illustrates the dilemmas involved in designing a capital city that would be friendly to its citizens and mindful of its cultural heritage yet advance national prestige and revolutionary values. The idea of tearing down the palace complex in the Forbidden City and the old alleys at Shichahai may offend our contemporary sensibility for historic preservation, but it is fetching to imagine the possibility of decentralizing city administration and linking Tiananmen Square—now a 109-acre empty space paved with concrete tiles—to a green park. The square was not predestined to be divorced from city life.

Tiananmen has become, however, a space unto itself. The square's design, dedicated to state functions, has not undergone any major changes since 1959, with the exception of adding Mao's mausoleum in 1977—even a reconstruction of Tiananmen Gate in 1970, without change to its original form, was kept secret for thirty-five years.[3] Although adjacent to the old city's commercial centers, the square is enclosed by monumental buildings that rupture the urban continuity. The square was transformed by the policy of sequestering it from daily life. Despite its central location, Tiananmen did not become the city center in the cultural or economic sense. It was marginalized as an urban site and was left in a policy limbo.

The square was forged into a national and at the same time an extraurban space, as illustrated symbolically by its autonomous administrative status, first under the police station nicknamed "The No. 1 Precinct Station under Heaven" (*Tianxia diyi paichusuo*) and since 2004 as a separate municipal district, the smallest of Beijing's seventeen districts and two counties—and the only one including no residential structures but rather a variety of state- and municipal-level protected buildings.[4] Tiananmen has been largely dissociated from Beijing's daily life. Insofar as it has served as a space of leisure, that use was claimed by citizens' initiative, independent of—and sometimes against—the authorities' interests.

Much attention has been given to Tiananmen as an emblem of the state and as what Henri Lefebvre calls a "monumental space," which supports purportedly eternal myths over the daily, ever-changing use of space.[5] Linda Hershkovitz notes that Tiananmen Square has become "a concrete representation of the hegemony of the Chinese state," and for this reason also the target of political dissidents, who have challenged the spatial practices at Tiananmen.[6] Yet the duality of state authority and dissident resistance might obscure an equally important distinction: the one between state symbolism and everyday urban life, that is, between the uses of space by design and those due to citizens' initiative. As I suggested in chapter 1, the emphasis on places of assembly and the celebration of residential spaces are not mutually exclusive but rather part of a dialectical logic essential to the new socialist city. This chapter investigates the interdependence between monumental and everyday spaces, state-imposed vision and personal gaze, national and urban identities.

The tension between the square's design as an emblem of the state and its use for citizens' spontaneous activities has been explored, and often instigated, by the cinema. Documentary and fiction films have intervened in shaping the material and symbolic layout of the square. Insofar as Tiananmen hosted spectacles made for display and dissemination, those images were reproduced and distributed mainly on film. State productions have propagated the images associated with the founding ceremony of the People's Republic in 1949. The site supported what may be called a *chronotope of perpetual revolution*, which stressed the perpetuity of Party ideology through the square's unchanging spatial practices. Since the death of Mao Zedong, films have juxtaposed the official images with the citizens' unscripted life. The square was reappropriated for the cinematic conventions of the anti-establishment hoodlum (*liumang*) and impromptu everyday activities. In creating normative images of state power and in reinstilling those images with new meanings, films played a major role in carving the square out of its urban context, or conversely in establishing it as a part of city life. The shift in the cinematic representation of Tiananmen illustrates in compact form the transformation of post-Maoist urban discourse in film, which I will detail in chapter 6.

This chapter is divided into three sections. The first examines how films have established Tiananmen Square as a space for state parades and spectacles. The normative image of the square as a national space harks back to the founding ceremony, captured in various media but, most important, in the film *The Birth of New China* (1949). The documentary, commissioned by the authorities, construes the ceremony as the culmination of the revolution and aligns Tiananmen with a national narrative. Later productions, up to the record of the 1999 parade, elaborate on the spatial patterns established in 1949. I also compare the images taken in 1949 with the docudrama *The Founding Ceremony* (1989), which restages the ceremony so it can correct the perceived imperfections of the original footage. The range of films that revisit the founding ceremony—up to the recent *Tiananmen* (2009)—attests to the sustained foundational status of the originary images.

The afterimages left on the collective retina continue to be central even in works that challenge propaganda, explored in the second section of this chapter. These films present a counterimage of the official view. *In a Land of Silence* (1979) and *Reverberations of Life* (1979) portray the student demonstrations of 1976, which reappropriated the state spectacles for political protest. More direct reflections on the parades, the cinematographic conventions involved, and their ideological message are found in *The Big Parade* (1986) and *Jerks Don't Say Fuck* (2000).

The chapter's final section discusses films that present an alternative to the official account by addressing the implications of urban policy at Tiananmen. It is no coincidence that the most prominent examples are documentary films, made independently of the official production system, using private funding and skirting the censored, state-run distribution system altogether. The TV series *Tiananmen* (1991) and the feature-length *The Square* (1994) shows the square as a space that resists total appropriation by the state. In all three approaches to the square—whether creating normative icons, countering and spoofing state symbols, or presenting an alternative in the form of the urban context—the task for filmmakers has been to define the cinema's role in creating a representation of space that transcends the boundaries of the site itself.

✤ CREATING A NORMATIVE IMAGE OF THE STATE

As soon as the People's Liberation Army entered Beijing (then Beiping), on January 31, 1949, the Communist leaders started rethinking the city's urban organization and political status. Governance of daily affairs accentuated the building of a socialist, productive city. The city was also chosen as the capital of the People's Republic, after the Nationalist regime had moved its seat of government to Nanjing. The celebration of residential neighborhoods signaled Beijing's restructuring as a functional city; the attention to Tiananmen Square, in contrast, marked the recognition of Beijing as the center of national power. The cinema played a key role in the Party's efforts to establish the square's status.

THE BIRTH OF NEW TIANANMEN

The iconic image of Tiananmen as an architectural symbol of the state was created on October 1, 1949, when Mao Zedong stood on the balcony on top of Tiananmen Gate and declared the founding of the People's Republic of China to the crowd at the square below. The site sustained its symbolic power largely due to the cinema. The founding ceremony was staged with an eye for the film cameras positioned around the square and created an indelible visual impression. *The Birth of New China*, the documentary that recorded the event—possibly the first film to dwell on Tiananmen—set a precedent for future cinematography of the square as a national emblem. The camera's point of view identified with Mao's gaze and his view of the spectacle. The film also separated the square from the urban context.

Tiananmen Gate lent its preexisting symbolism to the ceremony and at the same time acquired new significance. The structure, called Tiananmen (or Gate of Heavenly Peace) since 1651, had a long history as marking the border between the lay city and the imperial compound of the Forbidden

City to the gate's north. From here imperial edicts would be proclaimed, and since May 4, 1919, political protests typically gathered in front of the gate.[7] Mao's appearance on top of Tiananmen not only established the new leader as an emperor-like ruler but also elevated the site's status to an emblem of the socialist state. The gate was chosen as the central icon on the state insignia, since "on it the birth of New China was declared."[8]

The spectacle was carefully orchestrated for the cameras. The future premier, Zhou Enlai, chose the location, preferring it over Xiyuan airbase, because the parade could be viewed from the gate's high balcony.[9] The airbase had been used for the parade celebrating Mao's arrival in Beiping on March 25, which was recorded in the documentary *Chairman Mao and Commander-in-Chief Zhu Arrive in Beiping and Review the Military Parade* (1949). The film evidences that onlookers and photographers at Xiyuan had few vantage points higher than the tank turrets. Watching the footage, edited by the same director who would soon produce *The Birth of New China*, may have helped Zhou Enlai decide to hold the founding ceremony at Tiananmen instead of the airbase. In June, as soon as Tiananmen was chosen, preparations for the founding ceremony began.[10] A parade on July 7 (based on the protocol of a parade that had taken place on February 12)[11] featured many elements that would be reused in October—Mao appeared on the gate's balcony; the band played "March of the Volunteers" (*Yiyongjun jinxingqu*), originally the theme song for the film *Children of Troubled Times* (1935) and later the national anthem.[12] The founding ceremony was given a dress rehearsal, as it were.

Preparations to heighten the parade's visual impact on film began the square's symbolic restructuring. Placing the flagpole and laying the cornerstone for the Monument for the People's Heroes symbolically blocked Beijing's central axis, a thoroughfare at the heart of the symmetrical layout of the imperial city. Widening the gates on Chang'an Avenue to allow for the passage of military vehicles foreshadowed the avenue's future significance as an alternative east-west axis.[13] The founding ceremony laid the groundwork for placing the center of national government in the city and in particular for reconstructing Tiananmen Square as the new capitol, following the visual pattern established by *The Birth of New China*.

After choosing Beijing as the capital, the question remained, where the government headquarters should be located. Liang Sicheng and Chen Zhanxiang, two foreign-trained and highly regarded architects, argued that the old city center would be unable to accommodate the needs of a modern government, which instead should be housed west of the city walls, in a layout mirroring that of the Forbidden City. Liang and Chen were also interested in preserving the historic center. Their plan suggested converting the square into a shopping area and the presidential palace in Zhongnanhai into a park. Despite Liang Sicheng's reputation as China's leading architect, the plan was shelved. Soviet experts, modeling their vision on the rebuilt Moscow, argued in favor of making Beijing into an industrial city dotted with monumental buildings in an international socialist style.[14] The final design, chosen by Mao in person, was based on the plan by Hua Nangui, Zhu Zhaoxue, and Zhao Dongri, which placed the administrative headquarters near the square. The ideological decision had far-reaching implications for Beijing's development. Liang's and Chen's plan allowed for urban expansion and sought the preservation of the old city as an integral artifact. Liang and Chen calculated that to accommodate the government buildings 130,000 houses would need to be demolished—in hindsight, an estimate far too low. The plan adopted by Mao caused in the long run a congested and polluted city, constantly in need of denser construction at the expense of old architecture. Many of the problems detailed in chapters 3 and 6, such as the forced evacuation of old neighborhoods and the slapdash gentrification, hark back to the decision to use the ready-made monumentality of imperial architecture and turn Tiananmen Square into the capitol. Wu Liangyong, Liang Sicheng's student and a longtime advisor to the Beijing municipality, attributes Mao's decision to the symbolism established by the founding ceremony and to Tiananmen's new status as an emblem of the revolution.[15] Insofar as the choice was precipitated by the location of the founding ceremony at Tiananmen, recorded for posterity and for dissemination to the outlying provinces in *The Birth of New China*, the cinema played a crucial role in the development of Beijing, and especially in delegating to Tiananmen its irreconcilable functions as center of both government and city.

DISSEMINATING TIANANMEN

The Birth of New China's influence on high-level decisions about Beijing's plan is less surprising in light of the involvement of the Party leadership in the production and of the film's intended function as a disseminating vehicle for images of the founding ceremony and for revolutionary values generally.

The ceremony was designed to create new icons that would be recognized by citizens, the majority of whom were unfamiliar with Communist doctrine, policy, and even top leaders. Parades organized by the PLA sported prominently the effigies of Mao and the military commander Zhu De (the first parade in Beijing was held on February 3). The extravaganza of October 1 presented national icons not only for the attending foreign dignitaries or the local crowd of three hundred thousand. Through *The Birth of New China*, which distilled the events of 1949 into a forty-two-minute presentation, the government's efforts were made known far and wide. As Matthew Johnson comments, "documentary films of China's liberation helped in establishing and codifying China's geography through the moving image."[16] The images were distributed around the nation and the world.

Realizing the potential of the cinema, the highest echelons of the Communist Party took interest in filming the founding ceremony for posterity, and conceived even before the ceremony of a full-length documentary as the centerpiece of the propaganda effort. The leaders' intervention became most pronounced at the postproduction stage, as the director and editor Gao Weijin made modifications suggested by the Beiping Film Studio chiefs Qian Xiaozhang, Wang Yang, and Tian Fang, the Film Bureau head Yuan Muzhi, and the Bureau's Art Council member Cai Chusheng, all veteran filmmakers. In addition, Zhou Enlai himself wrote specific changes to make the narration more intelligible for a lay audience, and on the premier's instructions ten minutes were excised from the director's cut.[17]

The resources dedicated to the production were unprecedented. More than forty cameramen were enlisted. Unlike with almost all previous documentary films made by the Communist propaganda units, which were edited from frontline footage, the crew received detailed information ahead of time, toured the site, and arranged their equipment meticulously. Because of the event's importance, they were allowed liberal use of film, shooting close to ten times the amount used in the final cut, rather than the usual 4:1 ratio. (A similarly lavish policy applied to still photography—Hou Bo, who took some of the better-known photos of the occasion from her position on the gate's balcony, testifies that she used one roll after another.[18])

To head the large team, Beiping Film Studio chose Gao Weijin, a young documentary film editor with a revolutionary record. Gao, born in 1920, joined the Party in 1937, attended the Lu Xun School for the Arts in Yan'an, and acted in various stage productions. When the Yan'an Film Studio was established in 1946, Gao moved to filmmaking. She made her first movie in 1948, and since then edited documentaries; *The Birth of New China* was her ninth film. Gao could draw inspiration from only a handful of documentary films, mostly the Party-sponsored productions she saw in Manchuria in 1948. Kuomintang (KMT) footage and foreign documentaries—even those made by Westerners in Yan'an—were not available to her. *The Birth of New China* dovetailed with Gao's recent series of films about the Communist victories, such as *Liberating Tianjin* (1949) and *The Huaihai Campaign* (1949). As the culmination of Gao's war films, *The Birth of New China* suggests a narrative of ideological triumph.

In depicting the progress of the Communist forces, *The Birth of New China* anticipates its own distribution across the nation as a propaganda tool. The film proceeds from the proclamation on the Tiananmen balcony to the military parade below and finally to celebrations around the nation, as the people receive the news of the PRC's establishment. Grafting together footage collected from all over China, some taken by teams especially dispatched to remote areas, the film presents the jubilation of "children and old people, men and women, in small villages and large cities, from factories to the military, from north to south, from east to west." The narrator ends with the words, "The Chinese, a quarter of humankind, have risen. The PRC has proclaimed its establishment to the entire world. . . . We will turn an old and backward agricultural China into a self-sustaining, independent, industrialized, strong New China." In many places, the news of the founding of the PRC was conveyed through Gao Weijin's footage. *The Birth of New China* was screened all over the country; viewers were enthralled by their first chance to see a parade on film. The film disseminated images of the New China and its emblems, parading Tiananmen, as it were, to the ends of the land. The film has informed the cinematic imagination about Tiananmen and created a new representational space, one that extended the physical boundaries of staged spectacles and distributed the images—and the ideological vision—beyond the time and place it documented.

The emotional effect of being present at the founding ceremony was replicated through watching the film. Those who attended the ceremony were likely to share the feelings of the director, Gao Weijin, for whom the moment constituted the realization of her aspirations since joining the Party in 1937. The film makes extensive use of reaction shots (which Gao placed a camera inside the square to capture), allowing the viewers to identify with the crowd. The joy of the people in the square and of the film audience derives from participation. *The Birth of New China* manufactures a collective experience by showing the crowds shouting together, "Long live Chairman Mao!" By implication, each and every viewer could consider him- or herself vicariously to have been at Tiananmen. Gao's film created a community of viewers who despite their absence from the square on October 1 could identify the founding ceremony as their personal experience.

The Birth of New China does more than provide images of the event; it propagates a message. Like other Maoist documentaries, it provides an ideological story line, a narrative that placed events in a larger context and justified them. Until 1950, the Communist Party sponsored mostly documentary films because it lacked the resources to produce feature films, yet the documentaries were instilled with implicit plots. There is no clear dividing line between on-site records, such as *The Birth of New China*, and fictionalized accounts such as *Dragon Whisker Creek*. Gao's film foreshadows the growing use of documentary and docudrama to promote specific policies. Establishing the correct facts was less urgent in a system that gave the Party a monopoly on the production of truth. Rather, what was at stake was the creation of a unified historical perception consistent through various representations of the same event and common to all viewers. Rather than simply provide a descriptive record, *The Birth of New China* also prescribes how the founding ceremony, and Tiananmen's significance in general, should be represented and reenacted.

THE REVOLUTION RETOLD

The importance of Tiananmen has been reiterated through many productions that have either included parts of *The Birth of New China* or restaged the founding ceremony.[19] These films replicated Tiananmen's iconology time and again, with variances that only stressed the unchanging ideological message. Tiananmen became a steadfast marker of the revolution's accomplishment, in effect signaling a standstill that repeatedly reaffirmed the Communist vision's perpetuity.

Tiananmen's ideological significance, as established during the founding ceremony, was reinscribed through subsequent National Day parades. October 1 became a memorial day for the founding ceremony, commemorated by pageants that took place at the same location and in a similar format year after year.[20] Few cinematographic changes were introduced, although some technical aspects were improved—the high platforms were replaced with cranes, and cameras directed at the leaders were equipped with more powerful zoom lenses.[21] Party leaders were directly involved in procuring new equipment and deciding on camera placement, evidence of the importance they saw in recording the events.

Some of the ceremonies were distributed as full-length productions by the Central News and Documentary Film Studio (established in 1953). The films also recorded the changes in the square's layout through the 1950s. *Cosmic Renewal* (1956), documenting the 1956 celebration of workers' and peasants' newfound happiness, also attests to opening up Chang'an Avenue into a wide boulevard (1950) and the expansion of the square (1955–59).[22] The construction of the Great Hall of the People and the Museum of Revolutionary History, as part of the "Ten Great Buildings" project of 1959, is the subject of *Beijing's New Architecture* (1959); the buildings also figure prominently in *Celebrating a Decade with Joy* (1959), dedicated to the celebrations of the PRC's tenth anniversary. From our contemporary vantage point, these films serve as historical records. At the time of production and distribution, they were tools to impart knowledge of the square's design and political weight.

During the Cultural Revolution, the spectacles strengthened the identification of Tiananmen with Mao, who used the location to welcome the Red Guards in August 1966 and thereby launch the Cultural Revolution. It was, however, the events documented in *Chairman Mao Is the Red Sun in Our Hearts* (1967) that became emblematic of the Cultural Revolution (and were reproduced in countless films). Mao's funeral, also held in the square, largely followed the cinematic conventions of previous parades. As *The Great Leader and Chief Chairman Mao Zedong Will Never Wither* (1976) witnesses, the gate was turned into a makeshift altarpiece. The construction of the mausoleum for the leader's embalmed corpse at the square's center culminated the process of making Tiananmen into a place controlled by and dedicated to the state. The films helped reify Tiananmen as the material manifestation of the nation's political culture.

Even as the pageants became more elaborate and the documentaries more spectacular, no parade could match the emotional intensity of declaring the birth of New China. Filmmakers returned to the scene of the founding ceremony, restaging it in controlled sets for ideally placed cameras, to achieve a calculated effect that would improve on the originary images.

The "epic in music and dance" *The East Is Red* (1965) expanded and dramatized the revolutionary narrative presented in *The Birth of New China*, achieving its climax in the Founding Ceremony. *The East Is Red* was staged and filmed in October 1964, and released as a special coproduction of August First Film Studio, Beijing Film Studio, and the Central News and Documentary Film Studio on National Day (October 1) 1965. The piece starts with a shot of Tiananmen that pans to the Great Hall of the People, where the filmed performance took place in front of a live audience. The sixth and final act, representing the founding ceremony, is preceded by the proclamation, "The People's Republic of China is born! The Chinese people has arisen!" The cast salutes in front of Tiananmen as the flag is raised to the tune of the anthem. The camera zooms out to reveal the hall. The conductor turns to the audience, which stands up and joins in singing the Internationale. Standing in front of the stage set of Tiananmen, the audience takes the place of the crowd facing the gate at the parades. By implication, it is as if they were present at the founding ceremony. The spectacle is restaged to allow each spectator to share in experiencing the historic moment.

A full-fledged attempt to rethink the founding ceremony in cinematic terms is found in the docudrama *The Founding Ceremony*, planned for the fortieth anniversary of the PRC in 1989. The production of this and other movies was boosted by a call from the head of the Party's Propaganda Bureau for films that would underline the "main melody" (*zhu xuanlü*) of the period and privilege the political message. The call was made to the sound of a 10-million-RMB subsidy.[23] "Main melody" films included productions such as *The Meridian of War* (1990), about a company of young soldiers during World War II; *The Making of an Epoch* (1991), about founding the Chinese Communist Party in 1921; and *Mao Zedong and His Son* (1991), about Mao's relationship with his son Anying, who died in the Korean War. These films often insert documentary clips that blur the line between doctored propaganda and uncontested facts.

Like other "main melody" productions, *The Founding Ceremony* engages in a heavy-handed rewriting of history. It gives a particular spin to the last months of the civil war, concluding with a meticulous reconstruction of the founding ceremony. The film was given practically unlimited resources.[24] The production was granted massive help from army and navy units, and the score was recorded by the orchestra of the PLA's Political Section. As the film was released after the brutal suppression of the student protest at Tiananmen on June 4, the emphasis on the site's days of glory and its revolutionary aura came at a convenient time for the authorities, although it added difficulties for the filmmakers.

An account by the film's directors, Li Qiankuan and Xiao Guiyun, testifies to the special political and artistic challenges posed by the attempt to instill new content into the founding ceremony. As the directors readily acknowledge, politics played a large role in shaping the final product: "Under the specific historic conditions of midsummer 1989, when the film was completed, we had to edit out important parts of the script that would be otherwise unproblematic, such as Mao Zedong's talk of democracy as a weapon . . . and that 'only by winning over the hearts of people can we achieve control over the land.' "[25] The directors continue, "We realized that we could not recreate realistically the authentic founding ceremony of forty years ago. . . . for merely recreating the scene, one could watch documentaries, and we wouldn't have to rack our brains." Instead, the film aims to provide insight into the events. By focusing on the rivalry between Mao Zedong and Chiang Kai-shek, describing their parallel paths and drawing a contrast between the two—one "idolized" and the other "made grotesque"—*The Founding Ceremony* becomes a psychological drama that reveals the two characters' "inner state of the mind."[26] The presentation of Mao's and Chiang's campaigns side by side was a novelty—documentary footage shown in the PRC until that time was limited to that recording Mao's movements, and it would not be until the 1999 full-length documentary *China, 1949* that films from foreign sources would be integrated into a fuller presentation of the events leading to the establishment of the PRC. The directors of *The Founding Ceremony* were faced with the dilemma of all artists portraying revolutionary history: how to reiterate history and at the same time offer a novel perspective. The challenge was especially great in view of the drive to retain the practically sacrosanct images of the founding ceremony.

The Founding Ceremony faced a particular challenge in restaging the nine-minute-long sequence, depicting the ceremony itself, that serves as the film's emotional high point. The directors took artistic license and risked, in their view, "a daring experimentation" in shifting back and forth between documentary footage and reconstructed shots, "to make it difficult to distinguish between real and fake at the film's climax."[27] To ensure the seamless transition, the black-and-white documentary footage was converted to sepia, and the Eastman Kodak film used for the contemporary drama shots was developed with an attenuated signal to achieve a similar hue.[28] The considerations were partly practical—Party officials were willing to expend 2 million RMB to build a set of Tiananmen in Changchun, but it would have been difficult to bring in hundreds of thousands of people to reconstruct the military parade and crowds with accurate period details. More important, the combination of documentary and staged footage allowed the directors to express their artistic vision while paying tribute to *The Birth of New China*. The later production often recreates Gao's film shot by shot. The documentary material influences the overall structure, sets, framing, rhythm, transitions, filming technique, shooting angles, and length of shots.[29] The directors aim to improve on the original cinematography and at the same time preserve its guiding concepts.[30]

The directors often modify the mise-en-scène and soundtrack to produce clearer compositions and a stronger dramatic impact. For example, the beginning of the Founding Ceremony sequence, showing Mao's arrival at Tiananmen, diverges from the pomp in *The Birth of New China*, which plays at this point "The East Is Red"; instead, *The Founding Ceremony* integrates no exegetic music into the scene. Before cutting to a shot of Mao climbing up the stairs to the balcony, Li's and Xiao's film shows the leader in close-up, looking silently above. Doves fly in front of the gate, and the only sound is the batting of wings. The shots stress the importance of the moment ahead and Mao's awareness of history in the making (hearing "the wings of history" [*lishi de chibang*], as the Chinese expression goes). The next shots, modeled after *The Birth of New China*, show the retinue climbing the steps. The light refracts into a line of flares, and the scene is accompanied by an ethereal synthesizer score. The overall effect enhances the aesthetics and ideological message of the originary documentary film.

The doctoring of images is particularly clear in the sequence of the proclamation of the People's Republic. The frames shot in 1949 show Mao squeezed among, and sometimes dwarfed by, other leaders and camera crew, some of whom move unceremoniously back and forth; the view is also cluttered by cameras and microphones. Mao's body is awkwardly cropped (fig. 18). The dramatized sequence in *The Founding Ceremony*, on the other hand, is not only crisper, thanks to better film stock and controlled lighting, but also more clearly composed. In the reenacted shot, Mao stands in front; he is a head taller than the other leaders, with the exception of Liu Shaoqi to his right (Liu was associated with Deng Xiaoping, China's leader at the time of production; the shot rehabilitates Liu, who died during the Cultural Revo-

18.1 & 18.2 *The Birth of New China* (1949): Mao among the crowd on the Tiananmen balcony.

19 *The Founding Ceremony* (1989): A neater reenactment of *The Birth of New China* (compare to fig. 18).

lution). The microphones are neatly arrayed in front and do not disturb the composition (fig. 19). The rearrangement was inspired by the manipulated image of the same moment in Dong Xiwen's oil painting *The Founding Ceremony* (1953).[31] The film taps into the tradition of retouching historical documents to fit the political agenda of the day.

Reshooting the founding ceremony engaged in a cinematic dialogue with the visual precedents; in the directors' words, the documentary footage allowed them "to unite the real space filmed by the old generation of film-makers forty years ago and the artificial spaces filmed by us."[32] The new film also pays tribute to the makers of *The Birth of New China* by showing four photographers and two film cameramen—presumably Gao Weijin's crew—scurrying about the balcony to capture Mao's declaration (fig. 20). This eye-level original composition takes a step back from the balcony, as it were, to

20 *The Founding Ceremony* (1989): Frontal shot of Tiananmen Gate.
Notice the photographers in the foreground.

capture the filmmakers at work, arrayed neatly at the bottom of the frame, literally foregrounding their presence. The emphasis on the cinematographic dimension of the founding ceremony is also a metacinematic statement: historic images forge a self-referential lineage.

✥ BLURRED AFTER-IMAGES

The heavy-handed use of Tiananmen as a representative image of the state has given rise to an array of counterimages. Artists have turned the rich tradition against itself, making informed use of the symbolic iconology to challenge state ideology. As Wu Hung notes, "Unofficial art . . . turne[d] the square into a combat zone."[33] The filmmakers' goal is not to stage a crass (and impractical) defiance of the government but rather to claim a more personal expression within a frame of reference that resonates with individual perceptions of the square. Even though contesting the official view of Tiananmen does not amount to political dissent, it is part of a struggle for the right to contending narratives—of self, history, urban space, and visuality.

SPACES OF CONTENTION

The first major instance in which Tiananmen was reappropriated by unofficial groups, and its significance as an emblem of the state challenged, took place on March 23, 1976. The death of Premier Zhou Enlai that January 8 was followed by a filmed ceremony at the square. In late March, various organizations and individuals laid mourning wreaths for Zhou on the steps of the Monument to the People's Heroes, anticipating the Tomb-Sweeping Festival. By April 5 the square was filled daily almost to capacity, with a half million people staging a de facto demonstration against the leaders of the Cultural Revolution. It took a brutal suppression, followed by a staged spectacle of similar magnitude in support of the leaders, for the government to retake control of the square. The April Fifth movement foreshadowed and perhaps even enabled the overthrow of the so-called Gang of Four after Mao's death later that year. The events were recorded in *Celebrating with Joy the Great Victory* (1976). The documentary *Zhou Enlai* in 1990 and a docudrama of the same title the following year, both of which include documentary footage from 1976, evidence the Party's continuing need to present its version of the events.

In the late 1970s the demonstrations were lionized by Deng Xiaoping's government. Fictional portrayals of the April Fifth movement demonstrate, however, the potential of such protests to challenge the official image of Tiananmen altogether. Two films addressed the events—*In a Land of Silence* and *Reverberations of Life*, both produced in 1979. The two films show that the spectacles at Tiananmen can counter its official staging as a site of contained practices and an emblem of immutable history. The films venture an alternative spatial and temporal matrix to the chronotope of perpetual revolution.

In a Land of Silence, based on a stage play that swept the country in 1978, presents the story of two lovers torn apart by the Cultural Revolution. After the events of April 5, they reunite and turn their backs on the woman's father, who is associated with the Gang of Four.[34] As in the original stage play, the entire plot takes place in Shanghai, on a single day in 1976; the film—produced by Shanghai Film Studio and played by Shanghai actors—only adds a short flashback, using documentary footage of April 5. Although the film keeps within the discourse that regards Tiananmen exclusively as a stage for state affairs, the site's symbolism is rendered largely irrelevant, since it is left offscreen.

Reverberations of Life is set in Beijing. Presented in flashback, it tells how the violinist Zheng Changhe flees the henchmen of the Gang of Four in April 1976. He escapes with the help of Xu Shanshan, who recognizes the

21 *Reverberations of Life* (1979): The main characters at Tiananmen Square, during the mourning period for Zhou Enlai.

violinist also as the man she had met at Tiananmen the day before. Changhe eventually holds a concert in Zhou Enlai's memory and is promptly arrested, yet a couple of years later, after the downfall of the Gang of Four, Changhe is back onstage and receives loud applause. For film audiences familiar with the spectacles of the Cultural Revolution, the protagonist's return to the stage conveyed a powerful political message.

Reverberations of Life reminds the viewer that the people at Tiananmen do not appear out of nowhere. Unlike the state-sponsored festivities, for which participants are bused in to perform predetermined tasks, popular protest is conducted by citizens who use the square as part of a contiguous urban space. The film's opening sequence shows a bus driving westward on Chang'an Avenue, stringing Tiananmen Square with other familiar sights; the characters move about through Beijing landmarks such as Dongfeng Market (the revolutionary name of Dong'an Market from 1966 to 1988). *Reverberations of Life* stresses the continuum between Tiananmen and the city of Beijing.

The film—the directorial debut of Teng Wenji, to which Wu Tianming also gave his name—was especially daring for its time and was among those targeted in the clampdown of 1981.[35] The black-and-white film seamlessly incorporates footage from Zhou Enlai's funeral procession in front of Tiananmen as well as reconstructed scenes of April 5 (fig. 21). While the film is in tune with the ruling political agenda of extolling the triumph over the Gang of Four, it also demonstrates for the first time that the spaces and symbols of Tiananmen can be reappropriated by unstaged crowds and even spontaneous protests. Moreover, *Reverberations of Life* shows the official account to be manufactured. Significantly, the evildoer Weili is portrayed as using his camera to gather evidence against Changhe. The camera—and by extension, the film camera—becomes suspect. *Reverberations of Life* foregrounds the manipulative use of the medium and questions its previously uncontested claim to veracity.

CHALLENGING THE CINEMATIC AESTHETICS OF TIANANMEN

The developing rift between the contesting narratives of Tiananmen is evidenced in Chen Kaige's *The Big Parade* (1986). One of the earlier films made by so-called Fifth Generation directors, it is representative of the skepticism of Chen's generation toward the state. The story line follows a military company's training for the National Day parade at Tiananmen. The focus on specific soldiers is typical of post–Cultural Revolution plots, which emphasize the individual. The film illustrates Chen's criticism—made explicit in his autobiography—of the Maoist manipulation that made people believe they could only exist within the collective.[36] Chen hints at the inhumanity of military marching, which demands that all soldiers conform to the same stringent requirements (the importance of such uniform behavior had been stressed by earlier films about soldiers' education, for example in *Rookie Ma Qiang* [1981]). As Tony Rayns notes, *The Big Parade* beats earlier propaganda films at their own game, portraying a "collective protagonist" that can be read against the grain of selfless sacrifice for the collective.[37]

The impact of *The Big Parade* is fully understood, however, only in the context of earlier filming of National Day parades. Chen's film describes the preparations for the 1984 parade, a time when the National Day celebrations acquired a new meaning. The pageants were put on each year from 1949 to 1959, marking the year's achievements, but for the next twenty-five years, as a result of political and economic upheaval, the National Day festivities at Tiananmen did not include a military parade. It was only in 1984 that the parade was held again, to mark the thirty-fifth anniversary of the PRC.[38] Displaying an unprecedented amount of modern weaponry and a world record–setting array of infantry, it was the occasion for Deng Xiaoping to flaunt his firm hold on power and the success of his reforms. For the first time, a leader other than Mao presided over the parade, and Deng reenacted the Maoist spectacle, even imitating Mao's phrases.[39] According to a later documentary by China Central Television (CCTV), the 1984 parade was "a new point of departure for the people of China and the symbol of a new era."[40] The parade asserted both continuity with early PRC practices and a break with the Cultural Revolution. For Chen Kaige's generation, the 1984 parade was a novelty and at the same time a return to an experience known from documentary footage.

By Chen's time, images of *The Birth of New China* had worked their way into the collective imagination. Those who were present at the founding ceremony were idolized as witnesses to a unique historic moment. Among these were Chen's parents; as the director tells, "On October 1, 1949, when Mao Zedong proclaimed the founding of the state, they were two of the hundreds of thousands in the square." When Chen was a teenager in Beijing he could watch the ritual reenacted in the yearly celebrations. He describes them, however, from documentary footage: "In the documentary film on the National Day celebrations of 1965, before Mao appears, a long shot pans from the square to the Tiananmen wall. In that space containing a million people one could hear clearly the eight red flags flapping on the gate. This was the solemn moment before the gods' descent. Then the tune 'The East is Red' reverberated through the square in the midst of the salvos. . . . These were the sights of a golden age."[41] Chen observes the events with a filmmaker's eye, both to distance himself from the fervor of that period and to enhance the reader's appreciation of the enthusiasm that would engulf those present at the square. In *The Big Parade*, however, the experience of participating in the parade loses the luster of the halcyon days, making viewers question their own reminiscence of the Maoist era.

Under the director of cinematography, Zhang Yimou, *The Big Parade* challenges the accepted representation of the parades. Chen and Zhang had just filmed a TV drama about the 1984 parade, *Forcing through and Taking Flight* (1984). In adapting it into a film, the two young filmmakers sought to demonstrate their innovation.[42] Toward the film's ending, the military company that has undergone excruciating training at a remote base is transported to Beijing, where it marches in the parade. The scene appears to provide an uplifting conclusion, as the soldiers' hard work is rewarded by the chance to contribute to the motherland. Yet the sequence is anticlimactic. The vacuous parade does not compare to the heroic war scenes that end many Maoist films, such as the battle that evidences the protagonist's successful training in *Rookie Ma Qiang*. Moreover, the contrast between the long, arduous exercises and the short moment in which their task is completed calls for a more critical examination. A recent publication representing the official view describes the soldiers drilling in 1984 as "practicing in the cruel heat, unmoving in the blowing wind, staying composed in the beating rain."[43] Chen's film foregrounds that pain—only to suggest its futility. Moreover, the individual faces give way to a sea of undistinguishable figures. Similarly to the makers of *Reverberations of Life*, Chen grafts together footage from the 1984 parade with shots of his own making. The result is a seamless sequence showing the actors' faces and the masses of soldiers at Tiananmen. The photography shifts back and forth between long shots and close-ups; faces come into focus then dissolve again into abstract geometrical patterns. Including no establishing shot, and only an oblique shot of Tiananmen Gate, the sequence is spatially elusive. The scene exaggerates filmic conventions to reveal the hollowness if not inhumanity of that aesthetic, which harks back to Leni Riefenstahl's exultation of Nazi power in *Triumph of the Will* (1935). *The Big Parade* emphasizes the appeal of parade cinematography, which captures the shifting masses as pure choreographed form. Unlike the official documentary of the 1984 parade, which injects close-ups of leaders on the gate's balcony, Chen's sequence omits all reference to the eyes watching from above. The soldiers erase their own individuality even in the absence of visible surveillance.

The film uses innovative camera work that upsets practices followed since *The Birth of New China*. A medium shot of the marchers is taken from an extreme low angle; another marching sequence is projected in slow motion, turning the exhibition of military power into a dreamy ballet. These shots jolt viewers familiar with the official parade images and bring out a lyrical effect that stands out against the subject matter. The film's last shot, a twenty-two-second static close-up of a single soldier, his head silhouetted against the setting sun, stands in direct contrast to images of Maoist heroes such as Li Yuhe in *The Red Lantern* (1970)—unlike Li's radiant face, lit by the red light of Maoist faith, the facial features of the soldier in *The Big Parade* are darkened when backlit by the sun. In this shot, the parade is brought to an uncomfortable standstill. The sound, which starts with the soundtrack from the 1984 parade, including the national anthem, rifle salutes, and marching in unison, lapses into a slow if not outright mournful nondiegetic music and is eventually distilled into faint bugle taps. Chen Kaige, whose comments, quoted above, on the 1965 documentary demonstrate attention to the parade soundtrack, undercuts the message of earlier propaganda films at Tiananmen. The elegiac score and the slow motion create a dissonance between sound and image. The contrast was even more jarring in Chen's original script, which called for shooting an empty Tiananmen Square to the upbeat sound of the parade. The censors rejected the shot, which would portray the square as haunted, a place of ceremonial decorum and architectural grandeur that annihilates the people in it. A similar effect is achieved, however, in the film's first scene, a forty-seven-second tracking shot taken from a helicopter showing a vast asphalt strip during marching drills; the accompanying sound is that of rhythmic marching and a loud, ominous drone. The playful editing of the film's opening and finale teases the conventions of parade cinematography dominant since *The Birth of New China*.

The Big Parade not only provides political commentary but also turns into a statement on the role of post-Maoist film. In spoofing the official images of Tiananmen, *The Big Parade* reclaims the material space and filmic practices previously monopolized by Maoist cinema. Moreover, the reference to the renewed military parades, after their suspension between 1959 and 1984, reflects on the contemporary state of Chinese cinema. Like the parades, film production was put under strict political control from the late 1950s until the mid-1980s. Very few films were made between 1964 and 1979, and film education was halted. Chen's generation, which graduated from the reopened Beijing Film Academy in 1982, was entrusted with renewing Chinese film. *The Big Parade* is the counterimage of the 1984 parade in particular —whereas the parade sought to replicate and reassert the Maoist discourse at Tiananmen, Chen's film refers to the need for social reform by revising the symbolism of the square. The 1984 parade, as modified through Chen's lens, can be read as an allegory for the new Chinese cinema—still burdened by the Maoist conventions yet poised to challenge them.

TIANANMEN AS VIRTUAL SPACE

The relation between Tiananmen's appropriation by the state and the erasure of urban space is made explicit in Zhao Liang's *Jerks Don't Say Fuck* (2000).[44] I turn to Zhao's work, even though it is a short piece of video art, produced and exhibited through means very different from those of film, because it exemplifies the new visual sensibility of the 1990s. The looser government control over painting, still photography, and video art has made them the primary vehicles of critical portrayals of Tiananmen.[45] These media have developed largely in tandem with cinematic practices, and especially in response to the growing presence of CCTV in the square.

Like other works by Zhao, *Jerks* refers both to documentary film and to video games and MTV clips. The piece starts with a sequence, roughly forty seconds long, that cuts back and forth between sped-up footage of tanks rolling on Chang'an Avenue during the National Day parade and a construction worker demolishing a building, with a Forbidden City tower in the background. The two scenes depict some of the most familiar views of Beijing—parades and demolition. Zhao's work suggests that Tiananmen's official iconology and the rapid destruction of the architecture and skyline are complementary in that they are oppressive forces that invite ridicule and resistance.

The video consequently focuses on two sets of images which, put together, amount to a youthful rebellion against the normative images of Tiananmen. The piece presents a manifesto of sorts in computer-game fonts, set to the rock music of the band Sick Doctors: "Little punk, don't you start cussing. You're no more than a reborn pomegranate. Don't live like your parents, enveloped in the dark before dawn." A long-haired artist shakes his head violently; traffic signs flash their prohibitive messages: no smoking, no jogging, no U-turn, no entry. . . . Images of the parade are played back in loops, forcing themselves on the viewer. Gradually, the official images deteriorate as they are smeared and accelerated to a blur. In a manner reminiscent of the concluding sequence in Chen Kaige's *The Big Parade*, the official footage is manipulated to contradict its original message.

Zhao Liang spoofs the normative image of Tiananmen using outtakes from the 1999 National Day parade live broadcast (procured through a friend working at CCTV). Celebrating the fiftieth anniversary of the PRC, the 1999 parade subscribed to the conventions established by the founding ceremony and added pomp and extravagance, such as the release of half a million doves over the square. The celebrations were also the occasion for new landscape design, including new fountains, lawns, and night lighting.[46] The most extensive redesign was invisible—all the tiles at the square were torn out and replaced. Ironically, in line with upholding the immutability of Maoist iconology, the modern square underwent a preservation project more meticulous than most other old sites in the capital, many of which were being demolished at the same time. Citizens remarked that in changing the tiles, all material evidence of the 1989 bloodshed was eliminated. The architectural reconstruction was an exercise in historical revisionism. The subsequent parade, as a political spectacle, was an attractive target for parody.[47]

Insofar as the chronotope of perpetual revolution calls for constant reenactment of the founding ceremony, *Jerks* shows the return of the same images as a farce. Zhao pushes the propaganda aesthetics to the limit, at one point looping the same snippet over thirty times to the sound of techno music. The repeated image of goose-stepping infantry emphasizes the staged and aggressive nature of the parade. In another instance, the camera pans and captures another TV camera across the marching troops. The moment was excised from the official broadcast. In placing it back on view, time and again, *Jerks* questions the invisibility of the state apparatus in charge of generating the official image of the square.

Unknowingly, Zhao Liang taps into an issue that has haunted cinematography at Tiananmen ever since *The Birth of New China*. Gao Weijin's film features several sequences in which cameras are positioned in front of one another. In one shot, Mao occupies the middle front, but the upper half of the frame is taken by no less than three film cameras, belonging to Gao's crew and two crews sent from the Soviet Union to cover the founding of the sister communist republic.[48] Another image is part of the master shot that provided the iconic image of the founding ceremony—Mao stands in front of the microphones, holding up the resolutions of the central government of the PRC and reading them aloud. A camera—a three-lens handheld belonging to a Soviet crew—intrudes right behind Mao and aims almost directly at the Chinese camera. While some dignitaries move aside to allow the Soviet cinematographer a better view, the reading goes on undisturbed. The dialogue between the two cameras remains unacknowledged; the role of the cameras as they are caught in each other's lens is left unexplored. This shot was excised from practically all later excerpts from the film. The event is amplified by the presence of the cameras, yet the spectacle depends on their virtual invisibility—the officially approved images seem to require no guiding hand. The corresponding moment in *Jerks*, taken out of the edited version, evidences the continuation of the same dynamics that require the camera to remain invisible.

The last digitally manipulated shots trace the advance of the squadron of acrobatic human figures over the square (fig. 17; the original shots featured helicopters). Spoofing the familiar view of military aircraft in celebrations, starting with *The Birth of New China*, the shots in *Jerks* stage an imagined takeover of the space of the dehumanizing parades. The abiding control of the state over Tiananmen has made the camera an important agent in the battle of images.

⚡ THE CITY'S RESURGENCE

While films such as *Reverberations of Life* and *The Big Parade* challenge the official view by interpreting the government-sponsored events, other films present a radically different way of relating to the square. Although Tiananmen occupies a large area at the center of Beijing, the parades and their cinematic representation have largely ignored the square's urban context. For Tiananmen to function as a symbol of the state, government policy isolated the square from the city, and films fashioned it as an autonomous space. The movies discussed in this section expose the detrimental effects of the state's near-monopoly on Tiananmen and show how citizens can nevertheless use the space for everyday activities. Tiananmen is shown not only as a monumental space but also as a place subject to the dynamics of urban life. The art critic Li Xianting has recently expressed a wish for Tiananmen's transformation: "On the day when the gate becomes no more than the gate for the tourist destination of the Forbidden City, and when the square becomes no more than a space for sauntering and flying kites, then Tiananmen will no longer be the sacrificial altar of the Chinese, their spirit will become truly free, and they will achieve the ten thousand years of longevity [promised by the slogan on the gate]."[49]

RECLAIMING EVERYDAY LIFE

In accordance with the chronotope of perpetual revolution, the ideological significance of Tiananmen did not allow for material changes to the square, and undoing the official line had to be achieved by extra-architectural means. Any material intervention is left to fantasy, such as Ma Yansong's plan of 2006 for foresting the square and environs and turning them into "People's Park." Ma explains: "By 2050, a mature and democratic China will emerge, and spaces for massive political gathering and troop procession [military parades] like Red Square may no longer be necessary."[50] Ma's Beijing

2050 project resonates with many citizens' sentiments in early twenty-first-century China, yet it relegates the vision to the relatively distant future.

In the absence of the material modification of space, both the government and its critics have resorted to the cinema. Propaganda films have supported Tiananmen's extraurban status. *The Birth of New China* gradually zeroes in on the square, constructing the spatial context of the ceremony not by way of Beijing's landmarks but rather through a crescendo of crowd shots. The film situates Tiananmen within a self-contained frame of reference. Shots form static tableaux, imposing but at the same time disorienting. Most of the cameras either face the square or capture the gate without a clear spatial context.[51] Even a shot from a camera located inside an airplane scans the area starting with the gate and stopping at the southern end of the square, ignoring the city beyond. *The Birth of New China* invented a cinematic vocabulary, followed by later films, that divorces Tiananmen, as a political space, from Beijing as a lived city.

The moment of cinematic breakaway from the mold of propaganda films can be located in a specific production: the TV documentary *Tiananmen*, shot in 1988–89 and completed in 1991. *Tiananmen* is a milestone in Chinese documentary filmmaking, in ignoring overbearing narratives and creating an oral history of Beijing. The TV series is based on extensive interviews with eyewitnesses to Beijing's transformation, from a former court eunuch to a contemporary fashion model. The occurrence of the June Fourth incident just before the series' scheduled release in late 1989 resulted in shelving the production, originally commissioned by CCTV; it was completed independently by the directors and never aired.[52] The most politically sensitive is the eighth and final episode, which tells the history of Tiananmen. Historical footage, including from *The Birth of New China*, is interwoven with contemporary interviews, such as one with a woman who, as a girl in 1953, was chosen to hand flowers to Mao during the parade (a scene captured on film). Yet rather than presenting complementary versions, the interviews end up belying the earlier documentaries. Juxtaposing the testimony of a woman who orchestrated the slogan shouting during Mao's review of the Red Guards with the 1966 footage calls into question whether history can be gleaned from original material alone. When the filmmakers bring the woman to give her testimony on the balcony of Tiananmen, where she had stood during one of the Cultural Revolution's most notable moments, she cannot relive that experience; instead, she explains how she would have changed the slogans now. As a documentary, *Tiananmen* does not capture a purportedly objective history but rather allows for a reflection on the creation of narratives.

The eighth episode makes another important contribution to rethinking the documentary aesthetic by training the camera on material that was not previously considered legitimate subject matter. The solemn tone of Tiananmen is undercut by a conversation with a young child, who recognizes Mao's image but does not know who he was. Mao's imposing portrait is literally taken off its pedestal as *Tiananmen* follows the process of painting a fresh replica and hanging it up. Providing a stark contrast with the records of state affairs, lengthy sequences show children at the square throwing snowballs, flying kites, and taking photos. Photography is singled out as a way to capture life on the go at Tiananmen. The documentary includes a brief interview with the four Wang brothers, professional photographers who regularly take pictures at the square. As they explain it, the place "represents the people's joys and sorrows." Tiananmen figuratively parcels the experience of being in the square into short, private moments, as photos by the Wang brothers fill the screen, one at a time.

The documentary miniseries turns from Tiananmen's official use to the daily activities of regular people, a discursive shift enabled by the rise of critical thought during the "culture fever" of the late 1980s. Yet the TV series should be understood also as the outcome of a sea change in Beijing's urban planning and Tiananmen's place in the city. Since the end of the Cultural Revolution, coastal cities and Beijing in particular witnessed rapid if not uncontrolled urbanization. Inside the old city alone, 7 million square meters of new housing were built between 1974 and 1986.[53] The construction of large apartment buildings raised residential density; the city also attracted a large number of migrant workers, living in uncounted makeshift shacks. While fewer housing units provided spaces for relaxation and social interaction in the form of common courtyards and work unit facilities, more residents were taking part in the new culture of leisure, including shopping and strolling in public areas. Tiananmen, as an open and highly accessible space, was a natural choice for whiling away one's time. The square was also turning into a popular tourist destination. More people had the means for domestic travel, and many used the opportunity to visit the site that they had seen reproduced in various media. The government acknowledged the tourist impulse by opening the gate's balcony to visitors on January 1, 1988, at the then-exorbitant ticket price of ten RMB.[54] With little modification of its topography, the square's symbolic layout changed dramatically.

The independent production of *Tiananmen* signals the cinematic use of the square as an ideological battleground. Filmmakers who seek to tell a story different from the official line invade the square with their own cameras, literally changing the point of view from which the spectacle is seen and toward which it is staged. Whatever the new vision may include, it is no longer imagined only through Mao's omniscient gaze—or even as its direct foil. Beyond any filmic content, the very presence of multiple cameras in the square challenges the state's narrative.

THE CAMERA AND ITS DOUBLE

Since the late 1980s, many filmmakers have realized the potential for social criticism in questioning the official images of Tiananmen. The most spectacular confrontation with Maoist ideology, highlighting a different vision and bringing to the square an unprecedented number of camera crews, came in the protest movement of 1989 and the bloody military crackdown on the night of June 4. Yet the continuous live broadcast from the square, which CNN Bureau Chief Mike Chinoy called a "television revolution,"[55] had no tangible impact on Chinese cinema. Footage of the June Fourth movement was banned domestically, while PRC delegations overseas offered videocassettes of a documentary that presented the government's version. Direct cinematic reference to the events of June 4, such as in *Summer Palace* (2006), has been rare. Insofar as Chinese filmmakers in the 1990s called Tiananmen's iconology to question, they did so more obliquely than in earlier works such as *The Big Parade*.

In fact, even before June 4, 1989, Tiananmen retained only vestiges of its monumentality, not only because of many citizens' political disenchantment but also because of the rise of lighthearted popular culture. Films started to depict Tiananmen itself as reappropriated by the urban "hoodlum" (*liumang*) counterculture. In *Samsara* (1988), the hoodlum protagonist meets with two young women at the square. The three bond by taunting a guard in front of the gate and cracking jokes at the expense of the soldiers who look, they observe, like robots (fig. 22). Feng Xiaogang, as cowriter of *After Separation* (1992), hones his skills of spoofing Maoist iconology, later developed as a film director (see chapter 7). The male protagonist, Gu Yan (played by Ge You), sets a date with Lin Zhouyun (Xu Fan) under the pre-

22 *Samsara* (1988): Hoodlums at Tiananmen Square.

tense of being the author Wang Yue—a playful reference to the popular writer Wang Shuo. Gu is portrayed in shots that replicate *The Birth of New China*—he ascends the stairs and strikes a Mao-like pose in the middle of the balcony, facing the square. Lin immediately sees through Gu's pretense and brushes him off. The character who takes Mao's place is rejected for being a fake, but his offense is not that he fails to be as good as Mao; Lin is looking for someone like Wang Shuo, known for his lowbrow "hooligan literature" (*pizi wenxue*). Xia Gang and Feng Xiaogang bring Tiananmen into the fold of down-to-earth, irreverent city life.

Unlike *After Separation* and its flippant tone, Zhang Yuan's and Duan Jinchuan's *The Square* is a feature-length social study of Tiananmen, in line with what came to be known as the New Documentary movement.[56] As Chris Berry notes, the New Documentary movement is characterized by indirect reflection on June Fourth as a "structuring absence"; a focus on urban life, reflecting on the condition of the filmmakers and their social circles; spontaneous shooting; and independent production.[57] These elements are determining factors for the aesthetics and message of *The Square*. The Tiananmen incident of 1989 casts its shadow on the location; the square is understood through its urban context and in relation to the people who document it; the film's unscripted nature underlines Tiananmen's use for daily activities; *The Square* was not only made independently of the TV stations and film studios but also presents itself from the beginning as a foil to official productions.

After an establishing shot from the balcony, replicating the point of view identified with Mao, the film starts by showing a CCTV crew interviewing officers at the Tiananmen police station. In capturing the other crew's cam-

23 *The Square* (1994): A TV crew films schoolchildren
on the Tiananmen balcony. Courtesy of Zhang Yuan.

era, *The Square* draws attention to the fact that the square is subject to
contending visual and ideological representations. The TV crew is bolstering
the official line by preparing a program celebrating the forty-fifth anniversary of the PRC. In one instance, the TV director talks to young pioneers on
the Tiananmen balcony. He coaxes them to recite Mao's words at the founding ceremony, in an effort to demonstrate the young generation's identification with the symbols of the state (fig. 23). Like other propaganda pieces, the
official documentary attempts to return to the primal scene of the founding
of the People's Republic, reenacting national history in the present and
implying the continuity and immutability of the revolution. Zhang and
Duan, on the other hand, present their film as an alternative, stressing the
artificiality of the TV production.

Although the relationship between the directors of *The Square* and the
CCTV crew is more ambiguous and symbiotic than it may seem,[58] the contrast between the two productions is key to the film. Zhang sought to make a
movie that would counter preexisting images. He explains that since 1949
Chinese documentaries have always been used for political purposes—in
fact, they were not even perceived as bona fide films.[59] Zhang and Duan
were among the first to break away from the government-sponsored production system. Zhang had made *Beijing Bastards* (1993), an independent
film considered as the first movie of the so-called Sixth Generation; Duan

had worked for CCTV in Tibet and resigned on his return to Beijing. Shortly thereafter he made *The Square*. The two directors' disaffected attitude permeates their film.

Much of *The Square* is devoted to foregrounding the difference between the two modes of filmmaking. In contrast with the slick look of "main melody" films such as *The Founding Ceremony*, *The Square* uses a grainy black-and-white film stock, made for recording scientific experiments, which in Zhang Yuan's words feels "not entirely real"—presumably, the blurry texture counters realistic conventions (the choice of the domestically produced Baoding reels was also guided by financial concerns).[60] Whereas official productions glorify state events, *The Square* shows the disinterested looks of passersby and the return to daily hustle and bustle as soon as ceremonies (such as a salute to a visiting foreign dignitary) are over. Camera angles are awkward and unflattering, such as a rear view of the receding guard. Entire sequences, such as the flag raising ceremony, look like unpolished "making-of" films. These scenes impress on the viewer that propaganda films rely on a highly selective use of images.

The juxtaposition of the two cinematic approaches also suggests a different relation between film and urban space. In opening with the CCTV crew's interview of the police officers, *The Square* draws attention to the close connection between propaganda productions and the government's surveillance of the site. As the police commander notes, the Tiananmen station, rumored to be the largest in China with more than one hundred officers at the time, is nicknamed "No. 1 precinct station under Heaven" because of its central location. Zhang's camera, however, captures the policemen and military personnel in situations that compromise their control of space. Soldiers departing after the change of guards, the smartly dressed members of the elite unit, awkwardly straddle the chain surrounding the flagpole and walk through the crowd. The shot questions the borderline, symbolized by the chain, between state-regulated spaces and the people's use of the square for quotidian purposes. The scene is emblematic of how *The Square* marks the tenuous fault lines between public and private spheres, between monumental space and daily preoccupations.

The directors' choice of Tiananmen as the location of urban activities creates a cognitive dissonance between state symbolism and city life. As Duan Jinchuan tells, Zhang Yuan was inspired by the documentary filmmaker Wu Wenguang and was looking for a topic for a documentary of his own. On the same day that Duan showed Zhang a copy of Frederick Wiseman's *Central Park* (1989), Zhang decided to go along with a film on Tiananmen.[61] *Central Park* is exemplary of Wiseman's "thematic documentary," which structures non-premeditated footage around a theme. The film shows New Yorkers as they walk, jog, boat, bicycle, skate, read, bird-watch, and picnic, and as they enjoy music concerts, theater performances, and parades. *The Square* targets similar subject matter, showing the square as a place for popular leisure, a cement-covered park where children fly their kites (Zhang and Duan also take their cues from the TV series *Tiananmen*).[62] Wiseman also places citizens' behaviors in the larger context of urban policy, discussing the problems faced by the New York City Parks Department in maintaining the park and keeping it accessible to the public. Read against Wiseman's portrayal of the municipal workers' concern for Central Park, *The Square* shows that neither state functions nor citizens' usage of Tiananmen has much to do with an urban policy for sustaining a functional city. In observing the square—rather than municipal recreation spots less fraught with symbolism—Zhang and Duan stress how national politics takes over urban design at Tiananmen and how everyday life inevitably presents an alternative to the state's interpretation of the same space.[63] In the milieu of the 1990s, the subversive content of *The Square* created a buzz. The quasi-autobiographical narrator in Qiu Haidong's novel *City Tank* (1997) tells how he watched the film in an unofficial screening space, thick with smoke, with a crowd as interested in Zhang Yuan's aura as an underground director as in the film itself. *The Square* is mentioned in the same breath as iconoclastic performance art such as Zhang Huan's "Adding One Meter to an Anonymous Mountain," both symptoms of Beijing as breeding ground for limitless experimentation.[64]

CAMERA-READY TIANANMEN

The Square comments on the normative image of Tiananmen by focusing not only on the cinematic conventions associated with the square but also on the habits of still photography. Zhang and Duan devote a substantial portion of their film to the photo stall—in fact, it was the first sequence they shot—and to following people as they pose for a picture. Having one's photo taken in front of Tiananmen has become a ritual tribute to the state; yet *The Square* places photography at Tiananmen within a larger continuum, looking not at the artifact but rather at the process of negotiating between popular leisure and state control through the camera.

Photography at the square has undergone a transformation akin to that experienced by filmmakers. Since the founding ceremony, the authorities have produced and disseminated a large number of photos of Tiananmen during official celebrations. Like filmmakers, photographers have also used Tiananmen to challenge Maoist aesthetics and ideology. Beginning with the April Fifth movement in 1976, and especially since the mid-1980s, professional and amateur photographers took to the square to present their alternative points of view. Their subjects are unstaged, often caught by surprise.[65] Like the Wang brothers, interviewed for the *Tiananmen* TV series, an informal group of photographers calling themselves in jest the Photography Association of the Square (*Guangchang Yinghui*) seek to structure their spontaneous shots around well-defined subject matter.[66] Rejecting Maoist ceremonial photography, they regard the photographer as an auteur with a personal vision. The resulting works look for novel compositions and spatial configurations. Zhang Yuan, as the cinematographer for *The Square*, shares with the still photographers the attention to mundane subject matter and an interest in a fresh view of Tiananmen.

Zhang and Duan also address directly the most common photographic practice at Tiananmen: taking one's picture in front of the gate. As I have detailed elsewhere, the routine gesture developed in conjunction with the proliferation of Tiananmen's images in state propaganda.[67] The official photos of the leaders were mirrored by pictures taken by groups and individuals who performed what became known as "going to Tiananmen to see Chairman Mao."[68] They posed in front of the gate, under the leader's effigy, as a pilgrimage memento. Such images grew in popularity with Mao's personality cult during the Cultural Revolution, when photographers' posts were set up for the thousands of Red Guards who came to the square, often as the departure point for marches to the historic revolutionary bases. A Red Guard states her two goals for visiting Beijing: "one, to see Chairman Mao; two, to have my picture taken at Tiananmen."[69]

Many who could not afford to travel to Beijing availed themselves of Tiananmen backdrops in photographers' studios. (An example of this practice is found in the opening sequence of *Mongolian Ping Pong* [2005], where a Tiananmen mock-up is set up in the Mongolian steppes, introducing the film's theme of a displaced imagination of China.) Even such photos were expensive, and their existence demonstrates the perceived value of associating a memorable event in the family's life with the image of Tiananmen. The studio photos suggest the importance of Tiananmen, not only as a tourist spot but rather as a marker for the nation, independent of the original location. The site is reduced to a backdrop, and the intimate moment turns into a declaration of allegiance to a symbol of the collective.

Taking a photo of oneself asserts one's identity, in the spirit of Joseph Brodsky's phrase "Kodak ergo sum"; Zhang and Duan implicitly criticize the coupling of personal identity with Tiananmen as an emblem of the state. Rather than flattening Tiananmen to a backdrop and turning the photo into a fetish of revolutionary allegiance, *The Square* reveals the process of producing the photographic image. The workers of the state-run photography kiosk take the cart that serves as the stall out of storage, roll it into the square early in the morning, and set up the promotional display. The visitors to the square pose for pictures and react to the final product. Zhang's lens lingers on people as they tidy up and pose for the camera. While bystanders gawk, a man tries in vain to straighten his tie, and a woman is told to hide the receipt in her hand behind her back (fig. 24). The attempts to strike a proper appearance and comport with photographic conventions often seem ridiculous in view of the subjects' overall unkempt appearance and lack of camera savvy. The photographer, on the other hand, is smartly clad and self-confident, and he becomes the center of a spectacle in his own right. Within the full array of human interactions during the process, the snapshot loses its solemnity. The sequence portrays the square as a lived space, which lends itself to daily routines, extending to places near it (such as the stall storage locker) and to longer durations (including the time it takes to wait in line, prepare for the photo, and retrieve it from developing). Insofar as Tiananmen is a prop in the state's show of power, the mundane process of posing for a photograph contrasts with—and gives the lie to—the official extravaganzas. Zhang Yuan's camera strips activities in the square from the chronotope of perpetual revolution and its claim to immutability; *The Square* allows Tiananmen to regain a sense of temporal change. In spatial terms, Tiananmen is extracted from its monumentality and is located within contemporary Beijing's urban environment.

Zhang's and Duan's project is continued in other works, notably in *There Is a Strong Wind in Beijing* (1999). Ju Anqi's shoestring-budget documen-

24 *The Square* (1994): Cameras on the square—three young women have their photo taken in front of Tiananmen Gate.

tary is based on the premise of intruding into passersby's space with non-sequitur 2questions such as "Is there a strong wind in Beijing?" and eliciting impromptu social interaction. Ju's crew also goes to Tiananmen. The interlocutors in this scene, identified by their accents as domestic tourists or migrant workers, blurt out slogans such as "It's the country's capital, the heart of the PRC. It shows to the world China's strength" or "I hope that China will become even more powerful and prosperous." Against these hollow words, others reveal their down-to-earth concerns. A man says: "I have nothing to do so I came to loaf around; I have no work"; a woman sings "I love Beijing's Tiananmen" out of tune. Each has his or her own Tiananmen. The dialogues in the shadow of Tiananmen, forced and formulaic, demonstrate the site's abiding power to disrupt the spontaneous interaction between the camera and its subject.

Among the latest instances of reclaiming Tiananmen Square as a space of everyday life are Wang Wo's *Outside* (2005) and *Noise* (2007). Both documentaries, kaleidoscopic and avoiding any voiceover narration or interviews, juxtapose daily practices with the scripted activities of the official guard. Wang repeats the gesture of earlier films in focusing on the ritual of having one's photo taken (Wang has also addressed the subject matter in a series of still photographs).[70] In returning to the square, however, Wang demonstrates how, by the twenty-first century, the location is trite and much less burdened by ideological connotations. *Noise* aptly ends with the spontaneous celebrations, on July 13, 2001, of winning the bid for the 2008 Olympic Games—the moment that arguably best exemplifies the blurring of state-sponsored and citizen-initiated practices at Tiananmen.

Filmmaking at Tiananmen has not only recorded specific events but also become an active force in the site's spatial politics. Films have disseminated normative images of official celebrations, documented the architectural changes in the square, and turned themselves into visual monuments, reinforcing or contesting the ideological significance of the square. Paradoxically, Tiananmen, as an emblem of the state, lends itself more easily to manipulation by counterimages than the residential areas featured in the propaganda productions I considered in chapters 1 and 3. As a public space, Tiananmen can be used by citizens and visualized by filmmakers for their purposes. The filmic reappropriation of Tiananmen, hand in hand with the site's evolving function in the city's life, attests to the ever-fluctuating terms of the urban contract. The cinema is enlisted to support various political agendas and citizen initiatives. Images affect urban change, not by architectural restructuring but rather by tilting the balance of power—and not even Tiananmen is impervious to films' intervention.

FIVE

Angel Sanctuaries

Taipei's Gentrification and the Erasure of Veterans' Villages

TSAI MING-LIANG's twenty-five-minute short *The Skywalk Is Gone* (2002) focuses on the acutely felt absence of a familiar Taipei site, the bustling skywalk, now torn down, that used to serve those crossing Chung Hsiao West Road to the bus hub and railway station on the northern side. The titular phrase is spoken by a woman apprehended for jaywalking. Having hurled her large suitcase over the concrete separation and run through eight lanes of busy traffic (fig. 25), she responds to the policeman with indignation: "Why should I take out my ID? I was only crossing the street. The skywalk isn't there—you can't blame me for it! It's not like I'm not willing to take the skywalk. . . . It's because the skywalk is gone!" Never mind that a new, more convenient underpass was built in the skywalk's place. Law and order take second place to the woman's spatial memory. The bastards changed the rules—and it does not matter even if they told her. Everyday conduct remains dictated by a part of the city that has physically disappeared but remains etched in the citizens' minds.

The humorous portrayal of a daily occurrence turns into a commentary on urban change. Taipei is gentrified through slick planning that renders the connectors of the urban fabric invisible ("the skywalk is gone" is literally expressed as "the skywalk can be seen no more"). It is also a change in economic patterns—the skywalks used to be populated by hawkers displaying knickknacks and counterfeit merchandise in makeshift stalls, whereas now the underpasses host orderly malls; the underpass to Taipei Station in particular links to a maze of shops that stretches for miles. Yet the official regulation continues to be countered by citizens' reassertions of their spatial reasoning. Taipei's urban network can be understood only when one goes beyond what

25 *The Skywalk Is Gone* (2002): Jaywalking where the skywalk used to be.

meets the eye and instead treats the city as a palimpsest of simultaneously existing layers. Taipei's material spaces are merely the visible part of a city mostly submerged in memory.

The Skywalk Is Gone is also about Taipei's cinematic memory. The short is a sequel to Tsai's full-length feature *What Time Is It There* (2001) and a prequel to his *The Wayward Cloud* (2005), sharing the same protagonists (played by Lee Kang-sheng and Shiang-chyi Chen). The skywalk is a key location in the earlier film, where a young man peddles watches. He becomes obsessed with a young woman who bought a watch off his wrist and moved to Paris. The young jaywalker in *The Skywalk Is Gone* is the same woman, who is now looking for the watch vendor. The two eventually cross paths on the underpass staircase but fail to recognize each other. The camera follows the young woman as she looks to the place where the missing skywalk was, first at street level among the crowd, and then from a high-rise, gaining a bird's-eye view. The film retraces the ghostly vestiges of the skywalk—as a material structure, a social construct, and a cinematic image. Focusing on the area around the railway station, still under construction during the shoot, Cai's film shows the city in the process of being torn down and rebuilt—on the ground, in the citizens' imagination, and through the cinema.

The Skywalk Is Gone addresses, in the form of a condensed parable, the issues with which this chapter is concerned. The rapid urbanization of Taipei in the 1960s and '70s gave way beginning in the 1980s to gentrification, which sought to reverse the effects of the hurried construction. The architectural change also signaled the disappearance of a way of life. The transformation of the cityscape and the attendant social change gave rise to growing friction between the residents and the municipal authorities. At the same time, films have reproduced images of the disappearing landmarks, not to wallow in nostalgia but rather to emphasize the coexistence, in the collective memory, of the city in its past, present, and future forms.

THE VETERANS' VILLAGES AND URBAN DISCOURSE IN FILM

Joining the vibrant debates on Taipei's gentrification, filmmakers have referred in particular to the veterans' villages (*juancun*)—urban enclaves gradually evicted starting in the early 1980s—to draw attention to the social price paid for the municipal government's policy. The material vestiges of the veterans' villages, a phantomlike presence, resurge in filmic images.

Like any city rich with history, Taipei offers a palimpsest of layered growth, of which the veterans' villages and their destruction are a late phase. Taipei's architectural and symbolic contours reflect the expansion beyond the walled city. When it became the provincial capital under the Qing in the nineteenth century, Taipei acquired settlements to its west. During the Japanese occupation (1895–1945), the city wall was destroyed and new districts developed to the east, according to a city plan devised in the 1920s. The policy of Taipei's "Sinification" after 1945 included the demolition of many Japanese-style residences in favor of multistoried, functional housing of modernist design.[1] In the 1970s, the government strove to integrate the island into the global economy. Infrastructure was laid for the service sector (for example, in the form of the Ren Ai Road and Dun Hua Road parkways, built in the early 1970s). Developing a secondary urban center around Hsin Yi Road, formalized in a 1981 plan, was a turning point in rethinking Taipei's layout and implementing a postwar city plan.[2] The result was the Taipei Metropolitan Area, around a municipality that now covers 107 square miles with a population of more than 2.6 million people. The 1990s added yet another layer, with the drastic urban restructuring through reallocation of land use, including demolishing entire neighborhoods and designing new parks.

At the heart of the redevelopment that began in the mid-1980s were the veterans' villages. Like the old steel skywalks, which planners regarded as the crumbling remnants of an older urban vision, the veterans' villages become an eyesore to decision makers, and Taipei's gentrification entailed their systematic dismantlement. These urban divisions were built to house the military personnel and their dependents who accompanied Chiang Kai-shek and the Kuomintang (KMT, or Nationalist Party) in their retreat from mainland China in 1949. Unlike the identically named communities in the PRC, which offered privileged facilities for regular military units, the Taiwanese veterans' villages often suffered from poor upkeep. Top brass were given spacious single-family residences in orderly quarters, but low-ranking soldiers often had to build their own houses with minimal resources. The state invested little in long-term homes for a force ready, at least according to the slogan, to move out and "strike back at the mainland" (*fangong dalu*). As the temporary arrangements became ones of indefinite duration, bamboo and brick shacks became permanent housing. Soldiers established families and added makeshift rooms. In addition, many soldiers discharged during military downsizing were allowed to settle in vacant lots, and the authorities turned a blind eye to the illegal construction. Strictly speaking, these are squatter settlements rather than veterans' villages, but the distinction based on land use plans has little meaning on the ground.

These run-down divisions came to public attention in the late 1970s, as Taiwan's newfound affluence resulted in an unprecedented construction boom, driven by both the public and private sectors.[3] The evacuation of shantytowns in favor of modern buildings and recreational spaces was an integral part of the new policy. The fact that veterans' villages were built on land belonging to either the military or the municipal governments, combined with the illegal status of many constructions, facilitated the villages' evacuation beginning in the early 1980s. The central location of many veterans' villages made them a prime target for redevelopment, either into high-density housing compounds or into parks that would raise the value of adjacent property. The government cited the formal usage of the grounds, but in many cases the final park design was not the municipality's original intent. Notably, the locations that ended up as Taipei parks numbers 7, 14, 15, and 20 were designated for public use in the 1932 urban plan but later converted to "multipurpose use for public facilities" and "rewarding private investment"; only after citizen protest were they made into green spaces. As the authority of the KMT government waned, protests became a key vehicle for changing policy. When residents were evicted to inconvenient outlying locations and tightly knit communities were torn apart, demonstrations often turned violent.[4]

The involvement of the municipal government added a charged political dimension to urban redevelopment. The large-scale projects of construction and evacuation called for decisions by the mayor in person, in consultation with national leaders. The construction boom culminated in the mid-1990s, just as the DPP (Democratic Progressive Party, or Minjindang) was poised to take over the municipal government. Many saw the disregard for the veterans, Chiang Kai-shek's old retainers, as a betrayal by the defeated KMT politicians of now-expendable voters and an insensitive if not vengeful treatment by the DPP. The alleged discrimination along party lines further intensified and polarized the debate.

The plight of veterans' villages and the involvement of high-level politicians contributed to the development of urbanist activism. As the municipal government took a more active approach to changing the cityscape, professional planners were called on to design—and to justify economically and environmentally—new architectural patterns of housing, traffic, and leisure. Meanwhile, national politics was democratized, and the academy fostered activist planning. The resistance to the evacuation of the veterans' villages had direct impact on state spending and urban policy. Since 1994, the debates have been taken to the Legislative Yuan and to Taiwan's Supreme Court.[5] The fate of the veterans' villages provides a representative picture of Taiwanese society, politics, and urban aesthetics.

The veterans' villages offer an interesting comparison with housing projects in the PRC. The same circumstances that caused the de facto secession of Taiwan from the mainland in 1949 have also accounted for some similarities—the respective governments were burdened by the need to provide minimal living conditions for their loyal followers (whether the KMT military or the urban proletariat) under accelerated urbanization. The cities—especially the respective capitals—were seen as the state in miniature, and urban policy became part of nation building. The short-term measures of the 1950s and 1960s came to haunt the second generation of leaders, after Chiang Kai-shek's and Mao Zedong's deaths in 1975 and 1976, respectively. Whereas the PRC moved toward market-economy autocracy, Taiwan developed a combination of polarized democracy, strong-arm local government, and militant nongovernmental organizations (NGOS).

The political relaxation in Taiwan, leading to lifting of martial law in 1987, also allowed for a new filmmaking environment. Financing, production, and distribution grew increasingly independent from government supervision, and the film industry was inspired by former dissidents who became powerful opposition leaders. What might seem, in view of the directors' auteurist aura, as a disengaged artistic pursuit was in fact part of a civil movement to change existing policies. Filmmakers' criticism of urban policy could sway voting citizens and influence elected officials. In this respect, this chapter stands out from other chapters in this book, which deal with the more tightly controlled PRC film circles. Yet the Taiwanese example not only provides an instructive comparison; it has also influenced mainland filmmakers such as those I will consider in chapter 6, who seek to enhance public awareness of preservation policy or the lack thereof.

In Taiwan, the cinema plays an important role in excavating the urban palimpsest and linking between spatial and temporal perceptions of the city. The role of the archeologist, digging for Taipei's previous avatars, falls on filmmakers. To counter collective amnesia, the films foreground spaces that contain the signs of their recent or imminent erasure—construction and demolition sites, newly planted parks, rental apartments, makeshift market stalls, restaurants built too hastily to comply with fire codes, offices of bubble economy startups, and fashionable bars that cater to the floating population of expats and workers of multinational corporations. These locations present what may be called a *poetics of demolition*, which challenges Taipei's polished appearance and the government's engineering of memory. In the face of the erasure of older spaces under the new, gentrified city, films reclaim the ruins of the past. Where official narratives present the layers of reconstruction as a single-file progress toward a modern, global city, the films offer contending narratives using concurrent temporalities. The veterans' villages in particular mark what may be called a *chronotope of simultaneity*.

The films that address the demolition-and-relocation in the veterans' villages operate at the fringes of a civic dispute on the government's right to change the cityscape, and on the planners' role in changing it, in the face of socially established though legally nonbinding norms. Films focusing on the residents' plight question the official rhetoric of citizen participation, green aesthetics, and public usage of space. Although filmmakers were not directly involved in the negotiation between the residents and the authorities, the cinema outlines the borders of the public debate. I look at four films in particular. *Moonlight* (1983 [a.k.a. *Papa Can You Hear Me Sing*]) is a milestone portraying the social unrest of the early 1980s and in the veterans' villages in particular. *Vive l'Amour* (1994) presents the city as a battleground in ruins. *My Whispering Plan* (2002) lingers on the collapse of familial structures as a result of demolition-and-relocation. *Robinson's Crusoe* (2002) foregrounds the role of real estate speculators in shaping the city and their own vulnerability to the processes that they have set in motion.

Extensive studies of Taipei's cinematic representation have neglected the role of films in negotiating between the government, planners, and residents—the dynamics I have called the urban contract. Emilie Yeh and Darrell Davis have noted that existing studies focus on urban alienation, often set up as a red herring, and overlook cinematic style.[6] In other words, urban themes have been fetishized to the point of reducing films to the function of representing the city. Yet thematic studies have also diverted attention from the discursive context of Taipei's development and the institutional environment of urban policy in particular, both matrixes crucial to understanding the films' cinematic concerns. Taipei films are often blatantly allegorical and flamboyantly visual, yet their cinematic qualities are informed by debates on urban policy. The cinema has changed Taipei's perceptions of space, spatial practices, and spatial memory in the past twenty-five years.

✦ NEW TAIWAN CINEMA AS A NEW TAIPEI CINEMA

In the early 1980s, films on Taipei started addressing former taboos and questioning urban policy. The shift from the KMT-line "healthy realism" to the more critical trend that became known as New Taiwan Cinema had an immediate and profound impact on Taipei films. The city became a sign not of development but rather of the loss of a common history and collective memory. The films that marked the change are *Moonlight* and the short subject "The Taste of Apples," both released in 1983. The films break new ground by focusing on the aftermath of citywide planning and showing an urban environment built on the ruins of its former architecture and identity.

Until the early 1980s, Taipei was portrayed in film as a society striving for harmony. *Our Neighbors* (1963), the first production in Mandarin by Li Xing, imparts an atmosphere reminiscent of early films by Yasujirô Ozu and depicts poverty detached from any political factors. Even though the protagonist, Uncle Shi, is a garbage collector residing in a slum, the movie declares its message explicitly in the voiceover prologue: "This story takes place in one corner of the city. People who live there know no hatred, only love. . . . Only a society full of love can make real progress and entertain beautiful hopes."

Unlike later films, which emphasize incongruities with the past, *Our Neighbors* shows the residents driven by hope for a better future—in other words, citizens operating within a functional urban contract.

Other films also showed Taipei as the realization of earlier hopes. *Home, Sweet Home* (1970) weaves three plotlines that reaffirm Confucian family values and national pride. Despite its Chinese title, literally, "Taipei is our home," the city rarely appears onscreen. Local identity is conveyed in national terms, and the nation is defined through a larger framework of a pan-Chinese ideology that includes the diaspora (and implicitly the mainland). Significantly, the most prominent Taipei landmark in the film is the Sun Yat-sen Building in Yangmingshan. Built in 1966, it exemplifies the "new architecture in Chinese classical style" (*Zhongguo gudian shiyang xin jianzhu*), a design meant to convey a national Chinese heritage. As a critic explained at the time of construction, the cement monument "fully encompasses China's culture."[7] As Ching-chih Lee (Li Qingzhi) notes, films such as *Our Neighbor* and *Home, Sweet Home* associate Taipei with modernist glamour and reconstruction.[8]

More specifically, urban construction is portrayed in films of the 1970s as a symbol of vigor and upward social mobility. In *Family Love* (1970), a PRC spy tries to infiltrate Taiwan. She pretends to be the daughter of a construction contractor who works for the government. The film shows time and again a large construction site to underline the power of the new Republic of China in Taiwan and to foreshadow that the evil agent is bound to lose to the wheels of progress. A gravel-factory scene in *Home, Sweet Home* fulfills the same function. Another film of this period, *The Silent Lake* (1978), describes Xia Xiaonan's difficult choice between two women.[9] As his name hints, Xiaonan comes to "know the south" and goes to the southern city of Tainan to find his true love. Implicitly, a pan-Chinese vision (suggested by the surname Xia, which alludes to the Chinese nation)[10] is confronted with native Taiwan and comes to terms with it. It is of symbolic importance that Xia graduates in construction engineering and parts with his fiancée, the daughter of a wealthy contractor. The film suggests that Xia will now start his own business and that Taiwan will reconstruct on its own terms. A variation on this theme is found in "Frog" (1982), Ke Yizheng's contribution to the omnibus film *In Our Time* (1982), a harbinger of New Taiwan Cinema. The protagonist, Du Shilian (played by future dramatist Li Guoxiu), is intent on winning a swimming contest against the foreign students at National Taiwan University.

Du's plan also responds to his father's pressure to continue the family construction business. National pride is upheld in the sports arena just as it has been on the construction site.

Inasmuch as the films of the 1970s present construction as a symbol of progress, *Moonlight* marks a turning point. The movie was the first of Yu Kanping's Taipei films, including *Myth of a City* (1985) and *The Outsiders* (1986), all of which show aspects of the city's social underbelly. *Moonlight* stands out, however, in focusing on the changing cityscape. The plot spans the period from the late 1950s to the early 1980s and describes the relationship between a mute retired soldier (played by Sun Yue) and his adopted daughter, Ah Mei (Liu Ruiqi). In her meteoric rise to success, reflecting the fantasy of Taiwan's quick rise to riches, the daughter becomes a popular singer, but she fails to repay her father in kindness. As the film concludes, she rushes to the father's deathbed only to find out that he has already passed away.

At a pivotal moment, Ah Mei is asked about her father. Her impresario answers for her and conceals the singer's humble background by explaining that the father owns a big architecture firm in the United States. The occasion is especially humiliating to the father, who is present at the scene. As in earlier films, the trope of the master builder is used as a symbol of prosperity and high social status. In this case, however, commercial architecture is associated with arrogant pretense and shown to be a façade concealing unpalatable social reality. Moreover, the statement is ironic in view of the father's occupation. He trades in used bottles and uses some of the discarded glass to build the walls of his home in a veterans' village. In his modest way, he is in fact engaged in construction. A number of sequences in the film use the bottle walls for establishing shots or as a dominating backdrop. The old shack provides a warm home, but, unlike the more elegant apartment buildings erected in the construction boom of the 1970s and '80s, it is eventually swallowed up by the new cityscape. Significantly, the scene of the neighborhood's demolition, as part of a municipal modernization plan, starts with a shot of the bottle wall being smashed and knocked down. *Moonlight* associates new construction and the destruction of older spaces and values.

The motif of shattered glass signals the fate of a society to be dislocated in favor of a glitzy glass-and-steel city. In a family quarrel early in the film, the mute father's girlfriend breaks a bottle on his head before leaving forever.

Ah Mei's loss of virginity is captured in a cracked mirror. To advance her career, Ah Mei is made to change her name and at the same time move out into a modern apartment. Just before her father dies, she goes back to see him, only to find the entire division razed to the ground. She picks up a bottle shard, her only link to the past. Ah Mei briefly speaks to an unknown woman at the demolished site, and they part without ever realizing that the woman was Ah Mei's adoptive mother. Taipei's fragile spaces and the innocence of Taiwanese society are shattered at the same time, and they return later in the form of archeological finds, indexes of a past forgotten but never fully expired.

The symbolism of glass is explored in the theme song. *Moonlight* incorporates many songs, written by Hou Dejian and Wu Nien-jen, that became immediate hits.[11] Inspired by the recent success of *Fame* (1980), *Moonlight* uses the conventions of the Hollywood musical to bring together the major themes. While the woman singer's choreographed performances stand for cold, calculating commercialism, the lyrics often convey the dilemmas of fast-paced change in Taiwan. One song asks, "Who can tell me, is it we who changed the world or the world that changed you and me?" Morality, space, and identity are interwoven in the theme song: "Without heaven there is no earth; without earth there is no home; without home there is no you; without you there is no me."

The theme song, titled "Any Used Wine Bottles for Sale?" after the bottle peddler's street cry, signals Ah Mei's reconciliation with her father. The street cry was used by her schoolmates to mock her, but after her father's death she returns to a folk tune like those earlier dismissed by her agent and speaks the street cry onstage, thereby identifying with her native urban slums. The refrain is in Taiwanese while the rest of the lyrics are in Mandarin, creating a poetic symbiosis between the two languages and the two populations that they represent. Moreover, by adding the words to the street cry that the speech-impaired peddler could only signal with his trumpet, the singer voices the father's unuttered words and, by extension, expresses his unspoken emotions. The past is retrieved by invoking the glass bottles, the debris of now extinct architecture.

Moonlight presents the social conditions associated with the veterans' villages. The father is typical of the villages' low-income residents, engaging in simple trade. In most cases, the decommissioned soldiers came to Taiwan without their families and without money, and had neither social con-

26 *Moonlight* (1983): Veterans' village residents put up violent resistance during demolition-and-relocation.

nections on the island nor qualifications for good jobs. They often married indigenous Taiwanese women of even lesser financial means, resulting in households burdened with economic hardship and cultural misunderstanding. The mute father is typical of this sector.

The film focuses in particular on the residents' plight in the face of government decisions. The village idiot, one of the closest people to Ah Mei, perishes in a fire that spreads quickly through the neighborhood. His nephew Ah Ming, Ah Mei's closest childhood friend, dies when his house is torn down and collapses on top of him during the residents' violent protests (fig. 26). There is sarcasm in the incantation at his funeral service: "Mr. Li Ah Ming, taxi driver by vocation; his illegal structure was demolished, and he perished by accident." The prayerlike text is spoken in heavily accented Mandarin. It presents the events leading to Ah Ming's death in incongruously official lingo, in particular the reference to the "illegal structure." The policymakers' view accompanies Ah Ming to his grave. The multiple spatial and temporal matrices for interpreting the policy on the veterans' villages are expressed in the coexisting rhetorical styles.

Moonlight launches a pioneering criticism of the demolition-and-relocation policy then still in its early stages. The director, Yu Kanping, drew on personal experience, having witnessed the demolition-and-relocation of his native veterans' village.[12] *Moonlight* was produced at a historical turning point, when the veterans' villages were mostly intact but the evacuation was already underway. Many scenes were shot at the oldest veterans' village—

Forty-Four South Village, which had seen little change from 1949 to 1983. The film also offers a glimpse of the soon-to-be-demolished veterans' village of Jianhua Xincun, the future site of the Da-an Forest Park, thereby providing a visual record of the now-extinct neighborhoods. *Moonlight* is arguably the first film that critically documents the changes in Taipei's cityscape. It emphasizes not only the erasure of urban spaces but also the attendant loss of identity. Although overshadowed in critical reception by less commercially oriented contemporary works, *Moonlight* shares many themes associated with New Taiwan Cinema. The film proved very popular—it was nominated for eleven awards at the twentieth Golden Horse Film Festival (Taiwan's equivalent of the Academy Awards), ran in theaters for five months, and was rereleased eight times within a year.[13]

The success of *Moonlight* triggered a series of films scripted by Wu Nien-jen and typecasting Sun Yue as a kindhearted retired soldier of mainland origin who fails to adapt to life in Taiwan. *Old Mo's Second Spring* (1984) depicts an older mainlander who marries a Taiwanese aborigine; *Myth of a City* (1985) tells of Old Sun, a retired kindergarten bus driver, who takes over the bus without permission to give the children a one-day tour; *Old Ke's Last Day of Fall* (1988) portrays a retired soldier who robs a bank to draw attention to his plight; *People between the Two Chinas* (1988) achieves a closure for both the recurrent plotline and the subgenre when the protagonist, Sun Zhihao, returns to visit the mainland.

Curiously, *Moonlight* has enjoyed an afterlife on the mainland. The Taiwanese film was distributed in the PRC and was an audience favorite.[14] In 2005, the film was remade into a TV series of the same Chinese title (literally, "Riding the wrong car") starring Li Xuejian and set in Beijing. The remake was inspired by the demolition-and-relocation in full force in mainland cities, and in particular by the project at Jinyuchi that had been dramatized in the two BPAT stage plays I discussed at length in chapter 3.[15] As a mainstream production, the soap opera has eliminated the social criticism, instead indulging in an abstract and comfortable vision of the capital. A cryptic but more apropos reference to the original context is made in Jia Zhangke's *Still Life* (2006), which features the theme song "Any Used Wine Bottles for Sale?" in the midst of the demolition in preparation for the Three Gorges Dam. The transmigration of *Moonlight* to mainland screens illustrates the influence of Taiwan cinema on urban discourse in the PRC.

Yet *Moonlight*'s most notable contribution was to Taiwan cinema, signaling the rise to prominence of veterans' villages on the screen. Already in 1983, the year of *Moonlight*'s release, two other landmark films were made on the topic. Chen Kunhou directed *Growing Up*, about a man's troubled adolescence in a veterans' village. As Yeh and Davis note, the film signaled the end of "healthy realism" and the turn to "trauma, pain, and the difficulty of reconciliation."[16] The script is based on Chu Tien-wen's (Zhu Tianwen) short story, reflecting the author's experience of growing up in a veterans' village. Like Zhu's native neighborhood, the veterans' village in *Growing Up* is a legal military dependents' compound, with spacious Japanese-style houses (Chu notes, however, that the film has embellished the living conditions).[17] The social plight seems unconnected to the dilapidated state of the veterans' villages.

A more unsavory depiction of the crisis in the veterans' villages is presented in another 1983 production, "The Taste of Apples," the last of three shorts in the omnibus film *The Sandwich Man*. Shooting at the same location as *Moonlight*—the veterans' village of Jianhua Xincun—the short depicts it as a place slated for demolition and rife with potential civil unrest. The story provides a sarcastic look at U.S. neoimperialist privilege in Taiwan, seen through the benevolent but paternalizing treatment of a man hit by an embassy car. In an elaborate sequence, the American who was behind the wheel goes to find the family of the man he hit. The American is accompanied by a local liaison officer. A lengthy episode introduces the veterans' village and its tin shacks. The scene foregrounds the incompatible narratives through the simultaneous use of three languages—the American speaks only English, the liaison officer speaks no Taiwanese, and much of the residents' attitude, expressed in Taiwanese, is lost in translation through the intermediary Mandarin. The official interprets the American's surprise at the shantytown as an implicit criticism and says (in English): "Their new homes are nearly completed. Those apartments over there are new ones. Once they move these people out, they're going to put up a high-rise here." The remark may have been added to appease censors, but its incredibility ridicules the Taiwanese government's representation of relocation as fair, voluntary, and peaceful.[18]

Perhaps the most poignant social commentary is made through shots of Taipei and of the veterans' village in particular. The film starts with a high-angle shot of the city, followed by images of Taipei landmarks in the early morning, when the usually congested streets are eerily empty (similar sequences appear in the opening shots of *Super Citizen*, discussed below, and of *Terrorizers* [1986]). The montage of the ghostly city is followed by the accident sequence; the veterans' village is introduced through a lap dissolve that melds together the images of the village and the puddle of blood at the accident site. The film hints at the vulnerability of the slum as well as at the blood debt it might exact in the future.

The similar establishing shots of Jianhua Xincun, in *Moonlight* and "The Taste of Apples," are replicated in Wan Jen's 1985 production, *Super Citizen*. The opening sequence is a fast-paced slideshow of Taipei landmarks, in the manner of city films harking back to *Berlin, Symphony of a Big City* (1927). The inventory of Taipei's modern architecture conveys a certain elegance—but also, in view of the story line, outsiders' unrealistic fantasy of modern Taipei. The muted images cut abruptly to the noisy and smoggy city—the railway station, congested roads, and maze of skywalks. The next sequence opens with a zoom-out that reveals the slum at Jianhua Xincun. (Later in the film, the social problems at the veterans' village erupt when a local woman married to a mainlander kills herself and her children.) When one gets down to the nitty-gritty, *Super Citizen* implies, Taipei's reality is found not in sterile architectural monuments but in the slums of the veterans' villages.[19]

The films of the early 1980s establish urban themes, and the veterans' villages in particular, as microcosms of Taiwanese society. One should note that Taipei films emerged hand in hand with New Taiwan Cinema. In a dynamic similar to the response to Fifth Generation films in the PRC a couple of years later, New Taiwan Cinema was hailed for shifting attention to the countryside, in parallel with "native soil" (*xiangtu*) fiction. Yet as the films of the early 1980s evidence, urban issues were in fact at the heart of the new trend, and the veterans' villages served as prominent symbols of the need for social change. New Taiwan Cinema also entailed a new Taipei cinema.

⚡ TAIPEI, INVISIBLE CITY

In 1994, Taiwan's representative modern dance group, Cloud Gate Dance Theater, added to its repertoire *Invisible Cities*. The piece, by the Hong Kong choreographer Helen Lai (Li Haining), was inspired by Italo Calvino's novel of the same title. The portrayal of multiple views of the city, by residents and travelers, was welcomed by Taipei urbanites thinking of their own relation to the fast-changing city. When asked about the piece's relevance to Taipei, Lai responded, quoting Calvino's text: "Whatever city I may be talking of, I always describe my hometown"; a panel including the writer Ping Lu and the architect Kung Shu-chang (Gong Shuzhang) claimed that the dance resonated with Taipei.[20] In the same year, the cultural critic Ching-chih Lee wrote about the gigantic plastic dinosaur skeleton that had been hanging over the M Restaurant on Bade Road since 1989. Lee saw the dinosaur as an atavistic resistance to civilization, a monument to humanity's nearing extinction, since "fin-de-siècle Taipei is a city of extinct life."[21] Taiwan's cultural scene was engaged in an archeological excavation for the urban unconscious. Also in 1994, two films on Taipei's transformation, *The Red Lotus Society and Vive l'Amour*, were released and attained cult status. The urban turn in Taiwan culture in the 1990s, a discursive shift that placed urbanist issues at center stage, focused on the momentous change that was destroying all relics of Taipei's past.

During the 1990s Taipei's nature as a palimpsest of multilayered, invisible cities was underscored by accelerated construction. The old railway station (rebuilt in 1940) was razed to make room for the new station (inaugurated in September 1989) and the 244-meter-tall Shin Kong Mitsukoshi building (completed in October 1991); Zhonghua Market was demolished in 1992 to make way for a new raised freeway; architectural relics from the period of Japanese occupation, such as the Sanyezhuang building (constructed in 1907 and demolished in 1990), were torn down, and projects such as the new City Hall on Keelung Road (and later the adjacent Taipei 101 Tower, inaugurated in 2003) provided new focuses of urban activity. Yet the films of the 1990s no longer attach to monuments the importance observed in works such as *Home, Sweet Home*. Unlike the earlier montages of the city, the films released in 1994 use shots of Taipei not to orient the viewer but to juxtapose official design and individual reappropriation. Ambiguous spaces question the normative and legal uses of Taipei locations and the municipal government's vision of the city.

Critics have largely ignored the institutional background of Taipei films in the 1990s. The rise of Taipei cinema to genre status is indebted to scholarly inquiry into how films mirror social change—youth rebellion, familial disintegration, individual alienation, and the dislocation of desire.[22] Yet the urban turn in Taiwan culture, and especially in film, cannot be attributed simply to a fin-de-siècle impulse or millenarian anxiety. Taipei films concurred with a sea change in the power relations between citizens and the government, between planners and the government, and between the media and the government.

A quiet political revolution placed a more representative government in power after the 1988 general elections, and especially after the Taipei municipal elections of 1994, which brought to power Chen Shui-bian, the DPP's candidate. Citizens aired openly their dissatisfaction with inefficient policies, in mass protests and grassroots movements. The new municipal government, for its part, politicized urban space by commemorating previously suppressed history, in memorials such as the February 28 Peace Park (renamed in 1996) and the preservation of Forty-Four South Village, the veterans' village of the Forty-Fourth Armory (opened as a museum in 2002). Taipei identity was more than an alternative to national allegory.[23] As Huang Sun Chuan (Huang Sunquan) argues, Chen Shui-bian, as Taipei mayor, introduced "Taipei ideology" (*Taibei zhuyi*) as a way to gain support for the DPP.[24] Films on urban issues were inevitably enmeshed in the political debates.

The political change affected also urban planning circles. Alternative power centers to the municipal government sprang up in academic institutions and NGOs. The most notable is the Graduate Institute of Building and Planning (Chengxiang Suo), established as an independent institute at National Taiwan University in 1988. Under the leadership of Hsia Chu-joe (Xia Zhujiu), who subscribes to a proactive approach vis-à-vis policymakers, the institute has focused on "the social, economic, and political forces that shape and constrain the physical reality, the planning process, and the implementations of planning."[25] One of the common textbooks at the institute has been John Forester's *Planning in the Face of Power* (1988). Many students at the institute became involved in an NGO known as OURS (Organization of Urban Re-s), established in 1990. According to its website, OURS engages with the authorities—"finding ways to communicate, coordinate, and fight with the city government"—by criticizing official urban policy and calling for "reform, rediscovery, and reflection."[26] As I shall detail later, OURS has also used documentary filmmaking and movie screenings as tools to build a grassroots community.

The efforts toward increased transparency between the government, on the one hand, and citizens and planners, on the other, were also supported by the emergence of an engaged press and media in the early 1990s. Daily newspapers reported on resident dissatisfaction and demonstrations. The free weekly *POTS*, established in 1995 and edited by the OURS member Huang Sun Chuan, has raised public awareness of social issues beyond the reductive dichotomy between unification with the mainland and political independence. Interest groups have mobilized the Internet as a public forum for making known citizens' initiatives such as OURS.[27]

To inform the public of the conflict between the municipal policy and residents' interests, activists also turned to documentary filmmaking. One of the pioneers of the trend, Wu Yii-feng (Wu Yifeng), used his hallmark method of observing a subject for a long period to follow a group of elderly citizens at the veterans' village at Kangle Li, Taipei (at the intersection of Nanjing East Road and Lin Sen North Road). The resulting documentary, *Chen Tsai-gen and His Neighbors* (1996), gained poignancy when in September 1996 the municipal government slated Kangle Li for demolition and evacuated it by June of the next year. The fate of Kangle Li was representative of the gentrification policy—the space designated in the 1932 plan for parks numbers 14 and 15 was a godforsaken slum until the new greening policy called for turning it into the Lin Sen and Kangle Parks (total surface: 4.3 hectares; opened in 2002–3).[28] The full implications of the demolition-and-relocation plan are explored in Huang Sun Chuan's documentary *Green Bulldozer: The Rise of Your New Homeland* (1997). Huang, who was completing at the time his MA thesis at the Graduate Institute of Building and Planning, juxtaposed sketches of residents' daily lives with the concurrent plans for evacuation, civil protests, and eventual destruction of the veterans' village. Huang's documentary exemplifies how the media can empower citizens and planners in their struggle against the municipal government in the long and arduous process of negotiation and resistance.

⚡ FLIGHTS OF MEMORY

In the context of the new urban activism, fiction films may be regarded as yet another vehicle for opening up the debate on the policy that has rendered invisible entire parts of the city. The critical attitude was abetted by what Yeh and Davis call the transformation from "a cinema of authority"—that is, dictated by political fiat—to "a cinema of authorship."[29] Although the KMT-backed Central Motion Picture Corporation (CMPC) produced the early New Taiwan Cinema films, the studio's control over the final products was eroded by the rise of powerful directors, Hou Hsiao-hsien foremost among them, who stressed social and political criticism. Yet the importance of specific auteurs notwithstanding, New Taiwan Cinema was also the result of a novel vision of the power relations between filmmakers and policymakers.

One of the most extensive explorations on screen of how Taipei has been overwritten by new landmarks and its memories suppressed is found in *The Red Lotus Society* (1994). The film, the only made-for-screen production by Stan Lai (Lai Shengchuan)—the playwright, stage director, and founder of the drama troupe Performance Workshop—is a careful study of Taipei's politics of memory. As the Chinese title—literally "Ah Da the flying knight" —suggests, the plot revolves around a young man, about twenty years old, who becomes interested in the martial art of *qinggong*, which purportedly allows the practitioner to "vault," or hover and fly. The young man's search for the secret bearers of the vaulting tradition leads him through a series of formative experiences that adapt the ideals of martial arts to modern city life. As Ah Da wanders through Taipei, the place is revealed to be a monument for forgetting, a space of consumerism and speculation, a metropolis in the process of being demolished and reconstructed, a city that burns down and leaves room for neither personal memory nor collective identity. The film exposes the results of policies set on fast economic growth and unconcerned with the residents' sense of historical belonging.

Through the eyes of Ah Da, the film takes an inventory of Taipei's easily erased, memoryless spaces. His journey begins at a McDonald's, one of the many sterile franchises that dot the cityscape. Later Ah Da helps blind masseurs into hotel rooms rented by the hour to gangsters and call girls. Ah Da, who enters these dens by the service doors, becomes familiar with the affluent city's alternative geography of back alleys. Becoming an entrepreneur, he learns next the business of real estate in an almost virtual space linked to the outside world by a network of fax machines. When the boss's speculations turn sour, all that is left behind is the empty leased office. Ah Da learns how in Taipei's bubble economy busy spaces can be gutted in no time. He also visits an elegant Japanese restaurant, which goes up in flames. The scene resonates with Taipei of the late 1980s and early 1990s, when entrepreneurial greed and neglect by city regulators led to opening restaurants and karaoke bars in unfit quarters. The resulting fires, sometimes killing or injuring dozens of people, came to symbolize Taipei's unmonitored economic growth and governmental mismanagement. Toward the end, Ah Da returns to the park next to the History Museum, where an old mainlander used to tell the exploits of the mysterious Red Lotus Society. A younger man has taken over, telling the stories in a thick local accent. Taipei, Ah Da learns, is in perpetual flux.

The collective memory of Ah Da's community is in the process of receding. His father dies in a violent incident; the storyteller, who remains the only witness to the Red Lotus Society, suffers a stroke and loses his speech; Ah Da's urban odyssey ends in a restaurant fire that kills his boss, his childhood friend, and his lover. Ah Da copes with these losses by making his body into a repository of memories. A blind masseur tells him, "Our bodies are like our minds. They retain all sorts of memories. Especially traumatic memories will crystallize into lumps like this one. If you can work slowly and dissolve it, the horrible memory will disappear from the brain."[30] Ah Da searches Taipei's streets for lost memories and residual pain, and harnesses their energy for his art of vaulting. The director, Stan Lai, notes that the human body is weighed down by traumas: "If we could remember everything, we would fly."[31] Flight, in other words, denotes a total retention of the urban palimpsest. Ah Da gains this skill. As a series of incidents destroy his intimate spaces and kill his close friends, he is left an incognito vaulting master in a city that does not remember him and in which he has nothing and no one to remember.

Ah Da's vaulting suggests a particular form of visualizing the city. *Red Lotus Society* updates the flying knight myths of nineteenth-century martial arts novels and 1950s Hong Kong films.[32] The film grafts together the traditional martial arts lore, the modern myth of Superman, and the cinematic whimsy of navigating the futuristic city by air. The resulting combination envisions a modern knight-errant in the urban habitat, or as the marketing blurb on the videocassette jacket calls the film, "a filmic legend of the modern city" (*xiandai duhui chuanqi dianying*). Flying among Taipei's buildings is in fact not that far from reality—as several shots in *Red Lotus Society* remind the viewer, airplanes approaching Songshan Airport fly low over the city (fig. 27).[33] In the sky, Ah Da finds a space unregulated by land use laws, safe from the fluctuations of real estate, and devoid of any history that would weigh him down.

Earlier Taipei films have contrasted the establishing aerial shots, taken from an impersonal, God's-point-of-view high angle, with detailed portrayals of street-level existence; *Red Lotus Society*, on the other hand, inserts

27 *Red Lotus Society* (1994): A jet approaches Songshan Airport, Taipei.

human presence into aerial shots. Views of the entire city, whether from the surrounding mountains or from rooftops, are seen in over-the-shoulder shots, with Ah Da in the foreground. A key scene shows Ah Da exercising by climbing up roof stairs, in a low-angle shot that places Ah Da above the Shin Kong Mitsukoshi building. (The skyscraper offered its own bird's-eye view of the city from a balcony opened in January 1994, while the film was in production.) Other sequences show the vaulting Ah Da's point of view, at a dizzying proximity to rooftops and construction sites. These shots were taken by a remote-controlled minuscule helicopter, the "Redheaded Fly."[34] The resulting images show Ah Da's escapades as a cinematic fantasy in the spirit of Paul Virilio's poetic statement, "Cinema isn't I see, it's I fly."[35] Ah Da's out-of-body experience is tantamount to a human-sized airplane's foray into the city made visible again, if only for the lonely vaulter.

Vaulting, as shown through the helicopter point-of-view shots, is different from flying high above—the protagonist acquires a new familiarity with the city. Ah Da's stalking the rooftops and vaulting enact an individual liberation from the city, a liberation that depends on an intimate knowledge of urban space. Lin Wenchi argues that Ah Da's vaulting signals the loss of collective identity and the advent of Taiwan's "cultural schizophrenia"; looking at the city from the air becomes the last and only way to comprehend the city and its inhabitants as integral entities.[36] In this sense, *Red Lotus Society* is consistent with Stan Lai's stage plays, which often address Taiwanese identity through doppelgangers and split personalities.[37] Yet *Red Lotus Society* also shows that Taipei itself is haunted by a double, namely, the razed and forgotten cityscape. Vaulting is an attempt to reconstitute not only individual memory but also the mnemonic function of the urban environment.

The dissolution of memory in *Red Lotus Society* parallels the disappearance of Taipei's skyline. The film takes the viewer through sites of construction and demolition, reminding the viewer of the intensive remaking of Taipei through the 1980s and 1990s. The new landmarks celebrate a global city that responds to the expectations of the rising middle class at the price of erasing earlier landmarks. Whereas gentrification aims to show seamless modernization, *Red Lotus Society* reveals the temporal fault lines of the invisible Taipei.

Red Lotus Society addresses Taipei's gentrification and the attendant erasure of the city's architectural past by showing the city as a space of forgetting. Stan Lai stands out among New Taiwan Cinema directors in diverging from a linear, slice-of-life presentation—he seeks improbable points of view (via the Redheaded Fly) and uses flashbacks (in the sequences about the Red Lotus Society). Yet Lai's concerns are to a large extent representative of the new Taipei cinema, which zeroes in on spaces rendered invisible, inaccessible, or outright destroyed. Wan Jen makes the urban palimpsest visible in *Super Citizen Ko* (1995), where the transformed city—starting with the Shin Kong Mitsukoshi building—is seen through the eyes of a man just released from a long stay in a political prison. The earlier works of Edward Yang (Yang Dechang) feature sites declared out of bounds and at times transformed beyond recognition. An architect in Yang's *Taipei Story* (1985) says: "Look at these buildings—it's getting harder and harder for me to distinguish which ones I designed and which I didn't. . . . It's unimportant whether I exist or not." The building under construction in *Taipei Story*, the gang hideout in *Terrorizers*, and the shared apartment in *Mahjong* (1998) are visited and appropriated by various characters, none of whom claims ownership over the place or finds shelter in it.[38] Tsai Ming-liang is perhaps the most consistently interested in the erasure of Taipei's spaces. *Rebels of the Neon God* (1992) offers glimpses of the torn-down Chung Hua Road; *The Skywalk Is Gone* depicts a now-nonexistent overpass; *Goodbye, Dragon Inn* (2003) takes place in Fuhe Grand Theater in Yong-ho, designated for demolition and razed soon after the shoot. New Taipei cinema captures the particular economy of space, in which the city buries its past under its own structures.

The discourse on Taipei as haunted by its invisible double—a lingering and simultaneously existing past—finds an especially poignant manifestation in portrayals of the veterans' villages. Whereas in the mid-1980s films such as *Moonlight* and "The Taste of Apples" were motivated by the urgency of the coming evacuation, in the 1990s, the veterans' villages, mostly demolished, became the subject of nostalgia. In 1992, Chu Tien-hsin (Zhu Tianxin) published her essay "Thinking of My Veterans' Village Brothers." A section in Stan Lai's show (based on the traditional cross-talk form of comic dialogue) *Look Who's Cross-Talking Tonight* (1989) makes goodhearted fun of a veterans' village, describing it as not too different from a refugee camp, and laughing at the misunderstandings among residents speaking in the accents of their various provinces of origin. (A similar reminiscence of veterans' village life is found in the first part of the cross-talk show *Who's Pulling My Leg?* [1999], by the Xiangsheng Washe Group.) Lai's comic skit describes the veterans' village as a recreation of the mainland, ridiculing the KMT's rhetoric that saw Taiwan as a China in miniature. The veterans' villages were no longer considered a metonym for the nation but rather a sign of urban crisis.

In this context, Tsai Ming-liang's *Vive l'Amour*—shot at the same time as *The Red Lotus Society* and released a couple of months after Lai's film—presents a provocative return to the now-defunct spaces of the large veterans' village at Jianhua Xincun. Tsai, who had worked for a couple of days as a log keeper on the set of Yu Kanping's *Moonlight* at that village, returned to the same site in 1994, fully aware of its history.[39] The story line follows a female real estate agent, Ms. Lin, and two men: Xiaokang, who sells space for cremation jars in an interior burial complex, and Ah Rong, who vends smuggled goods at a makeshift sidewalk stall. They inhabit the spaces of an underground economy that developed in response to overpriced real estate. The two men live clandestinely in an apartment for sale, and their loveless triangle takes place in these temporary, borrowed, and impersonal places. The use of public space for personal purposes culminates in the film's last sequence, in which Ms. Lin cries her heart out in a nearly empty, open-air theater, making a spectacle of herself in the middle of the eight-hundred-seat arena. The lack of privacy marks the devaluation of the gaze, in a city that has rendered its residents invisible.

28 *Vive l'Amour* (1994): Ms. Lin walks through the newly opened Da'an Forest Park.

The seven-minute close-up on the weeping woman, a daring cinematic gesture, has drawn much critical attention as an expression of urban aliena-tion. Yet it is also important to note the location at the Da-an Forest Park (Da'an Senlin Gongyuan, opened in March 1994). Before arriving at the theater, Ms. Lin walks around the park; tracking shots, followed by a three-hundred-degree view of the park and its surroundings, orient the viewer. The park had just been constructed on the site of the demolished Jianhua Xincun—the same veterans' village that appeared in *Moonlight* and "The Taste of Apples." Tsai's camera captures the site at a point of transition, just as it opened to the public, still in the initial stages of landscaping. The park under construction presents upturned earth and bare cement, resembling bombarded ruins (fig. 28). Ms. Lin walks through a lunar landscape that still carries the scars of demolition.

The Da-an Forest Park, occupying a twenty-six-hectare block south of Hsin Yi Road and east of Hsin Sheng South Road, was at the center of debates in the late 1980s and the early 1990s. The place known before Taipei's expansion outside the walls as Long'anpo was designated in the Japanese city plan as Park Number 7. After 1949, it hosted the veterans' village known as Jianhua Xincun. In 1985, the municipal government decided to repossess the area, in a controversial process that would eventually be handled by four consecutive mayors and cost 21.8 billion new Taiwan dollars. Starting in April 1992, 1,348 houses, of which 1,257 were declared illegal, were demolished.[40] The large-scale project aroused widespread protest.

It is instructive to read side by side two accounts of the park. In one, Huang Dazhou, the mayor who initiated the project, explains the need for parks in a modern city, much like New York's Central Park.[41] Huang's book is a defense of the park's planners. Yet Huang dwells on a moot point—the importance of such green spaces has been widely recognized. After all, even with the completion of Da-an Forest Park, Taipei's parks comprised only 2.4 percent of the city's area, compared to Tokyo's 6.2 percent, New York City's 12.8 percent, and Paris's 26 percent.[42] What Huang ignores is that the design of public spaces at the city's center is necessarily political (a fact stressed also in Zhang Yuan's treatment of Tiananmen in *The Square*, coincidentally released in the same year as *Vive l'Amour*).

Unlike the former mayor, Huang Sun Chuan argues, in his master's thesis, that the environmentalist rhetoric, such as declaring 1989 the "year of greenifying" leading to Taipei as a "forest city," was a cover-up for rampant demolition. The "nature" promoted by municipal governments—whether under the KMT or the DPP—is no more than "institutionalized landscape," intended to increase the value of adjacent real estate. The talk of a picturesque city promoted, in fact, nationalist aspirations and capitalistic agendas. The word-laundering, using imported slogans such as "citizen participation," amounted to the municipal government's authoritarian use of power and exclusion of underprivileged groups from the debate by the force of what Huang Sun Chuan calls "the green bulldozer."[43] (Huang refers also to the color green's association with the DPP, which is in his view no more environmentally friendly than the KMT.) What one may call "painting the city green" has been as oppressive as the Maoist policy I have described as "painting the city red."

The Da-an Forest Park was part of an overall strategy of gentrifying Taipei through public works in the 1990s, which included the Keelung River Reclamation project and building the light rail transit. Taipei's greening also corresponded with a global trend—the rhetoric of "green lungs" was first used about New York's Central Park in 1987.[44] Yet the Da-an Forest Park plan stands out for having triggered the first of the "park movements" that pitted citizens against the municipal government and developed into the homeless movement Snail without Shell (*Wuke huaniu*) and its offspring

OURS.[45] In view of the publicity about the park project, when Ms. Lin sets foot in the park in *Vive l'Amour*, she enters spaces already associated with political bias, predatory urban policy, and disregard of city dwellers.

Vive l'Amour does not make direct reference to the veterans' village, but the plot and images are firmly rooted in the attendant social issues. Critics have already remarked that films present Taipei's parks as "locale[s] of deviant activities carried on outside the official orbit of the city life."[46] Yet the skeletal park in Tsai's film challenges the official narrative not because of the visitors' practices but because of the almost-invisible vestiges of another urban existence. It is precisely the allegorical register that allows *Vive l'Amour* to juxtapose the present-day park and the memory of the veterans' village, and to trace the identity crisis of the landless class to recent urban policy.

↯ THE LAST VETERANS' VILLAGE

As the veterans' villages were quickly disappearing from the cityscape in the 1990s, planners and filmmakers turned from chronicling the demolition-and-relocation projects to foregrounding the ghostly presence of past structures in the newly gentrified spaces. The transition from the lament of destruction in *Moonlight* to the resurgence of ruins in *Vive l'Amour* finds a compact expression in *My Whispering Plan*, which both documents the demolition at the veterans' village of Baozangyan and suggests that images of the razed buildings may linger and intrude into the present.

Baozangyan, known in English as Treasure Hill, is among the last remaining veterans' villages in Taipei. The area, formerly a military fortification, housed in the 1980s about two hundred households of meager means —veterans, senior citizens, students, and Southeast Asian immigrants. The helter-skelter buildings on the hillside give it a look, from afar, reminiscent of an Italian hill town. On December 4, 2001, the municipal government issued an order to evacuate and demolish the area in preparation for turning it into a public park. The first phase of demolition was carried out in April 2004, yet the municipal government declared the remaining residences as protected "historic buildings"[47] and halted the original project.

The demolition-and-relocation plan, similar to those at the sites of parks numbers 14 and 15 and later the Da-an Forest Park, was thwarted thanks to efforts spearheaded by the Graduate Institute of Building and Planning. Tense meetings between the institute's leaders and Mayor Ma Ying-jeou were followed by public petitions.[48] The institute has since acted through OURS, directed at the time by the institute's professor John Ke-chiang Liu. True to its mission to "actively promote fairness and equity in citizens' urban rights [and] participation in social movements of fragile communities,"[49] OURS offered an alternative plan.[50] Rather than becoming a green park, the neighborhood would retain its original character, supported by a social welfare program. The area would be cleaned up, the residents allowed to stay, and guest artist-activists given free lodging in the new Treasure Hill Artivists Co-op (*Gongsheng Yizhan*). According to Min-jay Kang, the first head of the project for OURS, the NGO had to persuade the Urban Planning Committee and the Historical Heritage Committee that preserving the site would not diminish Baozangyan's viability as a space for public use. To gain popular legitimacy and precipitate the legal procedure of rezoning, a publicity campaign stressed the site's artistic value: "Art might be a ticket to permanent residency, practically speaking."[51]

One of the major art projects for enhancing Baozangyan's profile was a multimedia presentation and performance designed by the Finnish architect Marco Casagrande in October 2003. A parade starting from Baozangyan proceeded through the city streets, rolling along pieces of junk, symbolically bringing Baozangyan into Taipei.[52] The walls of demolished houses were covered with larger-than-life photos of their previous inhabitants (fig. 29). When lit up at night, the walls facing the Xindian River looked as if the residents had returned. The memories of the place materialized in ghostly apparitions. Casagrande describes the artwork: "The project is eight floors high and touches all the mountain walls with the terraced houses—also the memories of the ripped-off houses. It is a parasite attached to the existing human values, human time and memories, a positive virus."[53] Baozangyan is fashioned as a space of contending memories and narratives.

To add to Baozangyan's visibility, OURS has also employed the cinema. Since 2002, weekly film screenings have taken place at "The Treasure Hill Family Cinema Club"—in fact, no more than an outdoor gathering area, with a whitewashed wall for a screen, an LCD projector, and Professor Liu's old loudspeakers; the place is darkened by placing a cardboard box over the streetlight.[54] OURS member Guo Boxiu made an amateur documentary about the screenings, *Come Watch Movies!* (*Lai kan dianying luo!* [2003]). The activists' efforts were largely successful—Baozangyan was placed under the auspices of the Department of Cultural Affairs of the Taipei city govern-

29 Installation art by Marco Casagrande at Baozangyan,
December 2003. Photo courtesy of Zhang Liben.

ment. After the site was recommended as a travel destination in the pages of
the *New York Times*, official recognition followed quickly.[55]

In the battle over Baozangyan, activists and the government have used
the same vocabulary. Although they have diverging interests—activists are
interested in preserving the community, and the government in efficient
land use—both parties have claimed to make the site visible and preserve
collective memory. A book published by the Department of Information of
the Taipei City Government in 2001 describes Baozangyan as a site of
nostalgia and hope: "The community at the illegal construction site of Baozangyan . . . will hopefully be preserved in the form of a cultural residential
park. . . . No matter how Taipei changes, I wish that it will become a city
where we will be able to read [the city's] history in tidy and seemly spaces."[56]
The description comports with the municipality's vision of Taipei as a lived
and livable city, evolving and keeping in touch with its past. Yet the wording
evades the stakes in the Baozangyan project. The book is careful to include
Baozangyan's story in the chapter "Destruction and Preservation" rather
than under the section heading "Veterans' Villages and State Residences."
The official publication insists on the term "illegal construction" (*weijian*),
although the area is in fact no different from the many other veterans'
villages, and stresses the need to "read history" in "tidy and seemly spaces"
—that is, to preserve the urban palimpsest in sterilized, regulated, and pret-
tified neighborhoods.

The government also tends to take all credit—municipal publications, statements, and websites mention the contribution of the Institute of Building and Planning but not that the institute had to intervene forcefully before the politicians conceded. Although progress has been made since planners and policymakers have started collaborating, the official discourse has largely ignored the issue of the existing community's livelihood. In contrast, the (now-defunct) Baozangyan website, sponsored by the Treasure Hill Artivists Co-op and significantly captioned "Taipei Visible and Invisible," explains its goal as "celebrating the hidden soul of the city. It is also a project to help citizens rediscover their natural environment and reconstruct a lost communal relationship."[57]

The portrayal of Taipei, and the veterans' villages in particular, as only liminally visible also takes after concepts that gained currency among architects at the time. The architect, experimental artist, and filmmaker Yan Chung-hsien (Yan Zhongxian) created in 1995 a multimedia installation titled "The Club of Aging Angels" (*Lao tianshi julebu*). Comprised of text, video art, and drawings and maquettes of fantastical structures, it invokes a gathering place for aging angels. According to the artist, the artwork challenges the borderline between the verbal and the visual and suggests that like flying angels, we can transcend spatial constrictions using our imagination.[58] The tropes of virtual structures, flying to escape the city's materiality, and the citizens' ghostly or angelic existence circulate back and forth between the architectural and cinematic discourses.

The rhetoric of in/visibility is helped by the distinctive scenery of the hillside settlement and the striking views it offers. Baozangyan has served as a shooting location for several feature films, from *Goodbye South, Goodbye* (1996) to *Spider Lilies* (2007). A more concrete reference to Baozangyan, recording the demolition phase and drawing attention to the loss involved in evacuation, is found in the 2002 film by Arthur Chu (Qu Youning), *My Whispering Plan*. The plot is firmly grounded in Baozangyan and the debate around its looming demolition, yet the film also comments in more general terms on the dislocation caused by demolition-and-relocation and the ghostly resurgence of the ruined veterans' villages.

My Whispering Plan follows Jane and her growing estrangement from her seventh-grade classmate, Sunny. Jane's family lives at Baozangyan, and the film records the neighborhood's transformation. Most of the film is shot in Baozangyan's alleys and residences. A handicam is used for intimate shots inside the neighborhood, while other shots present scenic views of the Xindian River and the Fu-Ho Bridge. Toward the end of the film, Jane's home is demolished and her family moves out. The camera captures in real time the massive destruction, dwelling on the grief-stricken expressions of residents—no outside actors appear in this scene—whose homes are being torn down. The film also shows the aftermath, as a large swath of Baozang-yan lies waste, filled with debris (fig. 30). The film spans the entire process, from the issuance of the demolition order to its execution.

My Whispering Plan does not, however, set out to be a truthful record. The images suggest total destruction, as Jane wanders in the picturesque hilly alleys that yellow hazard tape demarcates for leveling (fig. 31), yet in fact only the lower part of Baozangyan was designated for immediate demolition. The film touches only fleetingly on the residents' dissatisfaction and strug-gle against the municipal authorities. The activists' efforts are referred to obliquely, when Sunny walks in front of a sign that reads, "Creating a new scenery for Baozangyan: Taiwan's first artistic special zone park." These inaccuracies and omissions place in even sharper focus the oppressive force of urban change.

Any attempt to read the film as a historical document would be mislead-ing. Chu, who has worked with Tsai Ming-liang as first assistant director for *The Hole*, shares Tsai's allegorical approach. *My Whispering Plan* intervenes in urban discourse indirectly. A press release states that the film "reflect[s] the emptiness, loneliness, sense of peril, and uncertainty that the Taiwanese society is facing."[59] *My Whispering Plan* operates mainly through two tropes: the manga *Angel Sanctuary* and the yellow hazard tape.

Residents' unease with the changing cityscape is conveyed through Jane's troubled relationship with Sunny. Their sweet friendship slowly turns into possessive jealousy on Jane's part. As Sunny, prettier and more sociable, develops friendships with a number of classmates, Jane becomes estranged and irritable. Jane's unrealistic expectations to have Sunny all to herself result in violent fantasies. Jane imagines Sunny being run over by a car and stabbed to death. She records her fantasies in a notebook, manga style, and titles it "Murder Plan" (which is also the film's Chinese title). The trauma of being evacuated is shifted onto interpersonal relationships and encoded in the manga book.

The manga is central to understanding the story line. Jane's notebook, which causes the final rift between the two friends, sports on its cover the

30 *My Whispering Plan* (2002): Baozangyan after the first stage of demolition.

31 *My Whispering Plan* (2002): Jane and Sunny walk through a Baozangyan alley, flanked by hazard tape.

title of a popular Japanese manga series, *Angel Sanctuary*. Jane is a fan of the series, as attested also by a poster hanging in her room. Film viewers of Jane's age, at least, would recognize that Jane's fantasies take after the manga plot. First she makes angel costumes for herself and Sunny, casting them as the incestuous sisters Setsuna and Sara, and tells Sunny: "I'm your bodyguard." Yet after Sunny invites another girl to join their costume play, Jane retreats and makes herself up as the estranged twin brother Rosiel, with the iconic blue arabesque over the left half of her face. Rosiel, an androgynous angel, is a tortured soul who plots Sara's death. The arabesque signs are a symptom of his disintegration into an ugly and vile person. As Rosiel, Jane lets out her frustration and wishes for her own death. The final twist in *My Whispering Plan* takes place when Jane surprisingly commits suicide. Jane continues, in fact, to follow the path set by *Angel Sanctuary*— Rosiel chooses to end his suffering and die. Jane's fantasies are determined by *Angel Sanctuary*, and her nervous breakdown comports with her manga alter ego.

In conflating the manga plot with her life, Jane takes to the extreme the accepted conventions of enacting manga through fan cosplay (costume play). Jane's hallucinations, seeing Sunny and herself as reincarnations of manga characters, are both the symptom of her instability and the result of role-playing. *Angel Sanctuary* gives Jane a vocabulary for expressing emotional scarring, ghostly resurrection of the past, and traversing multiple temporalities—the symptoms of the urban palimpsest with which she tries to cope.

The manga provides Jane with a cultural matrix for interpreting her emotions, yet the source of her strained relationship with Sunny harks back to the impending demolition of Baozangyan. Jane's insecurity stands out next to Sunny's attitude toward urban space. Sunny is at first unfamiliar with Baozangyan and is easily scared by its dark spaces. She is a passing guest, sleeping at Jane's while her parents seem to care little about her. And yet Sunny has a home to which she can return, as she eventually does. The ending credits shot zooms out of Sunny's veranda to reveal a large apartment building with neighbors milling about and performing daily activities. Sunny's home is far from affluent, and the shot may allude to a community much more loosely connected than that at Baozangyan; yet her abode is at least a standard construction, not impacted by the massive demolition-and-relocation that takes place elsewhere. Jane's jealousy of her friend is also fueled by the poignant discrepancy between their living conditions.

The image of Sunny's apartment building—a frontal shot that places the girl firmly within the architectural context—stands in contrast with an earlier shot of Jane, standing at night on the rooftop of her Baozangyan abode overlooking the river. The girl looks desolately at car lights on the elevated freeway. Jane dons her angel outfit and faces the 1,666-foot Taipei 101 Tower, as if trying to fly away from the misery of her home. Unlike *Red Lotus Society*, where flying over high-rises results from total commitment to the city's memories, Jane wishes to escape her loneliness and estrangement.

32 *My Whispering Plan* (2002): Jane, now a pretty angel, sits in a room bearing the signs of a ouija board.

The winged Jane is an angel without a heaven to which to return and without the haven of a fixed home. She retreats into her cosplay role and finds safety in an imaginary sanctuary.

The film's final shot underlines the connection between Jane's fantasies and the demolition of her neighborhood. The credits are followed by a surreal image of the now-dead Jane, in angel outfit. She is mature and pretty; the costume sits well on her. She has turned into a veritable angel. By contrast, her old room shows the signs of neglect after the evacuation. The walls are covered with graffiti, similar to the scribbling the two girls used for a Ouija board–like game (fig. 32). As a building designated for demolition (or is it that the building, too, has already passed on?), the place bears the marks of ghostly existence. Human death, the disintegration of the community, and the crumbling of urban spaces are concurrent and coterminous.

THE PURLOINED HAZARD TAPE

The connection between the two students' troubled relationship and Baozangyan's anticipated dismantlement is conveyed through an unexpected reference to demolition in the cosplay scene. Jane, distraught and unable to find Sunny, wanders around the cosplay meeting place. As she makes her way through the crowd, she walks past a hazard tape extended across the large hall, used as a waist-level separation line. The tape, bearing the words "Danger, Construction! Do Not Approach!" is out of place, since no construction is in sight. The bright yellow tape haunts Jane, intruding on her field of vision as a subliminal yet forceful sign. The scene refers back to the film's beginning, in which Jane examines an evacuation order pasted on the wall. The entire alley is marked, on both sides, with yellow hazard tape. (The director may also be paying tribute to the park sequence in *Vive l'Amour*, in which Ms. Lin walks through terrain marked by a similar yellow tape—see fig. 28). The sign of demolition returns at the cosplay meeting, at the moment of Jane's separation from Sunny. Jane's insecurity in her friendship resonates with, and is compounded by, the menace of being uprooted from her home at Baozangyan.

The hazard tape, as if surfacing from Jane's unconscious, appears in a blur. Jane does not acknowledge the source of her unease. She walks away, returns to Baozangyan, strides past a similarly taped alleyway, and finds a place to sit down where the yellow tape is atypically absent. It is at this point that she sees for the first time her alter ego as an angel. Henceforth, reality and violent fantasy blend in Jane's mind, and the film spins into vertiginous visions of murder and death. With the introduction of the hazard tape, an indicator not so much of borderlines as of the disappearance of spatial landmarks, Jane's world falls apart.

The hazard tape, as an ever-present reminder of the coming loss, stresses Jane's willful blindness to demolition-and-relocation. The tape's message is "purloined" in the sense evoked in Edgar Allan Poe's "The Purloined Letter," in which a letter is concealed by being placed in plain view, only inside out. With the exception of Jane's first encounter with the tape at the beginning of the film, the warning printed on it is lost in blurs of frenzied motion. The ubiquity of the tape contributes, paradoxically, to its inconspicuousness. Like the veterans' village itself, the tape is visible and invisible at the same time.

Jane's repression of the sign of demolition and her eventual suicide, coinciding with the neighborhood's demolition, present Taipei's gentrification not only as the destruction of physical locations but also as the erasure of residents' memories. For demolition to wipe out the collective memory of place, the memory of demolition itself must also be erased. With the obliteration of Baozangyan's lower level, the hazard tape is removed together with the buildings it demarcated. In showing the hazard tape as unreadable and disposable, *My Whispering Plan* points to the odds stacked against collective memory in the absence of landmarks and communities to carry out the commemoration.

Conscious and constant work is needed to ensure that sites of memory do not slip into spaces of forgetting. The demolished swath at Baozangyan is now covered with grass and trees, and the rhetoric of the municipal government contributes to an amnesic version of the place's history. Even though the film shows real-time images of demolition, of poignancy unseen in Taiwanese film since *Moonlight, My Whispering Plan* suggests that direct representation is as elusive as the purloined hazard tape. Instead, the film focuses on the imprint of what has already vanished. Like Tsai Ming-liang before him, Chu resorts to spectral references. Baozangyan is portrayed as an angel sanctuary, a twilight zone that bears, in the film's last shot, the ghostly traces of a Ouija board. The challenge for new Taipei cinema lies not in documenting the city but rather in denoting its disappearance. Images of demolition are, so to speak, a pornographic representation of urban environment, stark visual images that ignore the desire for what cannot be visualized. The cinema is put to the test when required to represent the absence left by now-invisible structures, without recourse to nostalgia or the concomitant fetishizing of bygone landmarks.

✦ REAL ESTATE ISLAND

My Whispering Plan is arguably the most outspoken among a number of films that identify with citizens wronged by urban policy, and in particular the residents of veterans' villages. New Taipei cinema, however, has rarely described gentrification from the viewpoint of its enablers—architects, construction tycoons, investors, and real estate developers. A notable exception is found in *Robinson's Crusoe* (2002), a thoughtful portrait of the generation for whom the dismantled veterans' villages are childhood memories and who now are restructuring Taipei's real estate market.[60]

The story follows Robinson, a Taipei real estate developer, and his dream of purchasing and moving to Crusoe Island, an undeveloped retreat in the Caribbean. The characters are reminiscent of the alienated characters in Tsai Ming-liang's films (some roles are played by Tsai's favorite actors). Robinson is a loner, unwilling to get emotionally attached to people or places; he lives in a hotel, conducts his love affair in that leased space and in an apartment for sale, and flirts with all the women around him—only to recoil as soon as genuine sentiments are exposed. As a member of the transnational elite, he has no allegiance to the city in which he grew up. He is planning to relocate to Crusoe and surfs the island's website, introduced by the motto "La vie est ailleurs"—life is elsewhere.

Yet unlike Tsai's films, *Robinson's Crusoe* names explicitly the trauma and its roots. Robinson tells a colleague about his childhood at a veterans' village. His father, a general, was always waiting for repatriation after overtaking the mainland, which of course never occurred; the family later moved to the United States. As the director has explained, Robinson is typical of the rootless second-generation mainlanders, further estranged by urban change.[61] Robinson tells his experience to a woman colleague while standing at the exact site of his former Japanese-style house, now demolished to make room for a gentrified neighborhood. Memories of the disappeared spaces take over the present, as Robinson gestures with his hands, "That's where the garden used to be." The enigmatic images of childhood that appear in the film's opening sequence are understood, in retrospect, as part of a loss that has shaped Robinson into an alienated and emotionally handicapped person.

The trauma is encoded in spatial terms. Robinson exposes layers of the urban palimpsest as he returns to the location of his childhood home and relives his memories, even though the house is gone and the place has changed. In a previous scene, his colleague Xiuling tells him of her memories as she leads him to the transformed site of the place where she grew up. The two stand under an elevated highway, among tall buildings, while Xiuling recounts to Robinson how only small houses and a railroad used to be there. For her, too, the location is connected to loss and trauma—her father's suicide. The two imagine seeing and hearing the trains, and the film joins in with a nondiegetic train whistle. The sight of modern Taipei gives way to vivid memories of its buried past.

The sequence at Robinson's former home was shot at the site of a now-demolished veterans' village, Chenggong Xincun. This upscale, legal division on Ho Ping East Road (not far from the site of Da-an Forest Park) was designated for soldiers of Army headquarters and their families. Together with two other large veterans' villages, it was evacuated in 1982 into adjacent state housing (*guozhai*), and the site was further modernized in the first years of the twenty-first century.[62] Robinson's testimony places the current real estate glut in the historical context of Taipei's gentrification since the early 1980s. Today's insensitive tycoon is yesterday's evicted child. Taipei, as presented in *Robinson's Crusoe*, is caught in a vicious cycle of self-destruction.

The aftermath of Taipei's gentrification policy is a city in which memories have no healing power. Xiuling and Robinson reveal to each other their childhood experiences in a moment of intimacy that promises the beginning of a romance. Yet the exchange of memories tests Robinson's limits for interpersonal engagement. After Xiuling presents him with a book she has treasured during their eight-year-long friendship, he leaves it in the subway. Robinson returns to the site of his childhood only to put it behind him and depart for the remote island of Crusoe. Insofar as the veterans' village is Robinson's Rosebud, he refuses to acknowledge its impact on his present condition. Robinson is no Ah Da, who treasures his and others' past experience. The resurfacing of the urban palimpsest does not signal the emancipation of repressed emotions.

The film finds a material manifestation of Robinson's emotional repression in the cold operations of his office—its marketing strategies, land speculations, negotiations with competitors, and concessions to underground thugs. A number of scenes take place in Robinson's exhibition rooms, lined with maquettes of development projects. As I have explained in chapter 3 and will further discuss in chapter 7, such architectural miniatures give an illusion of power to planners and future residents alike, yet the models are no more than dreamscapes that idealize real estate as a desired commodity. It seems that precisely because Robinson lives on the surface, he can succeed as a real estate developer. Ironically, Robinson's disorientation in present-day Taipei gives him keen instincts for the market. Repressing his memories does not make him a better human being, but it certainly turns him into a more efficient businessman.

Lin Cheng-sheng's film indicts Taipei's gentrification and its enablers. The uninhabited dream island of Crusoe is the antithesis of the densely built Taiwan. Taiwan, formerly known as "treasure island" and "banana paradise" (appellations that have also served as English titles for films made in 1993 and 1989, respectively), has turned into a real estate island if not a construction hell. Films have countered by insisting on the city as a palimpsest, in which multiple pasts remain nearly visible, creating the temporal telescoping of the chronotope of simultaneity. Pierre Nora has labeled the locations emblematic of a community's history "sites of memory" (*lieux de mémoire*);[63] the veterans' villages—whether Jianhua Xincun, Baozangyan, or

Chenggong Xincun—are such sites. Taipei's gentrification has entailed, however, the erasure of these sites through their material destruction, evacuation of their inhabitants, and construction of new public facilities and private residences in their stead. In the absence of these sites of memory, Taipei cinema has striven to retain the memory of sites.

SIX

"This is the story of our street"

Urban Preservation and the Post-Maoist Politics of Memory

THE FILM DIRECTOR Ning Ying speaks with excited, broad gestures about the culture shock that inspired her Beijing trilogy. In the early 1990s, she made *For Fun* (1992) to capture her native Beijing—"ugly, rough, beautiful, exciting, and horrible, all at once." As soon as she started shooting, however, she realized that the city was changing too rapidly for her to establish a stable rapport with it. Buildings were being razed and new ones constructed overnight. Streets and roads were being torn up and replaced with new thoroughfares. In the absence of familiar landmarks, her memories were unanchored. Beijing no longer felt like her hometown. All that remained was the historical record kept by her camera. Ning made her next two movies, *On the Beat* (1995) and *I Love Beijing* (2000), in response to the quick urban transformation, documenting people's lives, architectural detail, and the urban layout.[1]

Ning's account of what has motivated her work as a director sums up how post-Maoist filmmakers have reacted to the changing cityscape and contributed to urbanistic debates. Since the Third Plenum of the Eleventh Party Congress Central Committee in 1978 endorsed urban development as official policy, and especially since Deng's drive for an economic transition, cities have experienced unprecedented growth. The approval of Beijing's master plan for 1991–2010 in 1993 accelerated new construction by emphasizing private enterprise, welcoming foreign investment, and designating a Central Business District.[2] Construction picked up further in preparation for the 2008 Olympics, in building not only sports facilities but also extravagant architectural landmarks, recreational spaces, large museums, and new subway lines (see also chapter 7). As Robin Visser notes, "Beijing [is kept] in a state of perpetual destruction and disruption."[3] The movies made since the mid-1990s are tinged with a fear for the future of memory, an anxiety for the loss of identity, and an urge to preserve images of the city.

Filmmakers' growing concern with documenting urban change paralleled wider social interest in the city as a repository of memory. Since the early 1980s, policymakers, planners, public intellectuals, and filmmakers have sought ways to preserve architectural and other visual records of the changing city. The terms of debate date back to the mass demolition and reconstruction of Paris under Georges-Eugène Haussmann in 1853–70, guided by the enthusiasm of the ruling classes for molding the urban environment through new technological means. Ever since, architects have sought to mitigate Haussmannian grand visions with a Renaissance reverence for architectural heritage and desire to express historical continuity. Planners have often seen themselves as guardians of local and national character, and integrated the mnemonic function of space as a guiding principle of urban design.[4] Similarly contradictory drives for demolition and for preservation in the PRC gave rise to the tension, which I have described in previous chapters, between modern monuments and vernacular architecture, manifest in the double emphasis on residential districts and large spaces for state functions. The rapid urbanization of the post-Maoist era has been counterbalanced by increased interest in preservation, both as a planning practice and as a cinematic strategy.

The response to urban change is akin to that observed by Ackbar Abbas in Hong Kong leading to the handover in 1997. An anxiety over the disappearance of Hong Kong as its residents had known it led to the production of "a culture of disappearance," which at the same time created a local cultural identity and lamented its purported approaching demise.[5] Unlike in Hong Kong, the disappearance of familiar spaces in Beijing was immediate and violent. Yet much like their Hong Kong counterparts, Beijing filmmakers struggled to make a difference despite their limited access to the decision-making process. Whereas earlier productions were released as an integral part of political campaigns, the post-Maoist movies cannot explicitly engage with official discourse—especially when they express disagreement over current policies. However, these movies are not passive representations of the city. In documenting the changing environment, the cinema draws attention to the need for urban preservation. Similar to their Taiwanese contemporaries I have just surveyed, and partly inspired by them, mainland directors have enlisted public opinion in support of policy change.

The discourse on urban preservation is largely critical of current urban policy. Yet the debates between "developmentalists" and "preservationists" are not tantamount to a showdown between the government and dissident resistance, as journalistic coverage tends to imagine. Instead, preservation has often been broached by placing urban development in a historical context. The films that express an interest in preservation take a course of action different from that of the stage plays I discussed in chapter 3. Whereas BPAT productions have waxed nostalgic about old courtyards only to justify their demolition in terms borrowed from urban planning, many films raise poignant questions about the human cost of demolition-and-relocation and inventory the vanishing city. In parallel with the rise of interest in preservation among urban planners, filmmakers have exhibited a documentary impulse for preserving the city, if only in image.

Insofar as state-sponsored drama has promoted commercial development through the upbeat illusion of an instantly rebuilt and modernized city—what I have called the chronotope of instantaneity—independent films have countered with an urgency to document the city before it changes. The cinema must act even more promptly than those who tear down the city. Ning Ying notes that she always hurries to start shooting as soon as possible, fearing that the object of her interest might disappear in the dust of demolition.[6] The documentary impulse is driven by what may be called a *preservational chronotope*, which is articulated through sites of demolition and construction and stresses their ephemerality. Against the developers' shortening of duration through ready-made models, the preservational chronotope slows down the events to lived time and turns the spectator into an eyewitness who moves through the city and records the change.

The documentary impulse has appeared hand in hand with an interest in new modes of realism. The crew members of *Neighbors* (1981), the earliest film I will examine in this chapter, described their approach as *jishi zhuyi*—"documentary realism," or in Chris Berry's translation, "on-the-spot realism"—a term associated with the contemporary reception in China of André Bazin's writing.[7] Another work mentioned in this chapter, *Demolition-and-Relocation* (1998), is associated with the New Documentary movement that started in the late 1980s. Wu Wenguang, the movement's leading figure, explains his work through the term *xianchang*, which refers to the filmmaker's work of recording in real time and on site.[8] Zhang Zhen notes that xianchang is bound to specific locations and often refers to the proliferation of construction sites (*shigong xianchang*) in the 1990s;[9] in this sense, the New Documentary movement is umbilically tied to urban development. Yet despite the affinity among the documentary impulse, "documentary realism," and the New Documentary movement, I am not arguing that urban films strive for a documentary aesthetics. They are at best what Bill Nichols calls "honorary documentaries," sharing an interest in effecting social change.[10] The documentary impulse is an attempt, much wider in scope than any genre, to understand films' function as visual records. In fact, fictional narratives are at the heart of the cinematic contribution to urban preservation.

Urban concerns appear in documentary and fiction films alike. Despite these topics' social sensitivity, they should not be aggrandized as the unique purview of edgy, purportedly dissident films. In fact, I argue that the much-touted genre of Urban Cinema, insofar as it denotes films depicting the alienation of the city dweller, presents a set of concerns very different from those of the documentary impulse. Meanwhile, films of all genres, critical and market-oriented productions alike, have engaged closely with urban policy. Zhang Zhen notes that what she calls "the urban generation" does not denote a cohesive movement but refers to unrelated filmmakers with common concerns for late twentieth-century urban society.[11] Furthermore, as we will see in this chapter, mainstream productions and lighthearted comedies have played a role as important as "underground films" in addressing official policy and developing a cinematic vocabulary for capturing images of urban transition. Across genres and styles, films have functioned as time capsules by training the camera on structures about to disappear. Moreover, in portraying the city as scarred by demolition, films unearth the traumas of urban development and give the wounds a visual form. In recording the erased architectural placeholders of memory, films become monuments to that loss.

Recent urban films are marked, in Zhang Zhen's words, by their "singular preoccupation with the destruction and reconstruction of the social fabric and urban identities of post-1989 China," presenting as their emblematic images bulldozers, building cranes, and urban ruins.[12] The centrality of ruins to both the imagery and the plotlines in many of the films examined here should be understood not only as a thematic concern but also as a critical strategy. Demolition sites reify the menace to the city and its memory. Images of entire districts being torn down, similar to those in contemporary Taiwanese cinema, instill a sense of urgency, as the present erases the past quickly and almost without trace.

This chapter outlines the cinematic involvement with demolition-and-relocation policies from the early 1980s to the present. The films have been as varied as the issues addressed. *Neighbors* and *Strangers in Beijing* (1996) document housing in the working unit system and linger on the problems in rapidly dilapidating communal buildings and the attendant social problems. Most films focus on older structures, especially Beijing's courtyards, some lamenting the passing of tradition, such as *Sunset Street* (1983) and *Farewell My Concubine* (1992), others showing the human attachment and trauma involved in moving, such as *No Regret about Youth* (1992), *A Tree in House* (1999), and *Meishi Street* (2006). A few movies allude to the problems awaiting the relocated population, as do *For Fun* (1992) and *Shower* (1999). All these works demonstrate the importance of film as record of, and evidence, a disappearing architectural and social environment. Whereas the stage plays and films discussed in previous chapters often insinuate that the urban environment is accessible primarily through cinematic representation, films adhering to the preservational chronotope acknowledge that the cities in their present form will survive only on film.

⚡ ELEGIES TO AN UNBUILT CITY

The rise of the city in post-Maoist films reflects not only the political support for urban growth but also the emergence of a cinematic effort to record the city. The changes in urban and cultural policy under Deng Xiaoping brought about a shift in the carefully monitored distribution of film subject matter. To remedy the neglect of urban drama, and in conjunction with an emphasis on previously denounced literary works, films took to the city. In 1982 film adaptations were released of literary and stage classics: Mao Dun's *Midnight*, which takes place in early twentieth-century Shanghai, Lao She's *Teahouse* and *Camel Xiangzi*, and the nostalgic *My Memories of Old Beijing*— all three depicting preliberation Beijing.

Contemporary plots included *Alley of Three Families* (1982), set in Guangzhou, and *As You Wish* (1982), set in Beijing. These productions did not amount to a cohesive statement about contemporary urban issues, yet they foregrounded the historical import of China's cities. *Midnight* raises the specter of commerce in elaborate depictions of the stock exchange, and *As You Wish* alludes to the devastation of the urban social fabric wrought by the Cultural Revolution. The return to Stanislavskian realism during the same period entailed meticulous attention to reconstructing everyday details. *Camel Xiangzi* was among the first productions to be shot on a special lot at the Beijing Film Studio designed for recreating Beijing's old alleys. The foundations of a cinematic aesthetics that emphasizes the documentation of everyday urban life were laid in the sets for these films.

Revisiting pre-1949 plots contributed to a sense of urban identity that had disappeared during the Cultural Revolution. The films made in the early 1980s rarely present contemporary issues and largely overlook the new Dengist emphasis on urban redevelopment. Yet by reinforcing stock images, such as Shanghai's Bund and Beijing's Drum Tower, the films fueled an emerging urban discourse. Professional planning also was being reestablished, in what Zhao Shixiu has called "the second spring" of Chinese urban planning (the first having taken place in the 1950s).[13] Planners' new visions and the shift in urban policy take center stage in two films, *Neighbors* (1981) and *Sunset Street* (1983).

THE REEMERGENCE OF URBAN DISCOURSE: *NEIGHBORS*

Neighbors, winner of the 1982 Golden Rooster Award for best picture, stands out as a pioneering exploration of Dengist urban reform. Produced by the Beijing Film Academy's Youth Film Studio, *Neighbors* gave voice to artists whose careers had been suspended by the Cultural Revolution, including the director Zheng Dongtian, the actress Zheng Zhenyao, and the playwright Xu Baogeng (credited under the pen name Da Jiangfu). The script often refers to the Cultural Revolution and to the tight bond among characters who suffered through it together before being rehabilitated.[14] The plot hones in, however, on the transition to new housing.

The story takes place in an unidentified city (the shooting locations included Beijing, Tianjin, and Hangzhou) and is filmed mainly inside a communal corridor building (*tongzilou*) that serves as the residential quarters of the Institute of Architecture and Construction.[15] The focus on the fictional Institute of Architecture and Construction allows the plot to dwell on details of urban policy. Since the tenants are also professional architects, they do not remain passive beneficiaries of development but rather play an active role in designing their new condos, even in advising the policymakers. The

33 *Neighbors* (1981): The communal kitchen at the academy dormitory.

film traces the entire process of relocation, including the city council decisions, professional planning, and oversight of construction. The film shows the implications of the economic reforms for housing conditions and foregrounds the mechanism for implementing housing reform.

The communal corridor building gives rise to the problems that impel the plot. This architectural form, initiated in the 1950s, was not only cheap but also allowed easy monitoring of the single entrance and mutual supervision by the tenants, who all shared lavatories and cooked in the corridor, next to one another. In *Neighbors*, the building was used as the university dormitory until the Cultural Revolution. When schools were shut down and students were sent to the countryside, the space was converted into housing for single teachers. As the teachers married and had children, the quarters became crowded.

The opening shot shows the congested corridor, which serves as the "communal kitchen," where each household has a small cooking area (fig. 33). This is a key space, as evidenced by the script's original title, *Chufang jiaoxiangqu* (The kitchen symphony).[16] The tenants repeatedly bump their heads into walls and equipment in the cooking area, and a young girl is scalded by spilled boiling water. The plot revolves around the expectations for new housing promised by the government.

The film was made at the transitional stage when the socialist work unit (*danwei*) system underwent restructuring. The system was a hallmark of

Maoist social organization and spatial regulation. Together with household registration (*hukou*), the work unit was established in the early 1950s and reinforced in 1958 as an urban version of the rural communes. It was the primary form of placing citizens within a framework that controlled all interactions between the individual and the state. Each citizen was affiliated with a place of employment, such as factory, school, or office. The work unit allocated food rations and housing, issued travel, marriage, and birth permits, and endorsed party membership, higher education, and military service. Based on Soviet urban planning, residential compounds (*xiaoqu*) were designed to overlap with work units. Not only was work unit housing a way to curb mobility, but it also became a leading principle in the layout of urban space. Members could stay within the unit's self-sufficient enclosures for work and recreation, socializing, and child education. The work units became cities within the city. The units often mimicked the pattern of the traditional courtyard, and Beijing's alleys gave way to the spatial logic of walled complexes.[17] The work unit left the residents no choice but to rely on a centralized housing system. (In fact, university work units such as the one depicted in *Neighbors* would often provide a mess hall for communal dining; the film stresses the blending of private and public spaces.) By the 1980s, urban work units suffered from the same problems that plagued city housing as a whole—the neglect of residential construction during the Maoist period led to a severe shortage. Extended families crammed into the space originally occupied by the elder generation. As the situation was addressed piecemeal, the media were mobilized to showcase the government's efforts.

The film sounds an upbeat note by contrasting the squalor of the old building with the elegant new development. The new quarters are located next to a modern hotel, designed by Professor Zhang from the Institute of Architecture and Construction. The rooms are spacious and bright, and each condo opens onto a balcony. Like the adjacent twenty-story hotel, the new housing compound signals progressive aesthetics and planning concepts, and the move symbolizes the modernization of China's cities.

In the vein of earlier Maoist plots, the story line is advanced by a difficulty that must be overcome, and a resolution is achieved through the benevolence and compassion of the Communist Party. The residents harbor doubts, not only about the availability of new housing but also about its fair distribution among awaiting candidates. New work unit housing could be assigned according to rank, seniority, or family size; residents developed a set of ethical standards, or a "moral economy," which sometimes clashed with the unit's decisions.[18] Following the formula known from works such as *Dragon Whisker Creek*, the residents question the possibility of fair treatment—in this case, they fear that there might be too many such housing problems to solve in the city, or that the promised new housing will be given to high-level cadres. (Here *Neighbors* addresses a side effect of the economic reforms, especially rampant in the 1980s: cadres took advantage of the construction boom and housing privatization to acquire better accommodations for themselves, in direct contradiction with the intent of policy meant to alleviate the shortage in apartments.)[19] The frustrated residents threaten to demonstrate and even prepare banners for the occasion. The solution is negotiated by the veteran cadre Old Liu, the retired institute secretary. Old Liu represents the selfless leader, confident in the final triumph of the correct ideology. He gives up the privilege of a new apartment until the entire dorm unit is moved. When confronted with pragmatic considerations he retorts, true to the Dengist spirit, "Reality, too, is created by people." To solve the housing crisis, Old Liu applies directly to his comrade-in-arms, the secretary of the municipal council, who explains that the problem lies with only a few people who abuse the Four Modernizations policy. Before Old Liu dies of cancer, he appoints a young and feisty man to replace him in a crucial council meeting. A new generation ensures the correct course of action, and the film ends with the residents' last meal in the old building, celebrating the imminent move. (The interpersonal problems arising subsequent to such a move are portrayed in Zheng's later film *Young Couples* [1987]). The film sides with the policies associated with Deng Xiaoping and his coterie of rehabilitated senior cadres, represented by Old Liu.

The film evidences a somewhat surprising willingness to face in public the pervasive and pressing housing problems. The subject matter was indeed deemed politically sensitive—several directors had expressed interest in the script before Zheng Dongtian did, only to be discouraged by their studios; the film was almost banned by the censors.[20] The film may have avoided the ban by attributing the lack of modern housing to the neglect of urban infrastructure during the now-reviled Cultural Revolution. *Neighbors* goes, however, beyond crass Dengist propaganda and introduces a fresh approach to chronicling housing reforms. The film confronts the poor conditions in the apartment blocks and mentions the abuse of housing privileges by cadres. *Neighbors* pays tribute to Party interests, but it is also committed to a new cinematic approach.

The filmmakers and their contemporary critics saw *Neighbors* as a milestone in introducing a new form of realism to the Chinese screen. The film was probably the first to be described with the term *jishi zhuyi*, or "documentary realism." The director Zheng Dongtian emphasized the focus on "reality [*zhenshi*], reality, and reality yet again." The prominent critic Li Tuo, citing Zheng, regarded the film as a landmark in relinquishing the revolutionary realism of the Maoist period and abandoning model characters, "living Lei Fengs," in favor of fallible personae.[21] *Neighbors* signaled a reaction to Maoist aesthetics by offering a credible record of post-Maoist urban policy.

The "documentary realism" of *Neighbors* is inextricable from its subject matter. The scriptwriters stress the importance of structural details: just as "a mountain is measured not by its height but by the immortals living in it," they explain, so is the less poetic communal corridor building not an abstract architectural form but rather a window on daily life.[22] The actor Wang Pei remarks that the dilapidated building is a reflection of the crumbling work unit as a social institution.[23] To foreground the connection between the building and the social commentary, the set designers took meticulous care in detailing the corridor and each of the one-room apartments.[24] The dexterous camera movement captures a complex spatial layout. Deep focus emphasizes elements such as the spacious and bright new apartments, and the last shot, a zoom-out from a single window to a bird's-eye view of an entire district, conveys the scale of urban reform. The documentary impulse, as established in *Neighbors*, is eminently urban and explicitly cinematic.

Neighbors demonstrates the debt of the post-Maoist documentary impulse to the realism of the early years of the PRC, as exemplified in Lao She's *Dragon Whisker Creek*. It stages the intricate urban environment not simply for documentary description but rather to vigorously engage in urban policy. *Neighbors* refers explicitly to the power of visual records in a scene in which the foreign reporter Agnes (played by Communist old-timer Betty Chandler) visits her friend Old Liu in the old dormitory. Even though Agnes's account in a U.S. newspaper is sympathetic, she describes the dorms as reminiscent of her days in Yan'an; by implication, urban housing has gained little over the cave dwellings used by the revolutionaries in the 1940s. The article, accompanied by a large photograph of the dorms, angers the municipal council secretary, who accuses Old Liu: "This is blackening the face of the Four Modernizations!" The article goads those in charge into action and contributes to the satisfactory resolution. By extension, the illustrated report shows the potential of the cinema. If a single journalistic piece can facilitate the completion of a housing project, the filmic representation of urban reform can explain to citizens the importance of the policy and at the same time ensure its proper implementation by the government.

THE DOWNFALL OF THE WORK UNIT:
STRANGERS IN BEIJING

Neighbors, documenting the beginning of urban transformation in the early years of Deng's reforms, holds a hopeful view of the new policies and at the same time is unable to imagine the more radical changes to come, which would encompass not only housing issues but also the work unit system. A different view is presented in *Strangers in Beijing* (1996), which bears witness to the dissolution of the work unit system and the concomitant stagnation in housing reform.

In the 1980s residents were troubled not only by relocation but also by the fear that their work units would be dismantled, as the transition from planned economy to market economy made the work unit system obsolescent. Many workers were laid off, and in some cases entire units were disbanded. As the "iron rice bowl" of secure employment broke, housing also became unreliable. Social and spatial disorientation went hand in hand. The conclusion of *Neighbors*, showing all the residents at the communal kitchen preparing for their collective move to the new dormitory, seems forced mainly because it represses the possibility that under the economic reforms the work unit would no longer take care of its members.

The fear only insinuated in *Neighbors*, that housing would disappear with the gradual demise of the work unit system, materializes with full force in *Strangers in Beijing*. The film, based on Hei Ma's novel of the same title (1992), was highly popular and won the Hundred Flowers Award for best picture for 1996.[25] *Strangers in Beijing* is comprised of vignettes on life in the residential building of a state-owned publishing house. The structure—as in *Neighbors*, a communal corridor building—has fallen into disrepair. In the absence of basic maintenance, the communal toilets overflow into the corridor, which also serves as the cooking space. A resident remarks with sarcasm, "To live in a derelict building like ours and still be patriotic, now *that's* a feat!" As the English title intimates, the residents come from other provinces. They are placed two per room, and any semblance of privacy is destroyed by gossip and malicious interference in each other's lives. Marriages are strained, and even a pregnant wife is not allowed to stay with her husband because she has no Beijing registration. The work unit system is shown to be crumbling from within.

Unlike *Neighbors*, which is aligned with the official optimism, *Strangers in Beijing* leaves no hope for reform within the unit. The film may be the first on urban housing that does not hold even the remote promise of a future move to newer quarters sponsored by the government or the unit. The publishing house takes no responsibility for the situation, and the tenants have no authority or power. When the housing officer arrives, the residents mob him and ask, "When will we move to new housing?" The question remains unanswered, and at the end of the film the workers return to their provinces of origin. The novel's epilogue even expresses the fear that the mean-spirited atmosphere of the communal corridor building will carry on in the protagonists' new environment.[26]

Facing such a bleak future, the characters feel a tinge of nostalgia. The last scene shows a couple waiting for a train that will take them away from the city. The man mutters, "To tell the truth, I still like Beijing best." A song plays in the background: "I've forgotten which road takes me home / I can't find it even in my dreams' geography / This isn't my home, that isn't my home either." The particular plight of migrant workers, who occupy a precarious physical and social space in the postsocial metropolis, foregrounds the bankruptcy of the current policies.

The capital is portrayed as a way station, with no viable housing plans for those who cannot find a place in the new, chaotic economy. Some of the workers devise moneymaking schemes, such as opening a private publishing house specializing in popular Taiwanese and Hong Kong literature. To make a living, the residents relinquish idealistic plans to write. *Strangers in Beijing* notes with some ambivalence the crumbling of the distinction between high- and lowbrow art under the market economy, foreshadowing later films that ridicule both the commercialization of culture and the intellectuals who fail to adapt. (I return to the blurring of low- and highbrow in chapter 7.)

Strangers in Beijing, with its bleak view of urban existence over a decade after the implementation of economic reforms, makes the cinema a venue for direct social criticism. Although the movie waters down Hei Ma's novel, it nonetheless exposes difficult problems in the derelict apartment block. As Hei Ma notes, the novel was difficult to publish, and the film adaptation—made with private funds and endorsed by the minor Fujian Film Studio—had to leave out much of the poignant criticism.[27] *Strangers in Beijing* is a milestone in onscreen challenges to urban policy. Amplifying the issues addressed in *Neighbors*, it portrays the deterioration of life in work unit housing to signal the downfall of Maoist urbanism. The films also break with the Maoist mode of representation, in favor of candid portrayal of social problems. Moving out of the communal corridor building and leaving the work unit mark the end of important architectural and cinematic aspects of the socialist era.

RESTRAINED NOSTALGIA: *SUNSET STREET*

The focus on the communal corridor buildings, recently built structures of little aesthetic allure, captures one facet of urban redevelopment. Many projects involved the evacuation and destruction of private courtyard houses (*siheyuan'r*), eliciting thorny issues of determining property rights, calculating land value, protecting vernacular architecture, and preserving cultural heritage.

As we saw in chapter 3, rapid urbanization and the attendant rise of land value for residential and business purposes brought about a mass-scale demolition of old quarters. At first, little cultural value was attached to residential architecture. Decisions after 1978 repeatedly recognized Beijing's status as a "historic city" and a "cultural center," but until the early 1980s, preservation was limited to isolated "cultural landmarks" (*wenwu*) and "relics" (*yizhi*), devoid of their urban context.[28] Terms such as *conservation* and *sustainability* were introduced into professional planning only in the late 1980s.[29] No one publicly questioned whether the redevelopment policy might undermine the integrity of cities, and Beijing in particular. The "aesthetics of city-scale preservation policy," as Daniel Abramson calls it, had been present already in Liang Sicheng's and Chen Zhanxiang's vision of Beijing in 1950, but the preservation of streets and districts and the development of an overarching concept of the city did not become part of official policy until 1986—arguably, when it was too late to save the city as "a planned whole," in Liang Sicheng's term.[30]

The discourse on preservation, when it finally emerged, became entangled in the policy of demolition-and-relocation (*chaiqian*). The dislocation of residents to make room for new housing and business centers, as well as wider roads, has often involved involuntary evacuation, unfair compensation, unkept promises about the quality of new facilities, unaffordable alternative housing, inconvenient distance of the new residences from the urban center, loss of community, and inadequate opportunity for legal appeal. The residents have been faced with powerful developers, the latter often backed by the government. By the 1990s, demolition companies disregarded the law and intimidated tenants, whose appeals to the courts were consistently dismissed.[31]

The policy favoring redevelopment, gentrification, and evacuation has left the residents with few choices. The official narrative presents the process as a straightforward replacement of a modernized city for an outdated urban layout. The slogans about trading the old for the new are exemplified by the twin mottos for the drive to rebuild Beijing: "Retreating from the second and entering the third" (*tui er jin san*) and "Retreating from the second and entering the fourth" (*tui er jin si*)—referring, respectively, to relinquishing manufacturing (the secondary sector) in favor of services (the tertiary sector), and to moving industrial enterprises currently located inside the second ring road to outside the fourth ring road.[32] This official rhetoric associates relocation with desirable restructuring of the urban economy.

The complex arguments for and against demolition-and-relocation became clear only gradually through the 1980s and 1990s. The first film to raise the issue was *Sunset Street*. Although the film praises the new policy of "reconstruction of hazardous and old houses," or *weigai*, it also mourns the disappearance of old Beijing. The film's treatment of the old alleys and courtyards underlines how the cinema documents sites where physical preservation is impossible. *Sunset Street*, influenced by contemporary courtyard stage plays but also seeking a uniquely cinematic approach, stands out as a new filmic engagement with urban development and preservation.

Sunset Street's plot takes place in 1980. It focuses on the eponymous alley, designated for demolition-and-relocation, and presents the entire process. The film follows the initial announcement by the head of the neighborhood committee, the registration for apartments, and the settlement in the new quarters. All the residents, some of whom have lived in the old city for more than sixty years, welcome the move to modern housing. Regret is registered only toward the end of the film, when the residents return to the now-abandoned alley on the eve of its demolition. One observes, "I will always feel as if I left something here"; another admits that a part of her will always stay behind and that she cannot let go (the exact same phrase is used in the 1983 version of the play *Small Well Lane* and in *Neighbors* to describe residents' relation to their old abodes). The loss incurred by demolition is justified, however, by the anticipated move to modern housing.

The nostalgia for the old and recognition of the advantage of the new are both implied in the title, which refers to the decline of Beijing's old way of life but also resonates with a popular adage about ephemerality, taken from a ninth-century poem by Li Shangyin: "The setting sun is boundlessly beautiful, yet it portends dusk" (*xiyang wuxian hao, zhishi jin huanghun*). Critics have noted the allusion, yet it is less known that the phrase is also rooted in the history of Beijing's urban planning. Zhou Enlai used the lines in a letter to Liang Sicheng, in response to Liang's warning against tearing down Beijing's memorial arches and wall towers.[33] In the context of Zhou's and Liang's correspondence, the poem acknowledges the beauty of the old architecture but associates it with a decrepit society that is bound to wane. In the same vein, the script for *Sunset Street* concludes: "The old always disappears and the new grows forth. Ah, Beijing, I wish you will change into a better place!"[34] Even in the playwright's view, Sunset Street, for all its beauty, is rightfully doomed to demolition.

The film seems ambivalent toward urban redevelopment. On the one hand, a character endorses change as inevitable, brought by "the tide of the times" (*shidai de chaoliu*; the expression evokes Sun Yat-sen's adage that "the tide of world events is mighty," quoted for the same purpose a decade later in *Beijing Pretenders*). To wit, the "Beijing and Countryside" tofu shop is torn down, only to reopen and preserve Beijing flavor in a more hygienic environment. As the director Wang Haowei explains, the film was made in more hopeful days, when demolition-and-relocation was introduced and before the policy's massive scale and social aftermath became known. On the other hand, *Sunset Street* alludes to the downside of relocation. Toward the end of the film, the doctor Zhou Yanyan and the bulldozer driver Wu Haibo return to the evacuated site on the eve of its demolition. The dialogue reveals that the childhood sweethearts are not destined to unite, since Zhou suffers from a fatal illness. She gives the key to her new apartment to Wu, establishing an analogy between the architectural destruction and human death. As the director commented later, Zhou Yanyan's death is tantamount to the end of an era and to the disappearance of old Beijing.[35] The film tones down a much more poignant situation: according to the original script, Wu Haibo is employed in the demolition work. Whereas in the final screen production, Wu is only shown moving gravel at a remote site, the uncensored script calls for detailed shots of his bulldozer toppling houses and for a close-up on Wu's hand as he operates the shovel.[36] The film version (which also excises a strongly nostalgic coda) does not linger on the pain of demolition.

Although *Sunset Street* is largely friendly to weigai and skirts the problems associated with it, the film gains social relevance by turning into a snapshot of everyday Beijing life and a record of contemporary urban renewal. Like *Small Well Lane* before it, *Sunset Street* does not foreground any lead character. Instead, the film provides what Wang Haowei calls "quick sketches of life." To recreate the Beijing alley, the crew paid attention to detail, such as typical street sounds and various courtyard layouts. (Wang's crew was hard-pressed to find courtyards that preserved their original form after the 1976 Tangshan earthquake, and three different locations were needed to put together the courtyard scenes.)[37] Like the post-Maoist courtyard plays, *Sunset Street* combines support for urban modernization at the courtyards' expense with nostalgia for the courtyard as a repository of Beijing's memories.

Sunset Street also pays tribute to old Beijing by making pigeon flocks an icon of the capital. The film shows Beijingers' love for the birds. Customarily, small whistles are tied to pigeons' necks, so that a flock produces a distinct sound as it flies over its home. The offscreen whistling, heard beyond the confines of the secluded courtyards, creates a continuum between private abodes and the urban environment, suggesting the city as seen from a bird's-eye view and imagined in flight. In later productions, the pigeon whistles signal nostalgia for the receding courtyards. The almost ghostly droning in films such as *On the Beat* and *Shower* accentuates the ephemerality of the city. By the twenty-first century, the sound has become a cliché, canned and overused in films such as *Beijing Bicycle* (2001). In *Sunset Street*, however, the pigeon whistles offer a fresh, poetic allusion to old Beijing.

It is worth noting that both the playwright, Su Shuyang, and the director, Wang Haowei, developed a lifelong interest in Beijing. Su had authored the script for *Next-Door Neighbors*, which helped establish the courtyard play genre.[38] As Su sees it, China's urban environment is a distillation of Enlightenment values and traditional culture.[39] Wang also grew up appreciating

Beijing drama, since her mother befriended the capital's leading actors. When Wang started making films after the Cultural Revolution (having graduated from the Beijing Film Academy in 1962), she chose to focus on Beijing, beginning with the urban comedy *What a Family* (1979) and later directing *Divorce* (1992) and the four-part documentary *Lao She* (1996). Wang energetically pursued Su's script, which was also coveted by another director, since she relished the challenge of a plot replete with Beijing flavor.[40]

The silver-screen record of Beijing created in *Sunset Street* is best understood in light of earlier, theatrical portrayals, especially Lao She's *Dragon Whisker Creek*. The film adapts Lao She's vision of socialist Beijing to the post-Maoist era. Like *Dragon Whisker Creek*—the first production of which Wang Haowei watched when she was ten—*Sunset Street* presents social restructuring through urban redevelopment. Yet the convenient division between preliberation evils and postliberation progress in *Dragon Whisker Creek* gives way to a more complex historical outline that acknowledges the havoc wreaked by the Cultural Revolution. As Su Shuyang puts it, *Sunset Street* raises the question, "Can we rehabilitate the best part of our lives?"[41] Some conflicts are never resolved, notably as personified by the egotistic Li Pengfei, who vows to remain in place until he gets a larger apartment. The shot of Li as he stubbornly walks through the rubble (fig. 34) not only refers to "stuck-nail tenants" (*dingzihu*), one of the biggest problems in the relocation process, but also captures on film for the first time the ruins of a longstanding PRC housing unit. The sequence is pregnant with symbolism—the revolution is in need of mending, in architectural as well as social terms. Thirty years after *Dragon Whisker Creek*, the promise of socialist urbanism still lies ahead.

The understanding of demolition-and-relocation as a temporary setback accentuates the value of *Sunset Street* as a record of the transitional period. The final shot zooms out of the new tofu shop and pans across the new compound to which the residents have been relocated (the cityscape captured on film is the new apartment buildings in Tuanjiehu, east of the third ring road). The narrator has the last word: "This is the story of our street. Who knows? This kind of everyday story must be taking place everywhere." The comment may be a tribute to the famous line in Jules Dassin's *The Naked City* (1948): "There are eight million stories in the Naked City; this has been one of them." It not only stresses the ubiquity of demolition-and-relocation, but also—especially when backed up by the expansive image of

34 *Sunset Street* (1983): Li Pengfei has turned into a "stuck-nail tenant."

endless housing units—claims that the film provides a representative picture of China's urban redevelopment. The shot combines the pretense of the courtyard plays to speak for the citizens at large (Li Longyun's *There Is a Small Courtyard* similarly opens with the words, "Who knows how many such small courtyards there are in Beijing?")[42] and the filmic convention of panning the skyline to place the camera as an unconcerned recording device (*Neighbors*, too, ends with a zoom-out, which recedes from the communal kitchen to the entire compound). *Sunset Street*, unable to provide a full justification of urban policy, turns to documenting the changing cityscape. The film foreshadows the later Urban Cinema, which distances itself from the official viewpoint, allows the filmmaker the critical position of an auteur, and regards the film camera as a tool for evidence gathering.

⌇ URBAN CINEMA: THE CITY AS METAPHOR

Although *Neighbors* and *Sunset Street* set important precedents, attention to urban subject matter picked up especially beginning in the mid-1980s, after the release of films addressing a different set of concerns. These films came to be known as Urban Cinema (*chengshi dianying*). Urban Cinema includes the best-known exemplars of Chinese films on the city, yet they deviate in important ways from my concern with the documentary impulse and the urban contract. We may thus discern two diverging trends in cinematic address of urban issues. Some directors have observed with a sense of urgency the need to record the changing city, leading to the documentary impulse, which in many forms engaged, albeit implicitly, with official discourses on urban preservation. Other filmmakers emphasized the protagonists' subjective experience—ignoring, if not outright resisting, the direct political associations and implications. This second tendency has received more popular and critical attention, at the expense of attention to city-scale structural issues. The independent filmmakers of the Sixth Generation, associated with urban films, have acquired an aura of youthful rebellion and detached cool by distancing themselves from policy-related films and emphasizing subjective affect. This section offers a concise discussion of the thematic concerns, aesthetics, ideology, and critical reception of Urban Cinema, only to place many of its exponents outside the cinematic discourse on preservation and documentation that continues in parallel.

URBAN CINEMA: THEMATIC AND IDEOLOGICAL CONCERNS

Scholarly discussion of recent films and the city in China has predominantly identified thematic concerns. The films address mostly young people's alienation from the material conditions in the quickly developing metropolises. These films give voice to a tormented modernity, in which the individual confronts the juggernaut of material transformation. It is not only, as the director Zheng Dongtian (of *Neighbors* fame) notices, that "the Sixth Generation grew up together with the cities" and was therefore familiar with the characters that appear in its movies, such as small business owners, unemployed youth, entertainers, and profiteers.[43] More significant, the films often focus on marginalized subcultures and self-marginalizing countercultures, including juvenile delinquents, the physically disabled, the mentally disturbed, and artist communities, to present the city as the battleground between oppressive collectivity and rebellious individuals.

As previous studies have noted, Urban Cinema may be characterized by specific thematic concerns. The earliest examples of the genre—Zhang Liang's *Yamaha Fish Stall* (1984) and *Juvenile Delinquents* (1985), Zhang Zeming's *Sunshine and Rain* (1987), and Sun Zhou's *With Sugar* (1987)—were produced and set in Guangzhou, which Deng's policies targeted for economic modernization modeled after the adjacent Hong Kong. Starting with *With Sugar*, urban films often depict the rock music and experimental art scenes. The rebellion of the avant-garde is presented in landmark works, from *Rock Kids* (1987) and *Obsession* (1988) to *Beijing Bastards* (1992), *Weekend Lover* (1993), *Dirt* (1994), *The Days* (1993), *Frozen* (1995), *The Making of*

Steel (1998), and *Quitting* (2001). Yingjin Zhang remarks that such films "articulate dissent and resistance." More broadly, they are instances of what Zhou Xuelin identifies as a Chinese variety of the international young rebel genre.[44]

Urban films also touch on the shady fringes of the unregulated market economy, including the sex industry, drugs, and pirated merchandise. A related theme is the lionizing of hoodlums (*liumang*), smooth operators (*wanzhu*), and hooligans (*pizi*) as heroic rebels. Whereas *Sunset Street* disapproved of the new phenomenon (a youngster is saved from socializing with punks at the Moscow Restaurant), films made shortly thereafter started celebrating the hoodlum as antihero.[45] Many urban films were based on the "hooligan literature" (*pizi wenxue*) of Wang Shuo, including *Samsara* (1988), *The Troubleshooters* (1988), and *In the Heat of the Sun* (1994). Other movies, such as *Keep Cool* (1997), followed suit.

Lastly, the focus on the alienated and marginalized coincided with the portrayal of unstable identities. The protagonists may be amnesiac, delirious, or clinically schizophrenic, as in *Red Beads* (1993), *Sons* (1996), *Frozen*, and *Quitting*, the last two of which also blur the line between real and performed identity. Female characters in particular appear as doubles, easily taken for each other, in *A Lingering Face* (1999), *Lunar Eclipse* (1999), and *Suzhou River* (2000). These films prize individual subjectivity and engage with urban discourse at an allegorical level.

Critics were quick to note the symbolism in urban films. Chris Berry already recognized in 1988 that in urban films "cities are not just something to be represented" and drew attention to the new trend's distinct "slice-of-life realism" and "absurdism."[46] In other words, Urban Cinema reacts against the mannered and self-important films of the socialist period. Zheng Dongtian, in a 1997 essay that established Urban Cinema as a genre-like category,[47] also defined Urban Cinema as antithetical to earlier paradigms. In Zheng's view, Urban Cinema rejects the Maoist vilification of cities as commercial centers (Zheng was likely alluding to films such as *A Married Couple* and *Sentinels under the Neon Light*, which I considered in chapter 2); Urban Cinema is also a corrective to Fifth Generation directors' initial exoticist focus on rural subject matter.[48] At its core, Urban Cinema is an alternative to Maoist cinematic practices; it is motivated by the attempt to foil the state-sponsored discourse of socialist ideals and nationalist collectivity.

Xiaobing Tang focuses on urban movies as indexes of an ideological shift.

He finds that in the films of the early 1990s "the urban landscape recedes, as it were, into the distance and turns simultaneously into an untranscendable historical condition and an experiential immediacy that together smother any coherent reception."[49] In other words, the materiality of the city remains a determining factor, but it is perceived only through individual experience—and a disorienting one at that. Through his reading of early exponents of Urban Cinema, Tang observes the formation of "modernist subjectivity" in Beijing in the late 1980s and joins mainland critics who find in such films "the experience of anomie and disorientation in . . . the age of market economy."[50] Urban Cinema is a manifestation of the political unconscious of the PRC in the 1990s.

FRAMING THE URBAN SUBJECT

Whereas critics identified the thematic and ideological concerns of Urban Cinema, its visual manifestations remain to be explored. A distinct cinematic idiom developed to emphasize the subjective position of the alienated individual, most prominently through shaky point-of-view tracking shots. To show the viewpoint of one person walking through the city, filmmakers turned to eye-level tracking shots using handheld steadycams. The first Chinese film to feature steadycam shots was *Black Snow* (1990).[51] The movie sought to replicate Beijing as portrayed in Liu Heng's novel of the same English title (*Hei de xue*, 1988). Both the novel and the film emphasize the material and social transformation of the post-Maoist city as reflected in the protagonist's inner psyche. Notably, the film's credit sequence features a take seventy-one seconds long that tracks Quanzi (played by Jiang Wen), a young man just released from prison, as he wends his way home through a run-down Beijing neighborhood. The inadequate natural lighting and bare soundtrack are complemented by an unedited steadycam shot. Xie Fei borrowed the only steadycam in China at the time from August First Film Studio, drawing critical attention and sparking widespread use of the technology.[52] The resulting shot conveys both eye-level familiarity with the city and a sense of jittery uncertainty. Insofar as the tracking shot presents Quanzi's subjective view, the over-the-shoulder camera position also shows the city closing in on the man and watching over him. (By contrast, when an escaped prisoner comes in while fearing police surveillance, he enters through the roof rather than following Quanzi's path.) The credit sequence is mirrored in the final scene, in which the fatally stabbed Quanzi staggers until he collapses in a public square. The tension between Quanzi's subjective point of view and the public space in which he dies anonymously and ignominiously shows the individual as shaped and obliterated by the urban environment.[53]

Black Snow, made by a veteran director just before the Tiananmen incident in 1989,[54] marks the end of the first wave of Urban Cinema. Younger filmmakers who have graduated since 1989 encountered a stricter censorship system and at the same time found venues of production outside state studios. Among the first Sixth Generation films was *Weekend Lover*, the directorial debut of Lou Ye, who graduated from the Beijing Film Academy in 1989 (made in 1993, the film cleared censorship and was released in 1996). Inspired by the camera work in *Black Snow* and *Farewell My Concubine* (1992), Lou's film features steadycam tracking shots (the camera was borrowed from the Shanghai Film Studio).[55] The film's opening shot—stylized and accompanied by a rhythmic score—follows the juvenile delinquent Axi (played by Jia Hongsheng) as he goes up and down a maze of stairwells, sometimes turning around, looking directly at the camera, to check that no one is pursuing him. The shot thereby underscores the protagonist's vulnerability. Toward the end of *Weekend Lover*, a similar shot tracks Axi's rival, Lala (Wang Zhiwen), who stumbles away from having murdered Axi. The shots that bracket the film may be read as a tribute to the opening and concluding scenes in *Black Snow*. Counterbalancing the frequent tracking shots, *Weekend Lover* is interspersed with immobile shots—of rooftop views of Shanghai, neon lights of nightlife locales, street signs, and traffic signs. These not only place the film in a concrete setting—Lou's script specifies exact Shanghai addresses for the shooting locations—but also stress that the characters are defined by navigating through the city. The last street sign, after the youths go their own ways, is blank. Subjective confusion and geographical disorientation resonate with each other.

The themes and film language of *Weekend Lover* are developed in Lou Ye's following feature, *Suzhou River*, also located in the run-down outskirts of old Shanghai, along the waterway known as Suzhou Creek. Elaborating on the camera work in *Weekend Lover*, the film's beginning sequence is a haunting collage of unsteady pans taken from a boat moving down Suzhou Creek. The ending sequence mirrors the beginning with a series of point-of-view shots down the same stream, resembling the increasingly erratic gaze of a drunken man. The sickeningly unsteady shots in *Suzhou River* are paradigmatic of Urban Cinema's subjective constructions. The rough and dynamic camera movement alludes to the protagonist's tenuous relation to the city and comments on film's role in recording that relation.

Suzhou River is a rare instance in which the concerns for objective documentation of urban space and for expressing a subjective point of view overlap and inform each other. The film may be read in relation to the nascent preservation policy in Shanghai. The beginning montage lingers on the warehouse district along the creek's southern bank (fig. 35). The large structures were built during the drive in the 1930s for "popular industry" (minzu gongye), as factories for everyday consumption goods, such as beer and cigarettes. In the late 1990s, some deserted factories were transformed into artists' studios, thanks to the initiative of the Taiwanese architect Teng Kun-yen.[56] During the Suzhou River shoot, the buildings were torn down to make room for a residential community, as part of a municipal plan to gentrify the area and attract foreign investment. A two-hundred-meter greenbelt was almost discarded due to the greed for real estate and only restored after public protest.[57] The construction took place in conjunction with an international project "to reduce pollution and restore the water quality in Suzhou Creek and its tributaries, and improve the environment, living conditions, and public health standards in the urban areas adjacent to the creek."[58] The beginning sequence exposes the destruction that accompanies Shanghai's urban restructuring despite the government's promises for preservation. Lou Ye's film not only portrays Suzhou Creek, in Zhang Zhen's words, as "a reservoir of urban memory,"[59] but also takes over this function.

At the same time, Suzhou River focuses on an individual identity crisis; in fact, the movie demonstrates the limits of the documentary impulse in the discourse on subjective perception. The film begins with a monologue by a cinematographer (narrated in Lou Ye's voice): "I can shoot anything . . . but . . . I'm telling you in advance: my camera doesn't lie." The phrase "My camera doesn't lie" has since been associated with an emphasis on objective, fly-on-the-wall documentation, but in the context of Lou Ye's films, it acquires an ironic undertone: as soon as the veridical camera is put into a filmmaker's hands, it will produce a lie, or at least a highly subjective account.[60]

The point-of-view tracking shot draws attention to the inner mindscape— what lies not in front of the camera lens but rather inside the camera obscura

35 *Suzhou River* (2000): The film is introduced by a montage
of the warehouse district near Suzhou Creek.

of the mind, looking for resonance in the urban environment. A poignant
variation on this device is found in *Good Morning, Beijing* (2003).[61] The plot
takes place during a single night and cuts back and forth between a man
trying to ransom his kidnapped girlfriend and a woman locked in an apartment, where she is forced into prostitution. The man spends the entire night
following the kidnappers' directions and driving from one landmark to
another, increasingly far from the capital's center. The woman endures her
fate in an indistinct, bare, and windowless apartment. Whereas the man's
path introduces the larger urban context, the woman's point of view is
confined to the claustrophobic space where she withdraws into herself.
Insofar as the two stories are interlinked—presumably, the young woman is
the man's kidnapped girlfriend—they present two complementary aspects of
the disorienting and entrapping city. The aesthetics dictated by the low
production values (nonprofessional actors, digital beta and digital video [DV]
formats, and a total budget of 100,000 RMB) is used to create a realism
evocative of documentaries. The grainy footage presents the underbelly of
the glitzy, gentrified metropolis.

The oppressive atmosphere persists though the movie's last shot, in
which the woman tears away the black cardboard covering the room that
was her prison (the scene may be read as an homage to Edward Yang's
Terrorizer [1986]). The torn cardboard reveals a full-wall window, through
which the woman watches, from atop a high-rise, an urban scene at dawn.
Much like the tracking shots in the films mentioned above, a slow zoom-in

36 *Good Morning, Beijing* (2003): The concluding shot superimposes the window and the film frame.

frames the woman in the urban environment, in this case a hazy cityscape of uniform apartment blocks and bleak high-rises under construction. She can only experience city life in muted form, as if it were a silent film in which she does not participate.

The woman's position as outside observer is enhanced by the fact that the exposed window is of the same proportions as a cinema screen, and the zoom-in ends by overlapping the frame with the window (fig. 36). In identi-fying the cinematographic frame with the woman's field of vision and set-ting her backlit silhouette against the skyline, the shot provides a parable on the relation between the individual and the filmed city. The woman is both part of the city and in the position of the cinematographer behind the lens. The exposure of the window-cum-lens takes place not in the manner of a quick opening of the shutter but rather through the laborious act of tearing the cover piece by piece. The final image retains the vestiges of that act, in the form of pointed black cardboard shreds at the window's edges. The protagonist and the city remain at a standoff.

The violent tension between the protagonists and the urban spaces in films such as *Black Snow, Weekend Lover*, and *Good Morning, Beijing* illus-trates the tendency of Urban Cinema to focus on subjective alienation to the point of taking the city for a metaphor rather than addressing concrete power structures. Robin Visser has noted a similar preoccupation in the urban fiction of the 1990s, which juxtaposes public life with the characters' withdrawal—both physical, to private spaces, and mental, to the self's interiority.[62] Paradoxically, the rise of a distinct urban consciousness since the late 1980s has been accompanied by disinterest in the professional and official discourses on urban planning. Filmmakers' concern with their subjective perception—some would argue, self-absorbed to the extreme[63]—shuns state- or city-level perspectives that might be associated with Maoist ideology and aesthetics.

The subjective emphasis in urban films resonates with the neo-Marxist insistence that historical awareness is created at the level of the individual subject. Yet looking at the city through the vision cone of the individual might leave in a blind spot an integrated perception of the urban environment. The narrow alley in *Black Snow*, the torn-down warehouses in *Suzhou River*, and the construction site outside the window in *Good Morning, Beijing* need to be appreciated both allegorically and in the geographical and historical context of the wholesale demolition of cities and the attendant tearing of the social fabric.

EXPOSING THE CITY'S SCARS

The urbanist debate on preservation raises the stakes for cultural mediators in the urban contract. For example, Wang Shuo—the novelist, scriptwriter, and film director—resists romanticizing the alleys, arguing explicitly against the preservation of old Beijing. In "Fan hutong" (Alley nuisance) he writes in a typically provocative manner, "The alley was mostly made up of rundown houses. . . . What joy was there to speak of? Every day people in the alley quarreled and cursed each other. . . . For all I care, if all of Beijing's alleys were to be flattened to the ground I wouldn't be sorry for it."[64] Wang's "hooligan literature" and the films it has inspired have helped create a vital urban identity that negotiates between local character and the authorities' pressure to conform—yet this apparently does not translate into concern for preservation. Other filmmakers felt compelled to protest the consequences of postsocialist urban policy, which has razed entire districts and displaced millions of residents. In parallel with the emphasis on subjective perception, a growing number of films since the 1990s have expressed the cinema's role in preserving China's old cities and their memories. A number of productions of the 1990s—*Farewell My Concubine, No Regret about Youth*, and Ning Ying's Beijing trilogy—signal a growing awareness of the scale of urban change and of the need to address it in film. The progression in Ning Ying's Beijing trilogy in particular shows how the visual emphasis turned increasingly to demolition. The salience of images of demolition may be better understood in light of filmmakers' awareness of their role in preserving a record of the vanishing cityscape. Demolition sites are seen as architectural scars and time capsules of urban history, and their cinematic representation aims to retain the spatial repositories of personal and collective memory. The films discussed in this section map out the cities' spaces as indexes of memory, thereby exposing the material wounds of urban development and giving visual form to the attendant psychological traumas.

PRESERVING THE CITY ON FILM: *FAREWELL MY CONCUBINE*

Chen Kaige's *Farewell My Concubine* (1992) marks a turning point in the discourse on urban memory. The film is an epic tale that follows the lives of two Beijing opera stars (Douzi and Shitou, later known as Dieyi and Xiaolou), beginning with their stage training as children and continuing through the civil war and the Cultural Revolution. Yet *Farewell* may also be viewed as the director's personal tribute to his native Beijing. Chen, acutely aware of the ongoing transformation of the city he has known, makes the film into a historical record. *Farewell* is a nostalgic reminiscence about Beijing before the social rupture of the Cultural Revolution and a cinematic monument to the courtyard houses of old Beijing. *Farewell* intervenes in the PRC politics of space and establishes the city as the middle ground between personal and collective history.

The dazzling images and sweeping narrative of *Farewell* might blind the viewer to the more intimate associations of the film's urban locations. Critics have accused the film of presenting a patronizing national allegory. *Farewell*'s epic plot, which takes place in the capital rather than in the rural setting of Chen's earlier films, was deplored as backsliding to an emphasis on the dominant national culture and as catering to the taste of an Orientalizing overseas audience for the exotic.[65] Yet *Farewell* uses political events as a backdrop for the story of a locale whose inhabitants strive to retain an identity free from the state's ideological manipulations. The director insists that the film is "not an epic. . . . It's a personal story about a few individuals."[66] *Farewell* continues Chen's project of reasserting individual spaces against those that the state rhetoric has claimed for the nation. His *The Big Parade* (1986) challenges the normative images of Tiananmen Square. *Farewell* turns away from the monumental space of Tiananmen to the more personal setting of Beijing's alleys and courtyards (although, as I showed in chapters 1 and 3, these also have been appropriated by government propaganda). By paying homage to the city's local culture, *Farewell* engages in personal reminiscences, contrapuntal and even conflicting with official history.

Farewell is perhaps first and foremost an exploration of the relation between personal and national memory.[67] Throughout the film, memories are rearticulated through intimate objects, bodily scars, and urban spaces, all of which resist the myths of the Chinese nation-state. Unresolved mental traumas constantly resurface through unhealed bodily scars—Douzi's chopped-off sixth finger, Shitou's bruised forehead, and Dieyi's final act of slitting his own throat. The film's final shot, in which Xiaolou relinquishes his dramatic persona as Hegemon King and calls the dying Dieyi by his childhood name Douzi, denotes the return of memory, in the form of a freshly opened wound.

The actors' reunion in a sports arena in 1977, a scene that brackets the film and ends with Dieyi's suicide, is key to understanding the importance of place and reminiscence in the plot. Unlike the description in the originary novel of the same name, which locates the reunion in Hong Kong, an intertitle (in the film's U.S. release version) specifies that the scene takes place in Beijing, even though the film has been set in Beijing from beginning to end.[68] The novel's allegory on the fraught relations between mainland China and Hong Kong is discarded. The two singers' friendship depended on the spaces of old Beijing. The modern, barren sports hall in the final scene underscores the irretrievable destruction of the capital's old structures and the attendant loss of its cultural values.

Chen Kaige sets out to capture old Beijing's flavor by recreating the capital's distinct architecture. Many of the structures are popular entertainment establishments, including a brothel that recalls the Bada Alley of the early twentieth century and, of course, opera houses. The film introduces the historic setting in an attenuated, sepia-tainted sequence featuring a marketplace reminiscent of the famed bazaar at Tianqiao, adjacent to Longxugou. Steadycam tracking shots (such as those that would later influence

Lou Ye) follow a woman as she makes her way through food and porcelain stalls, vendors of toys and musical instruments, and advertisers of foreign tobacco. Places extinct for the past fifty years reemerge on the screen.

At the heart of the film, visually and thematically, are the courtyard houses —the basic building block of Beijing's residential architecture from the thirteenth century to the 1990s. *Farewell* may have been the first movie to use the courtyards as the main visual sign of the city's grandeur. The film does not offer any grand vistas of Beijing, nor does it show many recognizable landmarks. The film was shot mostly in recreated alleys and courtyards on the Beijing Film Studio lot. Soon after Zhang Yimou turned to courtyard architecture in *Raise the Red Lantern* (1991), shot mostly at the Qiao Family Compound near Pingyao, Chen Kaige featured Beijing's residential design in *Farewell My Concubine*. Everyday life in the alleys is complemented by typical Beijing sounds, including street peddlers' cries and pigeon whistles. The film signals, however, the courtyards' swan song.

As I detailed in chapter 3, few courtyard houses have survived in their original form. Due to the housing shortage that began in the 1960s, descendants of the original inhabitants often built shacks inside the court, resulting in a slumlike maze (seen, for example, in *Black Snow*). The haphazard construction inside the courtyards was exacerbated by the Tangshan earthquake of 1976, which forced many citizens out of their homes (the process is illustrated in Zhang Yang's *Sunflower* [2005]). More recently, the acquisition of courtyards by wealthy investors has also resulted in destruction—the renovated buildings, in their stylized and gentrified form, were gutted of their original architectural logic.[69] As a result of the real estate boom of the 1990s, it was highly profitable to demolish these low-density constructions and replace them with multistory buildings. Since the government owned most of the land on which courtyards stood, demolition-and-relocation was carried out by quick administrative fiat, causing a severe impact on the historic cityscape.[70] At the time *Farewell* was produced, the architectural and social values of the old alleys and courtyards were disappearing.

By contrast with the actual conditions in the 1990s, *Farewell* features pristine courtyards, untouched by the ravages of time. These include the opera school, a three-court compound, which serves as a safe haven when political riots rage outside. The place keeps reminding the two actors of their bond, even when they are made to turn against each other. In one scene, the two grown-up actors return to the school courtyard to reenact punishment of each other; the ties between the actors and their teacher trump Xiaolou's wife Juxian, an outsider to the courtyard. In another scene, which takes place during the Cultural Revolution, Dieyi confronts his adopted son Xiaosi'r, who rebels and refuses to continue the operatic tradition. Xiaosi'r defies Dieyi and tells him that he is about to join the Red Guards. The adoptive son's betrayal is encoded in spatial terms—a shot/reverse shot sequence places Dieyi at the center of his courtyard abode and Xiaosi'r behind the "ghost screen" that protects the courtyard from outsiders looking in. By implication, leaving Beijing's traditional spaces is tantamount to turning one's back on the city's culture (and on one's father, a theme of poignant personal resonance for Chen Kaige).[71] Throughout the film, the contrast between courtyards and public spaces stands for the tension between individual and collective narratives.

Farewell sides consistently with personal memory, and the director's autobiographical accounts stress the importance of creating a record of old Beijing. Chen expresses his desire to return to live in a courtyard like the one in which he grew up and laments the recent gentrification of old courtyards, which have become status symbols for new entrepreneurs. He takes pride in his knowledge of the capital's history, which stood him in good stead in choosing shooting locations. "When shooting Farewell I felt an unknown force taking hold of me," Chen recalls. "I believe that I put into the film all my understanding of Beijing and all that old Beijing left in me."[72] Farewell may be seen as Chen's farewell to the city of his childhood, a city of whose layout, architecture, and culture he has become a connoisseur and which no longer exists in that form.

Recording personal recollections and recreating the lost city in Farewell signal a growing awareness of the need for urban preservation. Chen's nostalgic reference, above, to "old Beijing," as well as his acknowledgment of the devastation wrought by recent gentrification, situate the film in a larger effort to save the courtyard houses as part of the city's architectural heritage. Until the 1980s, preservation policy in the PRC referred only to monumental landmarks, such as palaces and temples. The recognition that courtyard houses should be targeted for preservation did not emerge until 1983, when the State Council proclaimed Beijing a "Renowned Historic and Cultural City." A year later, the list of protected sites included the first courtyard houses to be preserved for their architectural merits. Regulations enacted in 1985 and 1987 widened the scope of preservation by implementing "construction control zones" (*jianshe kongzhi didai*) around the protected courtyards. Dozens of courtyards have been saved and restored for their association with historical figures or even simply for their value as exemplars of Qing residential architecture. Despite the major setbacks to preservation I have already noted, protecting old buildings became a key component in post-Maoist urban planning.[73]

Until the late 1990s, however, preservation continued to be negotiated among high-level decision makers, away from public view. Insofar as a popular base of support was mobilized, it was through appealing to national and local pride by referring to buildings' historic value. In this context, memory has played an important role in urban discourse—a surge of nostalgic artifacts which established icons of "old Beijing." Drama was among the earliest exponents of urban nostalgia, through productions such as *The World's Top Restaurant* (1988) and *Bird Men* (1991). *Farewell* should be viewed in the context of the contemporary production of urban memory and the drive to replicate on studio lots and onscreen parts of the city that could not be preserved. The movie's plot, in which scars are repeatedly reopened, hints at the haunting presence of Beijing's architectural and cinematic past.

BEIJING'S CINEMATIC MEMORY

Farewell My Concubine comments on the role of film in creating urban memory by paying tribute to earlier movies. *Farewell* is better understood in conjunction with previous on-screen images and with Chen Kaige's later short, "Flowers Hidden Deep," which reaffirms the cinema as the only medium through which memory can survive.

Allusions to yet earlier films underline the director's commitment to documenting the city. *Farewell* follows *Fate in Tears and Laughter* (1932) in opening with shots of Tianqiao street performances. *Farewell* is also indebted to the classics *Stage Sisters* (1965) and *Opera Heroes* (1949). Both *Stage Sisters* and *Farewell My Concubine* rework the main themes of *Opera Heroes*. The 1949 film describes the careers of two male actors dedicated to the Communist cause. Yuan Wenguang drops out of high school to become an opera singer, under the stage name Yuan Shaolou, and teams up with female singer Liu Yanyun. Yuan is imprisoned by the Japanese, and Liu saves him at the price of her chastity. Liu drifts in and out of Yuan's life, but the latter becomes involved in political protest. The imagery as well as the plot of *Farewell* hark back to this and other earlier films. Chen's film features a scene of children training for Beijing opera reminiscent of the corresponding sequence in *Opera Heroes*. Insofar as *Farewell* is a tribute to the old capital and its vanishing spaces, the film also expresses longing for Beijing's early motion pictures.

In addition to borrowing themes and imagery, Chen casts his films to accentuate the affinity with earlier representations of Beijing. The film's funding by Hong Kong investors accounts for the choice of Leslie Cheung in the lead role, yet other characters are played by some of the capital's best-known actors, such as Zhang Fengyi as Xiaolou and Ge You as Master Yuan. Zhang rose to fame in films about the capital, from his debut in *My Memories of Old Beijing* and his lead role in *Camel Xiangzi* (both in 1982) to *No Regret about Youth* (1992). In his performances in *My Memories* and *Camel Xiangzi*, Zhang helped rehabilitate an image of Beijing that had been erased during the Cultural Revolution. Even though Chen's movie lacks the cool edge of Urban Cinema and the documentary-like realism of the films I will discuss later in this chapter, *Farewell* nevertheless joins those works in marking filmmakers' involvement with the city. *Farewell* is an important link in the shift from Fifth Generation directors' concern for collective memory to the Sixth Generation focus on individual identity.

The director's concern for how the cinema mediates urban memories and recreates the destroyed cityscape is made explicit in "One Hundred Flowers Hidden Deep," Chen's contribution to the omnibus film *Ten Minutes Older* (2002). The ten-minute short starts with a man hiring movers to relocate his belongings from an alley next to the Beijing Drum Tower. Driving first through the city's modern high-rises and then through an area in the process of demolition, they arrive at a vast area razed flat, with a single old locust tree standing in its middle. The man is revealed to be a madman who keeps pestering movers, and he insists that his house is still standing next to the tree. After he finds a memento of his old courtyard house, a small chime, his memories are visualized through an animation sequence of the house and neighboring alley. "Flowers Hidden Deep" is a parable on the trauma of demolition, barely concealed behind the city's new countenance.

The interaction between the movers and the madman is indicative of the popular attitude toward Beijing's architectural relics. The movers initially are indifferent, saying, "As long as you pay, we'll do anything." When the madman does not recognize the widened Ping'an Avenue—now a gentrified artery with fake Qing-style shop fronts—they remark, "It's the people

37 "One Hundred Flowers Hidden Deep" (2002): The demolished courtyard house is resurrected through a digitized dreamscape

who grew up in Beijing who now get lost in it." Yet the madman navigates as if by instinct. Even in the vast vacant lot he recognizes the former location of a filled-in creek. The people who make a buck off demolition-and-relocation are thick-skinned, and only madmen indulge in nostalgia. (Admittedly, the final scene tones down the message, as the man's longings stir the movers.)

Beijing as portrayed in "Flowers" is a city of make-believe, in which the madman continues to envision his demolished home; the movers humor him and entertain themselves, taking part in the illusion by pretending to move heavy furniture. The recent loss of the alleys and courtyards cannot be fully grasped and acknowledged; the destroyed structures continue to haunt the material world. Beijing's citizens are shown to exist in a posttraumatic condition, simulating normalcy. The madman—perhaps driven insane when uprooted from his old home—retains an exact image of the vanished city, and he calls on the movers to own up to the still-open wound.

The madman's recollection, visualized through the animation sequence, reconstitutes the entire courtyard from the chime found on site. The courtyard builds up around the remaining locust tree. One is reminded of the design for Ju'er Hutong and the staged rendition of the project in *Forsaken Alley*, where the old locust trees stand for continuity despite the gentrification that has removed all trace of the original structures. The animation sequence may be read as a comment on the director's role in erecting a monument to the demolished city; the scene employs an architect's imagination, as the courtyard is recreated through a computer-aided draft of the house's foundations, pillars, and beams (fig. 37). Whereas the scars in *Farewell* are linked only indirectly with the disappearing spaces of old Beijing,

"Flowers" makes the urban trauma explicit and shows the cinema as a facilitator of memory.

"Flowers" calls for placing the modernizing Beijing in a historical context. Like other contributions to *Ten Minutes Older*, Chen's short demonstrates the illusory nature of time. In Bernardo Bertolucci's contribution, a man experiences an entire lifetime only to find out that only ten minutes have passed. "Flowers" is a mirror image of Bertolucci's piece—the ten minutes represented on the screen encompass a lifetime's worth of memories. The demolition site is a time capsule, reopened in the process of redevelopment. In contemporary Beijing, everyone is a Rip Van Winkle—residents who find out that their city has become unrecognizable.

THE CITY AS A REOPENED SCAR:
NO REGRET ABOUT YOUTH

The analogy between demolition and scarring—bodily and psychological —is made explicit in Zhou Xiaowen's *No Regret about Youth* (1992). Released shortly before *Farewell*, *No Regret* places on the screen real-time images of the city demolished and rebuilt as residents look on. *No Regret* was the first of many PRC films to feature protagonists either observing demolition or wading through debris. As a cinematic trope, demolition sites not only reflect the contemporary urban condition but become symbols of the need to chronicle the city's transformation and reintroduce a historical memory.

No Regret redirects the focus away from the well-preserved courtyard houses featured in nostalgic films to mundane residences, the people who live in them, and the people who tear them down. The plot is set in a Beijing neighborhood where a ramshackle alley is evacuated and demolished to make room for a modern shopping center. The story revolves around a construction worker, Jianong (played by Zhang Fengyi), and a nurse, Qun (Shi Lan). She lives in a house that he is instructed to demolish; she administers the medical diagnosis for his severe headaches; eventually she becomes his lover. All these relations are framed by a shared experience—a few years before, during the Sino-Vietnamese war of 1979, the two served in the same army unit. A bomb destroyed their shelter, and when Jianong shielded Qun, his head was wounded. Jianong's description draws a parallel between his bodily injury and the building's collapse: "My wrist was broken . . . the building collapsed." The incident results in Jianong's amnesia, intertwining the destruction of memory and the demolition of buildings.

No Regret portrays Beijing in the throes of redevelopment. In 1979—incidentally, at the same time as the Sino-Vietnamese War that the film portrays as the source of trauma—the capital was thrown into a construction drive. The cityscape changed drastically, and more than 1 billion square feet of living space were added within sixteen years, three and a half times the growth of the previous thirty years combined.[74] In 1988 the reconstruction entered a new stage, with the municipal government's policy of "one shift, one emphasis, and four integrations" (*yige zhuanyi, yige weizhu, sige jiehe*). The bureaucratic lingo referred to the shift from building new areas to integrating new development and preservation; an emphasis on rebuilding old districts; and integrating reconstruction with (1) development of new districts, (2) reform in housing policy, (3) management of residential land, and (4) preserving the old city.[75] The euphemistic language concealed a sweeping license for mass demolition.[76] A major manifestation of the new policy was the huge project of the Asian Games Village (Yayuncun), which was modified after the 1990 Asian Games into the first modern gated communities (*xiaoqu*) and started the dramatic price rise in residential units (for theatrical references to the project, see chapter 3). The scale and speed of change led many—including Ning Ying, as I quoted her at the beginning of this chapter—to describe their experience as a culture shock.

It was not a matter of quantity alone. The makeover was radical in that it targeted largely the alleys and courtyard houses that had defined old Beijing. Until the 1990s, urban change was paradoxically highly visible but not widespread. Prominent monuments, such as the city wall razed in the late 1960s, made way for modern infrastructure, and yet the residences in the city's old alleys remained largely untouched.[77] It was only in the early 1990s that urban development began to be perceived as a threat to the old Beijing way of life. In 1998 Lao She's son Shu Yi expressed the cultural aspect of the devastation: "Beijing's second city wall is being torn down. The alleys and courtyards are Beijing's second city wall!"[78] The drive to modernize the city in the 1990s was experienced as the recurrence of a collective trauma.

Zhou Xiaowen, a Beijing native, was shaken by the dramatic changes and integrated them into the story line of *No Regret*. The kernel of the original plot is a love story, based on Wei Ren's novel *The Eroica Variations*, further inspired by Zhou's own life, and rendered into spirited dialogues by Wang Shuo. Yet in the process of searching for locations, Zhou decided to dedicate the film to Beijing's urban transformation. When he visited the construction site of the Asian Games Village, the sight of an entire neighborhood marked with the chalk sign "To be demolished" (chai), made a deep impression. He was reminded of how the city wall had been torn down. Zhou interviewed residents, who were of split opinions about the demolition-and-relocation, and feared that they were blind to the imminent social crisis of the "Fascist" wholesale demolition and construction of ugly high-rises in the name of modernization, as he saw it.[79]

No Regret portrays Beijing as a doomed space, waiting to be rebuilt into impersonal high-rises, shopping centers, and other shrines to new capital. The skyline is dominated not by buildings but rather by the bulldozers and cranes that surround them like scavengers and birds of prey. Houses appear in the film in two forms, either as structures still not demolished or as new buildings not yet completed. The protagonists' respective abodes represent these forms of space that rely on the imagination. Qun lives in an old house, yet her place cannot carry a lasting significance. It is neither comfortable nor elegant, and she never expresses any attachment to it. Her house bears the sign of its destruction, the word chai ("to be demolished") written over it and the neighboring buildings, putting them literally under the sign of erasure. Toward the end of the film, the house is reduced to rubble in less than a minute. In contrast with Qun's dilapidated house stands the apartment bought by her fiancé. It promises to be a modern high-rise condo, yet it is still under construction and looks much like Qun's ruined house. In both cases, the structures are indexes of change and disappearance—not only their own, but also of the inhabitants and their memories.

The third accommodation featured in the film, Jianong's current apartment, accentuates the transitory functions of space. When Qun is evacuated, Jianong's place serves as her jump station from the demolished building to her fiancé's new apartment. In a telling scene, Qun stands in Jianong's place and looks at her old house through binoculars, then turns around and directs the inverted binoculars at the sleeping Jianong. Both objects of observation recede fast and are soon going to disappear—one will be torn down, the other has a brain tumor. The bulldozer operator's demise, together with the buildings that he demolishes, underlines that the urban change has social as well as architectural consequences.

By chronicling the process of demolition, relocation, and new construction, Zhou's film challenges the official policy, which aims at forgetting the city's past, repressing its traumas, and displacing its memory. Ever since the founding of the PRC, the authorities have reconfigured urban space to suppress Beijing's prerevolutionary past. What Shu Yi calls the demolition of the second wall—alleys such as Qun's—also entailed a second wave of erasing memory. The bulldozer driver's fatal amnesia should be understood as an allegory for the destruction of Beijing's memories.

The city is hurtling toward the final transmogrification presented at the film's ending. A year after the demolition is completed and Jianong dies, Qun and Jianong's former wife meet at the new mall. (The film's shooting location was, in fact, an empty lot designated to become a shopping center.) One is reminded of Dai Jinhua's observation that the term "plaza" (*guangchang*) is fortuitously used for both public square and shopping mall. The word associated with Tiananmen Square's revolutionary and dissident history has come to denote the new consumer culture, thereby presenting a linguistic and spatial symbol of the ideological change in the 1990s.[80] The shopping mall erected over Qun's old neighborhood eliminates her and Jianong's shared experience without a trace. The new Beijing rises on the ruins of its former urban identity and of citizens' memory. *No Regret about Youth* portrays a city that contains no accurate record of its history.

No Regret is a landmark in the cinematic portrayal of urban redevelopment. At the same time that younger directors were becoming interested in the counterculture antihero, Zhou Xiaowen engaged images of demolition as a way to refer to the loss of collective memory. In what may be the first shots of demolition in progress in the history of PRC film, *No Regret* shows Jianong's bulldozer ripping through houses. As Zhou explains, he visited demolition sites and saw houses reduced to rubble within minutes. Realizing the power of these images, he decided to include them in the film.[81] In what is arguably the film's climactic moment, the camera lingers on Qun and Jianong as they sit shoulder to shoulder in the bulldozer cabin and pull together the lever to tear down Qun's old home (fig. 38). The emotionally powerful sequence is a rare visual illustration in mainstream Chinese media of a topic suppressed by official discourse.

The explicit portrayal of tearing down houses in *No Regret* does not, however, amount to a full condemnation of demolition-and-relocation. Like *Sunset Street* before it, *No Regret* laments the destroyed buildings only to the extent of showing the need to protect the memory of old Beijing. In fact, *No Regret* bears an uncanny resemblance to the original script of *Sunset Street*. Excised scenes in *Sunset Street* show Wu Haibo tearing down Zhou Yanyan's

38 *No Regret about Youth* (1992): The two protagonists proceed hand in hand to demolish the old house.

house and specify shots similar to those employed in *No Regret*. In both cases, the love between a woman radiologist and a bulldozer driver ends in the death of one of the lovers, soon after the demolition takes place. Neither film openly finds fault with Beijing's development at the expense of the city's old identity, although both tested censors' tolerance.

Zhou, who suffered many setbacks in his other films—four of which were entirely banned, leading to his retirement to TV production in 1998—expresses his disapproval of urban policy in circumspect ways. Qun, a "stuck-nail tenant," is depicted in a positive light, as a free and defiant spirit, fighting the inevitable evacuation and demolition of the old alley. Yet the film is also critical of residents like the two protagonists, who become willing participants in the project of forgetting. The scene in which the two tear down Qun's house suggests that they have resolved to let go of the past. Jianong dies without regaining his memory; Qun becomes an ordinary consumerist homemaker. As the title suggests, they express no regret—not for lost youth, not for a past that disappears without a trace.

No Regret is exemplary of the turn that Ni Zhen has called the "Post–Fifth Generation," toward filmmaking that no longer seeks to change Chinese society but rather tries to show it as it is. In the face of demolition, Zhou wanted at least "to leave a record on film" and tell the story of the demolisher and the demolished.[82] The director acknowledges explicitly his impulse to document, and *No Regret* makes a powerful statement by chronicling the disappearance of human life, space, and memory itself.

Whereas *No Regret* places the demolished alley in a nondescript location erected especially for the shoot, Ning Ying's films provide a more focused portrayal of the city's disappearance, referencing specific sites. Ning Ying stands out as an auteur with consistent thematic, aesthetic, and ideological concerns. Her films *For Fun* (1992), *On the Beat* (1995), and *I Love Beijing* (2000) may be regarded as a single, tripartite work that chronicles Beijing's transformation. As Ning explains, her Beijing trilogy uses the plots as vehicles to produce a visual record of the changes that span the decade.

The three films amount to an ever-widening exploration of the city. *For Fun* explores the life of the recently retired concierge of an opera company and his battle against bureaucracy to establish an amateur opera troupe featuring men like himself. The film dwells on the pastimes of old Beijingers, such as opera connoisseurship and bathhouse chats. Ning's next film, *On the Beat*, addresses the routine work of policemen responsible for the Desheng District. Patrolling by bicycle, they chase a rabid dog and apprehend petty criminals. A comic tone is struck by the juxtaposition of official slogans and administrative regulations, on the one hand, and the details of daily life, on the other. The last film in the trilogy, *I Love Beijing*, follows a taxi driver through his fleeting love affairs and sporadic encounters with underworld thugs and with the high society at Maxim's. The films mark a progression—first moving by foot, then by bicycle, and finally by car—to cover a small neighborhood, a district, and finally the entire city. The increasingly distant forays correspond to the growing scale of urban change.

The films present the city in flux by dwelling on images of demolition. The opera club in *For Fun* is housed in a courtyard that is eventually torn down to make room for a profitable karaoke bar. The dilapidated alleys where most of *For Fun* was shot, east of Fuxingmen, were indeed soon demolished and replaced by the skyscrapers of Capital Financial Street (Shoudu Jinrong Jie).[83] Parenthetically and ironically, the author of the original novel on which *For Fun* is based, Chen Jiangong, is less critical of the demolition. Although Chen has expressed reservations about the shift from courtyards to high-rises, in his book *Beijing Flavor* (1995), he notes: "If it weren't for the "demolish" sign at alley entrances, and if it weren't for the noisy bulldozers that came after them, the towering Capital Financial Street would not exist."[84]

On the Beat includes a poignant sequence that shows the demolition as a work in progress. A policeman introduces a newcomer to the new precinct (Ning notes that at the time policemen were assigned larger areas as a result of a manpower shortage). As the two patrol a large demolished lot, they observe that some six to seven hundred households were evacuated. Replicating the official rhetoric, they explain that the families must have benefited from the move to new apartment buildings. The next shot shows the two policemen dwarfed by heavy construction machinery bulldozing its way through the alley. The camera tilts up to view high-rises hanging menacingly over the old district—none other than the now-completed buildings of Capital Financial Street, at the location of *For Fun*.

I Love Beijing, in turn, records the architectural upheaval through which the city went as it prepared for the fiftieth anniversary of the PRC in 1999. Ning Ying compares the city in the late 1990s to a patient on the operating table, her guts pried open.[85] To complete the projects for the October 1 celebrations, construction continued twenty-four hours a day. Unceasing work was also going on at the site of the future Oriental Plaza (Dongfang Xin Tiandi), where old courtyard houses were quickly evacuated and torn down for the 2000 opening of a one-hundred-thousand-square-meter shopping mall.[86] The shoot took advantage of the ready-made locations. As Ning remarks, the changing scenery in the trilogy chronicles a growing alienation from the city. The city that hosts the intimate club in *For Fun* becomes oppressive in *I Love Beijing*, as the construction sites loom in the dark night, shapeless monsters in Ning's eyes.

The director relates her interest in documenting urban change to her personal experience. As her remarks quoted in the beginning of this chapter show, Ning was taken aback when she could no longer rely on her memory of Beijing. Insofar as a hometown is defined by its permanence, she felt like a stranger in her native city. Ning further elaborates on the swift change—whereas the capital remained largely untouched until the mid-1990s, it was as if within less than a decade old Beijing had been relegated to the ashbin of history. Ning mentions in particular two visual aspects of the transformation. In 1996, uniform private taxis were introduced. Streets previously dominated by officials' black limousines were at once yellow with taxis. Another change was the widening of roads and the placing of railings to stop pedestrians from jaywalking. As roads became obstacles to everyday mobility, like wide rivers to be forded, large neighborhoods were carved up into smaller blocks. The territory associated with one's identity shrank almost overnight. Ning Ying sees this condition, in which "taking a still photo of Beijing is impossible," as an opportunity for her as a filmmaker to record a unique and fleeting moment. Beijing's shift to a capitalist economy had implications for everyday life, architecture, and urban planning. Ning regards her films as periodic reports on the changing social system, basing her observations on wide knowledge of urban design and policy.

Perhaps more than any other director's films, Ning Ying's works represent a heightened awareness of planning discourse in the 1990s. Ning's neorealist sensibilities, combined with her access to Beijing's professional elite, allow her to criticize the planners' objectification of the city and neglect of its function as lived spaces. Her discussion of how large roads cut up the city echoes recent repugnance among planning circles toward the "wide rivers of asphalt."[87] In talking about her films, Ning repeatedly links planners' decisions and citizens' daily experience. Aware that Beijing's layout is the product of a unique city-scale plan, she sets special value in the architecture of the courtyard houses. She explains that the courtyards constituted retreats within the city. Their walls provided visual and acoustic protection that was violated once the second ring road was elevated, rising above the courtyards and subjecting them to noise and outside gazes.

Ning returns to the courtyard house in *Perpetual Motion* (2005). By the early twenty-first century, only a few hundred fully preserved courtyards, such as the one in which the entire film takes place, remained in the entire city. These courtyards stay intact in the midst of modern development, usually protected by their owners' high status (*Perpetual Motion* was shot in the courtyard abode of Zhang Hanzhi, Mao's personal translator and the widow of former Foreign Affairs Minister Qian Guanhua). Such miniature architectural reservations are jokingly referred to as "bonsai landscapes" (*penjing*). As Daniel Abramson observes, the gentrified courtyard houses are becoming a curiosity of little relevance to modern city life, "doomed to an unusually extreme kind of museumization."[88] Ning Ying is keenly aware of Beijing's destruction by dismantlement into preserved enclaves.

Ning underlines the changes in the rules and regulations that govern the city. *On the Beat* dwells on the role of the neighborhood committee in advising and monitoring the residents; the film also shows a hunt for pet dogs, prohibited by a recent policy. Urban films have repeatedly used the topic to foreground the tension between government and residents. Regulations against household animals and pets as part of the campaign "to keep the capital clean and beautiful," are featured in *Sunset Street*; the later *Cala My Dog* (2003), directed by Lu Xuechang, revolves around a police roundup of unlicensed dogs. Such details draw attention to the transformation of urban institutions. *I Love Beijing* also illustrates the transition, this time through a taxi drivers' meeting, which shows the cabbies—once under strict control—as indifferent and irreverent toward their superiors. The city is fraying at its architectural and social edges.

Ning Ying's films show Beijing in its messy complexity through seemingly unscripted camera work. As she notes, filming a version of the city with which she could identify, rather than a sterile representation, encountered two obstacles: the vestiges of Maoist aesthetics as upheld by censors and the market economy as promoted by investors. Unlike the many productions that feature beautiful, intact courtyards (such as *Farewell My Concubine*), Ning seeks to portray the ubiquitous derelict structures in danger of demolition. Her approach to urban issues has set her on a path of consistent confrontation with the censors. For her feature films, Ning has chosen to operate within the state system, although she has touched on even more controversial subjects in documentaries produced for U.N. agencies. Her films must therefore be approved by the State Administration of Radio, Film, and Television. As Ning explains, any film about contemporary Beijing is examined carefully by the board. Certain topics and sites are considered out of bounds; the censors often question even specific framings and camera angles. *I Love Beijing* in particular encountered objections. The Chinese title had to be changed, since *I Love Beijing* sounded too ironic; the traffic gridlock sequence that opens the film was deemed too negative; even the shots of morning exercise in a public park suggested to the censors an allusion to a nationwide psychosis. The final cut is relatively fast-paced, thanks to the censors' demand to excise entire shots and shorten others. The authorities' touchiness about Ning's faithful portrayal of urban material shows the high stakes in making such films.

The Beijing trilogy demonstrates the urgency of documenting urban change. The portrayal of subject matter such as police regulations and condemned houses, foregrounding the urban policies and their aftermath, reflects an ethical choice on the part of the director. The commitment to create a visual record is tantamount to turning filmmaking into memory work.

In elevating demolition to a metaphor, the cinema joins other media, such as photography, installations, performance art, and video. Notably, Zhan Wang's "Ruin Cleaning Project" (1994) "restored" a building designated for demolition and already half-destroyed. Photographs by the avant-garde artist Rong Rong capture torn-down structures and focus on mutilated pinup pictures in the debris. The vanishing urban spaces may be said to hold up to the viewer images that have already internalized their own ruin.[89] Another artist, Wang Jinsong, produced the series *One Hundred Signs of Demolition* (1999), which juxtaposes one hundred photos of the sign *chai* painted on houses to be demolished. Wang sees these signs as temporal marks that designate the liminal space between destruction and rebuilding.[90] In many cases, the multimedia works on demolition rely on photography, whether unprocessed or digitally manipulated, presented on its own merit or documenting performance art. Insofar as demolition sites encapsulate the ruin of memory, the camera becomes the only means of stopping or at least slowing down the process of forgetting.

Expanding on the photographic imagination, films feature demolition in many locations to refer to social issues at large. The last sequence in *Dirt* (1994) interjects shots of a Beijing demolition site in conjunction with the dissolution of a group of rebellious youth. Jia Zhangke's *Xiao Wu* (1997)— set in Fengyang, Shanxi, and based on a factual event—uses the demolition of a street of karaoke bars to emphasize the protagonist's sense of abandonment and betrayal.[91] The theme continues to haunt all of Jia's films up until *Still Life* (2006), shot in the Three Gorges area, and *24 City* (2008). Zhang Yuan's *Seventeen Years* (1999), set in Tianjin, alludes through the images of a demolished district to the force of postsocialist capitalism and the suppression of its devastating social effects. Huo Jianqi's *Life Show* (2000) traces a woman's fight for independence while her food stall is menaced by demolition (the plot is based on a controversial incident in which more than one hundred stalls in Wuhan's Jiqing Street were torn down on September 5, 1995). Beijing remains the predominant setting: the last shot in the original cut of *Happy Times* (2000) is situated in a demolition site, adding a hollow ring to the promise of a better future for the laid-off workers of a dissolved work unit. Li Shaohong's *Baober in Love* (2004) traces a young woman's suicidal thoughts to a childhood trauma of demolition-and-relocation (fig. 39). Yang Yazhou's *Loach Is a Fish, Too* (2005) stresses the disorientation of

39 *Baober in Love* (2004): A cityscape enhanced by computer-generated imaging transforms in seconds before the eyes of the traumatized girl. Courtesy of Li Shaohong.

migrant workers through poignant shots of renovating a site reminiscent of the Forbidden City and the parallel demolition of the migrants' shack. These and other films find in demolition a vehicle for expressing their concern about the erasure of the city's material and social structures.

THE LIMITS OF PUBLIC DEBATE

The proliferation of images of demolition attests to a heightened awareness, but not to a delusion that the cinema can change government policies or tip the balance of the urban contract in the residents' favor. The fate of Zhang Yuan's 1998 documentary *Demolition-and-Relocation* is a case in point. Zhang took advantage of the fact that he was living in Picai Alley, just northwest of Xidan, in an area to be torn down. Like all residents, he was constantly in touch with the Relocation Office (*Fangbansuo*) about receiving appropriate compensation for his two-room courtyard house. He knew neighbors willing to be filmed and was able to shoot fragments every now and then for over a year. Following the same "thematic documentary" approach and *xianchang* aesthetics that he had used in *The Square* (1994), Zhang created a slice-of-life record of living through the process of demolition-and-relocation. The film goes through each stage, from the announcement of pending demolition, to negotiation for new housing, to dealing with the threats of employees sent by the developer, to packing one's belongings, to moving into a new house. Zhang focuses on an old woman refusing to move, a "stuck-nail tenant," who is eventually evacuated forcefully (yet in compliance with the law). Zhang hoped that the documentary would run on TV stations and raise consciousness of the brutality with which developers treat residents. Yet TV stations refused to broadcast the film, which has to this date never been screened officially in the PRC. Zhang believes that the documentary could have had an impact. He became frustrated and decided that filmmaking of this sort was useless, since it could not stand up to the laws of the land.[92] Films were good for keeping a visual record, but not for countering the combined power of state authority and developers' capital.

The case of Zhang's *Demolition-and-Relocation* evidences how the cinema has been blocked from intervening directly in urban policy. While films such as Ning Ying's Beijing trilogy were testing the limits of what could be represented and preserved onscreen, filmmakers were barred from joining other public intellectuals in challenging government measures. The authorities ensured that relevant decisions would remain their prerogative and confined debate to professional planning circles. By 2003 reportage and discussion of demolition-and-relocation had been banned altogether.[93] Public discussion of the merits and drawbacks of preservation strategy was stifled. Films and other visual documentation of urban development have never been given the stage necessary to change current policies.

Filmmakers' circumspect engagement with the preservation discourse and their negligible impact on policy should be understood in the context of the limited effect of other intellectuals' appeal to public opinion and the media. I described the efforts of well-connected preservationists, such as Shu Yi, in chapter 3. Other attempts have been made by planners, such as the collective research that resulted in Fang Ke's dissertation, published in 2000, which contains evidence of policymakers' collusion with entrepreneurs in disregard of construction ordinances.[94] Fang's study is known to English readers through Ian Johnson's journalistic account, which describes it in heroic terms. Fang's achievement notwithstanding, it should be kept in mind that his book is not defiant but rather seeks a practical balance between political power and community-oriented planning.[95] Public debate seems to have made an impact on preservation only when combined with delicate negotiation with the authorities. Examples include projects by scholars at Tsinghua University in Beijing and Tongji University in Shanghai; journalistic work such as that of Wang Jun, a senior reporter at Xinhua News Agency and the author of a book on urban planning in Beijing in the early 1950s;[96] and the grassroots organization by activists such as Hua Xin-min, who has rallied support for preserving Beijing's courtyard houses.

One of the most adept people at using the media is the writer Feng Jicai, who became involved in urban preservation projects in the mid-1990s. When the old city of his native Tianjin was about to be torn down in 1994, Feng invited one hundred photographers to take pictures for a book that became the most complete record of the now-demolished quarters.[97] Other projects headed by Feng, such as a book involving an expert evaluation of each building in the city's old international concession, contributed to pro-tecting the area. Feng's books, unlike many nostalgic publications, do not prettify the buildings but rather urge respect for historic heritage. Most prominently, Feng has used his renown to protect Tianjin's Guyi Street, a commercial venue with a seven-hundred-year history and buildings dating to the early twentieth century. In his prolonged battle over the project with the municipal government, which issued a demolition order in December 1999, Feng turned to local and national media and organized resident pro-tests.[98] The campaign to save Guyi Street should be considered a milestone in mobilizing public opinion for urban preservation.[99] Although in the end Feng could not save the street, his work has created an accessible repository of visual memory. Feng says he is motivated by a sense of responsibility and urgency about the need to enhance popular awareness in the face of rapid and irreversible damage to China's cultural heritage.

Looking back at the Guyi Street campaign, Feng Jicai notes that it may have failed because fellow intellectuals did not support it. The novelist Zhang Xianliang, for example, said dismissively that while the common people lacked good houses to live in, Feng Jicai was busy appreciating ornamental architectural carvings. Even Liu Xinwu, a proponent of preserving old Bei-jing, claimed that demolishing early twentieth-century buildings in Tianjin was the precondition to progress. In Feng's eyes, such attacks are based on the same erroneous definition of culture that has guided the decision mak-ers. Directors such as Ning Ying and Zhang Yuan are the film world's equivalents of Feng—they aim to preserve the culture of the everyday, which does not enjoy the aura of century-old monuments. Policymakers ignorant of the cultural value of daily life and who have a vested interest in development bar filmmakers from accessing large audiences and stirring up debate. Inso-far as the cinema has impacted public opinion, it has done so through more commercial, lighthearted productions.

By the late 1990s, a number of factors had converged to create a new discursive environment. Political suppression of public debate intensified, but the sense of urgency for preservation increased. Beijing's twenty-year master plan, approved in 1993, laid the groundwork for modern development such as the Central Business District, but it also recognized the need for preservation, as part of turning the capital into a global city in time for the 2008 Olympics.[100] At the same time, disenchantment with elitist didacticism and the rise of commercial cinema, competing with the exposure to Hollywood productions, gave rise to entertainment-oriented movies. The grainy, hard-edged films of the Sixth Generation gave way to slick productions that celebrate the city and exploit the urban subaltern, in particular migrant workers, for melodramatic effect.

The commercially motivated trend known as New Urban Cinema (*xin chengshi dianying*) turned to feel-good films. The term was first promoted in early 2000, in publicity material and soon after in the journal *Popular Cinema* (*Dazhong dianying*). Essays credited New Urban Cinema with boosting box office revenues, claiming the popularity of *Poetic Times* (1999), Zhang Yuan's *Seventeen Years*, and Ning Ying's *I Love Beijing*.[101] The distinctions among "main melody" (*zhuxuanlü*) state propaganda, "art films" (*yishu pian*), and commercial "entertainment films" (*yule pian*) were becoming obsolete,[102] and New Urban Cinema further blurred the boundaries between highbrow avant-garde and market-oriented popular films. The critic Ling Yan (riffing on an earlier essay by Ni Zhen) found in films such as *Spicy Love Soup* (1997), *Beautiful New World* (1998), and *Love in the Internet Age* (1999) "myths for the new urban citizens."[103] Similar themes were also explored by more veteran directors such Zhang Yimou (in *Happy Times* [2000]) and previously experimental filmmakers like Wang Xiaoshuai (in *Beijing Bicycle* [2001]). Directors started to describe themselves as belonging to a generation of urban sensibilities.[104] The commercial aspect was emphasized by Zhang Yibai, the director of *Spring Subway* (2002), who claimed that his film, as New Urban Cinema, aimed at "reflecting and discovering the aesthetics of modern city life"; for Zhang, New Urban Cinema was the new mainstream.[105] The genre enjoyed the avant-garde aura of earlier urban films but did not commit itself to the same rhetoric of alienation and dissent.

On the one hand, New Urban Cinema as a whole takes few political risks. The trend fits in with the policy of giving cities brand-name recognition; there are even "main melody" New Urban films, such as *Bright Heart* (2002).[106] On the other hand, the commercial success of these productions allows filmmakers to touch on sensitive topics—for example, Zhang Yimou's *Happy Times* (2000) takes place at a defunct work unit and Feng Xiaogang's *Cell Phone* (2003) revolves around marital betrayal. The movies are both celebratory and mournful of the increasingly materialistic urban life. New Urban Cinema offers bittersweet depictions of dissolving social institutions, touching on employment instability, crumbling marriages, and households subjected to demolition-and-relocation.

A vivid and witty portrayal of the lifestyle wiped out by demolition-and-relocation, in the vein of New Urban Cinema, is found in *A Tree in House* (1999), directed by Yang Yazhou, who had previously collaborated with Huang Jianxin on four urban-theme films.[107] *A Tree in House* is based on Liu Heng's entertaining short story "The Happy Life of Chatterbox Zhang Damin" (1998) and stars the popular comedian Feng Gong. This commercial crowd pleaser relies on lowbrow humor and sharp quips. Feng, who received the Golden Rooster Award for this role, remakes the protagonist Zhang Damin, portrayed in Liu Heng's text as a witty half-wit, into a good-hearted and resourceful character. As the eldest of the five Zhang siblings who live with their mother, Damin resolves family trouble, the most urgent of which is their housing plight.

The film is set in contemporary Tianjin, and the opening sequence captures in multiple high-angle shots the old residential quarters of the city that Feng Jicai has been trying to preserve. The Zhangs live in a two-room house in an old courtyard, akin to the Beijing-style courtyard house. Since the siblings cannot afford to move out, once they start marrying space becomes increasingly tight. Elaborate scenes detail the calculation of every inch and the placement of flimsy partitions to protect a semblance of privacy. Damin uses the makeshift measures that have characterized inner city residences. The film's English title refers to Damin's eventual solution of building an additional room in the inner yard, around an old locust tree. Through underhanded negotiation with his neighbors, Damin gets their permission to tear down the outer yard wall and shift it into the public thoroughfare. The new space spares the Zhangs further conflict and provides room for a child. As with most courtyard houses in Chinese cities, the architectural integrity is sacrificed for more pressing needs.

The tree acquires a symbolic meaning as a marker of Damin's attachment to the old house. Damin avoids cutting down the tree not only because of the one-thousand-RMB fine involved but also because he wants to protect the tree. (The film resonates with the preservation of locust trees as part of the Ju'er Hutong project, discussed in chapter 3.) Zhang and his wife decorate the trunk, which sticks out from the middle of their bed, and wrap it in cloth. They name their son Little Tree, signaling the common destiny shared by the courtyard and its residents.

The promise of an organic bond between the family and its home is broken when the family is forced to move into a new apartment building. The film avoids showing the demolition, focusing instead on Damin's emotional reaction when he sees the new place for the first time—"The tree is gone," he says. The comment, expressing Damin's sense of loss, is typical of his seemingly idiotic yet meaningful chatter. After the move, the son's name, Little Tree, becomes an empty sign, the only reminder of the yard in which he grew up. In the concluding shot, Damin shoulders his son and expresses his wish that the child will grow up "without worries" (the colloquial phrase *meishi touzhele* is the film's Chinese title). The ending, despite its hopeful tone, alludes to the older generation's sense of dislocation.

A Tree in House does not criticize demolition-and-relocation explicitly, yet the images underscore the abrupt and disorienting change. When Damin refuses to sign a letter conceding his rights to the old place, turning into a potential "stuck-nail tenant," he is arrested. The demolition proceeds during his incarceration. As soon as Damin is released from jail, he moves into the family's new apartment. The ellipsis is emphasized in the editing, cutting from the street brawl with the developer's representatives directly to Damin's exit from prison. The gate closes behind, placing him in front of a black background. The past is symbolically shut off and erased forever. Even more than Zhang Yuan's never-released *Demolition-and-Relocation*, *A Tree in House* presents the long-duration view of urban redevelopment—lingering on life at the old location, the forced evacuation, and the accommodation to the new quarters. Since Yang Yazhou's movie adopted a humorous tone, it was approved for distribution and gained popularity. The film may, however, be read as a condemnation of official policy for failing to acknowledge the social alienation that accompanies demolition-and-relocation.

Yang's successful film inspired other work. Within a year, Beijing TV produced a series including twenty episodes and bearing the title of the originary short story, "The Happy Life of Chatterbox Zhang Damin." The story line is similar to the film's, adding episodes which seem inspired by *Red Suit* (1998). The stretched and diluted melodrama lacks the film's critical edge, however. Zhang Damin's house is placed this time in Beijing, exhibiting little local color (*A Tree in House* stresses the Tianjin location by using the local dialect). The series ends just before the family's potentially traumatic move to a new apartment. The saccharine conclusion, in which Damin's siblings are reminded of their past and recognize the elder brother's sacrifice, serves only to reaffirm the present and avoid the controversial aspects of demolition-and-relocation.

Some of the critical edge of the original film is retained in the silver-screen sequel, *Ordinary People's Life* (2000). Although released as a New Year's comedy, the Chinese title, literally "a beautiful home," is clearly sarcastic. Damin (played this time by Liang Guanhua) faces a series of setbacks at the new apartment, including leaking pipes, uncooperative neighbors, and a fraudulent remodeling contractor. Although the film suffers from the same slow pace and flat dialogues that plague the TV series, it is noteworthy for depicting the problems often faced by residents of new housing projects. Botched relocation has sparked widespread unrest. Residents sometimes find that their new homes lack title registration or are poorly constructed. Newspaper articles have suggested that the new houses are no better than the old buildings evacuated for being unsafe.[108] *Ordinary People's Life* moves beyond trauma and nostalgia to the down-to-earth problems of living in new housing.

URBAN MEMORY IN THE AGE OF ITS DIGITAL REPRODUCIBILITY
The cinematic contribution to urban discourse took new paths not only as a result of the rise of commercial cinema but also in response to the introduction of new digital media. Chinese documentary filmmakers have widely used camcorders since the 1980s and digital video (DV) since 1998.[109] DV was used for numerous records of demolition-and-relocation, such as Xu Dawei's *Requiem* (2001), a three-screen artistic rendering of demolition near Wangfujing. The advent of new media has forced filmmakers using traditional technology to contemplate the role of widespread and affordable formats in the collective effort to create visual repositories of memory. The appearance of cameras and camcorders on the screen, as part of the plot, may be read as a symptom of the growing awareness of the cinema's role in urban preservation.

Some films have referred to recording devices explicitly. *Suzhou River* is

40 *A Tree in House* (1999): The traditional "happy family" photograph has been substituted by real-time video recording.

told from the viewpoint of a cinematographer, who makes the sarcastic comment, "My camera doesn't lie." In other cases, the camera remains purportedly tangential to the plot, but its presence has disturbing implications. In *A Tree in House*, Damin's wedding celebration is attended also by a video cameraman, presumably hired to record the occasion (fig. 40). The scene draws attention to the fact that videos have replaced "happy family" (*quanjiafu*) still photos in marking such occasions and in shaping personal memories. Another example is found in the concluding sequence of *Stand Up, Don't Stoop* (1992). The Gaos leave their old apartment for a newly built condo. They are forced out by a bullying neighbor who takes over their apartment to tear down the separating wall, a situation reminiscent of forced demolition-and-relocation. At the last minute, a photographer is called in; the residents pose for the camera in recognition of the importance of the moment, and the photo is intended as a souvenir of the old house and neighbors (the custom of taking a photo in front of one's home before it is demolished is known also from other times and places;[110] it is featured also in *My Whispering Plan*, as discussed in chapter 5). Even though the relocation has not taken place yet, nostalgia has already set in, and a photo is required as a testimony to the harmonious living that has never existed. Insofar as the cameraman in this episode stands for the filmmaker chronicling demolition-and-relocation, his awkward work as he slips on a banana peel leaves a laughable, partial, and imperfect record.

The role of digital media in recording the urban transformation is explored in *Love in the Internet Age* (1999), mentioned by critics as a prominent example of New Urban Cinema. Divided into three parts, the film follows two Beijingers from their youth as students in 1988, to marriage in 1993, to blasé businesspeople in 1998. The likes of the protagonists Binzi and Maomao took part in the democracy movement of 1989, felt dislocated in the early 1990s, and ended up a few years later as the backbone of the new high-tech enterprises. For a short while, the independent film enjoyed cult status for encapsulating the spirit of the 1990s.[111]

The social change is also encoded in the spaces that the characters inhabit, from a dormitory in the first part, to a courtyard house in the second, to high-rises in the third. When the woman protagonist, Maomao, returns from the United States in 1998, she finds out that her former courtyard house has been razed to make way for a wider thoroughfare. "Everyone says it's going to be the road to prosperity," says Binzi with irony. The smartly clad woman stands at the demolished site, new buildings looming in the background, and takes a last shot of the place with her camcorder. Maomao's nonchalant gesture of whipping out the camcorder is a belated and ineffective attempt to stop the process of forgetting. Together with other failures to preserve a reliable memory in digital form—in audio files, a manipulated photograph, and e-mail—Maomao's amateur filmmaking shows the limitations of the new media as a viable form of recordkeeping.[112]

The demolition site and the camcorder are paired again in one of the most successful movies of the period, Zhang Yang's *Shower* (1999). The film focuses on the need of the protagonist, Liu Daming (played by Pu Cunxin), to come to terms with his family and childhood friends in an old Beijing neighborhood. After Daming reconciles with his aging father (Zhu Xu), the father unexpectedly dies, leaving Daming to take care of his mentally retarded younger brother Erming (Jiang Wu). Daming gradually learns to accept responsibility and to recognize his affection for his father and brother.

The story line finds architectural expression in identifying the father with Beijing traditions and his death with the city's demolition. The father lives in the old city (much of the shoot took place at the Shichahai area) and runs a traditional bathhouse, where people, mostly of the father's generation, come to relax and socialize, indulging in pastimes such as listening to opera, playing chess, and watching cricket fights. The bathhouse, like the elderly people's club in *For Fun,* becomes a symbol for communal cohesion. The psychologically soothing power of bathing is emphasized by comparing it to purifying rituals in the remote areas of Shaanxi and Tibet and contrasting it with Daming's habit of taking short showers. The film's opening credit sequence shows a man entering a fictional computerized shower booth that operates with the impersonal precision of a car wash. In the bathhouse, Daming immerses himself in the communal tub and washes away his alienated Shenzhen businessman mentality. He helps the father in mending the bathhouse roof during a stormy night—old houses are like old people, says the father. The bathhouse acquires a symbolic function, a nostalgic reference to the capital's disappearing neighborhoods and the old people who lived in them.[113]

Soon after the father dies, the bathhouse and much of the neighborhood are torn down (the original script describes the father's death as a reaction to the news that the place is going to be dismantled; the explicit condemnation of demolition was censored). Lengthy shots show the process of razing the structures. The director, Zhang Yang, who grew up in a courtyard house in the Shichahai area that was demolished in 1999, sees the plot as a reflection of his personal experience. Zhang's father was glad to give up his run-down home in exchange for an apartment in the three modern, six-story buildings that were erected on the same site. Yet the director laments the drastic transformation of Beijing since the early 1990s. Zhang notes that the courtyard houses were part of the century-old integral city plan, on a par with the imperial compounds, and comments: "The high-rises have gradually crushed the [old] city into an increasingly smaller place, until it has disappeared altogether."[114] The film underscores the sense of loss, as the residents go their own ways to unknown destinations and destinies—earlier, the bathhouse regulars note that some crickets were crushed to death during demolition, while others did not survive the relocation to an apartment building; by implication, the old men might suffer similar fates.

In a last attempt to keep a memento of their neighborhood, the old residents take a camcorder and chronicle the demolition process. They film from a tricycle—in fact, a common practice in low-budget documentaries such as *The Square* and *There Is a Strong Wind in Beijing.* A point-of-view shot, moving across a swath of debris, accentuates the magnitude of the demolition project, while the shaky image alludes to the amateur cameraman's intimate familiarity with the territory. Like the group photo in *Stand*

41 *Shower* (1999): The old residents use a camcorder to record their neighborhood during demolition.

Up, Don't Stoop, nostalgia sets in already at the moment of relocation, and the residents use the camcorder to chronicle the disappearing city (fig. 41). As in *Love in the Internet Age*, they are too late to capture the old abodes; they film the already-destroyed site.

The bathhouse patrons also film their old haunt being torn down. The camera's presence is foregrounded by a point-of-view shot of an elderly man approaching the camera and looking straight at it, as if suspicious of the new gadget's intrusion. They proceed to film Erming singing "O sole mio," a passionate adieu to the spaces being dismantled. The film's last shot zooms in on Erming. It is another point-of-view shot—this time the camera's mediation is stressed by the preceding close-up of the camcorder and the slow adjustment of focus. Zhang Yang's lens is one with the camcorder's, implying that the director shares the residents' attempt at chronicling the demolition. *Shower*, as a commercial film, takes up the task of home videos, distributing the images of urban change and showing the loss entailed in demolition-and-relocation.

Shower not only foregrounds the major stakes in the cinematic portrayal of predemolition Beijing and the post-relocation doldrums; it also brings together the issues that have preoccupied stage and silver-screen productions since the founding of the PRC. *Shower* may be viewed as a filmic variation on the BPAT productions discussed in chapter 3. The dialogues among the old bathhouse regulars resonate strongly with Beijing-flavor plays of the 1990s, such as *Bird Men*. (The connection is only natural, considering that the director Zhang Yang graduated from the Central Drama Academy of Drama and that two lead actors, Zhu Xu and Pu Cunxin, are affiliated with BPAT.) Moreover, *Shower* may be paying tribute to Lao She's *Dragon Whisker Creek*. Both *Dragon Whisker Creek* and *Shower* feature mentally challenged persons (Madman Cheng and Erming), who express their emotions in song. Yet whereas *Dragon Whisker Creek* concludes with Madman Cheng's ode to "new China, new Beijing," Ermin's swan song for the disappearing old Beijing bears witness to the environmental and social breakdown at the turn of the twenty-first century. *Dragon Whisker Creek* projects an idealized future; *Shower* laments the demise of an urban community that with its last breath creates a visual record of itself.

THE DOCUMENTARY IMPULSE AS GRAPHOMANIA

Shower points to the potential of the documentary impulse to elicit an information explosion, which forces us to rethink the nature and goals of filmmaking. In its radical manifestations, the documentary impulse may turn films from distilled parables to attempts to recreate reality on a scale of one to one, keeping a record of each urban location at each point in time. What started with Zheng Dongtian's relatively timid experimentation in documentary realism and Ning Ying's version of neorealism may be taking the form of an unedited and decentralized archive, the sum total of private citizens' footage of their neighborhoods' transformation.

The democratization of the image is already underway. Records of urban change are increased manyfold when numberless citizens own camcorders, keep day-by-day visual chronicles, and often post them online. Zhang Yuan's 1998 experiment, filming the demolition-and-relocation of the alley in which he was living, was more easily replicated a few years later. Shu Haolun's *Nostalgia* (2006), for example, documents the community where he grew up in the 1970s and '80s. It is a record of life in the unique architecture of Shanghai's *longtang*—colonial-period townhouses that open onto common lanes. Shu shot the film while aware that his longtang, like many around it, was slated for imminent demolition, and the film is permeated with a sense of displacement and disappearance. Shu, prodded into filmmaking because of his personal attachment to the doomed spaces, is conscious of his function as archivist.

Whereas Shu presents his project in neutral terms, as a nostalgic rumina-

42.1 & 42.2 *Meishi Street* (2006): Zhang Li covers his house with posters protesting the impending demolition and continues to shoot as the demolition crew approaches. Courtesy of Ou Ning and Cao Fei.

tion on the past, others use the camera to confront the predatory official discourse and practice. An example of aggressive visual recordkeeping is found in *Meishi Street* (2006).[115] The film focuses on the demolition in preparation for widening Coal Market Street, in Beijing's Dashalan'r (Dazhalan) neighborhood (in the Outer City, immediately southwest of Tiananmen Square). The documentary is a collaborative project overseen, produced, and edited by the visual artists Ou Ning and Cao Fei, who also provided additional camera work. The bulk of the material, however, was shot by Coal Market Street resident Zhang Jinli, who used a camcorder offered by Ou and Cao to chronicle his protest as a "stuck-nail tenant" up until the demolition of his house on October 21, 2005. Although Zhang explains that the film is a record that he will be able to watch decades from now, he is acutely aware of the present. Protesting the municipal policy and contributing to the film are inextricable from each other.

Zhang's filmic and nonfilmic activities alike may be described as graphomaniacal. Zhang provides meticulous visual evidence of every stage of his protest, his interaction with the authorities, and the measures taken by the police. Whenever he lays down his camera, he seems to be taking up his brush. He gives a full account of his violated property rights on large canvasses and paper posters. A large sign towers over Zhang's shop front, and the door is flanked by posters in the manner of a poetic couplet. A mannequin torso hangs from the eaves, wearing a T-shirt with more writing. The posters blend in with the writing by the authorities announcing the demolition. The windows are pasted with more papers in Zhang's handwriting, detailing Mao's protective policies ignored by the current government; other sheets cover almost every wall, exterior and interior, of Zhang's house. The posters claim that the demolition company has falsified documents, that the compensation is calculated according to obsolescent land survey data, and that the building lies partly outside the zone designated for demolition. The out-of-control proliferation of signs only underscores the predictable futility of Zhang's protest. Likewise, his incessant filming—of the house, of crowds looking on, of other acts of demolition, and finally of his house's destruction —may be taken for an obsession (fig. 42). Although the documentary as edited by Ou Ning and Cao Fei provides a clear and concise narrative, the images speak of an effusive joy in the act of filming, akin to Zhang's prolific calligraphy.

Zhang Jinli's calligraphic and filmic graphomania is an extreme case of the documentary impulse. Much like Zhang's posters, urban films offer formal supplications, intransigent protest, and architectural archives all at the same time. In pasting the posters all over the house designated for demolition, Zhang turns it into a treasury of historical and legal documents. Zhang is partly motivated by spite, flaunting his helplessness, but seems also to hope the calligraphy can provide a talismanic protective power. Likewise, the movies discussed in this chapter take urban architecture for the ultimate and final signifier of collective memory, repeatedly inscribing its image onto film.

SEVEN

The Day Trip of Your Dreams

Globalizing Beijing and the Postspatial City

IN THE YEARS leading to the 2008 Olympic Games, Beijing policy-makers were preoccupied with ensuring a well-run event and leveraging it to enhance the city's functionality and appeal to international investors. The infrastructure around the sports facilities would be the foundation for a multicentered metropolis, with widened arteries, larger shopping centers, and extended subway lines. The Olympics were seen as an opportunity to forge the city's image as a showcase for a wealthy nation and stable society under the government of the Communist Party. The marketing campaign of Beijing Municipality had called for a "green Olympics," a "high-tech Olympics" and a "humanistic Olympics." A 2002 essay collection undertook to fill the slogan "humanistic Olympics" with content; those attending the games would witness a city with a state-of-the-art transportation system, leisure centers such as Jianguomen and Sanlitun, and streamlined services to feed the hundreds of thousands of visitors. In addition to logistical improvements, policies aimed at human engineering—changing bad habits such as spitting, jaywalking, and insufficient smiling, as well as raising citizens' ethics and "human quality" (*suzhi*), and increasing their "global consciousness." Beijingers would bolster these traits with a heightened understanding of their city as a "historic site" (*lishi mingsheng*), enriched by a long heritage of urban planning. The preservation of imperial relics, vernacular architecture, and local way of life, or "Beijing-flavor culture" (*Jingwei wenhua*) was now a priority. Although politicians had often used the rhetoric of preservation and historical consciousness to suit their interests (see chapter 3), the "humanistic Olympics" slogan undeniably precipitated the restoration of relics, the organization of permanent and touring exhibitions, and the launch of education programs to make Beijingers of all ages experts on their cultural patrimony.[1] The Olympics not only changed Beijing; in many ways they reinvented the city.

The combination of sports, media, transnational capital, and urban policy—now a staple of international sporting events—appeared with a new twist in the Beijing Olympics, probably the first to be promoted directly through film and paracinematic events. Already in 2000, the TV miniseries *Count Me In* featured cameo appearances by many celebrities to support the Olympic bid made a year later. The film used the slogan that would later appear in media campaigns—"Count Me In for Volunteering for the Olympics"—to mobilize citizens' goodwill when Beijing would host the International Olympic Committee (IOC), at a time when many residents were doubting the benefit of the games for the average citizen.[2] To woo the IOC, the Chinese authorities commissioned a short from the internationally renowned film director Zhang Yimou (of *Raise the Red Lantern* fame). The clip—rumored to be the result of the officials' vision more than Zhang's—was a mishmash that boasted of the capital as a meeting place of business and pleasure, old and ultramodern architecture, local customs and global economy. The clip used visual clichés such as elderly people playing chess by Qianhai Lake juxtaposed with McDonald's golden arches. Zhang's contribution to the successful bid was rewarded when he was also assigned to choreograph the games' opening ceremony. The Chinese media played up Zhang's role—when Zhang sought the help of Steven Spielberg (who later resigned over China's Darfur policy), the Hollywood director was cast as Zhang's assistant, symbolizing China's rise to power. Zhang designed the opening ceremony as a sound-and-light extravaganza, including multiple screens—a live cinematic event that spilled into the city.

The promotion for the Olympics redefined the cinematic creative process as more than the production, screening, and interpretation of the filmic artifact. His expertise in creating mass spectacles has made Zhang an influential broker of Beijing's economy and culture to the world. As the crafter of Beijing's official image, Zhang in his recent career is exemplary of the key role filmmakers have taken in steering the city's transformation, and in particular its integration into the global economy.

This chapter addresses the response in films and filmmaking practices to Beijing's urban transformation since the late 1980s, hand in hand with the city's rise to a hub of the global economy. Globalization is not an indiscriminate force of nature; rather, entering the global economy has been encouraged and regulated by national and municipal policies. Similar integration with the global economy has been implemented in other Chinese cities, notably Shanghai, yet in Beijing the connection between urban restructuring and cultural engineering is especially salient.[3] Whereas the capital previously served primarily as a national center—with an emphasis on production since the 1950s and on culture since the 1980s—the national and municipal governments have taken measures since the mid-1990s to strengthen Beijing's ties with metropolitan centers around the world, seeking to make it a "global city."[4] The most visible of these steps both were taken in 2001, when China became a member of the World Trade Organization (WTO) and won the bid for the 2008 Olympics. The dynamics of globalization—reliance on international investment, on the one hand, and outsourcing manual labor, on the other—change the city's culture. Urban space turns into a commodity, marketed through iconic landmarks, brand-name architecture, and theme parks. These commodified spaces not only appear in films but also allude to a new relationship between the cinema and urban development, based on a shared entrepreneurial paradigm.

My main interest in this chapter is not to outline the new business models of filmmaking in China or the emergence of a distinct urban identity in film. Valuable studies have already addressed these issues.[5] Rather, I point out the changing role of the cinema in the urban contract—the way filmmakers act as intermediaries in the process of forging the city. The subjection of Beijing's development to global market dynamics allowed a new element to enter the fray, namely, local and international real estate moguls. These powerful developers coerce decision makers, recruit architects, and become role models for cultural producers. Whereas until the late 1990s directors negotiated principally between government agencies as the sole decision makers and the residents as the subjects of official policy, now filmmakers—like professional planners and other participants in the urban discourse—have to take into account private developers as a separate and often dominant force. Directors not only collaborate with these entrepreneurs but also compare themselves to real estate developers, as promoters of a new vision of the city.

The filmmaker's role finds expression also in Beijing's cinematic image. The urban environment, as forged in many new films, is experienced in simulated and mediatized forms, such as role-playing games, animation, and the Internet. It is not simply a matter of representing the city through new media; rather, the city is shown to operate as a parallel reality. Whereas the official line is supported by an illusion of instant development (see chapter 3), and the detractors of urban policy often rely on preservation through documentation (see chapter 6), the more recent response has been to look beyond conventional conceptions of space. In reaction to the architectural models that idealize recent urbanism, some films push modeling practices until they implode into a self-referential and patently virtual realm. Planned urban growth and social interaction alike are shown to depend on a nonmaterial space-time—a *postspatial chronotope*.

My main example for the filmmaker's new role in relating to spaces commercialized to the point of existing only in simulated form is the work of Feng Xiaogang. Feng's breakthrough film, *Dream Factory* (1997), tells of a business providing "the day trip of your dreams" (*hao meng yiri you*), during which the client, for a substantial fee, will escape everyday city life and, for one day, be transported to a make-believe environment of his or her choice. At least as poignant is Feng's *Big Shot's Funeral* (2001), a self-reflexive piece on the role of filmmakers as market manipulators and cultural brokers. When the main characters, a film director and an advertising entrepreneur, mull over their friends' ironic criticism—"You should have been running the Olympics!"—the joke is on Zhang Yimou as well as on Feng Xiaogang himself, as incorrigible and proud participants in the cultural economy.

Feng's films give new meaning to what I described in the introduction as "painting the city red." Feng's oeuvre fully acknowledges the extent of Communist image making; in fact, his films of the 1990s are encyclopedic collections of paraphrases of official discourse. Yet Feng's direct quotes from, and oblique references to, the Communist canon are in the form of spoof and carnivalesque indulgence in the new possibilities of the postsocialist era. Such irreverence toward Maoist symbols can be found already in earlier Urban Cinema (see chapter 6). For example, the hoodlum protagonist of *Samsara* (1988) whistles the 1950s tune "Socialism Is Good" while painting his room red—yet his individualistic behavior, and the psychedelic red paint he uses, bear little relation to Communist ideals. The same man uses official slogans to laugh at his girlfriend's unkempt hair, reprimanding her: "And the citizens have taken such pains to put in order the city's appearance!" Urban policy is reduced to meaningless witticisms. Likewise, Feng Xiaogang's characters have the day of their dreams and a night on the town because they are acutely aware of, and irreverent toward, the vestiges of Maoist hues.

Emptying Maoist symbols of their previous significance is not only a symptom of postsocialist disenchantment; it also acknowledges an existence that lays no claim to reality and an urban environment that does not depend on material spaces. The interest in virtual spaces is evident in Jia Zhangke's *The World* (2004). *Big Shot's Funeral* and *The World* might seem like a strange pairing: whereas Feng Xiaogang's comedies aim at a large domestic audience and embrace capitalist enterprise, Jia Zhangke provides a sober and critical look at the global economy that attracts a much smaller number of film aficionados, many of them at international film festivals. Yet Feng's and Jia's films also mirror each other. *The World* describes a theme park advertised with the slogan, "Give us a day and we'll show you the world." Like *Dream Factory* and its promise of "the day trip of your dreams," *The World* centers on the commodified, time-bound illusion of traversing space. Jia's film differs by focusing on the underbelly of the global economy, in particular the migrant workers who harbor more modest, yet even less attainable, ambitions.

Placed side by side, *Big Shot's Funeral* and *The World* show that in Beijing any space can be had for the right price—from the Forbidden City to the Eiffel Tower. Yet neither space is, of course, truly up for sale, and the inevitable breakdown of illusion leads the citizens to take refuge in virtual spaces. The incorporation in the works examined in this chapter of text messages, Internet-based multiuser dungeons, Flash animation, and Second Life communities should be seen in light of the collapse of spatial hierarchy in the globalizing Beijing. The *postspatial chronotope* emphasizes that the city can now be visualized only as cinematic, devoid of any reference to material space.

The postspatial chronotope challenges not only perceptions of space but also the technologies and aesthetics of celluloid-based cinema. The last section of this chapter, which may also be read as an epilogue to the book, examines the computer-generated video artworks *Q3* (1999) and *I • Mirror* (2007) and their construction of virtual cities. The postspatial ushers in the postcinematic.

Beijing's entry into the global market or, in Chinese parlance, turning into an "international city," has been anticipated, outlined, and regulated by official policies. Beijing's master plan for 1991–2010, approved by the state in 1993, was ambitious and visionary, presenting an outline that sounded almost unattainable at the time for rethinking the city's infrastructure, functions, and public image. The plan reiterated the policy set in 1980 that designated Beijing as the country's political and cultural center, implicitly reversing the Maoist drive toward urban industrialization. Most important, the plan stressed the goal of "building an international city."[6] Long-term as it was, the plan inevitably was modified and contained erroneous predictions (for example, projecting a population of 12.5 million by 2010, whereas in fact, by some accounts, Beijing already had 17 million residents by 2007). Such errors notwithstanding, the plan is key to understanding not only the rise of Beijing to a world city but also the ideological framework that determined the path of its globalization.

The master plan shows sensitivity to the city's image and tries to reconcile the tension between economic and cultural considerations.[7] The plan carefully notes Beijing's importance both as a "modern international city" (*xiandai guoji chengshi*) and "an ancient capital of world renown" (*shijie zhuming de gudu*). In other words, globalization should not impede efforts at preservation but rather reinforce Beijing's identity. Beijing's "traditional flavor" is mentioned frequently, in an effort to "allow Beijing's development and construction to comport with the needs of modern life and work, and at the same time preserve its unique historical and cultural characteristics."[8] The question remains, however, how both aspects of the policy may be combined in practice.

To a large extent, the plan's mention of local flavor is at best wishful thinking. As I discussed in chapter 3, municipal authorities have endorsed the preservation of vernacular architecture only as long as it enhanced real estate value. Although Chinese scholars have debated the benefits of globalization,[9] decision makers have as a whole adopted a neoliberal line, regarding globalization as an inevitable and mostly desirable process. Already in 1986, the Land Administration Act commodified land use rights in urban areas to accommodate foreign investment.[10] The 1993 plan links entry into the global economy and subjecting real estate values to market forces.

The immediate and highly visible result of the policy delineated in the master plan was the construction of new centers that would attract international investment, such as the Central Business District (CBD), Zhongguan-cun (known as "China's Silicon Valley"), and the Olympic Village. A new class of planners and entrepreneurs emerged to facilitate the urban transformation, including the Chinese-born architect Yung Ho Chang and real estate developer SOHO China. In Beijing as elsewhere, globalization has meant tapping into two forces that could endanger the city's heritage: transnational capital and international culture.

A parallel policy encouraging entry into the global market, triggering a systemic upheaval and giving rise to celebrity entrepreneurs, was implemented in the film industry in the 1990s. A series of gradual reforms decentralized the control of production and distribution, starting with giving film studios autonomy from the China Film Corporation in the late 1980s, welcoming foreign investment beginning in the early 1990s, abolishing the monopoly of state-run studios in 2002, and allowing foreign equity participation in media companies in 2004.[11] Commercial directors such as Zhang Yimou, Chen Kaige, and Huang Jianxin lauded joining the WTO in 2001; the critic Zhang Boqing went as far as to defy those who cried wolf: "The 'wolves' have come. Let's wrestle with them, welcome them in, dance with them, take on the challenge!"[12]

The single most influential director in turning the film industry into a commercially viable endeavor was Feng Xiaogang. In 1996 the producer Han Sanping—then the head of the Beijing Film Studio—urged Feng to provide an alternative to the unprofitable, state-funded "main melody" propaganda films. In response, Feng adapted Wang Shuo's novel *You're No Common Person* (*Ni bushi yige suren*) into the successful *Dream Factory* (1997).[13] Feng marketed *Dream Factory* as the first made-in-PRC New Year's movie (*hesuipian*). The ploy of releasing a comic film for the Chinese New Year had become standard practice in Hong Kong since 1982. The Film Bureau introduced the term to the PRC market when distributing Jackie Chan's *Rumble in the Bronx* under this rubric in 1995.[14] Following the success of *Dream Factory*, Feng has turned out increasingly popular movies every Spring Festival. The New Year's movies mark the maturation of a commercial film industry that has grown independent of state sponsorship.

Filmmakers such as Feng, who no longer identify with a supporting state apparatus, have turned to emulating their commercial sponsors. They have taken over not only production but also promotion and public relations. The transformation may be gleaned, for example, from Zhang Yimou's 2003 advertisement for Toyota, prefaced by the slide "directed by Zhang Yimou" and bearing the director's signature. Feng Xiaogang has appeared in person in his TV commercials, starting with the 2002 ad for Wahaha bottled tea. In that clip, Feng joins the Hong Kong "comedy king" Stephen Chow Sing-chi (Zhou Xingchi) in spoofing the martial arts film genre.[15] Directors have turned their name recognition into selling power.

Real estate developers and filmmakers, having risen at the same time to economic power and cultural icon status, have found opportunities for collaboration; moreover, public opinion has cast them in similar roles. Popular parlance refers to high-profile directors and real estate moguls alike as *dawan'r*.

The term *dawan'r* (literally "great wrist") originated in the circles of vernacular performers and denoted skilled and reputed artists.[16] In contemporary language, the term designates high-level players who create and mold markets. Jing Wang has remarked that the dawan'r were empowered by the rise of the cultural economy (*wenhua jingji*) policy, which rendered cultural capital and economic capital interchangeable. As I showed in chapter 3, various municipalities proclaimed cultural economy as a policy in the mid-1990s. Beijing municipal authorities endorsed it in March 1996 to cash in on cultural references and enhance the monetary value of commercial projects. The dawan'r have formed a new elite of "cultural brokers"—as anthropologists call those whose knowledge allows them to mediate between groups of differing cultural backgrounds. They mediate among various strata of culture, giving the lie to the distinction between high and low culture or, for that matter, between the Marxist state and capitalist ventures as contradictory market forces.[17] Filmmakers—like their counterparts in music distribution, art exhibition, and literary promotion—have benefited from their skills as producers of works of wide appeal and from their proximity to intellectual circles. Directors have expanded their activities to the realm of public celebrity, serving as influential middlemen. Aided by the emergence of new paradigms of advertising in the mid-1990s, the dawan'r packaged globalization in cultural terms, making commercial products more profitable.[18]

Cultural economy should not, however, be regarded only as cynical manipulation. Some directors have reflected on the consumerist society that created their new status. New Urban Cinema pieces (see chapter 6), including films by former iconoclasts—such as Wang Xiaoshuai's *Beijing Bicycle*

(2001) and Zhang Yuan's *Green Tea* (2003)—foreground the accelerated commercialization of urban spaces and the receding presence of Beijing's cultural heritage. Feng Xiaogang is of particular interest. Jason McGrath has noted that Feng's films provide "a reflexive commentary on the production and consumption of the very entertainment cinema" that they have exemplified and even generated.[19] *Big Shot's Funeral*, which bears the Chinese title *Dawan'r*, provides a wry portrayal of the protagonist—a filmmaker, advertising entrepreneur, and spatial manipulator—as a cultural broker.

✄ STRANGE BEDFELLOWS

Before turning to cinematic allegory, it may be instructive to examine the practices of real estate developers in the 1990s and their collaboration with filmmakers. As land values and construction have increased—most recently, in expectation of the Olympics—developers have become some of China's most powerful cultural brokers. The most visible company is SOHO China, owned and managed by Pan Shiyi and Zhang Xin. The ascendance of the husband-and-wife team has become a rags-to-riches legend.[20] Starting in 1998 with New Town SOHO—a profitable double-use project (the company's acronym stands for Small Office, Home Office)—they launched in February 2001 a complex of eleven villas and a clubhouse, known as Commune by the Great Wall. Originally planned to comprise up to fifty villas to be sold at half a million U.S. dollars each, the project stalled, and the villas are now rented as a boutique hotel. Yet the project was essential to establishing the company's name recognition and prestige. The buildings were designed by twelve Asian architects of (then) modest fame, and the result was a modernist, experimental complex. SOHO China submitted the Commune by the Great Wall to the Eighth International Architecture Exhibition of the Venice Biennale (2002), and Zhang Xin won for the project an unprecedented special prize for individual patronage of architectural works. The technical shortcomings and commercial failure of the Commune were dwarfed by the project's critical acclaim and international renown. In the recent business environment, which focuses not on a product's qualities but rather on its brand identity, SOHO China has managed to distinguish itself.[21]

The case of Pan Shiyi and Zhang Xin illustrates how players in the financial field make use of culture. Even Pan, seemingly the more practical of the two, fosters the aura of a cultural critic. In an interview for *Culture* magazine, he expatiates on a cultural comparison of Russia, China, and Japan.[22] Pan has even appeared in film, as the male lead in *Aspirin* (2005). SOHO China owes much of its success not only to marketing its products but also to promoting the company's image as a leader in setting cultural trends. SOHO China's slightly provocative yet ultimately noncontentious aesthetics—introducing, for example, Beijing's first brightly colored buildings in New Town SOHO—not only added novel ways of visualizing the urban environment but also became one of its most important financial assets. Its projects—including the SOHO Shang Du building by Lab Architecture Studio of Melbourne and a residential subdivision by Zaha Hadid—are wrapped in the glamour of foreign designers and recognition by the international art world. SOHO China has used art performances to accompany its project launches, in advertising terms fully "eventizing" a product release. Events such as an avant-garde poetry reading and installation art by Ai Weiwei were staged with SOHO's architectural landmarks as backdrops.[23]

Pan Shiyi and Zhang Xin are not only exemplars of the real estate dawan'r and an inspiration to the PRC's business elite; they have also established mutually beneficial relationships with filmmakers. The Commune by the Great Wall was presented in Venice through a video by the film director Ning Ying, who also shot other promotional pieces for SOHO China. The twelve-minute video (available on DVD on request and downloadable at SOHO China's website) associated SOHO China's products with Ning's reputation as an art film director and contributed to the project's success in Venice. Ning Ying's involvement with SOHO China is far from self-evident. The director is known for her Beijing trilogy (see chapter 6), which looks critically at urban change of the kind promoted by land speculators. Ning's video of the Commune by the Great Wall, however, comports with the commercial expectations. Smooth camera movement and a soundtrack comprised mostly of Muzak accompany a slick introduction to the Commune, including an on-site fashion show. Like many other directors who make their living by shooting commercials—and unlike Feng Xiaogang and Zhang Yimou—Ning Ying maintains a distance between her commercial gigs and personally motivated filmmaking. Nevertheless, Ning's collaboration with SOHO China points to the symbiosis between the real estate dawan'r and filmmakers.

A wide spectrum of entrepreneurial filmmakers have used their media savvy and cultural status to add prestige and monetary value to real estate projects. Perhaps the most unexpected instance involves the pioneer documentary filmmaker Wu Wenguang. In June 2001, Sino-Ocean Real Estate Development Company launched its Ocean Paradise (Yuanyang Tiandi) project. The housing complex for Beijing's new upper middle class was promoted as an entrance ticket to a post-WTO international lifestyle and was also marketed through the added value of culture—in this case, the Eastern Modern Art Center (Yuanyang Yishu Zhongxin), touted as a center for alternative art. The project was chosen by *Beijing Evening News* as one of the ten "star developments" of 2001. Two months into the presales, the Art Center hosted a much-publicized avant-garde performance, Wen Hui's "Dancing with Migrant Workers" ("Yu mingong yiqi wudao"). The rehearsal process, as well as the single public performance, were recorded by Wen's husband, Wu Wenguang, in a documentary bearing the same title.[24] Wu, the most prominent director of the New Documentary movement and a vocal proponent of using digital video to circumvent the state-controlled film industry, found in the commercial developer an alternative source of funding. The collaboration based on Wen's and Wu's avant-garde reputation shows how filmmakers and real estate developers can unexpectedly find themselves in each other's company.

⚡ FROM THE CINEMATIC TO THE POSTCINEMATIC

Feng Xiaogang, with a keen eye for the humorous in current social conditions, exaggerates the symbiosis of film art and commerce in a parodic portrait of an all-out cultural broker—film director, producer, advertising entrepreneur, and real estate developer in disguise. *Big Shot's Funeral* shows how the dawan'r leverage their film skills and location savvy to produce absurd scams, revealing the contradiction between the policies of economic globalization and cultural preservation. The plot starts as a famous Hollywood director, Donald Tyler (Donald Sutherland), arrives in Beijing to shoot a remake of *The Last Emperor* but soon falls into a coma. The cinematographer Yoyo (Ge You) takes to heart Tyler's request for a "comedy funeral" and plans an uplifting spectacle worthy of the director's reputation. To cover the costs, the cinematographer resorts to direct advertising and product placement. The body of the deceased director would be placed on sponsored furniture, surrounded by large product mock-ups, and dressed in sponsor brands (fig. 43). In the cinematographer's imagination, the funeral becomes the scaffolding for an elaborate moneymaking venture. Yoyo en-

43 *Big Shot's Funeral* (2001): The Forbidden City as advertising location.

lists his friend Louis Wang (Ying Da) to promote the enterprise. Louis comes up with a plan for eventizing the press launch and sales, building around them events such as an extravagant multimedia presentation, opera and rock performances, and a movie on Tyler's life. In a delirium, the producers later calculate DVD sales of the funeral and plan to place their business on the U.S. stock market. The crucial element in Yoyo's and Louis's scheme is that the funeral take place in the Forbidden City. As a site symbolizing Beijing's cultural heritage, it endows the event with not only luster but lucre.

Pulling off the implausible scheme distinguishes Yoyo as a cultural broker. The dawan'r, or "big shot," in the film's title is nominally Tyler. It is Yoyo, however, who becomes a dawan'r in the modern sense of a market shaper, and the story line follows his rise to become a savvy manipulator of cultural references. Originally hired only to shoot the "making-of" documentary (itself a mark of strategized DVD marketing) and explicitly denied any decision-making power by Tyler's producers, Yoyo negotiates an increasingly complicated deal.

The protagonist in *Big Shot's Funeral* is immediately recognizable as an updated version of the entrepreneurial fantasy providers in two earlier films, both played by Ge You, who also plays Yoyo. Jason McGrath, in a detailed reading of this cinematic genealogy, provides insight into the development of postsocialist irony.[25] The evolving characters can also be read as a history of the cultural broker, who is increasingly invested in creating a dream-space by cinematic means.

The earliest version appears in *The Troubleshooters* (1988), a prominent example of the 1980s Urban Cinema. The first movie based on a text by Wang Shuo, it exhibits the street savvy that has earned Wang's works the label "hooligan literature." The plot revolves around three young men who, in the spirit of the economic reforms, start their own enterprise, 3T. The company name alludes to its Chinese slogan, centered on three services: removing worries, solving difficult situations, and covering up for mistakes. The 3T trio finds itself in situations that require a resourceful redefinition of culture through its commodification.

The smooth operators in *The Troubleshooters* stage their make-believe schemes in theatrical settings. When a frustrated pulp fiction writer craves public recognition, they set up a free fashion show at the World Expo Center, at the end of which they assume the roles of scholarly judges and give the writer his long-awaited award. The episode of acknowledging in a mock-scholarly manner the works of an author rejected for his lowbrow writings questions the pretentiousness of high art and in particular the contemporary "root-seeking literature" (*xungen wenxue*) alluded to by the author's pen name, Zhiqing ("sent-down youth"). As behooves cultural brokers, the 3T further blur the line between low- and highbrow by including in the literary award ceremony a fashion show—a novel consumerist spectacle at the time —and crowding the runway with Beijing opera and modern drama characters, alluding to the declining status of both traditional and Maoist theatrical forms. The make-believe exploits of 3T soon branch into the cinema. Yu Guan (Zhang Guoli) takes on a stuntman's job, willing to risk his life in the name of making a Chinese movie as good as Hong Kong action flicks. The cultural broker's next stop, it is implied, is commercial filmmaking. Yet whether in the expo hall or in the film studio lot, the 3T men rely on well-known technologies of simulation and remain confined to the designated spaces of the stage arts.

The 3T trio is only partly successful; the protagonists are caught in the city's maelstrom. The title song identifies the transforming urban environment and the advertising business as threats to their identity. The song, by rock 'n' roll singer (and later music producer) Wang Di, goes: "I used to dream of modern urban life / But I don't know how to say what I feel now /

There are more high-rises by the day / It's not easy to live here / TV commercial time is increasing / It's as though you can't hold on to that golden moment / You can't do what you want / What you don't want comes in droves." The lyrics and accompanying montage of new buildings single out runaway construction and media excess as symptoms of the broken "dream of modern urban life." The 3T men, who end up in the unemployment line, also fall victims to the rapid social change.

Feng Xiaogang's first New Year's movie, *Dream Factory*, reworks *The Troubleshooters* and expands the scope of the playacting ploys. Four out-of-work film professionals form the company The Day Trip of Your Dreams, designed "to let the consumers have their dreams come true for one day." (The company name alludes to Feng's enterprise of the early 1990s—Haomeng, or "good dreams.") The Chinese title for *Dream Factory*, literally "Party A, Party B," refers to the contract drawn between the company and its customers, emphasizing how even dreams are commodified and reduced to commercial transactions.

The enterprising four successfully use their experience in the film industry to create movielike settings and a relatively seamless fantasy world. They conjure and spoof one film genre after the other: a bookseller stars in his own war movie modeled after Hollywood's *Patton*, and a cook is made the protagonist of a Qing-period costume drama. Whereas the 3T trio in *The Troubleshooters* fails to get into the movie business, the members of the *Dream Factory* foursome are industry veterans who find even more lucrative venues for their filmmaking expertise and talent. Their venture is *postcinematic*, both in the literal sense of coming on the heels of the state-run studios' collapse and in the sense of stretching make-believe beyond the screen, into customized reality shows.

In contrast with the portrayal of the protagonists in *The Troubleshooters* as "abnormal human characters and disturbing social phenomena," in the director's words, the entrepreneurs in *Dream Factory* are presented favorably, as ingenious, reliable, and compassionate.[26] Only in *Big Shot's Funeral*, however, do the con artists achieve the status of cultural brokers. Whereas the elaborate "Day Trip of Your Dreams" productions rely on traditional cinematic sets and make-believe, Yoyo's and Louis's 3W.com blurs the line between their schemes and city life. The savvy entrepreneurs make use of semipublic locations as the backdrop for their schemes; they integrate advertising seamlessly through product placement (called in Chinese *ruan-*

xing guanggao, or "soft advertising"—which reflects the practice of Feng Xiaogang and his producers, the erstwhile advertisement company Huayi Brothers, of bundling their films with product campaigns).[27] As a cultural broker, Yoyo does not simply create a make-believe space to advance his commercial vision; instead, he takes over Beijing and turns even the most improbable urban site into a commodity.

Yoyo is a more motivated, and more empowered, manipulator because—like Feng Xiaogang—he operates within the new global economy. Critics largely regard *Big Shot's Funeral* as a response to China's entry into the WTO, which took place on December 11, 2001, ten days before the film's release.[28] The plot and the making of the film itself feature transnational collaboration of unprecedented scope under a PRC director.[29] *Big Shot's Funeral* portrays the mediascape of post-WTO China, spoofing and at the same time participating in an extreme form of cultural economy; it introduces changes not only into film production models but also into brand-name consumption and even urban spatial practices.

⚡ BEIJING AS VIRTUAL SPACE

Feng Xiaogang's self-referential allegory on filmmaking in the face of globalization is also a commentary on Beijing's architectural heritage in the age of real estate speculation. The Forbidden City in *Big Shot's Funeral* is an exaggerated illustration of Beijing's integration into the global trend that Naomi Klein has called "No Space," where every public space is overtaken by brand advertisement.[30] The portrayal of filmmakers' and advertisers' manipulation of the Forbidden City is a parable for the tension between urban development and cultural preservation.

The process through which the Forbidden City turned into a film and advertisement location is emblematic of the transformation of the ideological, economic, and cinematic significance of Beijing spaces. The palace compound was first used as a film location in 1987, for Bernardo Bertolucci's *The Last Emperor.* Bertolucci realized the Forbidden City's marketing value and convinced the authorities to grant him permission to shoot on location, which greatly enhanced his film's appeal. A decade later, the Forbidden City opened for filmed cultural events—to be precise, the location was the Beijing Workers' Cultural Palace, the former imperial ancestral temple right outside the Forbidden City. The palace hosted events beginning with Yanni's concert in May 1997 (following his performance at the Taj Mahal) and, most famously, Giacomo Puccini's *Turandot*, conducted by Zubin Mehta and staged by Zhang Yimou in September 1998. These and other productions promoted Beijing's international image as a cultural center. Meanwhile, advertisers gained access to the Palace already in 1996, when Land Rover launched its campaign on the premises, and the Forbidden City has since become a popular location for advertising shoots. These occasions, condoned by the Beijing Cultural Relics Bureau, generated images exploited for economic and political purposes.

Big Shot's Funeral casts Yoyo and Louis retroactively as the producers of many of these events. After Tyler starts to film a remake of *The Last Emperor*, the two local brokers plan various performances, including Puccini's *Turandot*, directed by Zhang Yimou; most saliently, they imitate the practice of advertising at the Forbidden City. At the same time, *Big Shot's Funeral* flaunts Feng Xiaogang's own access to the place, on a par with Zhang Yimou and leading advertising agencies. More than Feng's admitted motivation "to break away from Bertolucci's images and present the Forbidden City in a novel way,"[31] the location also enhanced Feng's standing. The imagined funeral inside the Forbidden City foregrounds the ties binding commercial entrepreneurs, filmmakers, and policymakers.

The image of ads pasted all across the Forbidden City not only spoofs recent advertising practices but also challenges contemporary urban policy. In response to the large number of advertising and movie shoots in the Forbidden City, officials in 2004 enacted stricter regulation. In addition, a 1999 ban on commercial billboards on Chang'an Avenue and Tiananmen Square (affecting more than three hundred billboards) was expanded on October 1, 2004, to various cultural relics in the capital and even to vehicles entering Tiananmen Square.[32] The need for legislation indicates how far the advertising industry had been encroaching on cultural relics and state emblems. Evidently, promoters found it tempting to publicize their products in the vicinity of emblems of tradition and power. Leaders, on the other hand, must have found awkward the advertisers' association of cultural prestige, buying power, and political authority, which mirrored the state's appropriation of the same cultural symbols. *Big Shot's Funeral* exposes the uneasy connection between the government's use of symbolic space and the policy encouraging the commercialization of space.

The ban on street advertising reflects policymakers' reluctance to include Tiananmen in the urban texture (see chapter 4). Yet it also reflects particular sensitivity to the intrusion of icons of globalization into sites of symbolic national value. Similar concerns have led to the removal of a Starbucks franchise from the Forbidden City in 2007, after a seven-year presence. The teahouse that replaced it was touted for its traditional Chinese flavor.[33] One may recall Andy Warhol's wry summary of the contradiction between a city's distinctive aesthetics and the ubiquity of transnational brand logos: "The most beautiful thing in Tokyo is McDonald's. The most beautiful thing in Stockholm is McDonald's. The most beautiful thing in Florence is Mc-Donald's. Peking and Moscow don't have anything beautiful yet."[34] McDonald's opened in Pushkin Square and on Gorky Street in Moscow in 1990 and on Wangfujing in Beijing in 1991. With more than sixteen hundred golden arches expected in China by the Olympics,[35] Beijing should count now among the most beautiful cities in the world.

Big Shot's Funeral avoids the images of construction and demolition prevalent in the films I discussed in chapter 6, yet the focus on the Forbidden City, seemingly immutable and yet subjected to the ravages of globalization, makes the urban change even more poignant. The film is a reminder that even the Imperial Palace is real estate that can be put up for rent, if only for film locations and advertising campaigns. Yoyo and Louis talk of the Forbidden City as "the most expensive location in the world" only to show how the dawan'r can subject even the most inaccessible spaces to the market economy. Its cultural cachet and subsequent high price make the Forbidden City a perfect symbol for the new Beijing.

Big Shot's Funeral anticipates the advertising boom brought about by the Olympics and points to the Olympics as an incentive for commercializing cultural heritage.[36] The film alludes to the concert by the three tenors, Luciano Pavarotti, Plácido Domingo, and José Carreras, held in the Forbidden City to promote the Olympic bid on June 23, 2001, six months before the film's release. One scene in the film features thousands of people on the palace grounds holding up colored umbrellas to form an advertisement for "666" cigarettes (alluding to the popular brand 999). The situation imitates displays at Olympic Games ceremonies (as well as at National Day parades in Tiananmen Square since 1957).[37] In the same scene, when Yoyo shows his public relations savvy, Lucy remarks, "You should have been running the

Olympics!" Yoyo's character resonates with Zhang Yimou, chosen to choreograph shows at the Olympics, and Taylor's funeral is a thinly veiled allegory for the 2008 Games.

Even though *Big Shot's Funeral* spoofs the Olympics, it skirts the ongoing urban problems, discussed in previous chapters, entailed in the demolition-and-relocation policy, in particular the evacuation and destruction of an untold number of homes to make space for the Olympic Village.[38] Instead Feng's film takes part in advertising Beijing as a commodity. The Olympic bid was, after all, part of a larger drive for international exposure. Architectural landmarks and entire cities were promoted as if they were brand names; Kevin Roberts, chief executive officer of the worldwide advertising firm Saatchi and Saatchi, was even talking of "Brand China."[39] (In this light, the removal of billboards from Chang'an Avenue was ironically intended to facilitate turning the city itself into a product.) The New Urban Cinema of the early 2000s, featuring slick images of tourist sites such as Beijing alleys and Shanghai's Oriental Pearl TV tower, should also be understood in the context of city branding. Advertising campaigns and films alike trim the urban environment and show it as if in postcards, making spaces virtual and thus more marketable.

The city was explicitly reinvented in the Olympic Games slogan, "New Beijing, Great Olympics" (or in the Chinese version, "New Beijing, New Olympics"). "Selling Beijing to the world," as Anne-Marie Broudehoux calls it, included everything from blazing through new traffic arteries to installing public toilets and engineering more "civilized" residents.[40] *Big Shot's Funeral* toes the line in remolding the image of the Beijinger, as represented by Yoyo, as a dawan'r—a market-savvy, socially responsible, foreigner-friendly entrepreneur. Since Lao She's early twentieth-century novels, plays, and films have redefined "Beijing flavor" (*jingwei'r*); films such as *The Troubleshooters* and *Dream Factory* present what Yang Dongping calls "the new Beijing flavor."[41] In the spirit of the "humanistic Olympics," *Big Shot's Funeral* presents a new Beijing, in a *new* new Beijing flavor—a commodified, globalized, virtual city.

⚜ A WORLD APART

Whereas *Big Shot's Funeral* shows the Forbidden City, an emblem of Beijing culture, as a hollow façade for commercial transactions, *The World* shows that in consumerist and globalized Beijing, only patently unreal backdrops provide a makeshift refuge for the underclass. The plot follows workers at the Beijing World Park, a theme park that includes downscaled replicas of architectural monuments from around the world, such as the Pyramids of Egypt, St. Mark's Square in Venice, and the Eiffel Tower. Beijing World Park, opened 1993, is one of a number of such parks, notably the Window to the World Park in Shenzhen (opened in 1994, where much of *The World* was shot) and other icons of leisure culture, such as Shenzhen's Splendid China (opened in 1989), which exhibits elaborate miniature models of architecture inside China. In encapsulating the country and the world, the theme parks provide a semiofficial view of the nation and its place in global society,[42] which is in turn scrutinized in Jia Zhangke's film.

The world parks resonate with China's globalization policy. The park motto, "Give us a day and we'll show you the world," dovetails with the slogan for Deng's economic reforms, "Marching toward the world" (*zou xiang shijie*). National leaders' public endorsement of the world parks (Jiang Zemin, for example, wrote the calligraphy for the Shenzhen park's entrance) indicates that the allusion has not been lost on them. Moreover, the parks' version of opening up to the world, through a quick series of photo ops in front of decontextualized replicas, fits with planners' vision of uniform cities whose cultural heritage serves only as a tourist backdrop.

Perhaps the most eloquent proponent of such near-virtual cities is the architect Rem Koolhaas, who celebrates the "Generic City," geared toward functionality and unencumbered by plans for preserving local characteristics: "The Generic City is liberated . . . from the straitjacket of identity. The Generic City . . . is nothing but a reflection of present need and present ability. It is a city without history . . . serenity . . . is achieved by the *evacuation* of the public realm."[43] Koolhaas seems to express many Chinese policymakers' dream of massive demolition-and-relocation to make space for glass-and-steel corporate headquarters. In a generic city, devoid of history, land would be valued only according to its ability to sustain efficient construction and provide advertising space. Koolhaas was rewarded by being chosen to design the CCTV tower, one of the structures that reshaped Beijing's skyline for the Olympics. Following the logic of brand name consumption, Beijing's new identity is defined by landmarks by international star architects, turning China's capital into a theme park of world architecture.

The World gives the lie to the "international city" policy by highlighting the disparity between the park's fantasy and the workers' living conditions.

Globalization has created "transnational spaces"—business districts, air-ports, shopping malls, and corporate headquarters—that link the local and global economies. Since the 1980s, real estate developers sought to develop transnational spaces in Beijing.⁴⁴ The World Park, in contrast, caters to those who cannot afford to travel (the film quotes the park's promotional slogan: "Travel through the whole world without leaving Beijing"); instead, it offers an idealized view of the world—devoid of economic disparity, histor-ical difference, or political conflict. The park reduces to the absurd (as it were, miniaturizes to the absurd) transnational spaces, which privilege in-ternational corporations and the globetrotting class, ignoring local econo-mies and encouraging low-wage global outsourcing.

Like Jia Zhangke's previous film, *Platform*, *The World* portrays the every-day appropriation of cultural icons (in the case of *Platform*, Western pop songs) into a pastiche that only underlines the futility of the underclass's attempt to benefit from the cosmopolitan dream. *The World* focuses on a group of workers from China's destitute hinterland who have come to Bei-jing to earn a meager living. China's booming economy has generated a class of migrant workers, disadvantaged by their rural origins and often exploited by their employers. Out of Beijing's estimated 17 million residents in 2007, as many as 4 million were migrant workers, many of them working in construction related to the Olympic Games.⁴⁵ While globalization has made Beijing what Saskia Sassen has called a "global city"—the links that connect it profitably with other commercial hubs being stronger than the affinities to its immediate geographical surroundings—the same dynamics have also necessitated the migration of cheap labor to China's metropolitan areas and overseas.⁴⁶ It is emblematic of the global economy that the World Park fantasy is maintained through the labor of disenfranchised migrant workers. *The World* captures the irony, for example, in a shot of an airplane taking off over a construction site where one of the protagonists works and later meets his death (fig. 44).

The World joins a growing number of films that address migrant workers as a symptom of China's role in the global economy. State-sponsored films, from *The Girl from Huangshan* (1984) to *Going Home* (2004), have depicted benevolent though patronizing relationships between migrant workers and their urban employers. In particular, *Going Home*, a "main melody" propa-ganda movie by the PLA's August First Film Studio, addresses migrant workers' common grievance that their salary is often delayed for months

44 *The World* (2004): Two migrant workers look at a jet taking off, from the rooftop of a construction site.

on end. The plot places a construction worker and a newly appointed mayor in a stuck elevator, in a bonding experience that culminates when they save each other's lives. Subsequently, the mayor ensures that the worker and his companions get their salaries and are able to return home to celebrate the New Year with their families. The melodrama seeks to reassure viewers of the Party's fair treatment of migrant workers.

A much more critical discourse has developed in independent films, including fiction movies such as *Strangers in Beijing* (1996) and *Drifters* (*Erdi*, [2003]) as well as hard-hitting documentaries such as *Out of Phoenix Bridge* (1997) and *The Concrete Revolution* (2004). Jia Zhangke himself has been dubbed, due to his background as well as his thematic concerns, a "cinematic migrant worker" (*dianying mingong*). In fact, migrant workers have become a hallmark of urban films of various ideological hues. Zhang Zhen notes that "the figure of the migrant worker . . . registers the scale and intensity of the urbanizing process."[47] Off- and onscreen, migrant workers point to the changing rapport between urban environment and countryside, "global city" and rural hinterland, the dream of globalization and its victims.

The World presents the migrant workers in the park as trapped, able to survive only by taking part in the fantasy they help to maintain. Whereas visitors to the park live the world dream for a single day, the workers must live it every day, within the surreal mock-ups and in isolation from the world-class elegance of the adjacent Beijing. Nick Stanley notes that the Window to the World Park carries vestiges of the World's Fairs' exoticism and imperialist mindset.[48] The park workers in *The World* are similarly oppressed, and striking images juxtapose the simulated world of the theme park and the workers' wretched existence. Ironically, the world offered in the World Park is a reified, bounded, and inhibiting space.

The World Park creates, and then claims to satisfy, a desire for consumerist mobility. The visitor is imagined as a citizen of the world—that is, a member of the global elite—who avails himself of tourism and is given infinite choice. Lisa Nakamura notes that Microsoft's slogan "Where do you want to go today?" places the Internet-enabled consumer in the position of "the one who looks, the one who has access, the one who communicates."[49] Similarly, the World Park workers travel direct and nonstop between Tokyo, Paris, and New York, and they are incessantly typing instant messages into their cellphones. Yet ultimately they have no control of their movement, and eventually they can go nowhere.

Emblematically, the workers' only way of escape is through the virtual world of digital imaging. Using blue screen technology, they can see themselves flying on a magic carpet over their desired sites. The film further visualizes their existence within a make-believe space, parallel to rather than contiguous with the city, in animated sequences. To illustrate the protagonist's fantasies as she corresponds with her lover through text messaging, *The World* uses computer-generated animation.

The animated sequences in *The World* are based on Flash technology and made by the artist Wang Bo (a.k.a. Pi San). Wang notes that Flash art developed in China in the late 1990s, in tandem with the commercial leisure culture of the BoBos, or Bourgeois Bohemians. Flash animation, like the digital video (DV) filmmaking that took hold around the same time, provides an alternative to celluloid movies—affordable, requiring no formal training, and easily distributable online.[50] The Flash sequences in *The World* associate the protagonist's need to escape beyond the materiality of the city with new, postcinematic modes of visualization. Jia films, so to speak, in virtual space.

One may bear in mind that the Dengist slogan "Marching toward the world" was also used to describe the hope of the Internet. The phrase was the opening salvo of the Internet age in China. The first message e-mailed out of the PRC, on September 14, 1987, carried the words, "Across the Great Wall we can reach every corner in the world," an English rendition of the slogan *yueguo changcheng, zou xiang shijie*, more accurately translated as "Crossing the Great Wall and marching toward the world."[51] The globalization policy has promoted disjointed spatial references and the postspatial constructs of the Internet. With the subjugation of architectural heritage to market economy and the compromising of urban planning by the whims of transnational capital, space ceases to coincide with material place.

The downscaled buildings in the World Park mark more than the illusion of spatial control conveyed by the onstage maquettes discussed in chapter 3. They allude to a new understanding of space, adopted at the same time by urban planners, that decouples architecture from geographical context. Beijing's suburbs have become populated with developments imitating residences outside China, such as the Southern California–style "Orange County" tract homes, the construction of which was inspired by the Olympic bid.[52] The dislocated replicas in the World Park resonate with an urbanism that celebrates simulated spaces.

Big Shot's Funeral and *The World* explore the nexus of cinema, commerce, and space, based on new practices of image making, market shaping, and spatial design. Filmmaking becomes inseparable from advertising and real estate development. Together, they present spaces that can only exist in virtual form—in film, promotional material, miniature models, and cyberspace.

✦ THE POSTCINEMATIC AESTHETIC AND THE POSTSPATIAL CITY (A POSTSCRIPT)

The trajectory from the socialist city envisioned in *Dragon Whisker Creek* and *Sentinels under the Neon Lights* to the commercialized and virtual spaces of *Big Shot's Funeral* and *The World* outlines a transformation in cinematic practices. From films rooted in an acute sense of presence, theaterlike and even unmediated (one may recall director Jiao Juyin's insistence on making the audience feel the wriggling maggots onstage), filmmaking has ventured into virtual media, extending celluloid and digital video on-site recording to computer-aided and Internet-based image manipulation. These postcinematic technologies point to a new spatial perception, due to the geopolitics of globalization but also to a reconceptualization of the urban environment, in the form of the postspatial city.

Some planners have noted the recent turn to a "postspatial architecture." Anthony Vidler has proclaimed the advent of "the postspatial void," a paradigm couched in spatial terms—"virtual space" and "cyberspace"—only because of the challenge "to think the hitherto unthinkable (or rather the unthinkable within the frame of modernism) conditions of life without space."[53] In other words, the postspatial is a symptom of our anxiety in the face of an unimaginable virtual reality. Manesh Senagala explains that built environment no longer serves the function of communication. Planning must follow the conditions in which economic transactions (and, one should add, social interactions) are conducted "in an electronic, non-spatial form, flowing through the non-spatial channels that are not designed by architects. . . . Post-spatial approaches to architecture acknowledge this new reality."[54]

The postcinematic aesthetic recognizes, and engages with, the postspatial city. In *Big Shot's Funeral*, when Yoyo and Louis imagine the eventized and mediatized funeral, the narrative switches to an animated sequence. In parallel, the architectural heritage of the Forbidden City turns into advertising space—no more than scaffolding for changing billboards and a portal for globalizing consumerism. The frequent escapes in *The World* through the cellphone screen and into Flash animation reinforce the impression that for the protagonists the theme park is more real than the city. One may also recall Chen Kaige's "One Hundred Flowers Hidden Deep," which uses computer-generated graphics to visualize the madman's delirium of his now-demolished courtyard house, privileging digital imagery as a form of meaning (fig. 37).

Other works renounce celluloid altogether and construct a *hyperreal* space, one that does away with all reference to material urban existence and functions as a self-sufficient realm. The "hyperreal," in the sense used by Jean Baudrillard, has replaced not only the real but also all forms of imitation, duplication, and parody. It is not anchored to any ideal or territory.[55] The hyperreal offers the possibility of a representation of space that has no material counterpart and that can nevertheless be populated and overtaken, bought and sold. Hyperreal space challenges cinematic portrayals of the city by presenting a perfect facsimile—not a copy or model but rather a self-standing simulacrum.

The turning point, from real-time and real-space documentation to hyperreal cinema, is the subject matter of *Q3* (1999), a thirty-two-minute video artwork by Feng Mengbo.[56] *Q3* takes place inside the computer-generated sets of the video game Quake III Arena (QIII). QIII is a "first-person shooter" game, in which the player sees through a gun viewfinder and fires at animated figures. The arena is a multiuser dungeon (MUD) that can be accessed

45 *Q3* (1999): MONGBAT is killed. Courtesy of Feng Mengbo.

simultaneously by multiple players who communicate via the Internet. The film is divided into three sections, each starting with the noise of a dial-up "handshake" with an Internet server, foregrounding that the events take place on the Web. The first section ("hEAVEN") is a straightforward re-creation of a Quake III game. In the second section, CNN reporter Mengbo (pronounced to rhyme with Rambo and played by the artist) broadcasts from a battlefield indistinguishable from a QIII environment. Mengbo conducts a live interview, streamed via the Internet, with an animated figure answering to the name FILTH. One learns that the QIII animated figures are clones rebelling for freedom. After FILTH is shot dead during the interview, Mengbo decides to join the clones.

In the third and final section ("hELL"), the film returns to an extended first-person-shooter view of the QIII battleground. In light of the interview, the fight sequence is a brutal and even tragic fight among conscious beings. It ends when the first-person shooter comes across a player identified as GENOCIDAL MONGBAT and kills him at close range (fig. 45). The player's name sounds like a cyborgized Cantonese version of Mengbo. One may infer that the reporter has been fighting with the clones and has become a genocidal warrior, and that the last scene shows Mengbo's death.

Mengbo's decision to join the clones reflects his change of attitude toward the real. Initially, Mengbo disapproves of the clones' challenge to the boundaries of virtual reality. He taunts FILTH: "You think you can get out of here?

Clawing at the doors like all the rest . . ." and suggests to the clone to "get real." Mengbo's choice to leave HEAVEN and descend into HELL is a conversion from one who watches through the computer screen to one who lives inside cyberspace. Mengbo, now MONGBAT, joins the MUD community of borrowed identities, together with the murderous MAHATMA GANDHI, short-lived REMEMBER ME!!, and online gamer YOU ARE DISCONNECTED.[57] Like *The Matrix*, released in the same year, *Q3* features a battle that requires biocybernetic symbiosis with the simulated environment.

Mengbo's voluntary transformation, from a human reporter to a QIII clone, is indicative of the change from filmmaking committed to documenting reality to a postcinematic aesthetic. As a CNN reporter, Mengbo is the successor of Mike Chinoy, who in June 1989 reported live from Tiananmen Square, thereby establishing CNN as a world-class news provider.[58] Chinoy's reporting,—and, soon after, the coverage of the Gulf War, called the "videogame war" for the use of bomb-mounted cameras with first-person-shooter crosshairs—changed the definition of news.[59] Mengbo participates in the televisual revolution of post-Tiananmen media, which relies on real-time images. Like many directors in the 1990s, who subscribed to a documentary impulse as a way to counter the loss of collective memory, the interviewer in *Q3* fashions himself as a witness who places himself at the midst of events, chronicling and narrating them. With the help of video streaming—a technology of real-time and virtual-space reportage—his personal point of view is also, at the same time, a historical record.

The climactic moment of live reporting, when Mengbo's camera captures the filmed subject's death, is also the turning point at which Mengbo becomes MONGBAT, slipping from a firsthand witness to a first-person shooter. He does not fashion himself as a freedom fighter but rather as a man who gives in to the thrill of the virtual world: "I know it's stupid, but it's really a fuckin' game, anyway." As MONGBAT, he can celebrate virtual reality—and die by it. *Q3*, which starts by paying tribute to celluloid by imitating a scratched film reel, is later mediated through the reporter's camcorder and finally through the computer gamer's viewfinder. Feng Mengbo's video art encapsulates what Anne Friedberg has described as a historical trajectory from cinematic spectation, to televisual spectatorship, to the virtual gaze.[60]

The postcinematic is also postspatial. The virtual built environment in *Q3*, where the carnage takes place, can be read as a loose allegory for Beijing. The ready-made QIII dungeons bear little resemblance to any place, but the neoclassical monumental architecture resonates with Stalinist landmarks such as those at Tiananmen. Feng has commented on the resemblance between Chinese urban environment and QIII: "Have a look at our lovely cities. Do you think we can really find a way to save them from pollution? Maybe it is better to keep them like the scenes we see in Quake or Street Fighters: dark, dirty and ugly, with cold rain."[61] The QIII dungeons are not metaphors for the city, however; instead they refer to spaces that do not and cannot exist in material form.

Q3 may express the post-Tiananmen doldrums of the 1990s, finding in video games an alternative to Maoist heroism and the testimonial fervor of the 1980s. By the 2000s, however, virtual reality became a venue for addressing new concerns—primarily the commercialization of urban space. *I • Mirror*, a video art piece made for the Venice Biennale of 2007, follows the cyberspace exploits of China Tracy, the Second Life avatar of the artist and filmmaker Cao Fei. The artwork's subtitle, *"A Second Life Documentary Film,"* points to the possibility of making a film, and a documentary to boot, of one's parallel, Internet-based existence.

Feng Mengbo enters cybernetic existence by way of a series of increasingly virtualized forms that nevertheless refer to the author—the dial-up MUD user, the reporter Mengbo, and the clone MONGBAT. China Tracy, on the other hand, is self-sufficient and independent of Cao Fei. The piece, which starts by quoting the urbanist William J. Mitchell, "I am a spatially extended cyborg," records the adventures of China Tracy in a world composed of bytes and computer-generated graphics. Yet the opening images also speak of the material urban environment from which China Tracy is fleeing. She floats among high-end apartment buildings with a revolving dollar sign in front and among virtual high-rises, their contours delineated by the words "for sale" (fig. 46). A red flag in front of another lot for sale combines the Communist hammer and sickle with the Kmart logo. The images resemble China's California-style suburban developments and Beijing's gentrified high-rise compounds, such as Jianwai SOHO. Cao Fei, who has codirected documentaries on urban change in Guangzhou's Sanyuanli and Beijing's Dashalan'r, turns to the postcinematic and postspatial to address China's real estate dystopia.

In both form and content, *I • Mirror*—and Cao's subsequent Second Life project, *RMB City*—draw attention to the inadequacy of the cinema in dealing with the new paradigms of the city. Recent policy has relied on marketing and

46 *I · Mirror* (2007): Virtual buildings go up for sale.
Courtesy of Cao Fei.

eventizing the city; Broudehoux has argued that since the 1990s, Beijing urban planners have focused on creating and staging the "event-city."[62] Conveying the city through staged events reduces the urban environment to consumable spaces, and urban experience to marketable slogans. In reaction to the postspatial, Cao turns to postcinematic aesthetics—in her case, video art that relies on lifelong, or Second Life-long interaction with screen media. As I argued in the introduction, film does not function as a singular event, at the moment of encounter between spectator and screen; the postcinematic takes a further step in recognizing the limitations of film. Feng Mengbo's and Cao Fei's works turn the filmmaker into an architect and landowner of a space into which viewers enter through a binding contract—logging on, signing in, and assuming the persona of a first-person shooter or avatar. In so doing, they expose the dynamics of the urban contract.

As the lines blur between cinema and digital media, more films are permeated by the postspatial and postcinematic. In Jia Zhangke's *Still Life* (2006), a building can become a spaceship. The opening sequence of Li Shaohong's *Baober in Love* (2004) features a young girl traumatized by the rapid construction around her (fig. 39). Digitized animation stresses the amazingly fast urban growth, where an entire city is erected in the duration of the girl's single, piercing scream, within a single shot. Whereas the state productions mentioned in chapter 3 see instantaneous development as a blessing, the digital modeling in *Baober in Love* portrays future shock. The hyperrealist digital special effects (by Thomas Duval, of *Amélie* [2001] fame) present a city highly cinematic and yet beyond the reach of the camera lens.

The postcinematic and postspatial turns are only the latest forms of temporal manipulation of the perception of urban space. Beijing in particular has long been subjected to the dream of instantaneous change. *Dragon Whisker Creek* envisions the capital's regeneration as a socialist city in the early 1950s as "New China, New Beijing"; recent films responded to the updated slogan "New Beijing, Great Olympics." As long as planners and filmmakers must negotiate with power, the urban contract will remain an unfinished project.

INTRODUCTION Film and the Urban Contract

1 For more straightforward descriptions of art and power in the PRC, see, e.g., Barmé, *In the Red*; Kraus, *Party and the Arty*; and Link, *Uses of Literature*.

2 Pu Siwen, "Lao She xiansheng he ta de *Longxugou*."

3 Li Liyun, *Lao She zai Beijing de zuji*, 61–64.

4 *Dragon Whisker Creek* may be seen as Lao She's fatal involvement in politics. Lao She's cooperation with the political leaders paved his way to becoming one of the Communist government's main literary mouthpieces. Lao She had a painful awakening in 1957, when he began to encounter vehement political denunciations, which eventually turned to physical violence. *Dragon Whisker Creek* tells of a young girl who drowns in the filthy creek. In October 1966, following a brutal beating by Red Guards, the author drowned himself. The playwright's death, echoing that of his protagonist, may be seen as an implicit accusation of the failed revolution—little changed since Longxugou had run in the open and taken people's lives. The author's death ironically invokes the play's symbolism.

5 Lao She, "*Longxugou* de xiezuo jingguo," 9.

6 Becker, *Art Worlds*.

7 See, e.g,, Campanella, *Concrete Dragon*; Wang Jun, *Caifangben shang de chengshi*; and Visser, *Cities Surround the Countryside*.

8 Friedberg, *Window Shopping*, 134–35.

9 Castells and Borja, *Local and Global*, 253.

10 Forester, *Planning in the Face of Power*.

11 Campanella, *Concrete Dragon*.

12 Most of the people I interviewed are mentioned in the acknowledgments to this book; others prefer to stay anonymous.

13 Visser, *Cities Surround the Countryside*, introduction. Visser points especially to the building of urban planning exhibition halls; publication of journals such as the *New Urban China* (*Chengshi Zhongguo*) and *Shanghai City Development* (*Shanghai chengshi fazhan*); the translation of Western classics on urbanism; the collaboration between Chinese and Western

planners; and the strong presence of researchers such as Wang Xiaoming. Visser, *Cities Surround the Countryside*, introduction, chaps. 1 and 2.

14 Chu Weihua, *Zhongguo dushi pingmin dianying*; Chen Xiaoyun, *Dianying chengshi*.

15 Visser, *Cities Surround the Countryside*, introduction.

16 See, e.g., Zhang Zhen, "Bearing Witness," 7.

17 Friedmann, *China's Urban Transition*, xvi.

18 Kracauer, "Boredom," 331–32.

19 Benjamin wrote: "It is of the greatest importance for the philosophy of the future to recognize and sort out which elements of Kantian philosophy should be adopted and cultivated, which should be reworked, and which should be rejected." Benjamin, "On the Program," 101–2.

20 Walter Benjamin, "On Some Motifs in Baudelaire," 327, 328, 332. Compare Kant, *Critique of Judgment*, 94–109 (paragraphs 25–27).

21 Zhang, *City in Modern Chinese Literature and Film*, xvii, xviii, 3.

22 See, e.g., Braester, " 'If We Could Remember Everything' "; and Braester, "Tracing the City's Scars."

23 Bruno, *Streetwalking on a Ruined Map*; Gunning, "From the Kaleidoscope to the X-Ray."

24 Mulvey, "Visual Pleasure and Narrative Cinema"; Bordwell, "Case for Cognitivism"; Shaviro, *Cinematic Body*; Hansen, *Babel and Babylon*.

25 Hansen, "Benjamin, Cinema and Experience," 222; Hansen, *Babel and Babylon*, 91, 104, 90; Zhang Zhen, *Amorous History*, xxx, 1.

26 Braester, *Witness against History*, 16.

27 Jonathan Rosenbaum, for example, points to differences between the popular film *Saving Private Ryan* and the more critical but neglected *Small Soldiers*. Rosenbaum, *Movie Wars*, 62–77.

28 For Foucault, "the subject of discourse" is defined and constructed through procedures available only to those who possess a privileged knowledge. In the case at hand, the citizens become part of the urban matrix by acknowledging the power structure conveyed by planning and film. See Foucault, "Truth and Power."

29 Zhang Zhen's model has been called into question in Pang, "Walking Into and Out of the Spectacle."

30 Shiel, "Cinema and the City," 4, 3.

31 Hay, "What Remains of the Cinematic City," 216.

32 Ibid.

33 Clarke, "Introduction."

34 Eisenstein, "Problem of the Materialist Approach," 146.

35 Bazin, "Myth of Stalin," 23–40; Ellul, *Propaganda*; Baudrillard, *Simulacra and Simulation*.

36 See Jameson, *Geopolitical Aesthetic*, 3.

37 Braester, *Witness against History*, 106–30.

38 Altman, *Film/Genre*.

39 See Braester, "Political Campaign as Genre."

40 Abramson, "Urban Planning in China."

41 See Wang Jun, *Cheng ji*, 127–62.

42 Zhang, "Rebel without a Cause?" 53.

43 Pickowicz and Zhang, *From Underground to Independent*.

44 See Holquist, "Introduction."

45 While this book was being made ready for print, Michael Berry's *A History of Pain* was published. Berry too structures modern Chinese literature and film along the concept of the chronotope: " 'Chronotopes of pain' . . . redefine our very conceptions of the temporal and spatial boundaries of historical atrocity" (15). Berry invokes the chronotope to connote the reification of certain events as "entry points" for collective memory (379). My study, on the other hand, foregrounds the chronotope's instrumentality in associating specific sites with new historical metanarratives.

46 See Abbas, *Hong Kong*; Leung Ping-kwan, "Urban Cinema and the Cultural Identity of Hong Kong"; and Leung, *Undercurrents*.

47 Tweedie and Braester, "Introduction," 1.

48 Deleuze, *Cinema 2*, 272.

ONE New China, New Beijing

1 For examples of citation in urban planning sources, see Cao Hongtao and Zhu Chuanheng, *Dangdai zhongguo de chengshi jianshe*, 28; repeated also in Zhao Yongge and Wang Ya'nan, *Bainian chengshi bianqian*, 59. For use of the film as documentary footage, see *Goldfish Ponds* (2002).

2 Earlier plays shown at BPAT were restaged productions from the repertoire of the Liberated Areas and a translation of Soviet drama.

3 Ying Ruocheng, who took part in both *Dragon Whisker Creek* and *Teahouse*, reminisces that the first draft of *Dragon Whisker Creek* contained a teahouse scene that, although excised from the earlier play, was expanded into *Teahouse*. Ying Ruocheng and Conceison, *Voices Carry*, 138.

4 There are different versions of the play, starting with a number of drafts by the author, rewritten in response to the authorities' agenda and later to fit a film script format. The piece was first published in September 1950 and was revised twice before the publication of the final text in 1953. The script was modified by the stage director Jiao Juyin. Whereas the variances between Lao She's texts are negligible, Jiao's version is significantly different. The latter version (published in May 1951) served also as the foundation for the 1952 film script, by the director Xian Qun. On the various editions, see Shu Ji and Wang Xingzhi, "Lao She juzuo zhuyi mulu," 295; and Gan Hailan, *Lao She Nianpu*, 251–66. I could not access the first draft, preserved at the Beijing Library. The translation into English, *Dragon Beard Ditch*, was made from the final, 1953 version.

5 Lao She, "Wo re'ai xin Beijing," 6–7.

6 Cao Hongtao and Zhu Chuanheng, *Dangdai zhongguo de chengshi jianshe*, 26.

7 Dong, *Republican Beijing*, 22.

8 Zhao Yongge and Wang Ya'nan, *Bainian chengshi bianqian*, 58.

9 Ibid., 58–64.

10 Naquin, *Peking*, 269, 421.

11 My translation of Longxugou as "Dragon Whisker Creek," rather than the accepted "Dragon Beard Ditch," takes into account the whisker metaphor and the rivulet's origin in a natural creek.

12 Sun Xiuping, "Beijing chengqu quan xinshi maicang he, hu, gou, keng de fenbu ji qi yanbian," 222.

13 Zhao Yongge and Wang Ya'nan, *Bainian chengshi bianqian*, 59–60.

14 Cao Yanxing, "Guanyu Longxugou xiashuidao gongcheng wenti de baogao"; Zhao Yongge and Wang Ya'nan, *Bainian chengshi bianqian*, 59; Qu Yuanlin, "Guancha xin Zhongguo de yige shijiao."

15 Cao Yanxing, "Guanyu Longxugou xiashuidao gongcheng wenti de baogao."

16 The play was shown all over the country, from Guangzhou to Manchuria. Shu Yi, interview with the author, Beijing, October 24, 2003.

17 Li Bozhao, "Kan *Longxugou*," 3.

18 Li Bozhao, "Wei jin yibu xuexi he shijian Mao Zedong wenyi sixiang er fendou," 138.

19 Gan Hailan, *Lao She Nianpu*, 248, 250.

20 BPAT was restructured and formally inaugurated on June 12, 1952, from a troupe that included drama, song, and dance—the successor of the Art Department at the Central Party School of Art in Yan'an—to a strictly theatrical establishment under the supervision of the Beijing municipal government. Huang Weijun and Zhou Ruixiang, *Huihuang de yishu diantang*, 4–5; see also Ying Ruocheng and Conceison, *Voices Carry*, 220n19.

21 Gao Shen, *Longxugou de bianqian*. The play and the novel share many details, but neither is an adaptation of the other. I cannot establish which work inspired the other.

22 Mao Tse-Tung, "Talks at the Yenan Forum," 81.

23 Li Liyun, *Lao She zai Beijing de zuji*, 61.

24 Shu Yi, interview with the author, Beijing, October 24, 2003.

25 Gan Hailan, *Lao She Nianpu*, 251–52; Pu Siwen, "Lao She xiansheng he ta de *Longxugou*"; Lao She, "*Longxugou* de xiezuo jingguo," 9.

26 Pu Siwen, "Lao She xiansheng he ta de Longxugou"; Gan Hailan, *Lao She Nianpu*, 252.

27 Shu Yi, interview with the author, Beijing, October 24, 2003. The play was staged multiple times by BPAT as well as by troupes all over the country. See Liu Xiaowen and Liang Sirui, *1949–1984 Zhongguo shangyan huaju jumu zonglan*, 55.

28 Li Liyun, *Lao She zai Beijing de zuji*, 61–63.

29 Zeng Guangcan, *Lao She yanjiu zonglan*, 70–75.

30 Huang Wenlong et al., "Gongren huanying xiang *Longxugou* zheyang de zuopin."

31 One of the workers present is reported to have recounted his personal experience: "As soon as it rained, it was just like the Yellow River when the dykes are breached. Water all over the place, houses collapsing, crushing and drowning people to death. Melon rinds, greens, garbage, and various objects all swamped the streets. Once the water subsided, maggots were all over the beds and windowsills." Ibid.

32 Zhou Yang, "Cong *Longxugou* xuexi shenme?"

33 See, e.g., Gao Shen, *Longxugou de bianqian*.

34 See, e.g., Zhao Yongge and Wang Ya'nan, *Bainian chengshi bianqian*, 59.

35 Cao Yanxing, "Guanyu Longxugou xiashuidao gongcheng wenti de baogao."

36 Lao She, *Longxugou*, in *Lao She juzuo xuan* (1987 [1953]) (hereafter *Longxugou-1953*), 51.

37 Hu Hao, "Yu Longxugou dangdi jumin gongkan *Longxugou* yanchu."

38 Beijing Tebieshi Gongshu Gongwuju, memos concerning Zhang Qikui's petition for initiation works at Longxugou.

39 Lao She, *Longxugou* (1951) (hereafter *Longxugou-*DZSD), 43; *Longxugou-1953*, 45.

40 Lao She, "Longxugou de xiezuo jingguo," 10.

41 Lao She, "Mao zhuxi geile wo xin de wenyi shengming," 39.

42 Anagnost, *National Past-Times*, 31–32.

43 Huang Wenlong et al., "Gongren huanying xiang Longxugou zheyang de zuopin."

44 Lao She, "*Longxugou* paicaiben," 17; *Longxugou-*DZSD, 28; *Longxugou-1953*, 33.

45 See also *Longxugou-*DZSD, 3; *Longxugou-1953*, 8; Lao She, "*Longxugou* paicaiben," 18; *Longxugou-*DZSD, 30; *Longxugou-1953*, 35. Black Whirlwind's character is reminiscent of the bully punished by the new government in Zhao Shuli's short story of 1943, "Little Blackey Gets Married" ["Xiaoerhei jiehun"], in *Zhao Shuli daibiao zuo*, 1–16.

46 *Longxugou-*DZSD, 69; *Longxugou-1953*, 64; Lao She, "*Longxugou* paicaiben," 35.

47 Lao She, "*Longxugou* paicaiben," 25; *Longxugou-*DZSD, 49; *Longxugou-1953*, 50.

48 *Longxugou-*DZSD, 75; *Longxugou-1953*, 70.

49 Kwok, "Trends of Urban Planning," 165.

50 See, e.g., Jin Li, "Huigu *Longxugou* de pailian," 47.

51 *Longxugou-*DZSD, 77; *Longxugou-1953*, 71; Lao She, "*Longxugou* paicaiben," 38.

52 Lalkaka, "Urban Housing in China"; Sun Xiuping, "Beijing chengqu quan xinshi maicang he, hu, gou, keng de fenbu ji qi yanbian," 228.

53 Huang Wenlong, "Gongren huanying xiang Longxugou zheyang de zuopin."

54 *Longxugou-*DZSD, 41; *Longxugou-1953*, 44; Lao She, "*Longxugou* paicaiben," 26; Lao She, "*Longxugou* paicaiben," 10; *Longxugou-*DZSD, 10; *Longxugou-1953*, 15.

55 Lao She, "Longxugou de xiezuo jingguo," 9.

56 "Liyong dufan taowa Longxugou jihua."

57 Shi Mingzheng, *Zouxiang jindaihua de Beijingcheng*, 122.

58 "Liyong dufan taowa Longxugou jihua."

59 Beijing Tebieshi Gongshu Gongwuju, Memos concerning Zhang Qikui's petition for initiation works at Longxugou.

60 Lao She, "Mao zhuxi geile wo xin de wenyi shengming," 44.

61 Dong, *Republican Beijing*, 304.

62 Lao She, "*Longxugou* de xiezuo jingguo," 10.

63 Lao She, "*Longxugou* de renwu," 13.

64 See, e.g., Zhong Dafeng, Zhen Zhang, and Yingjin Zhang, "From *Wenmingxi* (Civilized Play) to *Yingxi* (Shadowplay)."

65 Details on the production of *This Life of Mine* and interviews with actors are included in the TV documentary *Beijing, oh Beijing*.

66 The play mentions that the site was originally the barracks of the Manchu Blue Banner (*Longxugou*-DZSD, 40; *Longxugou*-1953, 43). On the architecture and social significance of the *zayuan'r*, see Bai Quequn, *Lao Beijing de juzhu*, 68.

67 Lao She, "Yao re'ai ni de hutong."

68 In a long essay, Jiao refers to his experience in directing *Dragon Whisker Creek* only to launch into a long exposition on the Stanislavsky method. Jiao Juyin, "Longxugou daoyan yishu chuangzao de zongjie." For Jiao's explanation of the Stanislavskian implications for stage sets, see Jiao Juyin, "Lun huaju wutai meishu de minzuhua wenti."

69 Chen Yongxiang, "Cong shenghuo dao wutai," 230.

70 Many sources comment on the actors' stay at Longxugou; the story is confirmed in interviews with the actors for *A City without Rain*, the TV documentary on *Dragon Whisker Creek*.

71 Chen Yongxiang, "Cong shenghuo dao wutai," 240, 239. Li Bozhao also emphasizes how the performance blurs the distinction between life and art: "When I watched the general rehearsal, it was as if I was no longer watching a play and actors but rather was transported into the drama, experiencing the characters' joys and sorrows": Li Bozhao, "Cong *Longxugou* kan Beijing," 3.

72 Chen Yongxiang, "Cong shenghuo dao wutai," 258.

73 The actor Li Daqian tells how Lao She guided him in speaking with a standard Beijing accent. Gan Hailan. *Lao She Nianpu*, 257.

74 *Longxugou*-DZSD, 49; *Longxugou*-1953, 49; Lao She, "*Longxugou* paicaiben," 25.

75 Dong, *Republican Beijing*, 172–207.

76 The novelist Zhang Henshui, who lived in Beijing between 1919 and 1937, reported on Tianqiao in several of his writings. See, e.g., Zhang Henshui, *Zhang Henshui shuo Beijing*, 99.

77 Zhao Shuli, "Li Youcai banhua" [Rhymes of Li Youcai], in *Zhao Shuli daibiao zuo*, 17–60.

78 Yu Shizhi, "Yanyuan riji zhaichao zhi yi," 179.

79 Lao She, "Beijing," 5.

80 On the touristy use of these observation points during the Qing, see Naquin, *Peking*, 492–93.

81 Dong, *Republican Beijing*, 256.

82 Li Bozhao, "Cong *Longxugou* kan Beijing."

83 *Longxugou*-DZSD, 4; *Longxugou*-1953, 8; see also Lao She, "*Longxugou* paicai-ben," 8.

84 Lao She, "*Longxugou* paicaiben," 6. A similar warning was given to the BPAT actors when they visited Longxugou. Jin Li, "Huigu Longxugou de pailian," 48.

85 Lao She, "*Longxugou* de renwu," 13.

86 *Longxugou*-DZSD, 36; *Longxugou*-1953, 40.

87 Lao She, "*Longxugou* paicaiben," 23.

88 *Longxugou*-DZSD, 51; *Longxugou*-1953, 51.

89 Naquin, *Peking*, 632.

90 *Longxugou*-DZSD, 42; *Longxugou*-1953, 45.

91 Broudehoux, *Making and Selling of Post-Mao Beijing*, 96–104.

92 Lao She, "*Longxugou* paicaiben," 26.

93 Lao She feared that in its original form "the play wasn't enough of a Sprout Song–like performance." Pu Siwen, "Lao She xiansheng he ta de *Longxugou*," 85.

94 Lao She, "*Longxugou* paicaiben," 38; Lao She, *Longxugou*-1953, 72.

95 In fact, Zhao Shuli, as a member of the Municipal Literary Association, suggested after the general rehearsal to add more actors onstage. "*Longxugou* diyici caipai" (1951), 1.

96 Zha, *China Pop*, 63.

97 The chimney seems to appear first as an icon of modernity in the paintings of Claude Monet, who nevertheless took care not to associate industrial images with labor. T. J. Clark, *Painting of Modern Life*, 184–90.

98 Widdis, *Visions of a New Land*, 80, 81, 84, 175.

99 Wang Jun notes the impracticality of this vision, based on Soviet experts' analogy with Moscow. Whereas 25 percent of the Soviet capital's residents were laborers, only 4 percent of Beijing's citizens were involved in industry. Wang Jun, *Cheng ji*, 82–83.

TWO A Big Dyeing Vat

1 Shanghai Shi Lishi Bowuguan, *Zou zai lishi de jiyi li*, 126, 136.

2 "Yongyuan baochi jianku fendou de geming jingshen," 1–2.

3 Yusuf and Weiping Wu, *Dynamics of Urban Growth*, 48.

4 Des Forges, *Mediasphere Shanghai*, 19.

5 Cheng Tongyi, "20 shijimo dansheng de Zhongguo Nanjing lu xue," 670–84; see Cochran, *Inventing Nanjing Road*.

6 Paul Clark, *Chinese Cinema*, 48–52.

7 The description is based on the documentary film *The Birth of New China* [1949] and footage reproduced in the documentaries *China, 1949* and *New China*, both of which aired in 1999. On the days following the PLA's entry into the city, see extended reports in the *Liberation Daily* of October 9, 1949, as well as *Xin shanghai bianlan*, 461–63; Shanghai Huangpu Qu Geming Weiyuanhui Xiezuozu,

Shanghai waitan Nanjing lu shihua, 185–91; Shanghaishi Dang'anguan, *Shanghai jiefang*; and *Dangdai Zhongguo de Shanghai*, 1:91–94.

8 Gao Weijin, interview with the author, Beijing, July 12, 2001.

9 Chen Huangmei, *Dangdai Zhongguo dianying shi*, 2:6–11.

10 Zhang Zhen, *Amorous History*, 52–64.

11 Vampley, *Turf*, 12, 135.

12 Yang Jiayou, *Shanghai lao fangzi de gushi*, 368–71.

13 Braester, "Shanghai's Economy of the Spectacle."

14 Coates, *China Races*.

15 As T. J. Clark notes, the fiction of suburban idyll developed in conjunction with Paris's urbanization in the nineteenth century, giving rise to a new perception of the *banlieux*. Clark, *Painting of Modern Life*, 152.

16 *Shanghai chengshi guihua zhi* Bianzuan Weiyuanhui, *Shanghai chengshi guihua zhi*, 92, 462–63.

17 Cheng Jihua, *Zhongguo dianying fazhan shi*, 2:243; Zhao Ming, *Ju ying fuchen lu*, 128–33.

18 On the cartoon, see Farquhar, "Sanmao," 109–25.

19 Zhao Ming, *Ju ying fuchen lu*.

20 *Shanghai chengshi guihua zhi* Bianzuan Weiyuanhui, *Shanghai chengshi guihua zhi*, 90–96.

21 Pan Xulan, *Xin Zhongguo wenxue cidian*, 633. Su Yemu's text is available at www.bookhome.net. Accessed August 20, 2006.

22 Yang Jiayou, *Shanghai lao fangzi de gushi*, 124–28.

23 Mao Zedong, "Zai Zhongguo gongchandang diqijie zhongyang yuanhui dierci quanti huiyi shang de baogao" [Report at the second plenum of the seventh Central Committee of the Chinese Communist Party]; quoted in Nie Wei, "*Nihong deng xia de shaobing*."

24 Yang Dongping, *Chengshi jifeng*, 306.

25 Gu Weili, *Zhao Dan*, 166–67.

26 Qi Xiaoping, *Xianghua ducao*, 93–109.

27 See Salaff, "Urban Communes."

28 See Li Xiao, *Shanghai huaju zhi*, 202.

29 "Shiwei youxing shengkuang."

30 "Shanghai renmin yi wubi reqing relie huanying renmin Jiefangjun," 2; for more details, see Braester, " 'Big Dying Vat.' "

31 Barber, *Fall of Shanghai*, 142.

32 Wasserstrom, *Student Protests*, 275.

33 See *Shanghai jiefang shinian* [Ten years to the liberation of Shanghai], ed. *Shanghai jiefang shinian* Zhengwen Bianji Weiyuanhui [The Essay Solicitation and Editorial Committee of Ten Years to the Liberation of Shanghai], esp. Zhang Chunqiao, "Pandeng xin de shengli gaofeng."

34 Mao Tse-Tung, "On the Correct Handling of Contradictions."

35 *Shanghai chengshi guihua zhi* Bianzuan Weiyuanhui, *Shanghai chengshi guihua zhi*, 90–96.

36 Hua Lanhong, *Chongjian Zhongguo*, 45.

37 Yang Dongping sees in the film's reference to "Greater Shanghai" a sign of the end of Shanghai's reputation as "the Paris of the East." Yang Dongping, *Chengshi jifeng*, 312.

38 Naughton, "Third Front."

39 Wang Youhai, " 'Nanjing lu shang hao balian' chengming jingguo." The company was first known as the First Company of the First Battalion of the Special Regiment of the Eastern Arena Guard Brigade.

40 Lü Xingchen, "Nanjing lu shang hao balian"; Cheng Tongyi, "Malu zhi jia."

41 Zhang Zheming, " 'Nanjing lu shang hao balian' chengming qianhou."

42 Wang Youhai, " 'Nanjing lu shang hao balian' chengming jingguo."

43 Bennet, *Yundong*, 33, 38–40.

44 "Shanghai renmin yi wubi reqing relie huanying renmin Jiefangjun."

45 Lü Xingchen, *Nanjing lu shang hao balian de gushi*.

46 Gongqingtuan Shiwei Xuanchuanbu, "Benshi qingnian xuexi 'Nanjing lu shang hao balian' de qingkuang fanying."

47 Zhongguo Renmin Geming Junshi Bowuguan, "Nanjing lu shang hao balian shiji guatu," second leaf.

48 "Wubi baochi jianku fendou de zuofeng"; "Jianku zuofeng, daidai xiangchuan"; " 'Hao balian' de gushi shuobuwan."

49 Wang Chuanyou and Wang Jingwen were assigned to the Shanghai Military Command headquarters. Zhang Zheming, " 'Nanjing lu shang hao balian' chengming qianhou."

50 Cheng Tongyi, "Malu zhi jia," 568.

51 Gongqingtuan Shiwei Xuanchuanbu, "Benshi qingnian xuexi 'Nanjing lu shang hao balian' de qingkuang fanying."

52 Shanghai Shi Zonggonghui Xuanchuanbu, "Tongzhi."

53 Gongqingtuan Shanghaishi Weiyuanhui, "Guanyu zai quanshi qingshaonian zhong guangfan kaizhan xuexi 'Nanjing lu shang hao balian' de jiaoyu huodong de tongzhi."

54 Ibid.

55 "Yongyuan baochi jianku fendou de geming jingshen"; "Zhongguo renmin Jiefangjun zong zhenzhibu guanyu 'Nanjing lu shang hao balian' zhengzhi sixiang gongzuo jingyan de jieshao."

56 Lü Xingchen, *Nanjing lu shang hao balian de gushi*; Du Xiulin, *Nanjing lu shang hao balian*. On the comic book, see Xu Ping and Yu Xiangyang, " 'Nanjing lu shang hao balian' de youlai."

57 For additional images, see Braester, " 'Big Dying Vat.' "

58 Gongqingtuan Shanghaishi Weiyuanhui, "Guanyu zai quanshi qingshaonian zhong guangfan kaizhan xuexi 'Nanjing lu shang hao balian' de jiaoyu huodong de tongzhi," 2–3.

59 Zhongguo Caimao Gonghui Shanghaishi Weiyuanhui, "Guanyu Zhongbai si dian, yiyao yi dian, Huamei fuzhuang dian sange danwei xuexi Lei Feng, xuexi Nanjing lu shang hao balian de qingguang huibao."

60 Cheng Tongyi, "Malu zhi jia," 564.

61 See MacFarquhar, *Origins of the Cultural Revolution*, 334–48.

62 Bennet, *Yundong*, 38–40.

63 See Jieming Zhu, *Transition of China's Urban Development*, 15.

64 "Yongyuan baochi jianku fendou de geming jingshen," 1–2.

65 Cheng Tongyi, "Malu zhi jia," 563–64. Circumstantial evidence of the campaign's impact may be found in the fact that all the references I have encountered to the events of 1949 mention the company by its later name. Even informed eyewitnesses to Shanghai's liberation described to me the orderly occupation of the city by the PLA in phrases almost identical to state propaganda and referred, anachronistically, to the Good Eighth Company.

66 Zhongguo Renmin Geming Junshi Bowuguan, "Nanjing lu shang hao balian shiji guatu," leaf no. 12.

67 Nie Wei, "*Nihong deng xia de shaobing.*"

68 Gu Yubao, "*Nihong deng xia de shaobing* 'si' er fusheng ji." Some discrepancies exist concerning the performance dates in Beijing; I have followed Gu's account throughout.

69 Gongqingtuan Shanghaishi Weiyuanhui, "Guanyu zai quanshi qingshaonian zhong guangfan kaizhan xuexi 'Nanjing lu shang hao balian' de jiaoyu huodong de tongzhi."

70 Wang Youhai, "'Nanjing lu shang hao balian' chengming jingguo"; Xu Renjun, "Qin Hualong mengyuan shimo."

71 Ge Yihong et al., *Zhongguo huaju tongshi*, 431–32, 437; Gu Yubao, "*Nihong deng xia de shaobing* 'si' er fusheng ji"; Song Zhao, *Mama de yisheng*, 160.

72 Wang Youhai, "'Nanjing lu shang hao balian' chengming jingguo," 13–18; Song Zhao, *Mama de yisheng*, 161.

73 Chen Qingquan, "*Nihongdeng xia de shaobing* zai Shanghai kaipai," 27; Song Zhao, *Mama de yisheng*, 151, 161.

74 Song Zhao, *Mama de yisheng*, 162.

75 Nan Shao, "Lishi chelun cao zai shei shou?"

76 Sun Keyu, "*Bu ye cheng* waiqu le lishi zhenshi"; Xi Longxiang et al., "*Bu ye cheng* mosha jieji douzheng xuanyang touxiang zhuyi."

77 Shanghai Dianying Xitong Da Pipan Xiezuo Zu, "Chedi cuihui zichan jieji de *Bu ye cheng*," 46.

78 Zi Zhongyun, "The Clash of Ideas," 238.

79 Wang Youhai, "'Nanjing lu shang hao balian' chengming jingguo," 13–18.

80 Nie Wei, "*Nihong deng xia de shaobing.*"

81 For a detailed discussion of *The Young Generation*, see Tang, *Chinese Modern*, 163–95.

82 Zhang Zhengyu, "Wutai meishu pingdian"; Sun Haoran, "San kan *Shaobing.*"

83 "Shanghai zui zao fanhua de malu."

84 Kinouchi Makoto, *Shanhai rekishi gaidomappu*, 5.

85 Fang Xiang, "Diguo zhuyi zai yuandong de da duqu."

86 "Diguo zhuyi de xingwei yaobude."

87 Song Zhao, *Mama de yisheng*, 166–67.

88 Pang, *Building a New China in Cinema*, 179–82.

89 On the *huaji* production, see the Shanghai municipal local gazetteer office website: www.shtong.gov.cn. Accessed August 30, 2006.

90 E.g., *Are You Satisfied?*; and *Forced Draft*.

91 "Jiefang Shanghai diyiri."

92 Song Zhao, *Mama de yisheng*, 162.

93 Sun Shaoyi, "Dushi kongjian yu Zhongguo minzu zhuyi," 43.

94 For a synopsis of *Humanity*, see Cheng Jihua, *Zhongguo dianying fazhan shi*, 1:190–91.

95 See Jones, *Yellow Music*. Mao Dun's novel *Midnight* (1932) opens with a reference to "a gigantic neon sign."

96 Song Zhao, *Mama de yisheng*, 166–68.

97 Shang Jingwen, *Nanjing lu shang hao balian*, 33.

98 For details on the 1976 Guangzhou revival, see "Tizhe naodai paiyan *Nihong deng xia da shaobeng*," www.gzlib.gov.cn/shequ_info/ndgz/NDGZDetail.do?id= 18464. The 2001 play was filmed by Shanghai TV Station, and the TV series was distributed by Hunan Jinfeng Video Publications.

99 Fu Gengzhen, "Cong *Jiashen sanbai nian ji* dao *Nihong deng xia de shaobing*"; on the various anniversary celebrations of the Good Eighth Company, see Xu Ping and Yu Xiangyang, " 'Nanjing lu shang hao balian' de youlai."

THREE Mansions of Uneven Rhyme

1 Li Longyun, *Wanjia denghuo*, promotional jacket.

2 Huang Weijun and Zhou Ruixiang, *Huihuang de yishu diantang*, 169; Chen, *Acting the Right Part*, 185–86.

3 See, e.g., Yu Qing, "Shei ye dangbuzhu qianjin de chaotou"; and Chen Baichen, "Chong du *Xiaojing hutong*."

4 Some sources claim that *Next-Door Neighbors* was also titled *The Big Courtyard* (*Da yuan'r*). In fact, the latter was a play by another playwright that was rejected by BPAT. Su Shuyang, interview with the author, Beijing, July 23, 2006.

5 Ibid.

6 Huang Weijun, "Xiaoyuan chunqiu."

7 Ibid. Huang concedes, however, that the political message already seemed dated in 1981.

8 Quotations based on recorded performance by BPAT in 1980. Video CD.

9 Su Shuyang, interview with the author, Beijing, July 23, 2006.

10 Li Longyun, *Small Well Lane*, 72.

11 Li Longyun, *You zheyang yige xiaoyuan*. *There Is a Small Courtyard* features the character Zheng Jiaxing, a former actor who recites lines from various plays on Beijing, such as Tian Han's *Guan Hanqing* (1958) and *Dragon Whisker Creek*. In

portraying Zheng as an actor who went mad during the Cultural Revolution, just as Lao She portrayed Madman Cheng as a victim of "feudal" society, Li Longyun condemns yet again the "ten years of chaos." The repeated references to *Dragon Whisker Creek*, showing that the promise of socialism has not been fulfilled yet, seems directed against the Gang of Four. Xiaomei Chen sees in the play also an implicit criticism of the contemporary conditions of the early 1980s. Chen, *Acting the Right Part*, 211.

12 Li Longyun, *You zheyang yige xiaoyuan*.

13 Li Longyun, *Small Well Lane*, 19. Li's mentor, Chen Baichen, describes the play explicitly as adhering to revolutionary realism. "Chong du *Xiaojing hutong*."

14 For a discussion of *Small Well Lane* as oral history, see Jiang and Cheek, "Introduction."

15 Li Longyun, *Xiaojing hutong*, 402.

16 Chen Baichen, "Chong du *Xiaojing hutong*."

17 On the National Construction Committee's decision, see Wang Dehua, *Zhongguo chengshi guihua shigang*, 163.

18 Wu, "China's Changing Urban Governance," 1084.

19 The 1983 script diverges significantly from the 1980 version (published in 1981 and available in English translation) and from the censored script as staged in 1985 (circulated on video CD). The play was staged in 1983 (original version, in a performance for officials only) and in the censored version in 1985 and 1993. Li Longyun gives a full account of the various rewritings in "Wei *Xiaojing hutong* xi san."

20 Li Longyun, *Xiaojing hutong*, 402.

21 Chen, *Reading the Right Part*, 16–17.

22 Chen, *Acting the Right Part*, 327.

23 Quotations based on recorded performance by BPAT in 1991. Video CD.

24 Conceison, *Significant Other*, 128. Conceison provides detailed background on the staging of *Bird Men* and insights into its themes; ibid., 120–36.

25 Guo Jia, "*Cesuo* haobi dunzhe de *Chaguan*."

26 Jing Wang, " 'Culture' as Leisure," 71.

27 An official publication states the following facts: "Total savings deposits of urban and rural residents had just reached 500 billion yuan in 1989; they now exceed 8.7 trillion yuan; . . . The overall scale of consumption continues to grow. In 2001, total retail sales of consumer products in China were 3.5 times the level of 1990, at a value of 3,759,500 billion yuan. Consumption patterns have undergone radical changes. Urban families' average per capita expenditure on food, as a proportion of total spending, dropped from 54.2 per cent in 1990 to 37.9 per cent in 2001; rural families' dropped from 58.8 to 47.7 per cent." United Nations Economic and Social Council, "Implementation of the International Covenant on Economic, Social and Cultural Rights," 40.

28 Quotations based on recorded performance by BPAT in 1991. Video CD.

29 Tong Daoming, "*Beijing daye* xiqi."

30 The script emphasizes the analogy between the courtyard and other architectural treasures, whereas the 1994 draft avoids state symbols and mentions only Qianmen (Zhengyangmen) Gate.

31 Jia Fulin, "Beijing de ye."

32 Friedmann, *China's Urban Transition*, 33.

33 Abramson, "Beijing's Preservation Policy."

34 Fang Ke, *Dangdai Beijing jiucheng gengxin*, 24–25.

35 Friedmann, *China's Urban Transition*, 23.

36 United Nations Economic and Social Council, "Implementation of the International Covenant on Economic, Social and Cultural Rights," 40.

37 Ian Johnson, *Wild Grass*, 87–182; Friedmann, *China's Urban Transition*, 106–8.

38 Wang Dehua, *Zhongguo chengshi guihua shigang*, 195–216.

39 Abramson, "Aesthetics of City-Scale Preservation Policy."

40 Abramson, "Beijing's Preservation Policy."

41 Urban planning in China remains a nascent field, trying to catch up quickly with Western theories and train a sufficient number of practitioners. Visser, *Cities Surround the Countryside*, chap. 1.

42 Wang Dehua, *Zhongguo chengshi guihua shigang*, 159–70.

43 On Feng's activities, see Braester and Zhang, "Future of China's Memories."

44 Shu Yi, talk at Peking University, October 2003.

45 For a transcript of the TV show, see 202.114.166.22/bmp/shss/shss_13.htm (Google cache).

46 Xie Xizhang, "*Beijing daye.*"

47 Ibid.; She Ran, "Siheyuan li de shidai zheguang," 29.

48 "*Beijing daye*: Beijingren de ganga."

49 Xie Xizhang, "*Beijing daye,*" 11.

50 Yang Dongping, "*Beijing daye.*"

51 Zhong Jieying, "Juben gousi xunji," 26.

52 Shu Yi, "Daye? Daye?"

53 Zhong Jieying, "Zhi yuan shen zai ci shan zhong."

54 The bannermen concept is an old one. The Qing dynasty originated with the Manchu—a northern tribe considered alien at the time of the invasion, in the early seventeenth century. The Qing court relied on Manchu retainers, who were organized into "banners" (erstwhile military divisions). By the late nineteenth century, banners had lost much of their significance. Many Beijing families can trace their origins to the banners, but other than granting a vague sense of superior pedigree, this heritage means simply that they are of Manchu origin.

55 "*Beijing daye*: Beijingren de ganga."

56 Shu Yi, "Daye? Daye?"

57 See Zhou Siyuan, "Xijian Beijingren chongshen ziji"; Xie Xizhang, "*Beijing daye,*" 11.

58 See, e.g., Xu Chengbei, *Jiudu xinxie*; Hua Mengyang and Zhang Hongjie, *Lao*

Beijingren de shenghuo; Zeng Zhizhong and You Deyan, *Zhang Hengshui shuo Beijing*; Han Xiaohui, *Chengshi piping*; Zhang Qi, *Beijingren he Shanghairen qutan*; and Lu Xun et al., *Beijingren, Shanghairen*.

59 *Beijing lao Tianqiao*; *Beijing lao chengmen*.

60 Wang Zengqi, "Hutong wenhua."

61 Jing Wang, "'Culture' as Leisure."

62 Quotations based on recorded performance by China Youth Theater in 1997. Video CD.

63 Braester and Zhang, "Future of China's Memories," 148.

64 Zhang Donglin and Wang Chao, "Lixing, ganxing, Beijing kuashiji zhuzhai."

65 Li Longyun, *Wo suo zhidao de Yu Shizhi*, 111.

66 For a short biography of Lan Yinhai, see the online *Shijie renwu cihai* [Lexion of world people]: www.worldpersondictionary.com. Accessed October 23, 2006.

67 Zhang Zuomin, "Gao chang shidai tongxinqu."

68 Yu Kui, "*Gala'r Hutong* ABC."

69 Wang Hongbo, "*Gala'r Hutong* qishilu."

70 Quotations based on recorded performance by China Youth Theater in 1997. Video CD.

71 The play may also have been inspired by the construction in Debao District and Huaiboshu jie (Locust Tree Street). Yu Kui, "*Gala'r Hutong* ABC."

72 Wu Liangyong, *Rehabilitating the Old City of Beijing*, 130.

73 Gao Fuyuan, "Beijing shishu—guouhai."

74 Zhang Zuomin, "Gao chang shidai tongxinqu."

75 Ren Ming, interview with the author, Beijing, July 10, 2002.

76 "Fang+gai weigai yinling chaiqianhu zoushang anju lu"; He and Wu, "Property-Led Redevelopment"; Jianshebu Zhengce Yanjiu Zhongxin, *Zuixin chengshi fangwu chaiqian zhinan*.

77 Ma Qiang, "Weigai haishi qiangqie?"

78 Fang Ke, *Dangdai Beijing jiucheng gengxin*. On the reception of Fang Ke's book, see also Ian Johnson, *Wild Grass*, 110–22.

79 He and Wu, "Property-Led Redevelopment."

80 Wang Guangtao, *Beijing lishi wenhua mingcheng de baohu yu fazhan*, 93.

81 Ibid., 94–95.

82 For a review of the Beijing Sixth Development and Construction Company, see the site of the Beijing Federation of Trade Unions: www.bjzgh.gov.cn. Accessed June 27, 2009.

83 "Chongwenqu Jinyuchi shequ."

84 He Depu, "Beijing Jinyuchi xiaoqu huiqianhu de fennu."

85 Goldfish Ponds resident, interview with the author, Beijing, August 2004.

86 He Depu, "Beijing Jinyuchi xiaoqu huiqianhu de fennu."

87 Goldfish Ponds resident, interview with the author, Beijing, August 2004.

88 Unger and Chan, "Memories and the Moral Economy."

89 Descriptions of the play follow my viewing of the play in July 2001; quotations based on the unpublished rehearsal script.

90 Peng Yongjie, Zhang Zhiwei, and Han Donghui, *Renwen Aoyun*.

91 Duan Muqi, "Zhongguo fangdichan jingguan sheji xianzhuang yu fazhan."

92 See, e.g., *Zhongguo fangdichan guanggao nianjian*.

93 Wu Qiong, interview with the author, Beijing, July 10, 2002.

94 "Cong *Longxugou* dao *Jinyuchi*."

95 "*Longxugou* jinri pu xinbian *Jinyuchi* zuowan shouyan."

96 Information on Jinyuchi is given on the Chongwen district government's official site: www.cwi.gov.cn. Accessed December 11, 2005.

97 Wang Jun, "Beijing Jinyuchi baixing yuan le zhufang meng."

98 The Chongwen district government website featured for a while a dedicated Jinyuchi portal, at www.cwi.gov.cn/cwi_zt/jyc/jyc.htm. Accessed December 11, 2005.

99 My discussion of *A Myriad Lights* is based on two versions of the play: the original written script, in Li Longyun, *Wanjia denghuo*, 1–164, and the staged version, available on DVD.

100 Li Longyun, "*Wanjia denghuo* chuangzuo de qianyin houguo"; Li Longyun, "Yu shi gejue de sanshi tian," 165.

101 Li Longyun, "*Wanjia denghuo* chuangzuo riji houji."

102 Li Longyun, interview with the author, Beijing, September 10, 2005; Lin Zhaohua, informal conversation with the author, Beijing, September 9, 2005.

103 Li Longyun, "Yu shi gejue de sanshi tian," 175.

104 Li Longyun, *Xiaojing hutong*, 402.

105 Duan Muqi, "Zhongguo fangdichan jingguan sheji xianzhuang yu fazhan."

106 Wang Dehua, *Zhongguo chengshi guihua shigang*, 299–304.

107 Keane, *Created in China*, 114.

108 See, e.g., Wang Shaoqiang, *Zhongguo fangdichan guanggao nianjian, 2003*; and Wei Chenglin, *Beijing zhongchouxian chengshi sheji*.

109 Wu Liangyong, *Rehabilitating the Old City*, 192–93.

FOUR The First Precinct under Heaven

1 Dong Guangqi, *Gudu Beijing*, 27–41.

2 Chen Wenqian, "Kuqiang Beijingcheng."

3 "Tiananmen 35 nian qian ceng mimi chongjian."

4 In 2003, an urban supervisory department (*chengguan fenju*) was given control of "Tiananmen region" (*Tiananmen diqu*), made autonomous to "avoid a vacuum." Regulation No. 144 of Beijing Municipality, issued on April 20, 2004, citing incidents of public unrest (including demonstrations over demolition-and-relocation), established Tiananmen District. The area includes the National Museum (formerly the Museum of the Revolution) east of the Square, the Great Hall

of the People to the west, Zhengyangmen (Qianmen) Gate to the south, and all the way north to Meridian Gate, the entrance to the Forbidden City. The district is under the jurisdiction of the Administrative Committee of Tiananmen Region (Tiananmen Diqu Guanli Weiyuanhui), originally a small unit in charge of the upkeep of the Tiananmen Gate structure. Ou Yangbin, "Tiananmen guangchang bainian libian." See also the Tiananmen District Committee's website, www .tiananmen.org.cn. Accessed June 1, 2008.

5 Lefebvre, *Production of Space*, 38–39, 200–206, 225.

6 Hershkovitz, "Tiananmen Square," 399.

7 Wang Yushi, *Tiananmen*, 1–10, 36–60; Sit, *Beijing*, 50–52, 77; Hou Renzhi, "Beijing jiucheng pingmian sheji de gaizao"; Hou Renzhi, "Tiananmen guang-chang"; Hou Renzhi, "Transformation of the Old City of Beijing"; Hershkovitz, "Tiananmen Square," 405; Wang Yushi, *Tiananmen*, 25–27; Wu Hung, "Tiananmen Square," 91–93.

8 Wen Fu, *Tiananmen jianzheng lu*, 524.

9 Wang Yushi, *Tiananmen*, 65.

10 See Wu Shibao, "Kaiguo dadian shang de bubing fangdui."

11 At the February parade, local leaders surveyed the troops from the Tiananmen balcony: Wang Yushi, *Tiananmen*, 62–63; see also Wen Fu, *Tiananmen jianzheng lu*, 423–29. That was also the first time a portrait of Mao Zedong (side by side with one of Lin Biao) was hung on the gate. Wen Fu, *Tiananmen jianzheng lu*, 435–36.

12 Wang Hongzhi, *Tiananmen guangchang geming jianshi*, 47; Wen Fu, *Tiananmen jianzheng lu*, 453–54.

13 Wu Hung, *Remaking Beijing*, 64–65. See also Wang Hongzhi, *Tiananmen guang-chang geming jianshi*, 60; Wen Fu, *Tiananmen jianzheng lu*, 479–84; Wang Yushi, *Tiananmen*, 93.

14 Tung, *Preserving the World's Great Cities*, 158–60; Wang Jun, *Cheng ji*, 82–96.

15 Wu Liangyong, *Rehabilitating the Old City*, 16–23.

16 Matthew Johnson, "State Cinema and Sovereign Form."

17 Details about the filming and screening of *The Birth of New China* are based on my interview with director Gao Weijin on August 8, 2001, at her Beijing residence.

18 Hou Bo, "Kaiguo dadian," 15.

19 Two recent examples of special notice are the TV documentary series *The Story of 1949* (1999) and *Founding the Nation* (2004). *The Story of 1949* recreates the narrative of *The Birth of New China* in a series that includes one hundred episodes and presents the events literally day by day; *Founding the Nation* (in four episodes) combines original footage of the days leading to the Founding Ceremony—practically all taken from *The Birth of New China*—with recent interviews with eyewitnesses.

20 Wu Hung details the changes to the spectacle, including floats since 1952 and large patterns made of flowers carried by people since 1957, in his *Remaking Beijing*, 100–101.

21 The parades precipitated, in fact, the use of telephoto lenses. Yu Huiru, a Xinhua News Agency photographer assigned to the parades since 1953, tells how in 1954 a platform made of reeds was raised at the square's northeastern corner. Jokingly called "the artillery battery," it was equipped two years later with a high-resolution camera. Yu Huiru, "Tiananmen qian jia 'dapao.'" As Mao summoned the Red Guards for parades in 1966, new solutions were needed, especially as the Mao cult required ever-larger portraits of the Great Leader. Since only Xinhua News Agency owned a zoom lens, other photographers first borrowed lenses— no organization could refuse lending them for the purpose of capturing Mao's image—and later imported them from Japan. With a 2000mm lens, the *People's Daily* boasted close-ups of unprecedented quality, but the agencies continued to compete for the best view of the balcony. Wang Dong, "Jinshuiqiao tou de 'paoqun,'" 66.

22 Zhang Jinggan, *Beijing guihua jianshe wushi nian*, 59.

23 Chris Berry, "A Nation T(w/o)o," 27.

24 Li Qiankuan and Xiao Guiyun, "Nuli zai yinmu shang shuxie shidai fenliu," 37.

25 Ibid., 36.

26 Ibid., 32, 43.

27 Ibid., 39, 41.

28 Ibid., 40.

29 Ibid., 40.

30 The success in creating an identity between the documentary footage and the 1989 film is evidenced also by the fact that when *The Birth of New China* was issued on video CD in 1997, the cover photo was taken—without acknowledgement—from *The Founding Ceremony*.

31 The original script of *The Founding Ceremony* called for opening the film with a shot of Dong's work. Li Qiankuan and Xiao Guiyun, "Nuli zai yinmu shang shuxie shidai fenliu," 40. For a detailed analysis of Dong's painting, see Wu Hung, *Remaking Beijing*, 171–74. The political travails of the various versions of the painting are discussed in Chen Lüsheng, *Xin Zhongguo meishu tushi*, 183; and Andrews, *Painters and Politics*, 80–86.

32 Li Qiankuan and Xiao Guiyun, "Nuli zai yinmu shang shuxie shidai fenliu," 40.

33 Wu Hung, *Remaking Beijing*, 165.

34 On the play's exceptional reception, see Chen, *Acting the Right Part*, 197–201; and Li Xiao, *Shanghai huaju zhi*, 215–16.

35 Paul Clark, *Chinese Cinema*, 160–67. I also thank Wu Tianming for details he gave me during a conversation in Seattle on November 16, 2006.

36 See, e.g., Chen Kaige, *Longxieshu*, 80–81.

37 Chen Kaige and Rayns, *King of the Children*, 28–32; on the production of *The Big Parade*, see also Paul Clark, *Reinventing China*, 146–51.

38 *Celebrations of the Fiftieth Anniversary of the People's Republic of China*, TV documentary.

39 Wen Fu, *Tiananmen jianzheng lu*, 1069.

40 Ibid.

41 Chen Kaige, *Longxieshu*, 11, 10.

42 Huang Xiaoyang, *Yinxiang Zhongguo*, 49–51.

43 Wen Fu, *Tiananmen jianzheng lu*, 1041.

44 Many of Zhao Liang's works, including *Jerks*, can be viewed at art.mofile.com/en/SVFK8YNL. Accessed June 6, 2008.

45 See Wu Hung, *Remaking Beijing*; and Braester, "Photography at Tiananmen."

46 Broudehoux, *Making and Selling of Post-Mao Beijing*, 168.

47 The official line on the 1999 parade is presented in the DVD *China's Fiftieth National Day Parade*.

48 The footage was later integrated into two coproductions by Moscow's Central Documentary Film Studios and Beijing Film Studio: *New Beijing* and *Liberated China*, both released in 1950.

49 Li Xianting, "Tiananmen."

50 "Beijing 2050, Beijing, August 2006." See also Jiang Jun, "Why MAD Is Mad."

51 Two cameras were placed right under the gate, facing the balcony (the camera to the east was manned by the director Gao Weijin; the one to the west was equipped with a zoom for close-ups of the leaders). Two other cameras were situated farther from the gate, south of Chang'an Avenue, to capture the military parade (the one to the east was mounted on a high platform; neither could see beyond the massive triple gates on the avenue). A couple of cameras were perched on top of the square's surrounding walls, providing an overview. A seventh camera, closer to the square's center, filmed prearranged performances. In addition, a number of mobile, soundless cameras were deployed for filming impromptu compositions, such as the dignitaries on the balcony and viewers' reactions inside the square. Gao Weijin, interview with the author, Beijing, August 8, 2001.

52 Li Xin, Liu Xiaosa, and Wang Jifang, *Bei yiwang de yingxiang*, 246–396.

53 Wu Liangyong, *Rehabilitating the Old City*, 51; Lü Junhua, Rowe, and Zhang Jie, *Modern Urban Housing*, 195–207.

54 By comparison, a ticket to the Forbidden City cost only 0.5 RMB at the time. An Ge, *Shenghuo zai Deng Xiaoping shidai*, 222.

55 Chinoy, *China Live*.

56 In the same year, Jia Zhangke made his first short, *One Day, in Beijing*, at Tiananmen. The copy has since been lost.

57 Chris Berry, "Facing Reality."

58 It was through Duan Jinchuan's connections at CCTV that he (as soundman) and Zhang (as cinematographer) were allowed to accompany the TV crew. Since Zhang and Duan arrived with the officially approved crew, no one asked for their credentials and they shot without any hindrance. Zhang Yuan also mentions that he felt at the time that the TV crew were acting for his camera. Li Xin, Liu Xiaosa, and Wang Jifang, *Bei yiwang de yingxiang*, 81.

59 Ibid., 78.

60 Zhang Yuan, interview with the author, Beijing, July 2006.

61 Li Xin, Liu Xiaosa, and Wang Jifang, *Bei yiwang de yingxiang*, 210–14.

62 Shi Jian showed his work, as well as Wu Wenguang's *Bumming in Beijing*, in a workshop held in late 1991: Wu Wenguang, "Just on the Road," 132–38.

63 Zhang also follows Wiseman by claiming that he would let the camera take in any sight and add his narrative through editing. The director of *Central Park* says: "The final film resembles fiction although it is based on un-staged, un-manipulated actions. . . . you structure it." Aftab and Weltz, interview with Frederick Wiseman.

64 Qiu Haidong, *Chengshi zhanche*, 95–97.

65 Wu Hung, *Remaking Beijing*, 211; Li Xiaobin, " 'Shangfangzhe' ji qita," 125; Li Xiaobin, "Guanyu 'Shangfangzhe' de paishe ji qita."

66 Chen Penggui, "Guangchang shang de zheibang ge'rmen."

67 Braester, "Photography at Tiananmen."

68 Jia Yingting, Ye Xiaoyong, and Lu Ye, *Tiananmen bainian jujiao*, 212.

69 Zhang Haiping, " 'Changzheng dui' zhanyou," 78–79.

70 See Wang Wo and Wang Chao, *Renmin wansui*.

FIVE Angel Sanctuaries

1 Allen, "Reading Taipei."

2 Lin Qianrong, *Dushi sheji zai Taiwan*, 58, 99.

3 Ibid., 60–61.

4 Huang Sunquan, "Lüse tuituji," 9–10.

5 Ibid., 31; "DPP to Protest against Amendment Favoring Veterans."

6 Yeh and Davis, *Taiwan Film Directors*, 220, 224.

7 Sun Ke, "Zhonghua wenhua yimiao xiangcheng guanghui canlan wangu chuangxin," *Xianggang shibao*, November 17, 1966; quoted in Fu Zhaoqing, *Zhongguo gudian shiyang xin jianzhu*, 275.

8 Li Qingzhi, "Construct and Transformation," 28.

9 *The Silent Lake* involves figures who would continue to contribute to New Taiwan Cinema. The art director is the future director Wang Tong, and the script is written by Xiaoye, who would also write the script for Edward Yang's *Terrorizer*.

10 Xia is the name of the ancient dynasty from which the Chinese nation purportedly stems. It is used as a common literary allusion to national allegories.

11 The crew included many people who would become famous filmmakers, such as Chris Doyle as photographer, Tsui Hark as director of the Hong Kong crew, Sylvia Chang as production designer, and Wu Nien-jen as coscriptwriter. Wu Nien-jen's lyrics for "The Same Moonlight" were credited to the popular singer Lo Ta-yu for commercial reasons. Wu Nien-jen, informal remarks during the "Island of Light" symposium on Taiwan cinema, University of Wisconsin, Madison, March 7–9, 2002; Yu Kanping, telephone interview with the author, April 20, 2008.

12 Yu Kanping, interview with Lin Wenchi, 2007 (unpublished; my thanks to Lin

Wenchi for providing me with the transcript); Yu Kanping, telephone interview with the author, April 20, 2008.

13 For more on the film's reception, see Kuan Liguang and Li Yuzhi, *Taiwan Xianggang dianying mingpian xinshang*, 178–813; and Yeh and Davis, *Taiwan Film Directors*, 74.

14 Wang Xiaoying, "Hongdong Taiwan de *Da cuoche*."

15 A screening of the entire series was given to a focus group of Jinyuchi residents. "Youru yitai qinggan zhizaoji Dacuoche jixu cuilei."

16 Yeh and Davis, *Taiwan Film Directors*, 156.

17 Chu Tien-wen, informal conversation with the author, May 3, 2008.

18 On the controversy around the film, see Yeh and Davis, *Taiwan Film Directors*, 62.

19 The unchanged appearance of the veterans' village, still a slum, irked the censors, which evidences the sensitivity of policy on veterans' villages. Ibid., 62.

20 "Invisible Cities."

21 Li Qingzhi, *Niaoguo kuang*, 35, 132–33.

22 These topics are explored extensively and repeatedly in the special issue accompanying the 1995 Golden Horse Film Festival retrospective "Focus on Taipei through Cinema": Chen Ruxiu and Miao Jinfeng, *Xunzhao dianying zhong de Taibei* [Focus on Taipei through cinema], ed. Chen Ruxiu and Miao Jinfeng (Taipei: Wanxiang, 1995).

23 See, e.g., Lin Wenqi, "Jiuling niandai Taiwan dushi dianying zhong de lishi, kongjian yu jia/guo."

24 Huang Sunquan, "Lüse tuituji," 64.

25 The institute's self-description was posted on its former website: www.eng.ntu.edu.tw/eng/english/department.asp?key=bp. Accessed February 23, 2007.

26 "Organization of Urban Re's." See also Liu and Lu, "Toward a City for Citizens."

27 See the POTS website at www.pots.com.tw; the Treasure Hill website, associated with OURS, at http://mymedia.yam.com/treasure_hill; and Huang Sun Chuan's blog site at heterotopias.org. Accessed February 10, 2007.

28 Data posted on the website of the Household Registration Office, Zhongshan District of Taipei City: www.cshr.taipei.gov.tw/pk-05.htm. Accessed June 15, 2007.

29 Yeh and Davis, *Taiwan Film Directors*, 6.

30 The relation between memory and modern Taiwan's identity is consistently examined in Stan Lai's work. Stephen Chan observes that episode 4 ("Memory and Amnesia") of Lai's *Na yi ye, women shuo xiangsheng* [That evening, we had a cross-talk show, 1985] implies that all experience recedes into forgetting unless it becomes part of a collective historical narrative. Chan, "Temporality and the Modern Subject." The plot of *Red Lotus Society* also resonates in many ways with Lai's previous film, *Peach Blossom Land* (1992, adapted from the 1986 stage play), which is also preoccupied with the relation between contemporary Taiwan and the experience of aging mainlanders.

31 Stan Lai, interview with the author, Taipei, September 2, 1999.

32 Liu Damu, "Cong wuxia xiaoshuo dao dianying."

33 Ching-chih Lee discusses in detail the fantasy of flying in Taipei and sees it as an escape mechanism from urban stress. Li Qingzhi, "Construct and Transformation," 160–61.

34 Lü Yuezhu, "Hongtou cangying zhen lafeng"; Lan Zuwei, "Yaokong feiji + 35mm sheyingji."

35 Virilio, *War and Cinema*, 11.

36 Lin Wenqi, "Jiuling niandai Taiwan dushi dianying zhong de lishi, kongjian yu jia/guo."

37 Braester, "In Search of History Point Zero."

38 For a discussion of Yang's *Mahjong*, see Braester, "Tales of a Porous City."

39 Tsai expressed interest in the veterans' villages, recalling his work for Yu Kan-ping. Tsai Mingliang, public talk, Taipei, December 2003.

40 Huang Sunquan, "Lüse tuituji," 51–2; Taibeishi Zhengfu Gongwuju Gongyuan Ludeng Gongcheng Guanlichu, "Taibeishi da'an Qihao gongyuan jianjie."

41 Huang Dazhou, *Tuobian*.

42 Lin Chongjie, "Jingying chengshi de xinling," 119.

43 Huang Sunquan, "Lüse tuituji," 5–8, 36, 63.

44 Ibid., 8.

45 Ibid., 58.

46 Chang and Wang, "Mapping Taipei's Landscape of Desire," 115.

47 "Gongsheng yizhan."

48 The correspondence in support of their project, addressed to Mayor Ma Ying-jeou (including a public letter by the author), has been published online on the Treasure Hill website, http://www.treasurehill.org (now http://mymedia.yam .com/treasure_hill). Accessed February 10, 2007.

49 Self-description of OURS, as previously posted on its website: www.ours.org.tw. Accessed May 2, 2007.

50 OURS has recently been involved with the veterans' village at Yangmingshan, where it tries to balance an overzealous development plan with "more sensitive, sustainable, and participatory planning." Ibid.

51 Kang, "Altered Space."

52 Momphard, "Battle of Treasure Hill."

53 Quoted in Wide, "Baozangyan," 169. English text modified to comply with standard grammar.

54 The Family Cinema Club may have drawn inspiration, both as an idea and in design, from the Fremont Outdoor Cinema in Seattle. Min Jay Kang wrote his PhD dissertation on Fremont.

55 See Gross, "Going to Taipei"; and "Treasure Hill," a feature on the site of the Taipei City Government Department of Cultural Affairs, posted October 27, 2006: English.taipei.gov.tw/culture. Accessed June 15, 2007.

56 Xu Yunbin, *Zhanqian guhou*, 189.

57 Treasure Hill website, taipei.treasurehill.org.tw (now http://mymedia.yam.com/ treasure_hill). Accessed June 15, 2003.

58 Yan Zhongxian, *Yizhong jianzhu de shuoshushu*, 95–117.
59 "Sharen jihua" (My Whispering Plan). Publicity pamphlet, 2002.
60 The film failed, to a large extent, due to inexpert marketing. It was Lin's first movie after breaking up with the producer Peggy Chiao Hsiung-ping.
61 Lin Cheng-sheng, interview with the author, Seattle, October 6, 2006.
62 Information on Chenggong Xincun can be found in a report on a project by the National Taiwan University Department of Geography, on its website: www.geog .ntu.edu.tw/course/rs/92final/team7/webpage/new_page_3.htm.   Further information on Taipei's veterans' villages can be found in "This Is My Land," a project of the Ming Hu Junior High School of Taipei: librarywork.taiwanschool net.org/gsh2006/gsh4294. Accessed June 21, 2007.
63 Nora, "Between Memory and History."

SIX "This is the story of our street"

1 Based on Ning Ying's talks at the University of Washington Exploration Seminar in Beijing, August 30, 2004, and August 24, 2005.
2 Wang Dehua, *Zhongguo chengshi guihua shigang*, 195–216; Zhang Zhen, "Bearing Witness," 5.
3 Visser, *Cities Surround the Countryside*, chap. 3.
4 Kostof, "His Majesty the Pick."
5 Abbas, *Hong Kong*, 7.
6 Ning Ying, talk with the audience after screening *On the Beat* at the Walter Reade Theater, New York City, February 2001.
7 Chris Berry, "Facing Reality." On the relationship between *jishi zhuyi* and Bazin, see Zheng Dongtian's recent interview, "Chunzhen niandai."
8 Wu Wenguang, "*Xianchang*." See also Braester, "Excuse Me."
9 Zhang Zhen, "Bearing Witness," 21; Zhang Zhen, "Transfiguring the Postsocialist Chinese City."
10 Nichols, "Strike."
11 Zhang Zhen, "Bearing Witness," 8.
12 Ibid., 2, 3.
13 Leaf and Li Hou, " 'Third Spring,' " 560.
14 See Ma Lin, Da Jiangxia, and Zhu Mei, "*Neighbors*."
15 The shoot took place at the dormitory of the Beijing Institute of Aeronautics and Astronautics; the campus filmed was that of Zhejiang University: Zheng Dongtian, telephone interview with the author, February 7, 2009.
16 Ma Lin, Da Jiangxia and Zhu Mei, "Zunxun shenghuo de qishi," 201. The scriptwriter Zhu Mei was personally acquainted with such buildings, since he lived at the Tsinghua University dormitory. Zheng Dongtian, telephone interview with the author, February 7, 2009.
17 Yang Dongping, *Chengshi jifeng*, 249–58. For a partial translation, see Dutton,

Streetlife China, 212–13. On the work unit system, see Lu and Perry, *Danwei*; and Bray, *Social Space and Governance*.

18 See Unger and Chan, "Memories and the Moral Economy." Unger and Chan discuss work unit housing in the 1990s, but the situation harks back to the 1980s.

19 Lü Junhua, Rowe, and Zhang Jie, eds., *Modern Urban Housing in China*, 202.

20 The fashioning of the most positive character as a retired rather than active cadre set the script apart and constituted the most politically sensitive element. Zheng Dongtian, telephone interview with the author, February 7, 2009.

21 Li Tuo, "*Linju* chuangzuo de qishi."

22 Ma Lin, Da Jiangxia, and Zhu Mei, "Zunxun shenghuo de qishi," 194.

23 Wang Pei, "Yuan Yifang chuangzao duanxiang," 259.

24 Liu Guang'en, Wang Honghai, and Yin Li, "*Linju* meishu sheji de liangge wenti."

25 On the relation between the originary novel and the film—which spurred sales of the novel—see Hei Ma, "Fidelity and Betrayal."

26 Hei Ma, *Hun zai Beijing.*

27 Hei Ma, "Fidelity and Betrayal."

28 Wang Dehua, *Zhongguo chengshi guihua shigang*, 202; Wang Jinghui, Ruan Yisan, and Wang Lin, *Lishi wenhua mingcheng baohu lilun yu guihua*, 10.

29 Tsinghua University teams started studying urban conservation in 1986; *sustainable development* became a buzzword after the Brundtland Report of the World Commission on Environment and Development was submitted in 1987. Wu Liangyong, *Rehabilitating the Old City of Beijing*, 64, 106.

30 Abramson, "Aesthetics of City-Scale Preservation Policy."

31 See Fang Ke, *Dangdai Beijing jiucheng gengxin*, 51, 37.

32 Jianshebu Zhengce Yanjiu Zhongxin, *Zuixin chengshi fangwu chaiqian zhinan*, 41.

33 The poem was mentioned by Huang Shixian of the Beijing Film Academy in a forum on *Sunset Street*. "Yingtan de yisheng chunxun," 185; Yang Dongping, *Chengshi jifeng*, 200.

34 Su Shuyang, "*Xizhao jie*," 186.

35 Wang Haowei, interview with the author, Beijing, July 8, 2006.

36 Su Shuyang, "*Xizhao jie*", 117, 118, 152, 183.

37 Wang Haowei, "*Xizhao jie* paishe huigu"; Wang Haowei, interview with the author, Beijing, July 8, 2006.

38 Wang Haowei first offered the character of Li Pengfei to the BPAT actor Lin Liankun, impressed by his performance in *Next-Door Neighbors*. Wang Haowei, interview with the author, Beijing, July 8, 2006.

39 Su Shuyang, interview with the author, Beijing, July 23, 2006.

40 Wang Haowei, interview with the author, Beijing, July 8, 2006.

41 Su Shuyang, interview with the author, Beijing, July 23, 2006.

42 Li Longyun, *You zheyang yige xiaoyuan*, 1.

43 Zheng Dongtian, "Chengzhang de fannao."

44　Zhang, "Rebel without a Cause?" 61; Zhou Xuelin, *Young Rebels.*

45　On the "apotheosis" of the liumang, see Barmé, *In the Red*, 62–98.

46　Chris Berry, "Chinese Urban Cinema."

47　Zheng's promotion of Urban Cinema may be understood as a way to distinguish it as art film. Braester, "From Urban Films to Urban Cinema."

48　Zheng Dongtian, "Chengzhang de fannao."

49　Tang, *Chinese Modern*, 249.

50　Wei Xiaolin, *Benmingnian* de renzhi jiazhi" [The cognitive value of *Black Snow*], *Dianying yishu* [Film art] no. 212 (1990): 51; quoted in Tang, *Chinese Modern*, 251.

51　The film was to be titled after Liu Heng's novel *Black Snow*, whose original Chinese title is *Benmingnian* (literally, "zodiac year of birth"). The lead actor, Jiang Wen, suggested the new title since the shooting took place in a year without snow. Xie Fei, interview with the author, Beijing, July 10, 2006.

52　Ibid.

53　See also Xiaobing Tang's analysis of the opening sequence, in his *Chinese Modern*, 257–58.

54　Shooting for *Black Snow* took place between March and May, 1989. The film crew came to encourage the hunger strikers at Tiananmen Square, and a photo of their production truck threatened to land the production in trouble. Xie Fei, personal interview with the author, Beijing, July 10, 2006.

55　Lou Ye, conversation with the author, Seattle, November 15, 2006.

56　For a survey of the creek's history and the artist communities on its southern bank, see Han Yuqi and Zhang Song, *Dongfang de Saina zuo'an*. The information is also based on my interviews with Han Yuqi (Shanghai, July 2003 and June 2004), Zhang Song (Shanghai, July 2003), and Qiao Yanjun (Shanghai, June 2004).

57　The protest was led by the artist Han Yuqi, who appealed to the media and at the same time mobilized urban planners to write a report with an alternative plan for rehabilitating the area. It is now treated similarly to the twenty sites slated for preservation in Shanghai. For documentation of Han Yuqi's actions, see Han Yuqi and Zhang Song, *Dongfang de Saina zuo'an*.

58　"Report and Recommendation of the President to the Board of Directors," ii.

59　On the production of *Suzhou River*, see Zhang Zhen, "Urban Dreamscape, Phantom Sisters."

60　For a detailed analysis of *Suzhou River* in relation to Shanghai's urban identity, see also Visser, *Cities Surround the Countryside*, chap. 4.

61　Pan Jianlin's film should not be confused with another film that bears the same English title, *Beijing, ni zao* (*Good Morning, Beijing*, 1990).

62　Visser, *Cities Surround the Countryside.*

63　Paul Pickowicz describes the individual identity in crisis in Sixth Generation films as follows: "I'm homeless. I'm a prostitute. I'm a club singer. I'm a homosexual. I'm confused. I'm a drug addict. I'm a lesbian. I'm a migrant. I'm really confused. I'm a bohemian. I'm a con artist. I have AIDS. I'm a criminal. I'm crazy. I'm confused beyond imagination." Pickowicz, "Social and Political Dynamics," 15.

64 Quoted in Wang Jun, *Cheng ji*, 16.

65 See, e.g., Kwok Wah Lau, "*Farewell My Concubine*"; Liao Binghui, "Shikong"; and Lin Wenqi, "Xi, lishi, rensheng."

66 Zha, *China Pop*, 98.

67 A longer version of my discussion of *Farewell* explores the personal stakes for Chen and the crucial role of memory in his later *The Emperor and the Assassin* (1999). Braester, "*Farewell My Concubine*."

68 The author of the 1985 novel, Li Bihua (a.k.a. Lillian Lee), collaborated with Chen Kaige on the script. Following the film's success, Li published a revised edition of the novel in 1993. Li's novel retains scenes excised from or modified in Chen's film. Li Bihua, *Farewell My Concubine*, 352.

69 Abramson, "Beijing's Preservation Policy."

70 Ibid.

71 On the importance of the father figure in Chen's films, see Braester, "*Farewell My Concubine*."

72 Chen Kaige, "Zhangda youshi zhishi yishunjian de shi," 253. On Chen's childhood in Beijing and his memories thereof, see Ni Zhen, *Memoirs from the Beijing Film Academy*, 13.

73 Abramson, "Beijing's Preservation Policy."

74 Zhang Jinggan, *Beijing guihua jianshe zongheng tan*, 52.

75 Ibid., 178–79.

76 See Fang Ke, *Dangdai Beijing jiucheng gengxin*, 59–62.

77 Abramson, "Aesthetics of City-Scale Preservation Policy." On the process leading to the demolition of the city wall, see Wang Guohua, *Beijing chengqiang cunfei ji*.

78 Quoted in Fang Ke, *Dangdai Beijing jiucheng gengxin*, 39.

79 I thank Zhou Xiaowen for his detailed account of the production of *No Regret*. Zhou Xiaowen, interview with the author, Beijing, July 13, 2007. On the autobiographical background in Zhou's film, see Chai Xiaofeng, *Xiaowen ye fengkuang*, 49; and Lu Wei, "Shuoshuo Zhou Xiaowen," 348.

80 Dai Jinhua, *Yinxing shuxie*, 259–75.

81 Zhou Xiaowen, interview with the author, Beijing, July 13, 2007.

82 Ibid.

83 The club scenes were shot at a location in the Jiaodaokou area.

84 Quoted in Wang Jun, *Cheng ji*, 16. See also Zha, *China Pop*, 55.

85 Reference to Ning Ying's descriptions throughout this section are based on Ning's talks at the University of Washington Exploration Seminar in Beijing and Program in Chinese Film History and Criticism in Beijing. I thank Ning Ying for the insights gained during more than ten hours of interviews and talks, spanning five years.

86 The forceful evacuation at the site of Oriental Plaza is described in Ian Johnson, *Wild Grass*, 89–182.

87 Ivana Benda, "Organized Chaos and Design of Large Architectural and Urban Complexes" [unpublished report], quoted in Visser, *Cities Surround the Countryside*, chap. 1.

88 Abramson, "Beijing's Preservation Policy."

89 Wu Hung, *Transience*, 108–19.

90 Huang Du and Bingyi, *Hou wuzhi*, 62. See also Lu, "Tear Down the City."

91 Jia Zhangke has often commented on the importance of demolition in his films. See, e.g., Michael Berry, *Speaking in Images*, 182–207.

92 Zhang Yuan, talk at the University of Washington Exploration Seminar in Beijing, September 7, 2004.

93 "Zhongguo meiti beiling tingzhi baodao chaoqian wenti."

94 Fang Ke, *Dangdai Beijing jiucheng gengxin*.

95 Ian Johnson, *Wild Grass*, 89–182. My thanks to Fang's wife, the urban planner Zhang Yan, as well as to Dan Abramson for clarifying the nuances lost in Johnson's account.

96 Wang Jun, *Cheng ji*.

97 Feng Jicai, *Jiucheng yiyun*.

98 Feng published a book about the process: Feng Jicai, *Qiangjiu laojie*. See also Feng Jicai, *Shouxia liuqing*.

99 The account of Feng's actions and opinions is based on an interview I had with him in Tianjin on July 3, 2001. For the full version, see Braester and Enhua Zhang, "Future of China's Memories."

100 Wang Dehua, *Zhongguo chengshi guihua shigang*, 195–216.

101 Sun Chen, " 'Xin chengshi dianying' miaozhun dushi qingnianren"; Xiao Ji, " 'Xin chengshi dianying' fuchu shuimian."

102 Zhang, "Rebel without a Cause?" 49.

103 Ling Yan, "Xin dushi shimin shenhua." Ling's point and his examples are uncannily similar to those in Ni Zhen's essay "Shouwang xinsheng dai."

104 Li Yan, "wto laile women zenme ban?"

105 Qian Chunlei, "Dushi youzou."

106 Suosuo, "Xin chengshi dianying de zhu xuanlü."

107 Yang acted in Huang's *The Wooden Man's Bride*, served as Huang's assistant in *Signal Left, Turn Right*, and codirected with Huang *Back to Back, Face to Face* and *Surveillance*.

108 Fang Ke, *Dangdai Beijing jiucheng gengxin*, 45, 47.

109 Yiman Wang, "Amateur's Lightning Rod."

110 Kostof, "His Majesty the Pick," 10.

111 Guo Xiaolu, "Yige feizhiye bianju de silu."

112 For an extended discussion of *Love in the Internet Age*, in the context of the Internet's introduction in China, see Braester, "From Real Time to Virtual Reality."

113 A critical debate raged over the inaccurate though symbolically powerful portrayal of the bathhouse, in a special issue of *Dangdai dianying* [Contemporary cinema], no. 1 (2000). See the reprinted articles Zheng Guoen and Qi Hong,

"Jiadingxing zhong xunqiu zhenshigan," 292; and Hu Ke, "Jingqiao de xushu yishu," 278.

114 Zhang Yang, talk at the University of Washington Exploration Seminar in Beijing, August 31, 2005.

115 I thank Cao Fei and Ou Ning for providing me with a copy of their film. For Zhang's film and other documentation projects at Dashalan'r, see www.dazhalan-project .org/video-cn/video-cn.htm. Accessed November 30, 2006.

SEVEN The Day Trip of Your Dreams

1 See Yang Chenguang, "Yangtang zasui yu Man-Han quanxi"; Yang Chenguang, "Chengshi de 'xuemai' "; Chang Runjie, "Kan Aoyun, you Beijing"; Ge Chenhong, "Wenming Beijingren xingxiang suzao gongcheng"; An Hongkun, "Xin Beijing, xin Aoyun, xin shimin"; Hu Xiaoqin, "Liaojie shijie, zuo shijie gongmin"; Chang Runjie, "Jingqiang Jingwei de Beijing"; Hu Xiaoqin, "Ganshang Beijing de bufa"; and Xin Xu, "Modernizing China," 98–99.

2 For representative uses of the slogan "Count Me In," see Hou Jianmei, "Meili Beijing, you wo yige"; "Zhiyuan Aoyun, you wo yige," for events organized by the Communist Youth League; and Luo Xianming, "Zhiyuan Beijing, you wo yige," for the participation of the real estate mogul Pan Shiyi. As for grumbling about the Olympics, I can attest from personal experience that it was the talk of the day in 2001; Anne-Marie Broudehoux notes a similar sentiment during the 1993 bid. Broudehoux, *Making and Selling of Post-Mao Beijing*, 158.

3 See Wei, Leung, and Luo, "Globalizing Shanghai: Foreign Investment and Urban Restructuring"; Yusuf and Wu, "Pathways"; and Walcott, "Science Parks."

4 For the significance of "global cities," see esp. the writings of Saskia Sassen, beginning with *The Global City*.

5 Of special interest are the essays in Zhang Zhen, *Urban Generation*, and Robin Visser's *Cities Surround the Countryside*. For a survey of the institutional transformation from a state-led film industry to commercial production, see Zhu, *Chinese Cinema*, esp. chap. 5, "Post-Wave: 'It's the Economy, Stupid!' " An entire volume was dedicated to comments by leading scholars and filmmakers on joining the WTO and the subsequent "dancing with wolves," as the critic Zhang Boqing put it. See Zhang Boqing, " 'Yu lang gongwu.' "

6 *Beijing chengshi zongti guiha (1991 nian zhi 2010 nian)*

7 The sensitivity to public opinion is evidenced by the fact that the plan calls on leaders specifically to "spread the word about the master plan [*jiaqiang dui zongti huihua de xuanchuan*], enhance the awareness of planning of all citizens, to consciously implement the master plan and related regulations and intensively support and participate in the building and management of the city." Ibid.

8 Ibid.

9 Gu Xuewu notices three approaches to globalization in the PRC: some embrace it (Yan Xuetong, a professor of international relations at Tsinghua University,

projects a future homogenization of all world cultures); some deplore it (Han Deqiang points out that major local industries are unprepared for the competition); others simply take stock of the pros and cons, using the rhetoric of "a double-edged sword." Gu, "China and Its Reactions to Globalization."

10 Presas, "Transnational Urban Spaces."

11 Zhu, *Chinese Cinema*, 72–83; Brent, "China's Film Industry Steps Out of the Shadows"; Shen, "Tom Buys 35% of Huayi Brothers."

12 Zhang Boqing, " 'Yu lang gongwu,' yingjie tiaozhan," 220. See also the other essays in Zhang Zhenqian and Yang Yuanying, *WTO yu Zhongguo dianying*.

13 See Feng Xiaogang, *Wo ba qingchun xian gei ni*, 102–19.

14 Braester, "New Year's Movie."

15 On Li Geng, see Zheng Xin'an, *Jingtou li de shangpin*, 70–90; on the collaboration between Chow and Feng, see "Zhou Xingchi + Feng Xiaogang."

16 "He wei 'dawan,' 'dakuan'?"

17 Jing Wang, " 'Culture' as Leisure." On the term *cultural broker*, referring to a person who mediates between groups of differing cultural backgrounds, see, e.g., Geertz, "Javanese Kijai."

18 On the new model for advertising, see Po, "Repackaging Globalization"; and Jing Wang, *Brand New China*, 8.

19 McGrath, *Postsocialist Modernity*, 178.

20 See Zha, "Turtles."

21 Naomi Klein argues that the U.S. advertising industry turned from product promotion to brand identity in 1993; Klein, *No Logo*, 5–26. China soon followed suit, as the data in Jing Wang's *Brand New China* suggests.

22 Fang Zhenming, "Zhongguo haishi yao kafang."

23 Inwood, "Live Spaces and Urban Environment."

24 Welland, "Ocean Paradise." See also Cosco's website: www.cosred.com/cosred/index.php. Accessed October 10, 2004.

25 McGrath, *Postsocialist Modernity*, 165–202. For a more detailed version of the current discussion, see Braester, "Chinese Cinema in the Age of Advertisement."

26 Mi Jiashan, "Discussing *The Troubleshooters*."

27 See Jing Wang, *Brand New China*, 212.

28 "Galaxy of Stars Come Out."

29 Shujen Wang sees both the plot and the film itself as a response to anxieties about China's entry to the WTO. Shujen Wang, "*Big Shot's Funeral.*"

30 Klein, *No Logo*, 5.

31 Feng Xiaogang, interview with the author, Beijing, July 19, 2002.

32 "Beijing Gets Tough on Relics Protection"; Broudehoux, *Making and Selling of Post-Mao Beijing*, 165; Di Fang, "Outdoor Ads Banned"; Liu Li, "Beijing to Continue Ban."

33 "New Coffee Shop Replacing Starbucks."

34 Warhol, *Philosophy of Andy Warhol*, 71.

35 "McDonald's in China."

36 See Elliott, "Advertising for Olympics."

37 Wu Hung, *Remaking Beijing*, 101.

38 See Coonan, "China Aims to Win the Charm Olympics."

39 Roberts, "Brand China, Beijing."

40 Broudehoux, *Making and Selling of Post-Mao Beijing*, 148–207.

41 Visser, *Cities Surround the Countryside*, chap. 3.

42 Ann Anagnost argues that within the clear boundaries of the Splendid China park, the nation-state is presented as a timeless totality. Anagnost, *National Past-Times*, 162–63.

43 Koolhaas and Mau, *S.M.L.XL.*, 1249–51.

44 Presas, "Transnational Urban Spaces."

45 Visser, *Cities Surround the Countryside*, chap. 1.

46 Sassen, "Introduction," 2–37; Sassen, "Identity in the Global City."

47 Zhang Zhen, "Bearing Witness," 6.

48 Stanley, "Chinese Theme Parks."

49 Nakamura, *Cybertypes*, 89.

50 Wang Bo, *FLASH*, 20–21, 77–78.

51 Li Nanjun, "Zhongguo jieru hulianwang de zaoqi gongzuo huigu."

52 Wu, "Transplanting cityscapes"; Rosenthal, "North of Beijing."

53 Vidler, *Warped Space*, 234.

54 Senagala, "Post-spatial Architectures," 43, 45–46.

55 Baudrillard, *Simulacra and Simulation*, 2.

56 For a more detailed discussion of Q3, see Braester, "From Real Time to Virtual Reality."

57 Feng explains in an interview that the dungeon figures were manipulated by friends who logged in in coordination with the artist. Feng Mengbo, interview with the author, Beijing, August 2001.

58 At the time, direct satellite connection was yet unavailable, not to mention video streaming over the web. Chinoy recounts how tapes were flown to Hong Kong or transmitted digitally on a slow phone connection using a Pixelator; Chinoy, *China Live*, 255. Nevertheless, CNN was identified with the events of June 4 long after. On the tenth anniversary of the Tiananmen massacre—as Feng Mengbo was working on his video art—the Public Security Bureau ordered CNN to shut down its signal between June 2 and 8. Ibid.; "Beijing Authorities Shut Down CNN Signal."

59 Baudrillard, *Gulf War*; Taylor, *War and the Media*.

60 Friedberg, *Window Shopping*, 146.

61 Feng Mengbo, "Taking Mt. Doom by Strategy."

62 Broudehoux, *Making and Selling of Post-Mao Beijing*, 148–207.

24 City [*Ershisi chengshi*]. Dir. Jia Zhangke, 2008. Shanghai Film Group; Shanghai Film Studio.

After Separation [*Da saba'r*]. Dir. Xia Gang, 1992. Beijing Film Studio.

Alley of Three Families [*San jia xiang*]. Dir. Wang Weiyi, 1982. Pearl River Film Studio.

Amélie [*Le fabuleux destin d'Amélie Poulain*]. Dir. Jean-Pierre Jeunet, 2001. Victoires Productions; Tapioca Films; France 3 Cinéma; MMC Independent.

Are You Satisfied? [*Manyi bu manyi*]. Dir. Yan Gong, 1963. Changchun Film Studio.

Aspirin [*Asipilin*]. Dir. Yan Bo, 2005. Shengshi Fenghua.

As You Wish [*Ruyi*]. Dir. Huang Jianzhong, 1982. Beijing Film Studio.

Back to Back, Face to Face [*Bei kao bei, lian dui lian*]. Dir. Huang Jianxin and Yang Yazhou, 1994. Xi'an Film Studio.

Banana Paradise [*Xiangjiao tiantang*]. Dir. Wang Tong, 1989. Central Motion Pictures Corporation.

Baober in Love [*Lian'ai zhong de Baobei'r*]. Dir. Li Shaohong, 2004. Rosat Film and TV Productions.

The Battle for Shanghai [*Zhan Shanghai*]. Dir. Wang Bing, 1959. August First Film Studio.

Beautiful New World [*Meili xin shijie*]. Dir. Shi Runjiu, 1998. Imar Film; Xi'an Film Studio.

Beijing Bastards [*Beijing zazhong*]. Dir. Zhang Yuan, 1993. Beijing Bastards Film Team.

Beijing Bicycle [*Shiqi sui de danche*]. Dir. Wang Xiaoshuai, 2001. Arc Light Films; Beijing Film Studio.

Beijing, oh Beijing [*Beijing ah Beijing*]. Dir. Yang Shupeng, 2004. TV documentary on *This Life of Mine*, part of the series *Film Legends* [*Dianying chuanqi*] (first aired August 13, 2004).

Beijing's New Architecture [*Beijing xin jianzhu*]. Dir. Zhang Jianzhen and Li Kun, 1959. Central Newsreel and Documentary Film Studio.

Berlin: Symphony of a Big City [*Berlin: Die Sinfonie der Großstadt*]. Dir. Walter Ruttmann, 1927. Deutsche Vereins-Film.

The Big Parade [*Da yuebing*]. Dir. Chen Kaige, 1986. Guangxi Film Studio.

Big Shot's Funeral [*Dawan'r*]. Dir. Feng Xiaogang, 2001. Columbia Pictures; Huayi Brothers and Taihe Film.

The Birth of New China [*Xin Zhongguo de dansheng*]. Dir. Gao Weijin, 1949. Beiping Film Studio.

Black Snow [*Benmingnian*]. Dir. Xie Fei, 1990. Youth Film Studio.

Bright Heart [*Mingliang de xin*]. Dir. Hao Ran, 2002. Changchun Film Studio.

Cageman [*Longmin/Lung man*]. Dir. Chi Leung Jacob Cheung, 1992. Filmagica Productions.

Cala My Dog [*Kala shi tiao gou*]. Dir. Lu Xuechang, 2003. Huayi Brothers.

Camel Xiangzi [*Luotuo Xiangzi*]. Dir. Ling Zifeng, 1982. Beijing Film Studio.

Celebrating a Decade with Joy [*Huanqing shinian*]. 1959. Central Newsreel and Documentary Film Studio.

Celebrating with Joy the Great Victory [*Huanqing weida de shengli*]. Dir. Zhang Mengqi et al., 1976. Central Newsreel and Documentary Film Studio.

Cell Phone [*Shouji*]. Dir. Feng Xiaogang, 2003. Huayi Brothers and Taihe Film.

Central Park. Dir. Frederick Wiseman, 1989. Independent production.

Chairman Mao and Commander-in-Chief Zhu Arrive in Beijing and Review the Military Parade [*Mao zhuxi Zhu zongsiling liping yuebing*]. Dir. Gao Weijin, 1949. Beiping Film Studio.

Chairman Mao Is the Red Sun in Our Hearts [*Mao Zhuxi shi women xinzhong de hong taiyang*]. Dir. Guan Shiyuan, 1967. Central Newsreel and Documentary Film Studio.

Chen Tsai-gen and His Neighbors [*Chen Caigen de linjumen*]. Dir. Wu Yifeng/Wu Yiifeng, 1996. Fullshot Video Workshop.

Children of Troubled Times [*Fengyun ernü*]. Dir. Xu Xingzhi, 1935. Diantong Film.

China, 1949 [*Zhongguo, 1949*]. Dir. Zhao Pingyang, 1999. Central Newsreel and Documentary Film Studio; Shanghai Oriental Film.

China's Fiftieth National Day Parade [*Wushi zhounian guoqing xunyou dadian*]. 1999. CCTV; Beijing TV.

Chungking Express [*Chongqing senlin/Chung hing sam lam*]. Dir. Wang Jiawei/Wong Kar Wai, 1994. Jet Tone Production.

Cityscape [*Dushi fengguang*]. Dir. Yuan Muzhi, 1935. Diantong Film.

City without Night [*Bu ye cheng*]. Dir. Tang Xiaodan, 1957. Jiangnan Film Studio.

A City without Rain [*Wu yu zhi cheng*]. Dir. Yang Shupeng and Liu Tuanjie, 2004. TV documentary on *Dragon Whisker Creek*, part of the series *Film Legends* [*Dianying chuanqi*] (first aired January 22, 2005).

Come Watch Movies! Documentation of the Treasure Hill Family Cinema Club [*Lai kan dianying luo! Baozangyan jiating dianying julebu huodong jishi*]. Dir. Guo Boxiu, 2003. Independent production.

The Concrete Revolution [*Qianru routi de chengshi*]. Dir. Xiaolu Guo, 2004. Xiaolu Guo Ltd.

Cosmic Renewal [*Wanxiang gengxin*]. Dir. Xu Xiaobing and Lei Zhenlin, 1956. Central Newsreel and Documentary Film Studio.

Count Me In [*You wo yige*]. Dir. Zheng Jianfeng, 2000. TV miniseries.

Crows and Sparrows [*Wuya yu maque*]. Dir. Zheng Junli, 1949. Kunlun Film.

Dancing with Migrant Workers [*Yu mingong yiqi wudao*, a.k.a. *Dancing with Farm-workers*]. Dir. Wu Wenguang, 2001. Wu Documentary Studio.

Daybreak [*Tianming*]. Dir. Sun Yu, 1932. Lianhua Film.

The Days [*Dongchun de rizi*]. Dir. Wang Xiaoshuai, 1993. Shu Kei's Creative Workshop; Image Studio.

Demolition and Relocation [*Dingzi hu*]. Dir. Zhang Yuan, 1998. Hoso Bunka Foundation.

Dirt [*Toufa luan le*]. Dir. Guan Hu, 1994. Inner Mongolia Film Studio.

Divorce [*Lihun*]. Dir. Wang Haowei, 1992. Beijing Film Studio.

Dragon Whisker Creek [*Longxugou*]. Dir. Xian Qun, 1952. Beijing Film Studio.

Dream Factory [*Jiafang yifang*]. Dir. Feng Xiaogang, 1997. Beijing Film Studio.

Drifters [*Erdi*]. Dir. Wang Xiaoshuai, 2003. Purple Light Films.

The East Is Red [*Dongfang hong*]. Dir. Wang Ping, 1965. August First Film Studio.

Fame. Dir. Alan Parker, 1980. United Artists; MGM.

Family Love [*Gesheng meiying*]. Dir. Wu Xuan, 1970. Taiwan Film Studio.

Fang Zhenzhu. Dir. Xu Changlin, 1952. Da Guangming Film.

Farewell My Concubine [*Bawang bie ji*]. Dir. Chen Kaige, 1992. Tomson Film, Hong Kong; Beijing Film Studio.

Fate in Tears and Laughter [*Tixiao yinyuan*]. Dir. Zhang Shichuan, 1932. Mingxing Film.

Footsteps of Youth [*Qingchun de jiaobu*]. Dir. Yan Gong and Su Li, 1957.

Forcing through and Taking Flight [*Qiangxing qifei*]. Dir. Chen Kaige, 1984. CCTV.

For Fun [*Zhao le*]. Dir. Ning Ying, 1992. Beijing Film Studio.

For Peace [*Weile heping*]. Dir. Huang Zuolin, 1956. Shanghai Film Studio.

The Founding Ceremony [*Kaiguo dadian*]. Dir. Li Qiankuan and Xiao Guiyun, 1989. Changchun Film Studio.

Founding the Nation [*Kaiguo*]. Dir. Wei Baohe and Liu Yong, 2004. Documentary series by CCTV-10.

"Frog" ["Tiaowa"]. Dir. Ke Yizheng, 1982. In *In Our Time* [*Guangyin de gushi*], 1982. Central Motion Pictures Corporation.

The Fountainhead. Dir. King Vidor, 1949. Warner Bros. Pictures.

Frozen [*Jidu hanleng*]. Dir. Wang Xiaoshuai, 1995. Shu Kei's Creative Workshop.

The Girl from Huangshan Mountain [*Huangshan lai de guniang*]. Dir. Zhang Yuan and Yu Yanfu, 1984. Changchun Film Studio.

Goddess [*Shennü*]. Dir. Wu Yonggang, 1934. Lianhua Film.

Going Home [*Mingong huijia*]. Dir. Wang Jia, 2004. August First Film Studio.

Goldfish Ponds [*Jinyuchi*]. Dir. Ma Zhiyi, 2002. Video CD produced jointly by the Propaganda Bureau of the Chinese Communist Party in Chongwen District and the Chongwen District News Center.

Goodbye, Dragon Inn [*Bu san*]. Dir. Cai Mingliang/Tsai Ming-liang, 2003. Home-green Films.

Goodbye South, Goodbye [*Zaijian Nanguo zaijian*]. Dir. Hou Hsiao-hsien, 1996. 3H Films; Shochiku.

The Good Eighth Company of Nanjing Road [*Nanjing lu shang hao balian*]. Dir. Lu Fang, 1960. August First Film Studio.

Good Morning, Beijing [*Beijing, ni zao*]. Dir. Zhang Nuanxin, 1990. Youth Film Studio.

Good Morning, Beijing [*Zao'an Beijing*, a.k.a. *Sejie*]. Dir. Pan Jianlin, 2003. Independent production, distributed by Xiamen Audio and Video Publishing House.

The Great Combat: The Big Battle over Ningbo, Shanghai, and Hangzhou [*Da jinzhan: Dazhan Ning Hu Hang*]. Dir. Wei Lian, 1999. August First Film Studio.

The Great Leader and Chief Chairman Mao Zedong Will Never Wither [*Weida lingxiu he daoshi Mao Zedong zhuxi yong chuibuxiu*]. Dir. Wang Yingdong et al., 1976. Central Newsreel and Documentary Film Studio.

Green Bulldozer: The Rise of Your New Homeland [*Women jia zai Kangle li*]. Dir. Huang Sunquan/Huang Sun Chuan, 1997. OURS.

Green Tea [*Lücha*]. Dir. Zhang Yuan, 2003. Asian Union Film.

Growing Up [*Xiao Bi de gushi*]. Dir. Chen Kunhou, 1983. Evergreen.

The Happy Life of Chatterbox Zhang Damin [*Pinzui Zhang Damin de xingfu shenghuo*]. Dir. Shen Haofang, 2000. Beijing TV.

Happy Times [*Xingfu shiguang*]. Dir. Zhang Yimou, 2000. Guangxi Film Studio.

The Hole [*Dong*]. Dir. Cai Mingliang/Tsai Ming-liang, 1998. Haut et Court; La Sept ARTE; Arc Light Films; China Television; Central Motion Pictures Corporation.

Hollywood, Hong Kong [*Xianggang you ge Helihuo/Heung gong yao gok Hor Lei Wood*]. Dir. Chen Guo/Fruit Chan, 2001. Media Suits; Movement Pictures.

Home, Sweet Home [*Jia zai Taibei*]. Dir. Bai Jingrui, 1970. Central Motion Pictures Corporation.

House of Seventy-Two Tenants [*Qishier jia fangke/Chat sap yee ga fong haak*]. Dir. Chu Yuan/Chor Yuen, 1973. Shaw Brothers.

The Huaihai Campaign [*Huaihai zhanyi*]. Dir. Gao Weijin, 1949. Central Newsreel and Documentary Film Studio.

Humanity [*Rendao*]. Dir. Bu Wancang, 1932. Lianhua Film.

I Love Beijing [*Xiari nuanyangyang*]. Dir. Ning Ying, 2000. Eurasia Communications; Happy Village.

I • Mirror. China Tracy [Cao Fei], 2007. Video art.

In a Land of Silence [*Yu wusheng chu*]. Dir. Lu Ren, 1979. Shanghai Film Studio.

In the Face of Demolition [*Weilou chunxiao/Aau lau chun hiu*]. Dir. Lie Tei/Lee Tit, 1953. United Film Enterprises, Hong Kong.

In the Heat of the Sun [*Yangguang canlan de rizi*]. Dir. Jiang Wen, 1994. Dragon Film.

Jerks Don't Say Fuck [*Xiaozi bie shuo taicao*]. Zhao Liang, 2000. Video art.

Juvenile Delinquents [*Shaonian fan*]. Dir. Zhang Liang, 1985. Shenzhen Film.

Keep Cool [*You hua haohao shuo*]. Dir. Zhang Yimou, 1997. Guangxi Film Studio.

Lao She. Dir. Wang Haowei and Li Chensheng, 1996. Beijing Film Academy Video Publications.

The Last Emperor. Dir. Bernardo Bertolucci, 1987. Yanco Films; TAO Film.

Liberated China [Osvobozhdyonnyy kitay]. Dir. Sergei Gerassimov and Ivan Dukinsky, 1950. Central Studio for Documentary Film, U.S.S.R.

Liberating Tianjin [Jiefang Tianjin]. Dir. Gao Weijin, 1949. Central Newsreel and Documentary Film Studio.

The Life of Wu Xun [Wu Xun zhuan]. Dir. Sun Yu, 1950. Kunlun Film.

Life Show [Shenghuo xiu]. Dir. Huo Jianqi, 2000. Beijing Film Studio.

A Lingering Face [Feichang xiari]. Dir. Lu Xuechang, 1999. Beijing Film Studio.

Loach Is a Fish, Too [Niqiu yeshi yu]. Dir. Yang Yazhou, 2005. Flying Dragon Movie and Teleplay Cultural Medium.

Love in the Internet Age [Wanglu shidai de aiqing, a.k.a. Love in Cyberspace]. Dir. Jin Chen, 1999. Xi'an Film Studio.

Lunar Eclipse [Yueshi]. Dir. Wang Quan'an, 1999. Atika Films; Beijing Film Studio.

The Making of an Epoch [Kaitian pidi]. Dir. Lie Xiepu, 1991. Shanghai Film Studio.

The Making of Steel [Zhangda chengren]. Dir. Lu Xuechang, 1998. Beijing Film Studio.

Mao Zedong and His Son [Mao Zedong he ta de erzi]. Dir. Zhang Jinbiao, 1991.

A Married Couple [Women fufu zhi jian]. Dir. Zheng Junli, 1951.

The Matrix. Dir. Andy Wachowski and Larry Wachowski, 1999. Warner Bros. Pictures.

Mayor Chen Yi [Chen Yi shizhang]. Dir. Huang Zuolin, 1981. Shanghai Film Studio.

Meishi Street [Meishi jie]. Dir. Ou Ning, 2006. Alternative Archive.

The Meridian of War [Zhanzheng ziwu xian]. Dir. Feng Xiaoning, 1990. Beijing Film Studio.

Midnight [Ziye]. Dir. Sang Hu and Fu Jinggong, 1982. Shanghai Film Studio.

A Million Heroes Descend on Jiangnan [Baiwan xiongshi xia Jiangnan]. Dir. Qian Xiaozhang, 1949. Beijing Film Studio.

Mongolian Ping Pong [Lü Caodi]. Dir. Ning Hao, 2005. Kunlun Brother Film and TV Productions.

Moonlight [Da cuo che, a.k.a. Papa Can You Hear Me Sing]. Dir. Yu Kanping, 1983. Cinema City.

My Memories of Old Beijing [Chengnan jiushi]. Dir. Wu Yigong, 1984. Shanghai Film Studio.

A Myriad Lights [Wanjia denghuo]. Dir. Shen Fu, 1948. Kunlun Film.

Myth of a City [Taibei shenhua]. Dir. Yu Kanping, 1985. Feiteng Production.

My Whispering Plan [Sharen jihua]. Dir. Qu Youning/Arthur Chu, 2002. Oxygen Film.

The Naked City. Dir. Jules Dassin, 1948. Universal International Pictures.

National Day at Ten o'Clock [Guoqing shi dian zhong]. Dir. Wu Tian, 1959. Changchun Film Studio.

Neighbors [Linju]. Dir. Zheng Dongtian and Xu Guming, 1981. Youth Film Studio.

New Beijing [Novyy Pekin]. Dir. Sergei Gerassimov, 1950. Central Studio for Documentary Film, U.S.S.R.

New China [*Xin Zhongguo*]. Dir. Wang Xuan et al., 1999. CCTV.

New Woman [*Xin nüxing*]. Dir. Cai Chusheng, 1934. Lianhua Film.

Noise [*Renao*]. Dir. Wang Wo, 2007. Independent production.

No Regret about Youth [*Qingchun wuhui*]. Dir. Zhou Xiaowen, 1992. Xi'an Film Studio.

Nostalgia [*Xiangchou*]. Dir. Shu Haolun, 2006. Film Spirit Productions.

Obsession [*Fengkuang de daijia*]. Dir. Zhou Xiaowen, 1988. Xi'an Film Studio.

Old Ke's Last Day of Fall [*Lao Ke de zuihou yige qiutian*]. Dir. Li Youning, 1988. Scholar Film.

Old Mo's Second Spring [*Lao Mo de di'er ge chuntian*]. Dir. Li Youning, 1984. Gaoshi Film.

Once upon a Time in Shanghai [*Shanghai jishi*]. Dir. Peng Xiaolian, 1998. Shanghai Film Studio.

"One Hundred Flowers Hidden Deep." Dir. Chen Kaige. In *Ten Minutes Older*, 2002. Matador Pictures; Odyssey Films London; Road Movies.

On the Beat [*Minjing gushi*]. Dir. Ning Ying, 1995. Eurasia Communications.

On the Docks [*Haigang*]. Dir. Xie Tieli and Xie Jin, 1972. Beijing Film Studio; Shanghai Film Studio.

Opera Heroes [*Liyuan yinglie*, a.k.a. *Erbaiwu xiaozhuan*]. Dir. Zheng Xiaoqiu, 1949. Datong Film.

Ordinary People's Life [*Meili de jia*]. Dir. An Zhanjun, 2000. Beijing Forbidden City Film.

An Orphan on the Streets [*Sanmao liulang ji*]. Dir. Zhao Ming and Yan Gong [uncredited], 1949. Kunlun Film.

Our Neighbors [*Jietou xiangwei*]. Dir. Li Xing, 1963. Independence Film.

Out of Phoenix Bridge [*Huidao fenghuang qiao*]. Dir. Li Hong, 1997. Independent production.

Outside [*Waimian*]. Dir. Wang Wo, 2005. Independent production.

The Outsiders [*Niezi*]. Dir. Yu Kanping, 1986. Long Shong Pictures.

Patton. Dir. Franklin J. Schaffner, 1970. Twentieth-Century Fox.

Peach Blossom Land [*Anlian—Taohuayuan*]. Dir. Lai Shengchuan/Stan Lai, 1992. Long Shong Pictures; Performance Workshop Films.

People between the Two Chinas [*Haixia liang'an*]. Dir. Yu Kanping, 1988. Long Shong Pictures.

Perpetual Motion [*Wuqiong dong*]. Dir. Ning Ying, 2005. Happy Village.

Platform [*Zhantai*]. Dir. Jia Zhangke, 2000. T-Mark; Artcam International.

Poetic Times [*Shiyi de niandai*]. Dir. Lü Yue, 1999. Beijing Forbidden City Film.

Q3. Feng Mengbo, 1999. Video art.

Quitting [*Zuotian*]. Dir. Zhang Yang, 2001. Imar Film; Xi'an Film Studio.

Raise the Red Lantern [*Da hong denglong gaogao gua*]. Dir. Zhang Yimou, 1991. ERA International.

Rebels of the Neon God [*Qingshaonian Nazha*]. Dir. Cai Mingliang/Tsai Ming-liang, 1992. Central Motion Pictures Corporation.

Re-cycle [*Gui cheng/Gwai wik*]. Dir. Pang brothers, 2006. Universe Entertainment; Matching Motion Pictures; Magic Head Film Production.

Red Beads [*Xuanlian*]. Dir. He Jianjun, 1993. Fortissimo Films.

The Red Lantern [*Hongdeng ji*]. Dir. Cheng Yin, 1970. August First Film Studio.

The Red Lotus Society [*Feixia Ada*]. Dir. Lai Shengehuan/Stan Lai, 1994. Long Shong Pictures; Performance Workshop Films.

Red Suit [*Hong xifu*]. Dir. Li Shaohong, 1998. Beijing Film Studio.

Requiem. Xu Dawei, 2001. Video art.

The Reunion [*Da tuanyuan*]. Dir. Ding Li, 1948. Qinghua Film.

Reverberations of Life [*Shenghuo de Chanyin*]. Dir. Teng Wenji and Wu Tianming, 1979. Xi'an Film Studio.

Riding the Wrong Car [*Da cuo che*]. Dir. Gao Xixi, 2005. Beijing Oriental Zheng Yi Film and TV Communication.

RMB City. Cao Fei, 2008. Video art.

Robinson's Crusoe [*Luobinsun piaoliu ji*]. Dir. Lin Zhengsheng/Lin Cheng-sheng, 2003. Central Motion Pictures Corporation.

Rock Kids [*Yaogun qingnian*]. Dir. Tian Zhuangzhuang, 1987. Beijing Film Studio.

Rookie Ma Qiang [*Xinbing Ma Qiang*]. Dir. Yu Qing, 1981. Beijing Film Studio.

Rumble in the Bronx [*Hongfan qu/Hong faan kui*]. Dir. Stanley Kwai-lai Tong, 1995.

Samsara [*Lunhui*]. Dir. Huang Jianxin, 1988. Shanghai Film Studio.

Sanmao Studies Business [*Sanmao xue shengyi*]. Dir. Huang Zuolin, 1958. Tianma Film Studio.

Saving Private Ryan. Dir. Steven Spielberg, 1998. Amblin Entertainment; Dream-Works; Paramount Pictures.

Sentinels under the Neon Lights [*Nihong deng xia de shaobing*]. Dir. Wang Ping, 1964. August First Film Studio.

Seventeen Years [*Guonian huijia*]. Dir. Zhang Yuan, 1999. Xi'an Film Studio.

Shanghai Bride [*Shanghai xinniang*]. Dir. Shi Fenghe, 1997. Shanghai Film Studio.

Shanghai Fever [*Gu feng*]. Dir. Li Guoli, 1994. Xiaoxiang Film Studio; Impact Films.

Shower [*Xizao*]. Dir. Zhang Yang, 1999. Imar Film; Xi'an Film Studio.

Signal Left, Turn Right [*Hong deng ting, lü deng xing*]. Dir. Huang Jianxin, 1996. Xi'an Film Studio.

The Silent Lake [*Ningjing hai*]. Dir. Lin Fudi, 1978. Win's Films.

The Skywalk Is Gone [*Tianqiao bu jian le*]. Dir. Cai Mingliang/Tsai Ming-liang, 2002. Homegreen Films; Le Fresnoy.

Small Soldiers. Dir. Joe Dante, 1998. Amblin Entertainment; DreamWorks; Universal Studios.

Sons [*Erzi*]. Dir. Zhang Yuan, 1996. Beijing Expression Culture Communication Center.

Spicy Love Soup [*Aiqing malatang*]. Dir. Zhang Yang, 1997. Imar Film; Xi'an Film Studio.

Spider Lilies [*Ciqing*]. Dir. Zhou Meiling, 2007. 3rd Vision Films.

The Spring River Flows East [*Yi jiang chunshui xiang dong liu*]. Dir. Zheng Junli, 1947. Kunlun Film.

Spring Subway [*Kai wang chuntian de ditie*]. Dir. Zhang Yibai, 2002. Electric Orange Entertainment.

The Square [*Guangchang*]. Dir. Duan Jinchuan and Zhang Yuan, 1994. Independent production.

Stage Sisters [*Wutai jiemei*]. Dir. Xie Jin, 1965. Tianma Film Studio.

Stand Up, Don't Stoop [*Zhanzhi luo, bie paxia*]. Dir. Huang Jianxin, 1992. Xi'an Film Studio.

Still Life [*Sanxia haoren*]. Dir. Jia Zhangke, 2006. Shanghai Film Studio.

The Story of 1949 [*1949 nian de gushi*]. Dir. Chen Hu, 1999. Documentary series by Beijing TV.

Strangers in Beijing [*Hun zai Beijing*]. Dir. He Qun, 1996. Fujian Film Studio.

Street Angel [*Malu tianshi*]. Dir. Yuan Muzhi, 1937. Mingxing Film.

Strong Criticism against the Revisionist Film "City without Night" [*Chedi pipan fandong yingpian "Bu ye cheng"*]. No director credit, 1967. Dongfanghong [East Is Red] Film Studio [formerly Tianma Film Studio].

Summer Palace [*Yiheyuan*]. Dir. Lou Ye, 2006. Laurel Films; Rosem Films.

Sunflower [*Xiangrikui*]. Dir. Zhang Yang, 2005. Beijing Film Studio; Fortissimo Films; Ming Productions.

Sunset Street [*Xizhao jie*]. Dir. Wang Haowei, 1983. Beijing Film Studio.

Sunshine and Rain [*Taiyangyu*]. Dir. Zhang Zeming, 1987. Pearl River Film Studio.

Super Citizen [*Chaoji shimin*]. Dir. Wan Ren/Wan Jen, 1985. Cinema City.

Super Citizen Ko [*Chaoji da guomin*]. Dir. Wan Ren/Wan Jen, 1995. Wan Jen Films.

Surveillance [*Maifu*]. Dir. Huang Jianxin and Yang Yazhou, 1996. Xiaoxiang Productions.

Suzhou River [*Suzhouhe*]. Dir. Lou Ye, 2000. Essential Film; Dream Factory.

Taipei Story [*Qingmei zhuma*]. Dir. Yang Dechang/Edward Yang, 1985. Evergreen.

"The Taste of Apples" ["*Pingguo de ziwei*"]. Dir. Zeng Zhuanxiang. In *The Sandwich Man* [*Erzi de wan'ou*], 1983. Central Motion Pictures Corporation.

Teahouse [*Chaguan'r*]. Dir. Xie Tian, 1982. Beijing Film Studio.

Terrorizers [*Kongbu fenzi*]. Dir. Yang Dechang/Edward Yang, 1986. Central Motion Pictures Corporation.

There Is a Strong Wind in Beijing [*Beijing de feng hen da*]. Dir. Ju Anqi, 1999. Trench Group. Independent production.

This Life of Mine [*Wo zhei beizi*]. Dir. Shi Hui, 1950. Wenhua Film Company.

Tiananmen. Dir. Shi Jian and Chen Jue, 1991. Commissioned by CCTV and completed as an independent production.

Tiananmen. Dir. Ye Ying/Yip Ying, 2009. China Film Group Corp.; China Movie Channel.

Treasure Island [*Zhi yao wei ni huo yitian*]. Dir. Chen Guofu/Chen Kuo-fu, 1993. City Films.

A Tree in House [*Mei shi touzhe le*]. Dir. Yang Yazhou, 1999. Xi'an Film Studio.

Triumph of the Will [*Triumph des Willens*]. Dir. Leni Riefenstahl, 1935. Reichspropagandaleitung der NSDAP.

The Troubleshooters [*Wanzhu*]. Dir. Mi Jiashan, 1988. Emei Film Studio.

The Undying Transmission [*Yong bu xiaoshi de dianbo*]. Dir. Wang Ping, 1958. August First Film Studio.

Unity for Tomorrow [*Tuanjie qilai dao mingtian*]. Dir. Zhao Ming, 1950. Shanghai Film Studio.

Vive l'amour [*Aiqing wansui*]. Dir. Cai Mingliang/Tsai Ming-liang, 1994. Central Motion Pictures Corporation.

The Wayward Cloud [*Tianbian yiduo yun*]. Dir. Cai Mingliang/Tsai Ming-liang, 2005. Arena Films; Homegreen Films.

Weekend Lover [*Zhoumo qingren*]. Dir. Lou Ye, 1993. Fujian Film Studio.

What a Family [*Qiao zheyi jiazi*]. Dir. Wang Haowei, 1979. Beijing Film Studio.

What Time Is It There [*Ni neibian jidian*]. Dir. Cai Mingliang/Tsai Ming-liang, 2001. Arena Films; Homegreen Films.

With Sugar [*Gei kafei jia dian tang*]. Dir. Sun Zhou, 1987. Pearl River Film Studio.

Women of the Great Leap Forward [*Wanzi qianhong zongshi chun*]. Dir. Shen Fu, 1959. Haiyan Film Studio.

The Wooden Man's Bride [*Wu Kui*]. Dir. Huang Jianxin, 1993. Long Shong Pictures.

The World [*Shijie*]. Dir. Jia Zhangke, 2004. Shanghai Film Group; Shanghai Film Studio; Xinghui Production, Hong Kong.

Xiao Wu. Dir. Jia Zhangke, 1997. Hu Tong Communications; Radiant Advertising.

Yamaha Fish Stall [*Yamaha yudang*]. Dir. Zhang Liang, 1984. Pearl River Film Studio.

Young Couples [*Yuanyang lou*]. Dir. Zheng Dongtian, 1987. Youth Film Studio.

The Young Generation [*Nianqing de yidai*]. Dir. Zhao Ming, 1965. Tianma Film Studio.

Zhou Enlai. Dir. Wang Yonghong, 1990. Central Newsreel and Documentary Film Studio.

Zhou Enlai. Dir. Ding Yinnan, 1991. Guangxi Film Studio.

Zhuazhuangding [*Forced Draft*]. Dir. Chen Ge, 1963. August First Film Studio.

Beijing Pretenders [*Beijing daye*]. Playwright: Zhong Jieying. Premiered by
BPAT in 1995, dir. Ren Ming. Live performance viewed by the author in
1995. Video CD. Beijing: Beijing Pujiao Yinxiang Chubanshe, 1997.

Bird Men [*Niaoren*]. Playwright: Guo Shixing. Premiered by BPAT in 1993, dir.
Lin Zhaohua. Live performance viewed by the author in 1995. Video CD.
Beijing: Beijing Dianshi Yishu Zhongxin Yinxiang Chubanshe, 1997.

Chess Men [*Qiren*]. Playwright: Guo Shixing. Premiered by the China Experimental Theater in 1995, dir. Lin Zhaohua. DVD. Beijing: Beijing Wenhua
Yishu Yinxiang Chubanshe, 2004.

A Courtyard with a Backyard [*Dai houyuan de siheyuan'r*]. Playwright: Zheng
Xiaonong. Premiered by the China Youth Theater in 1985, dir. Zhou
Guozhi. Video CD. Beijing: Beijing Weixiang Yinxiang Chubanshe, 2000.

Dragon Whisker Creek [*Longxugou*]. Playwright: Lao She. Premiered by BPAT
in 1951, dir. Jiao Juyin.

Fang Zhenzhu. Playwright: Lao She. Premiered by the China Youth Art Theater in 1951, dir. Shi Yu.

Fish Men [*Yuren*]. Playwright: Guo Shixing. Premiered by BPAT in 1989, dir.
Lin Zhaohua and Ren Ming. Video CD. Beijing: Beijing Dianshi Yishu
Zhongxin Yinxiang Chubanshe, 1999.

Forsaken Alley [*Gala'r Hutong*]. Playwright: Lan Yinhai. Premiered by BPAT in
1993, dir. Gu Wei. Video CD. Beijing: Beijing Dianshi Yishu Zhongxin
Yinxiang Chubanshe, 1997.

Goldfish Ponds [*Jinyuchi*]. Playwright: Wang Zhi'an. Premiered by BPAT in
2001, dir. Ren Ming. Live performance viewed by the author in 2001.

Guan Hanqing. Playwright: Tian Han. Premiered by BPAT in 1958, dir. Jiao
Juyin and Ouyang Shanzun.

Invisible Cities [*Kanbujian de chengshi*]. Choreographer: Li Haining/Helen
Lai. Premiered by the City Contemporary Dance Company of Hong Kong
in 1992. Performed by Cloud Gate Dance Theater in 1994. Live performance viewed by the author in 1994.

Look Who's Cross-Talking Tonight [*Zhei ye, shei lai shuo xiangsheng*]. Premiered
by the Performance Workshop in 1989, dir. Lai Shengchuan/Stan Lai.
DVD. Taipei: Performance Workshop, c. 2000.

A Myriad Lights [*Wanjia denghuo*]. Playwright: Li Longyun. Performed by BPAT in 2002, dir. Lin Zhaohua and Li Luyi. Live performance viewed by the author in 2007. DVD. Guangzhou: Qiaojiaren, 2005.

Next-Door Neighbors [*Zuolin youshe*]. Playwright: Su Shuyang. Performed by BPAT in 1980, dir. Jin Li. Video CD. Beijing: Beijing Dianshi Yishu Zhongxin Yinxiang Chubanshe, 1999.

Peking Man [*Beijingren*]. Playwright: Cao Yu. Premiered By the China Youth Art Theater in 1941, dir. Zhang Junxiang. Performed by BPAT in 1990, dir. Xia Chun. Video CD. Beijing: Beijing Dianshi Yishu Zhangxin Yinxiang Chubanshe, c. 1999. Performed by BPAT in 2006, dir. Li Liuyi. Live performance viewed by the author in 2006. Beijing: Beijing Wenhua Yishu Yinxiang Chubanshe, 2007.

Sentinels under the Neon Lights [*Nihongdeng xia de shaobing*]. Playwrights: Shen Ximeng, Mo Yan, and Lü Xingchen. Premiered by the Nanjing Military Command's Frontier Theater Troupe in 1963, dir. Mo Yan. Performed by an ad hoc cast in 2001, dir. Chen Xinyi. Video CD. Shanghai: Shanghai Luxiang, 2001.

Shanghai's Battle Song [*Shanghai zhan'ge*]. Playwright: Du Xuan. Premiered by the Shanghai People's Art Theater in 1959, dir. Kou Honglie.

Small Well Lane [*Xiaojing hutong*]. Playwright: Li Longyun. Premiered by BPAT in 1983, dir. Shao Guangtan. Video CD [1985 performance]. Beijing: Beijing Dianshi Yishu Zhangxin Yinxiang Chubanshe, 1999.

Street of Foul Talk [*Huaihua yitiao jie*]. Playwright: Guo Shixing. Premiered by the China Experimental Theater in 1998, dir. Meng Jinghui. Video CD. Beijing: Beijing Weixiang Yinxiang Chubanshe, 2000.

Teahouse [*Chaguan'r*]. Playwright: Lao She. Premiered by BPAT in 1957, dir. Jiao Juyin. Performed by BPAT in 1992, dir. Jiao Juyin and Xia Chun. Video CD. Beijing: Beijing Pujiao Yinxiang Chubanshe, 1997. Performed by BPAT in 1999, dir. Lin Zhaohua. Live performance viewed by the author in 2005. Video CD. Beijing: Beijing Dianshi Yishu Zhongxin Yinxiang Chubanshe, 2000.

There Is a Small Courtyard [*You zheyang yige xiaoyuan*]. Playwright: Li Longyun. Premiered at the China Children's Art Theater in 1979, dir. Zhou Lai and Li Ding.

Toilet [*Cesuo*]. Playwright: Guo Shixing. Premiered by the National Theater of China in 2003, dir. Lin Zhaohua. Live performance viewed by the author in 2003. DVD [2004 performance]. Beijing: Beijing Wenhua Yishu Yinxiang Chubanshe, 2007.

Uncle Doggie's Nirvana [*Gou'r ye niepan*]. Playwright: Jin Yun. Premiered at BPAT in 1986, dir. Shao Guangtan and Lin Zhaohua. Video CD. Beijing: Beijing Dianshi Yishu Zhongxin Yinxiang Chubanshe, 1997.

We're All Beijingers [*Quan shi Beijingren*]. Playwright: Liu Jinyuan. Premiered by China Youth Theater in 1997, dir. Wang Gui. Video CD. Beijing: Beijing Weixiang Yinxiang Chubanshe, 2000.

Who's Pulling My Leg? [*Shei hulong wo?*]. Performed by the Xiangsheng Washe Group in 1999. Video CD. Taipei: Sony Entertainment (Taiwan), 1999.

The World's Top Restaurant [*Tianxia diyi lou*]. Playwright: He Jiping. Premiered by BPAT in 1988, dir. Xia Chun and Gu Wei. Video CD. Beijing: Beijing Pujiao Yinxiang Chubanshe, 1997.

Abbas, Ackbar. *Hong Kong: Culture and the Politics of Disappearance*. Minneapolis: University of Minnesota Press, 1997.

Abramson, Daniel Benjamin. "The Aesthetics of City-Scale Preservation Policy in Beijing." *Planning Perspectives* 22.2 (April 2007): 129–66.

——. "Beijing's Preservation Policy and the Fate of the Siheyuan." *Traditional Dwellings and Settlements Review* 13.1 (Fall 2001): 7–22.

——. "Urban Planning in China: Continuity and Change." *Journal of the American Planning Association* 71.1 (Spring 2006): 197–215.

Aftab, Kaleem, and Alexandra Weltz. Interview with Frederick Wiseman. *Film West* 40. www.iol.ie/~galfilm/filmwest/. Accessed August 28, 2006.

Allen, Joseph. "Reading Taipei: Cultural Traces in a Cityscape." *Harvard Studies on Taiwan* 3 (2000): 1–21.

Altman, Rick. *Film/Genre*. London: British Film Institute, 1989.

Anagnost, Ann. *National Past-Times: Narrative, Representation, and Power in Modern China*. Durham, N.C.: Duke University Press, 1997.

Andrews, Julia. *Painters and Politics in the People's Republic of China, 1949–1979*. Berkeley: University of California Press, 1994.

An Ge. *Shenghuo zai Deng Xiaoping shidai: Shijue 80 niandai* [Living in the Deng Xiaoping era: Visualizing the 1980s]. Guangzhou: Yangcheng Wanbao Chubanshe, 2001.

An Hongkun. "Xin Beijing, xin Aoyun, xin shimin" [New Beijing, new Olympics, new citizens]. In *Renwen Aoyun*, ed. Peng Yongjie, Zhang Zhiwei, and Han Donghui, 495–98.

Bai Quequn. *Lao Beijing de juzhu* [Old Beijing residences]. Beijing: Beijing Yanshan Chubanshe, 1999.

Barber, Noel. *The Fall of Shanghai*. New York: Coward, McCann, and Geoghegan, 1979.

Barmé, Geremie. *In the Red: On Contemporary Chinese Culture*. New York: Columbia University Press, 1999.

Baudrillard, Jean. *The Gulf War Did Not Take Place*. Bloomington: Indiana University Press, 1995.

———. *Simulacra and Simulation*. Trans. Sheila Faria Glaser. Ann Arbor: University of Michigan Press, 1994.

Bazin, André. "The Myth of Stalin in the Soviet Cinema." In *Bazin at Work: Major Essays and Reviews from the Forties and Fifties*, ed. Bert Cardullo, trans. Alain Piette and Bert Cardullo, 23–40. New York: Routledge, 1997.

Becker, Howard S. *Art Worlds*. Berkeley: University of California Press, 1982.

"Beijing 2050, Beijing, August 2006." Computer-generated renderings and text describing project. www.world-architects.com. Accessed September 25, 2008.

"Beijing Authorities Shut Down CNN Signal." CNN website, www.cnn.com. Accessed September 16, 2001.

Beijing chengshi zongti guiha (1991 nian zhi 2010 nian) [Master plan for Beijing City (1991 to 2010)]. Posted on the Beijing municipal government website: zhengwu.beijing.gov.cn. Accessed December 12, 2007.

"*Beijing daye*: Beijingren de ganga" [*Beijing Pretenders*: Beijingers' embarrassment]. *Zhongguo tupian bao* [China illustrated], June 29, 1995.

"Beijing Gets Tough on Relics Protection." Article on site of China Internet Information Center (authorized government portal), July 30, 2004. www.china.org.cn/english. Accessed January 7, 2005.

Beijing lao chengmen [Beijing's old city gates]. Beijing: Beijing Chubanshe, 2002.

Beijing lao Tianqiao [Beijing's old Tianqiao]. Beijing: Wenjin Chubanshe, 1993.

Beijing Tebieshi Gongshu Gongwuju [Public Works Bureau of the Beijing Special Municipality]. Memos concerning Zhang Qikui's petition for initiation works at Longxugou. File at the Beijing Municipal Archives. Compiled September 11, 1939.

Benjamin, Walter. "On Some Motifs in Baudelaire." Trans. Harry Zohn. In *Selected Writings*, vol. 4: *1938–1940*, ed. Howard Eiland and Michael W. Jennings, 313–55. Cambridge: Harvard University Press, 2003.

———. "On the Program of the Coming Philosophy." Trans. Mark Ritter. In *Selected Writings*, vol. 1: *1913–1926*, ed. Marcus Bullock and Michael W. Jennings, 100–110. Cambridge: Harvard University Press, 2004.

Bennet, G. A. *Yundong: Mass Campaigns in Chinese Communist Leadership*. Berkeley: University of California Press, 1976.

Berry, Chris. "Chinese Urban Cinema: Hyper-realism versus Absurdism." *East-West Film Journal* 3.1 (December 1988): 76–87.

———. "Facing Reality: Chinese Documentary, Chinese Postsocialism." In *Reinterpretation: A Decade of Experimental Chinese Art (1990–2000)—The First Guangzhou Triennial*, ed. Wu Hung, Wang Huangsheng, and Feng Boyi, 121–31. Guangzhou: Guangdong Museum of Art, 2002.

———. "A Nation T(w/o)o: Chinese Cinema(s) and Nationhood(s)." *East-West Film Journal* 7.1 (January 1993): 24–51.

Berry, Michael. *A History of Pain: Trauma in Modern Chinese Literature and Film*. New York: Columbia University Press, 2008.

———. *Speaking in Images: Interviews with Contemporary Chinese Filmmakers*. New York: Columbia University Press, 2005.

Bordwell, David. "A Case for Cognitivism." *Iris* 9 (Spring 1989): 11–40.

Braester, Yomi. " 'A Big Dying Vat': The Vilifying of Shanghai during the Good Eighth Company Campaign." *Modern China* 31.4 (October 2005): 411–47.

——. "Chinese Cinema in the Age of Advertisement: The Filmmaker as a Cultural Broker." *China Quarterly* 183 (September 2005): 549–64.

——. "Excuse Me, Your Camera Is in My Face." In *The New Chinese Documentary Film Movement: For the Public Record*, ed. Lisa Rofel, Chris Berry, and Lü Xinyu. Forthcoming.

——. "*Farewell My Concubine*: National Myth and City Memories." In *Chinese Films in Focus: Twenty-Five New Takes*, ed. Chris Berry, 89–96. London: British Film Institute, 2003.

——. "From Urban Films to Urban Cinema: The Emergence of a Critical Concept." In *A Companion to Chinese Cinema*, ed. Yingjin Zhang. Blackwell, forthcoming.

——. "From Real Time to Virtual Reality: Chinese Cinema in the Internet Age." *Journal of Contemporary China* 13.38 (February 2004): 89–104.

——. " 'If We Could Remember Everything, We Would Be Able to Fly': Taipei's Cinematic Poetics of Demolition." *Modern Chinese Literature and Culture* 15.1 (Spring 2003): 29–61.

——. "In Search of History Point Zero: Stan Lai's Drama and Taiwan's Doubled Identities." *Journal of Contemporary China* 17.55 (November 2008): 689–98.

——. "New Year's Movie." In *Encyclopedia of Modern China*, ed. David Pong, 4 vols., 3:36–37. Detroit: Charles Scribner's Sons, 2009.

——. "Photography at Tiananmen: Pictorial Frames, Spatial Borders, and Ideological Matrixes." *positions: east asia cultures critique*. Forthcoming.

——. "The Political Campaign as Genre: Ideology and Iconography during the Seventeen Years Period." *Modern Languages Quarterly* 69.1 (March 2008): 119–40.

——. "Shanghai's Economy of the Spectacle: The Shanghai Race Club in Liu Na'ou's and Mu Shiying's Stories." *Modern Chinese Literature* 9.1 (Spring 1995): 39–57.

——. "Tales of a Porous City: Public Residences and Private Streets in Taipei Films." In *Contested Modernities in Chinese Literature*, ed. Charles Laughlin, 157–70. New York: Palgrave, 2005.

——. "Tracing the City's Scars: Demolition and the Limits of the Documentary Impulse in New Urban Cinema." In *Urban Generation*, ed. Zhang Zhen, 161–80.

——. *Witness against History: Literature, Film and Public Discourse in Twentieth-Century China*. Stanford, Calif.: Stanford University Press, 2003.

Braester, Yomi, and Enhua Zhang. "The Future of China's Memories: An Interview with Feng Jicai." *Journal of Modern Literature in Chinese* 5.2 (January 2002): 131–48.

Bray, David. *Social Space and Governance in Urban China: The Danwei System from Origins to Reform*. Stanford, Calif.: Stanford University Press, 2005.

Brent, William. "China's Film Industry Steps Out of the Shadows." *China Business Review*, November–December 2003. www.chinabusinessreview.com. Accessed May 18, 2008.

Broudehoux, Anne-Marie. *The Making and Selling of Post-Mao Beijing.* New York: Routledge, 2004.

Bruno, Giuliana. *Streetwalking on a Ruined Map: Cultural Theory and the City Films of Elvira Notari.* Princeton, N.J.: Princeton University Press, 1993.

Campanella, Thomas J. *The Concrete Dragon: China's Urban Revolution and What It Means for the World.* New York: Princeton Architectural Press, 2008.

Cao Hongtao and Zhu Chuanheng, eds. *Dangdai zhongguo de chengshi jianshe* [Urban construction in contemporary China]. Beijing: Zhongguo Shehui Kexue Chubanshe, 1990.

Cao Yanxing. "Guanyu Longxugou xiashuidao gongcheng wenti de baogao" [Report on the engineering problems in the Longxugou sewage canal]. Internal Municipal Government memo, October 9, 1950. Beijing Municipal Archives.

Castells, Manuel, and Jordi Borja. *Local and Global: The Culture of Cities in the Information Age.* London: Earthscan, 1997.

Chai Xiaofeng. *Xiaowen ye fengkuang* [Xiaowen too is mad]. Changsha: Hunan Wenyi Chubanshe, 1997.

Chan, Ching-kiu Stephen. "Temporality and the Modern Subject: Effects of Memory in Lai Sheng-ch'uan's *The Other Evening, We Put Up a Show of 'Hsiang-sheng.' " Tamkang Review* 18.1–4 (1989): 1–37.

Chang, Hsiao-hung, and Chih-hung Wang. "Mapping Taipei's Landscape of Desire: Deterritorialization and Reterritorialization of the Family / Park." In *Xunzhao dianying zhong de Taibei* [Focus on Taipei through cinema], ed. Chen Ruxiu and Miao Jinfeng, 115–25. Taipei: Wanxiang, 1995.

Chang Runjie. "Jingqiang Jingwei de Beijing" [Beijing of a Beijing accent and Beijing flavor]. In *Renwen Aoyun*, ed. Peng Yongjie, Zhang Zhiwei, and Han Donghui, 422–25.

———. "Kan Aoyun, you Beijing" [Watching the Olympics, touring Beijing]. In *Renwen Aoyun*, ed. Peng Yongjie, Zhang Zhiwei, and Han Donghui, 426–30.

Chen, Xiaomei. *Acting the Right Part: Political Theater and Popular Drama in Contemporary China.* Honolulu: University of Hawai'i Press, 2002.

———. *Reading the Right Part: An Anthology of Contemporary Chinese Drama.* Honolulu: University of Hawai'i Press, 2003.

Chen Baichen. "Chong du *Xiaojing hutong*" [Rereading *Small Well Lane*]. *Zhongshan* 29.2 (1984): 237–40.

Cheng Jihua, ed. *Zhongguo dianying fazhan shi* [History of the development of Chinese cinema]. 2 vols. Beijing: Zhongguo Dianying Chubanshe, 1998.

Cheng Tongyi. "20 shijimo dansheng de Zhongguo Nanjing lu xue" [The birth of Nanjing Road studies at the end of the twentieth century]. In *Kaibu: Zhongguo Nanjing lu 150 nian* [Building the city: One hundred and fifty years to China's Nanjing Road], 670–84. Beijing: Kunlun Chubanshe, 1996.

———. "Malu zhi jia: Nanjing lu shang hao balian" [A home on the road: The Good Eighth Company of Nanjing Road]. In *Kaibu: Zhongguo Nanjing lu 150 nian*

[Building the city: One hundred and fifty years to China's Nanjing Road], 563–70. Beijing: Kunlun Chubanshe, 1996.

Chen Huangmei, ed. *Dangdai Zhongguo dianying shi* [A history of contemporary Chinese cinema]. Beijing: Zhongguo Shehui Kexue Chubanshe, 1989.

Chen Kaige. *Longxieshu* [The dragon-blood tree]. Hong Kong: Cosmos, 1992.

——. "Zhangda youshi zhishi yishunjian de shi" [Sometimes growing up takes only an instant]. In *90 niandai de "diwudai"* ["The Fifth Generation" in the 1990s], ed. Yang Yuanying, Pan Hua, and Zhang Zhuan, 251–60. Beijing: Beijing Guangbo Xueyuan Chubanshe, 2000.

Chen Kaige and Tony Rayns. *King of the Children and the New Chinese Cinema*. London: Faber, 1989.

Chen Lüsheng. *Xin Zhongguo meishu tushi, 1949–1966* [An illustrated history of art in the New China, 1949–1966]. Beijing: Zhongguo Qingnian Chubanshe, 2000.

Chen Penggui. "Guangchang shang de zheibang ge'rmen" [This bunch of buddies at the square]. In *Tiananmen qian* [In front of Tiananmen], ed. *Dazhong dianying* [Popular cinema], 152–54. Beijing: Jiefangjun Wenyi Chubanshe, 1999.

Chen Qingquan. "*Nihong deng xia de shaobing* zai Shanghai kaipai" [*Sentinels under the Neon Lights* is being shot in Shanghai]. *Dazhong dianying* [Popular cinema], May 1964, 27.

Chen Wenqian. "Kuqiang Beijingcheng" [Beijing of the Wailing Wall]. *Zhongguo shibao* [China times], August 16, 2005. Reposted on the Internet forum *Sishu luntan*: www.sishu.cn. Accessed June 27, 2009.

Chen Xiaoyun. *Dianying chengshi: Zhongguo dianying yu chengshi wenhua (1990–2007 nian)* [The cinematic city: Chinese cinema and urban culture (1990–2007)]. Beijing: Zhongguo Dianying Chubanshe, 2008.

Chen Yongxiang. "Cong shenghuo dao wutai" [From life to the stage]. In *"Longxu-gou" de wutai yishu* [The stage art of *Dragon Whisker Creek*], ed. Jiang Rui, 230–43. Beijing: Zhongguo Xiju Chubanshe, 1987.

Chinoy, Mike. *China Live: People Power and the Television Revolution*. Lanham, Md.: Rowman and Littlefield, 1999.

"Chongwenqu Jinyuchi shequ" [The community at Goldfish Ponds, Chongwen District]. Part of the website of the Committee for Establishing the Capital's Spiritual Civilization (Shoudu Jingshen Wenming Jianshe Weiyuanhui): www.bjwmb.gov .cn/v2003/wmdwgongshi/nr.asp?id=8922. Accessed December 11, 2005.

"Chunzhen niandai: Xin shiqi dianying chuangzuo huigu" [The age of purity: Looking back at the cinematic creation of the New Era] (Zhang Wei interviews Zheng Dongtian). blog.sina.com.cn/s/blog_ccd4ee301000a9v.html. Accessed October 21, 2008.

Chu Weihua. *Zhongguo dushi pingmin dianying* [The cinema of Chinese urban citizens]. Beijing: Zhongguo Dianying Chubanshe, 2008.

Clark, Paul. *Chinese Cinema: Culture and Politics since 1949*. Cambridge: Cambridge University Press, 1987.

———. *Reinventing China: A Generation and Its Films*. Hong Kong: Chinese University Press, 2005.

Clark, T. J. *The Painting of Modern Life: Paris in the Art of Manet and His Followers*. New York: Knopf, 1985.

Clarke, David B. "Introduction: Previewing the Cinematic City." In *The Cinematic City*, ed. David B. Clarke, 1–18. London: Routledge, 1997.

Coates, Austin. *China Races*. Hong Kong: Oxford University Press, 1983.

Cochran, Sherman. *Inventing Nanjing Road: Commercial Culture in Shanghai, 1900–1945*. Ithaca, N.Y.: Cornell University Press, 2000.

Conceison, Claire. *Significant Other: Staging the American in China*. Honolulu: University of Hawai'i Press, 2002.

"Cong *Longxugou* dao *Jinyuchi*: Yi bu nongsuo Beijing chengshi fazhanshi" [From *Dragon Whisker Creek* to *Goldfish Ponds*: A concentrated history of Beijing's urban development]. *Beijing wanbao* [Beijing evening news], June 29, 2001.

Coonan, Clifford. "China Aims to Win the Charm Olympics." *Independent*, February 21, 2008. www.independent.co.uk. Accessed May 10, 2008.

Dai Jinhua. *Yinxing shuxie* [Invisible writing]. Nanjing: Jiangsu Renmin Chubanshe, 1999.

Dangdai Zhongguo de Shanghai [Shanghai in contemporary China]. 2 vols. Beijing: Dangdai Zhongguo Chubanshe, 1993.

Deleuze, Gilles. *Cinema 2: The Time-Image*. Trans. Hugh Tomlinson and Robert Galeta. Minneapolis: University of Minnesota Press, 1989.

Des Forges, Alexander. *Mediasphere Shanghai*. Honolulu: University of Hawai'i Press, 2007.

Di Fang. "Outdoor Ads Banned in Beijing's Special Areas." *China Daily*, September 13, 2004. www.chinadaily.com.cn/english. Accessed June 30, 2009.

"Diguo zhuyi de xingwei yaobude: Oulifu chuju yi san tian" [Imperialist behavior is intolerable: Olive put in detention for three days]. *Jiefang ribao* [Liberation daily], July 10, 1949.

Dong, Madeleine Yue. *Republican Beijing: The City and Its Histories*. Berkeley: University of California Press, 2003.

Dong Guangqi, ed. *Gudu Beijing: Wushi nian yanbian lu* [The old capital of Beijing: A record of fifty years of evolution]. Nanjing: Dongnan Daxue Chubanshe, 2006.

"DPP to Protest against Amendment Favoring Veterans." Article on site of Government Information Office, Republic of China (Taiwan): www.taiwanheadlines.gov.tw. Accessed February 9, 2007.

Duan Muqi. "Zhongguo fangdichan jingguan sheji xianzhuang yu fazhan" [The current state and future development of Chinese real estate landscape design]. Talk at a conference on real estate landscape design, Beijing, August 17–19, 2002. Posted on the real estate portal house.sina.com.cn. Accessed June 27, 2009.

Du Xiulin. *Nanjing lu shang hao balian* [The Good Eighth Company of Nanjing Road]. Illustrated by He Youzhi et al. Shanghai: Shanghai Renmin Meishu Chubanshe, 2003 [1963].

Dutton, Michael. *Streetlife China*. Cambridge: Cambridge University Press, 1998.

Eisenstein, Sergei. "The Problem of the Materialist Approach to Form." In *Film Theory: Critical Concepts in Media and Cultural Studies*, ed. Philip Simpson, Andrew Utterson, and K. J. Shepherdson, 142–48. London: Routledge, 2003.

Elliott, Stuart. "Advertising for Olympics, China's Marketers Are Showing Their Pride." *New York Times*, November 14, 2007. www.nytimes.com. Accessed June 1, 2008.

Ellul, Jacques. *Propaganda: The Formation of Men's Attitudes*. New York: Vintage, 1973.

"Fang+gai weigai yinling chaiqianhu zoushang anju lu" [Redevelopment by housing reform gives relocated residents hope for stable housing]. *Beijing chenbao* [Beijing morning news]. house.sina.com.cn/n/b/2001–10–19/4098.html. Accessed December 11, 2005.

Fang Ke. *Dangdai Beijing jiucheng gengxin: Diaocha, yanjiu, tansuo* [Contemporary redevelopment in the inner city of Beijing: Survey, analysis, and investigation]. Beijing: Zhongguo Jianzhu Gongye Chubanshe, 2000.

Fang Xiang. "Diguo zhuyi zai yuandong de da duqu: Paomating" [The great gambling den of imperialism in the Far East: The Race Course]. In *Shanghai de gushi* [Shanghai stories], ed. Li Jiashou, 128–40. Shanghai: Renmin Chubanshe, 1982.

Fang Zhenming. "Zhongguo haishi yao kafang: Fang SOHO Zhongguo dongshizhang Pan Shiyi" [China still has to open up: An interview with Pan Shiyi, General Manager of SOHO China]. *Wenhua* [Culture], September 2004.

Farquhar, Mary Ann. "Sanmao: Classic Cartoons and Chinese Popular Culture." In *Asian Popular Culture*, ed. John Lent, 109–25. Boulder, Colo.: Westview, 1995.

Feng Jicai. *Jiucheng yiyun: Tianjin lao fangzi* [Resonances left of an old town: Old Tianjin buildings]. Tianjin: Yangliuqing Huashe, 1995.

——. *Qiangjiu laojie* [Saving an old street]. Beijing: Xiyuan Chubanshe, 2000.

——. *Shouxia liuqing: Xiandai dushi wenhua de youhuan* [Have mercy: The anxiety of modern urban culture]. Shanghai: Xuelin Chubanshe, 2000.

Feng Mengbo. "Taking Mt. Doom by Strategy." member.netease.com/~mbgame/page/tmdc9.htm. Accessed September 16, 2001.

Feng Xiaogang. *Wo ba qingchun xian gei ni* [I gave you my youth]. Wuhan: Changjiang Wenyi Chubanshe, 2003.

Forester, John. *Planning in the Face of Power*. Berkeley: University of California Press, 1989.

Foucault, Michel. "Truth and Power." In *Power/Knowledge: Selected Interviews and Other Writings, 1972–1977*, ed. Colin Gordon, 109–33. New York: Random House, 1980.

Friedberg, Anne. *Window Shopping: Cinema and the Postmodern*. Berkeley: University of California Press, 1993.

Friedmann, John. *China's Urban Transition*. Minneapolis: University of Minnesota Press, 2005.

Fu Gengzhen. "Cong *Jiashen sanbai nian ji* dao *Nihong deng xia de shaobing*." [From

The Three-Hundred-Year Memorial to Jiashen to *Sentinels under the Neon Lights*]. *Qiushi* [Seeking truth], no. 18 (1996): 43.

Fu Zhaoqing. *Zhongguo gudian shiyang xin jianzhu: Ershi shiji Zhongguo xin jianzhu guanzhi wenhua de lishi yanjiu* [New architecture in Chinese classical style: A historical exploration of the institutionalization of new architecture in twentieth-century China]. Taipei: Nantian Shuju, 1993.

"Galaxy of Stars Come Out for Film Awards in China." *People's Daily Online*, October 22, 2003. english.people.com.cn. Accessed December 20, 2004.

Gan Hailan. *Lao She Nianpu* [A chronology of Lao She]. Beijing: Shumu Wenxian Chubanshe, 1989.

Gao Fuyuan. "Beijingshi shishu—guohuai" [The city tree of Beijing: The national locust tree]. Essay at the Beijing municipal government popular science portal: www.bjkp.gov.cn. Accessed December 11, 2005.

Gao Shen. *Longxugou de bianqian* [The transformation of Longxugou]. Beijing: Tianxia Chubanshe, 1951.

Ge Chenhong. "Wenming Beijingren xingxiang suzao gongcheng" [The process of creating the image of the civilized Beijinger]. In *Renwen Aoyun*, ed. Peng Yongjie, Zhang Zhiwei, and Han Donghui, 489–94.

Geertz, Clifford. "Javanese Kijai: The Changing Role of a Cultural Broker." *Comparative Study of Society and History* 2 (1960): 228–49.

Ge Yihong et al., eds. *Zhongguo huaju tongshi* [History of modern Chinese drama]. Beijing: Wenhua Yishu Chubanshe, 1997.

Gongqingtuan Shanghaishi Weiyuanhui [The Chinese Communist Youth League Shanghai Council]. "Guanyu zai quanshi qingshaonian zhong guangfan kaizhan xuexi 'Nanjing lu shang hao balian' de jiaoyu huodong de tongzhi" [Announcement on educational activities to launch a widespread study of the Good Eighth Company of Nanjing Road among youth all over the city]. Internal document, signed April 19, dated April 23, 1963 [Shanghai Municipal Film Archives].

Gongqingtuan Shiwei Xuanchuanbu [Propaganda team of the Chinese Communist Youth League Shanghai Council]. "Benshi qingnian xuexi 'Nanjing lu shang hao balian' de qingkuang fanying" [State of affairs and response to the city's youth study of "The Good Eighth Company of Nanjing Road"]. Internal memo draft, April 30, 1963 [Shanghai Municipal Film Archives].

"Gongsheng yizhan: Baozangyan lishi juluo shezhi yishucun jihua weituo guihua" [Artivist village: Plan proposal for establishing an artists' village at the historical settlement of Baozangyan]. Unpublished booklet. Prepared by the ROC Team for Urban Reform, May 5, 2003.

Gross, Matt. "Going to Taipei." *New York Times*, February 12, 2006.

Gu, Xuewu. "China and Its Reactions to Globalization." Article on site of Bundeszentrale für Politische Bildung. www.bpb.de/files/E4SM4X.pdf. Accessed December 12, 2007.

Gunning, Tom. "From the Kaleidoscope to the X-Ray: Urban Spectatorship, Poe, Benjamin, and *Traffic in Souls* (1913)." *Wide Angle* 19.4 (1997): 25–61.

Guo Jia. "*Cesuo* haobi dunzhe de *Chaguan*" [*Toilet* is tantamount to *Teahouse* in a crouching position]. *Beijing qingnian bao* [Beijing youth daily]. Republished on the News Guangdong website: www.southcn.com. Accessed June 27, 2009.

Guo Xiaolu. "Yige feizhiye bianju de silu" [A nonprofessional scriptwriter's thoughts]. In *Zhongguo dianying meixue, 1999* [Chinese film aesthetics, 1999], ed. Hu Ke et al., 77–80. Beijing: Beijing Guangbo Xueyuan Chubanshe, 2000.

Gu Weili. *Zhao Dan: Diyu tiantang suoyizhu* [Zhao Dan: Looking for pearls of art in heaven and hell]. Shanghai: Shanghai Jiaoyu Chubanshe, 2000.

Gu Yubao. "*Nihong deng xia de shaobing* 'si' er fusheng ji" [Records of the "death" and revival of *Sentinels under the Neon Lights*]. Posted on the *Hebei Daily* website: skb.hebeidaily.com.cn/200517/ca484811.htm. Accessed October 20, 2006.

Hansen, Miriam. *Babel and Babylon: Spectatorship in American Silent Film.* Cambridge: Harvard University Press, 1994.

——. "Benjamin, Cinema and Experience: 'The Blue Flower in the Land of Technology.' " *New German Critique* 40 (Winter 1987): 179–224.

Han Xiaohui, ed. *Chengshi piping: Beijing juan* [Urban criticism: Beijing]. Beijing: Wenhua Yishu Chubanshe, 2002.

Han Yuqi and Zhang Song. *Dongfang de Saina zuo'an—Suzhouhe yan'an de yishu cangku* [The Rive Gauche of the Orient: The art warehouses on the bank of Suzhou Creek]. Shanghai: Shanghai Guji Chubanshe, 2004.

" 'Hao balian' de gushi shuobuwan" [The story of the Good Eighth Company cannot come to an end]. In *Nanjing lu shang hao balian*, 41–84.

Hay, James. "Piecing Together What Remains of the Cinematic City." In *The Cinematic City*, ed. David B. Clarke, 209–29. London: Routledge, 1997.

He, Shenjing, and Fulong Wu. "Property-Led Redevelopment in Post-reform China: A Case Study of Xintiandi Redevelopment Project in Shanghai." *Journal of Urban Affairs* 27.1 (February 2005): 1–23.

He Depu. "Beijing Jinyuchi xiaoqu huiqianhu de fennu" [Residents returning to Beijing's Goldfish Ponds neighborhood are angry]. July 8, 2002. Published at Boxun News, a site for independent "citizen journalism": www.boxun.com/hero/hdp/29_1.shtml. Accessed December 11, 2005.

Hei Ma. "Fidelity and Betrayal: Adapting Novel into Film in a Political-Commercial Context." *Scope: An Online Journal of Film Studies*, special issue on Asian cinema, 2003. www.scope.nottingham.ac.uk. June 27, 2009.

—— *Hun zai Beijing* [Strangers in Beijing]. Harbin: Beifang Wenyi Chubanshe, 1993.

Hershkovitz, Linda. "Tiananmen Square and the Politics of Place." *Political Geography* 12.5 (September 1993): 395–420.

"He wei 'dawan,' 'dakuan'?" [What are "dawan" and "dakuan"?]. *Zhongguo Gonghui Caihui* [Trade Union Financial Affairs of China], no.1 (1994): n.p.

Holquist, Michael. "Introduction." In Mikhail Bakhtin, *Speech Genres and Other Late Essays*, ed. Caryl Emerson and Michael Holquist, trans. Vern W. McGee, ix–xxiii. Austin: University of Texas Press, 1986.

Hou Bo. "Kaiguo dadian" [The founding ceremony]. In *Tiananmen qian* [In front of Tiananmen], ed. *Dazhong dianying* [Popular photography magazine], 15. Beijing: Jiefangjun Wenyi Chubanshe, 1999.

Hou Jianmei. "Meili Beijing, you wo yige: Renwen Aoyun yu zhiyuanzhe" [Beautiful Beijing, count me in: Humanistic Olympics and the volunteers]. In *Renwen Aoyun*, ed. Peng Yongjie, Zhang Zhiwei, and Han Donghui, 525–28.

Hou Renzhi. "Beijing jiucheng pingmian sheji de gaizao" [Reconstructing the surface design of Beijing's old city]. In *Lishi dilixue de lilun yu shixian* [Theory and practice of historical geography], ed. Hou Renzhi, 205–26. Shanghai: Shanghai Renmin Chubanshe, 1979.

———. "Tiananmen guangchang: Cong gongting guangchang dao renmin guangchange de yanbian he gaizao" [Tiananmen Square: Evolution and reconstruction from imperial square to the people's square]. In *Lishi dilixue de lilun yu shixian* [Theory and practice of historical geography], ed. Hou Renzhi, 227–50. Shanghai: Shanghai Renmin Chubanshe, 1979.

———. "The Transformation of the Old City of Beijing, China." In *World Patterns of Modern Urban Change*, ed. Michael P. Conzen, 217–39. Chicago: University of Chicago, Department of Geography, 1986.

Hua Lanhong. *Chongjian Zhongguo: Chengshi guihua sanshi nian, 1949–1979*. Trans. from the French by Li Ying. Beijing: Sanlian Shudian, 2006.

Hua Mengyang and Zhang Hongjie, eds. *Lao Beijingren de shenghuo* [The life of the people of old Beijing]. Taian: Shandong Huabao Chubanshe, 2000.

Huang Dazhou. *Tuobian: Da'an senlin gongyuan de dansheng* [Metamorphosis: The birth of the Da'an Forest Park]. Taipei: Zhengzhong Shudian, 2001.

Huang Du and Bingyi. *Hou wuzhi* [The postmaterial]. Beijing: Shijie Huaren Yishu Chubanshe, 2000.

Huang Shixian et al. "Yingtan de yisheng chunxun: Shoudu wenyijie renshi zuotan *Xizhao jie*" [Spring declared unanimously by the film circles: A forum on *Sunset Street* with Beijing literary celebrities]. In *Bu siliang, zi nanwang: Wang Haowei yanjiu wenji* [Immeasurable and unforgettable: Collected research writings on Wang Haowei], ed. Wang Renyin, 185–87. Beijing: Zhongguo Dianying Chubanshe, 2002.

Huang Sunquan [Huang Sun Chuan]. "Lüse tuituji: Jiuling niandai Taibei de weijian, gongyuan, ziran fangdichan yu zhiduhua dijing" [Green bulldozer: Squatters, parks, nature estate, and institutionalized landscape in 1990s Taipei]. MA thesis. National Taiwan University, submitted 1997.

Huang Weijun. "Xiaoyuan chunqiu: Kan huaju *Zuolin youshe*" [Annals of a small courtyard: Watching the modern play *Next-Door Neighbors*]. *Beijing ribao* [Beijing daily], February 26, 1981.

Huang Weijun and Zhou Ruixiang. *Huihuang de yishu diantang: Beijing renmin yishu juyuan wushi nian* [A resplendent art hall: Fifty years of the Beijing People's Art Theater]. Beijing: Zhongguo Shudian, 2002.

Huang Wenlong et al. "Gongren huanying xiang *Longxugou* zheyang de zuopin"

[The workers welcome pieces such as *Dragon Whisker Creek*]. *Renmin ribao* [People's Daily], March 18, 1951.

Huang Xiaoyang. *Yinxiang Zhongguo—Zhang Yimou zhuan* [Impressions of China: A biography of Zhang Yimou]. Beijing: Huaxia Chubanshe, 2008.

Hu Hao. "Yu Longxugou dangdi jumin gongkan *Longxugou* yanchu" [Watching a performance of *Dragon Whisker Creek* together with residents of Longxugou]. *Renmin ribao* [People's Daily], n.d. [ca. February 18, 1951; clipping in Beijing People's Art Theater archives].

Hu Ke. "Jingqiao de xushu yishu" [An ingenious art of narration]. In *Zhongguo dianying meixue, 1999* [Chinese film aesthetics, 1999], ed. Hu Ke et al., 275–84. Beijing: Beijing Guangbo Xueyuan Chubanshe, 2000.

Hu Xiaoqin. "Ganshang Beijing de bufa" [Catching up with Beijing's stride]. In *Renwen Aoyun*, ed. Peng Yongjie, Zhang Zhiwei, and Han Donghui, 519–24.

——. "Liaojie shijie, zuo shijie gongmin" [Understanding the world, becoming citizens of the world]. In *Renwen Aoyun*, ed. Peng Yongjie, Zhang Zhiwei, and Han Donghui, 514–18.

"Invisible Cities." Program notes for the performance of *Invisible Cities* by Cloud Gate Dance Theater. 2004.

Inwood, Heather. "Live Spaces and Urban Environment in China's Contemporary Poetry Scene." Paper presented at the conference "Literature, Media, and the Environment." Chengdu, August 6, 2007.

Jameson, Fredric. *The Geopolitical Aesthetic: Cinema and Space in the World System*. Bloomington: Indiana University Press, 1992.

Jia Fulin. "Beijing de ye" [Beijing's *ye*]. Posted on Ma Jin's website of literary texts: majin.uiii.net. Accessed October 19, 2005.

Jiang, Hong, and Timothy Cheek. "Introduction: Sense of Place, History, and Community in *Small Well Lane*." In Li Longyun, *Small Well Lane*, 1–24.

Jiang Jun. "Why MAD Is Mad." In *MAD Dinner*, ed. Brendan McGetrick and Chen Shuyu, 350–57. Barcelona: Actar, 2007.

"Jianku zuofeng, daidai xiangchuan" [The attitude of arduous work is transmitted from generation to generation]. In *Nanjing lu shang hao balian*, 18–40.

Jianshebu Zhengce Yanjiu Zhongxin [Policy Research Center of the Construction Bureau], ed. *Zuixin chengshi fangwu chaiqian zhinan* [The new guide to demolition and relocation of urban houses]. Beijing: Zhongguo Jianzhu Gongye Chubanshe, 2004.

Jiao Juyin. "*Longxugou* daoyan yishu chuangzao de zongjie" [A summary of the artistic creativity in directing *Dragon Whisker Creek*]. *Renmin xiju*, June 10, 1951.

——. "Lun huaju wutai meishu de minzuhua wenti" [On making modern theater art comport with national style]. In *Wutai meishu wenji* (Selected writings on stage art), ed. Zhongguo Yishu Yanjiuyuan Xiqu Yanjiusuo [Theater Program at the China Research Institute of Art], 188–97. Beijing: Zhongguo Xiju Chubanshe, 1982.

Jia Yingting, Ye Xiaoyong, and Lu Ye, eds. *Tiananmen bainian jujiao* [Centenary focus on Tiananmen]. Beijing: Zhongguo Duiwai Fanyi Chuban Gongsi, 2000.

"Jiefang Shanghai diyiri" [The first day of Shanghai's liberation]. *Jiefang ribao* [Liberation daily], July 9, 1949.

Jin Li. "Huigu *Longxugou* de pailian" [Reminiscing on rehearsing *Dragon Whisker Creek*]. In *"Longxugou" de wutai yishu* [The stage art of *Dragon Whisker Creek*], ed. Jiang Rui, 38–79. Beijing: Zhongguo Xiju Chubanshe, 1987.

Johnson, Ian. *Wild Grass: Three Stories of Change in Modern China.* New York: Pantheon, 2004.

Johnson, Matthew D. "State Cinema and Sovereign Form: Wartime Documentary Filmmaking and Its Aftermath." Unpublished paper, 2007.

Jones, Andrew F. *Yellow Music: Media Culture and Colonial Modernity in the Chinese Jazz Age.* Durham, N.C.: Duke University Press, 2001.

Kang, Min Jay. "Altered Space: Squatting and Legitimizing Treasure Hill, Taipei." Paper presented at Cultural Development Network forum, "Artivism: The Role of Arts in Regeneration," Melbourne, Australia, June 23, 2006. culturaldevelopment.net.au. Accessed June 15, 2007.

Kant, Immanuel. *Critique of Judgment*, trans. James Creed Meredith. Oxford, U.K.: Clarendon, 1992.

Keane, Michael. *Created in China: The Great New Leap Forward.* London: Routledge, 2007.

Kinouchi Makoto. *Shanhai rekishi gaidomappu* [Guidemaps to Shanghai's history]. Tokyo: Taishukan, 2001.

Klein, Naomi. *No Logo.* New York: Picador, 2002.

Koolhas, Rem, and Bruce Mau. *S.M.L.XL.* New York: Montacelli, 1995.

Kostof, Spiro. "His Majesty the Pick: The Aesthetics of Demolition." In *Streets: Critical Perspectives on Public Space*, ed. Zeynep Çelik, Diane Favro, and Richard Ingersoll, 9–22. Berkeley: University of California Press, 1994.

Kracauer, Siegfried. "Boredom." In *The Mass Ornament: Weimar Essays*, ed. and trans. Thomas Y. Levin, 331–32. Cambridge: Harvard University Press, 1995.

Kraus, Richard Curt. *The Party and the Art in China: The New Politics of Culture.* Lanham, Md.: Rowman and Littlefield, 2004.

Kuan Liguang and Li Yuzhi, eds. *Taiwan Xianggang dianying mingpian xinshang* [Appreciating famous Taiwan and Hong Kong films]. Taiyuan: Shanxi Jiaoyu Chubanshe, 1996.

Kwok, R. Yin-Wang. "Trends of Urban Planning and Development in China." In *Urban Development in Modern China*, ed. Laurence J. C. Ma and Edward W. Hanten, 147–93. Boulder, Colo.: Westview, 1981.

Kwok Wah Lau, Jenny. "*Farewell My Concubine*: History, Melodrama, and Ideology in Contemporary Pan-Chinese Cinema." *Film Quarterly* 49.1 (1995): 16–27.

Lalkaka, Dinyar. "Urban Housing in China." *Habitat International* 8.1 (1984): 63–73.

Lan Zuwei. "Yaokong feiji + 35mm sheyingji: Guopian feiqilai luo!" [Remote-controlled plane + 35mm-camera: Chinese film has taken off!]. *Lianhebao* [United daily news], January 12, 1994.

Lao She. "Beijing." In *Wo re'ai Beijing* [I dearly love Beijing], 4–7. Beijing: Beijing Chubanshe, 1979.

——. *Longxugou* [Dragon Whisker Creek]. Beijing: Dazhong Shudian, 1951.

——. "*Longxugou*" [Dragon Whisker Creek]. In *Lao She juzuo xuan* [Selected drama by Lao She], 1–72. Beijing: Renmin Wenxue Chubanshe, 1987 [1953].

——. "*Longxugou* de renwu" [The characters in *Dragon Whisker Creek*]. *Wenyibao* [Literature and arts] 3, no. 9 (1951). Rpt. in "*Longxugou*" *de wutai yishu* [The stage art of *Dragon Whisker Creek*], ed. Jiang Rui, 12–16. Beijing: Zhongguo Xiju Chubanshe, 1987.

——. "*Longxugou* de xiezuo jingguo" [The experience of writing *Dragon Whisker Creek*]. *Renmin ribao* [*People's Daily*], February 4, 1951. Rpt. in "*Longxugou*" *de wutai yishu* [The stage art of *Dragon Whisker Creek*], ed. Jiang Rui, 9–11. Beijing: Zhongguo Xiju Chubanshe, 1987.

——. "*Longxugou* paicaiben" [Script for the general rehearsal of *Dragon Whisker Creek*]. Revised by Jiao Juyin. Supplement to *Renmin xiju* [People's drama], May 10, 1951.

——. "Mao zhuxi geile wo xin de wenyi shengming" [Chairman Mao gave me a new artistic life]. *Renmin ribao* [*People's Daily*], May 21, 1952. Rpt. in *Wo re'ai Beijing* [I dearly love Beijing], 39–46. Beijing: Beijing Chubanshe, 1979.

——. "Wo re'ai xin Beijing" [I dearly love the new Beijing]. *Renmin ribao* [*People's Daily*], January 25, 1951. Rpt. in "*Longxugou*" *de wutai yishu* [The stage art of *Dragon Whisker Creek*], ed. Jiang Rui, 5–8. Beijing: Zhongguo Xiju Chubanshe, 1987.

——. "Yao re'ai ni de hutong." [You should love your alley]. In *Wo re'ai Beijing* [I dearly love Beijing], 8–9. Beijing: Beijing Chubanshe, 1979.

Leaf, Michael, and Li Hou. "The 'Third Spring' of Urban Planning in China: The Resurrection of Professional Planning in the Post-Mao Era." *China Information* 20.3 (November 2006): 553–85.

Lefebvre, Henri. *The Production of Space*. London: Basil Blackwell, 1991.

Leung, Helen Hok-Sze. *Undercurrents: Queer Culture and Postcolonial Hong Kong*. Vancouver: University of British Columbia Press, 2008.

Leung Ping-kwan. "Urban Cinema and the Cultural Identity of Hong Kong." In *The Cinema of Hong Kong: History, Arts, Identity*, ed. Poshek Fu and David Desser, 227–51. Cambridge: Cambridge University Press, 2000.

Liao Binghui. "Shikong yu xingbie de cuoluan: Lun *Bawang bie ji*" [Time and space and gender disorder: On *Farewell My Concubine*]. *Zhongwai wenxue* [Chung-Wai literary monthly] 22.1 (1993): 6–18.

Li Bihua. *Bawang bie ji* [*Farewell My Concubine*], new ed. Hong Kong: Tiandi Tushu, 1993.

Li Bozhao. "Cong *Longxugou* kan Beijing" [Seeing Beijing from *Dragon Whisker Creek*]. *Guangming ribao* [Guangming daily], February 4, 1951.

——. "Kan *Longxugou*" [Watching *Dragon Whisker Creek*]. *Renmin ribao* [*People's Daily*], February 4, 1951. Rpt. in "*Longxugou*" *de wutai yishu* [The stage art of

Dragon Whisker Creek], ed. Jiang Rui, 3–4. Beijing: Zhongguo Xiju Chubanshe, 1987.

———. "Wei jin yibu xuexi he shijian Mao Zedong wenyi sixiang er fendou: Beijing renmin yishu juyuan 1950 nian gongzuo zongjie baogao" [Struggle to advance another step in studying and practicing Mao Zedong's thought on art and literature: A concluding report on Beijing People's Art Theater's work in the year 1950]. In *Fazhan zhong de Beijing wenyi* [Emerging Beijing literature and arts], ed. Beijing Municipal Literary Association, 136–45. Shanghai: Chenguang Chubanshe, 1951.

Li Liyun. *Lao She zai Beijing de zuji* [Lao She's traces in Beijing]. Beijing: Beijing Yanshan Chubanshe, 1986.

Li Longyun. *Small Well Lane: A Contemporary Chinese Play and Oral History*. Trans. and ed. Hong Jiang and Timothy Cheek. Ann Arbor: University of Michigan Press, 2002.

———. *Wanjia denghuo* [A myriad lights]. Beijing: Zhongguo Qingnian Chubanshe, 2004.

———. "*Wanjia denghuo* chuangzuo de qianyin houguo" [The cause and result of composing *A Myriad Lights*]. In Li Longyun, *Wanjia denghuo*, 1–3.

———. "*Wanjia denghuo* chuangzuo riji houji" [Afterword to the diary of composing *A Myriad Lights*]. In Li Longyun, *Wanjia denghuo*, 228.

———. "Wei *Xiaojing hutong* xi san" [Giving *Small Well Lane* three cleansings]. In Li Longyun, *Huangyuan yu ren* [Wasteland and man], 171–77. Beijing: Zhongguo Shehui Kexue Chubanshe, 1993.

———. *Wo suo zhidao de Yu Shizhi* [Yu Shizhi as I knew him]. Beijing: Zhongguo Qingnian Chubanshe, 2004.

———. *Xiaojing hutong* [*Small Well Lane*]. Xin shiqi wenxue ershi nian jingxuan: Huaju juan [Selection from the twenty years of literature of the new period: Drama]. Shanghai: Shanghai Jiaoyu Chubanshe, 2002.

———. *You zheyang yige xiaoyuan* [There is a small courtyard]. Zhengzhou: Henan Renmin Chubanshe, 1979.

———. "Yu shi gejue de sanshi tian: *Wanjia denghuo* chuangzuo riji" [Apart from the world for thirty days: A diary of composing *A Myriad Lights*]. In Li Longyun, *Wanjia denghuo*, 165–227.

Li Nanjun [Werner Zorn]. "Zhongguo jieru hulianwang de zaoqi gongzuo huigu" [Remembering the early work for China's entry to the Internet]. media.people.com.cn/GB/40628/5076637.html. Accessed December 12, 2007.

Lin Chongjie. "Jingying chengshi de xinling: Taibei de dushi kaifang kongjian jihua" [Administrating the city's soul: Planning open urban spaces in Taipei]. In *Shimin de chengshi* [City of the urban citizens], ed. Lin Chongjie et al., 118–23. Taipei: Chuangxing Chubanshe, 1996.

Ling Yan. "Xin dushi shimin shenhua" [The myths of the new urban citizens]. *Dianying wenxue* [Film and literature], November 1999, 11–14.

"*Linju*": *Cong juben dao yingpian* [*Neighbors*: From script to film]. Zhongguo Dianying Chubanshe, 1984.

Link, Perry. *The Uses of Literature: Life in the Socialist Chinese Literary System*. Princeton, N.J.: Princeton University Press, 2000.

Lin Qianrong. *Dushi sheji zai Taiwan* [Urban design in Taiwan]. Taipei: Chuangxing
Chubanshe, 1995.

Lin Wenqi. "Jiuling niandai Taiwan dushi dianying zhong de lishi, kongjian yu
jia/guo" [History, space, and home/state in Taiwan urban film of the 1990s].
Zhongwai wenxue [Chung-Wai literary monthly] 27.5 (1998): 99–117.

———. "Xi, lishi, rensheng: *Bawang bie ji* yu *Ximeng rensheng* zhong de guozu
rentong" ["Drama, History, Life: National Identity in *Farewell My Concubine* and
The Puppetmaster"]. *Zhongwai wenxue* [Chung-Wai literary monthly] 23.1 (1994):
1139–56.

Li Qiankuan and Xiao Guiyun. "Nuli zai yinmu shang shuxie shidai fenliu: *Kaiguo
dadian* de daoyan chuangzuo tihui" [Striving to depict the *air du temps* on the silver screen: The personal experience of the directors of *The Founding Ceremony*].
In *Zaixian geming lishi de yishu: Geming lishi ticai dianying yanjiu lunwen ji* [The
art of representing the revolutionary history: Research papers on film on revolutionary history material], 31–45. Beijing: Zhongguo Dianying Chubanshe, 1993.

Li Qingzhi. "The Construct and Transformation of Taipei's City Image." In *Xunzhao
dianying zhong de Taibei* [Focus on Taipei through cinema], ed. Chen Ruxiu and
Miao Jinfeng, 20–33. Taipei: Wanxiang, 1995.

———. *Niaoguo kuang: Shijimo Taibei kongjian wenhua xianxiang* [Birdland craze: Spatial culture in fin-de-siècle Taipei]. Taipei: Chuangxing Chubanshe, 1994.

Li Tuo. "*Linju* chuangzuo de qishi" [Revelations from the making of *Neighbors*].
Wenyibao [Literature and arts], no. 8 (1982). Rpt. in "*Linju*": *Cong juben dao yingpian*, 367–75.

Liu, Hsin-Jung, and Bing-Yi Lu. "Toward a City for Citizens: Two Community Organizations in Taiwan." In *Democratic Design in the Pacific Rim: Japan, Taiwan, and
the United States*, ed. Randolph T. Hester and Corrina Kweskin, 250–57. Men-
docino, Calif.: Ridge Times, 1999.

Liu Damu. "Cong wuxia xiaoshuo dao dianying" [From chivalric fiction to martial
arts]. In *Xianggang wuxia dianying yanjiu (1945–1980)* [A study of Hong Kong
swordplay film, 1945–1980], 33–46. Hong Kong: Urban Council, 1996.

Liu Guang'en, Wang Honghai, and Yin Li. "*Linju* meishu sheji de liangge wenti"
[Two problems in the set design for *Neighbors*]. In "*Linju*": *Cong juben dao yingpian*, 286–93.

Liu Heng. "Pinzui Zhang Damin de xingfu shenghuo" [The happy life of chatterbox
Zhang Damin]. Beijing: Huayi Chubanshe, 1999.

Liu Li. "Beijing to Continue Ban on Ads in Tian'anmen." *China Daily*, April 13,
2004. www.chinadaily.com.cn/english. Accessed January 7, 2005.

Liu Xiaowen and Liang Sirui, eds. *1949–1984 Zhongguo shangyan huaju jumu zonglan* [Survey of spoken drama staged in China, 1949–1984]. Chengdu: Bashu Shushe, 2002.

Li Xianting. "Tiananmen: Xiandai zhongguoren de jingshen jitan" [Tiananmen: The sacrificial altar of the modern Chinese]. In Wang Wo and Wang Chao, *Renmin wansui*.

Li Xiao, ed. *Shanghai huaju zhi* [Gazetteer of Shanghai's spoken drama]. Shanghai: Baijia Chubanshe, 2002.

Li Xiaobin. "Guanyu 'Shangfangzhe' de paishe ji qita" [On taking "Visitor from the Countryside" and other matters]. In *Lao zhaopian* [Old photographs], 15:126. Jinan: Shandong Huabao Chubanshe, 2002.

———. " 'Shangfangzhe' ji qita" ["Visitor from the Countryside" and other matters]. In *Tiananmen qian* [In front of Tiananmen], ed. *Dazhong dianying* [Popular photography magazine], 124–25. Beijing: Jiefangjun Wenyi Chubanshe, 1999.

Li Xin, Liu Xiaosa, and Wang Jifang. *Bei yiwang de yingxiang* [Forgotten images]. Beijing: Zhongguo Shehui Kexue Chubanshe, 2006.

Li Yan. "WTO laile women zenme ban?" [What should we do when WTO arrives?]. *Dazhong dianying* [Popular cinema], June 2000, 50–55.

"Liyong dufan taowa Longxugou jihua" [Plan for using drug-use convicts for dredging Longxugou]. Folder at the Beijing Municipal Archives containing internal memos of the Beiping Municipal Government, compiled June 28, 1935.

"*Longxugou* diyici caipai zhuanjia zuotan jilu" [Record of a professional's talk at the first dress rehearsal of *Dragon Whisker Creek*]. Internal BPAT memo, January 26, 1951.

"*Longxugou* jinri pu xinbian *Jinyuchi* zuowan shouyan" [*Goldfish Ponds*, the new version of *Dragon Whisker Creek*, premiered yesterday evening]. *Beijing chenbao* [Beijing morning news]. ent.sina.com.cn/h/48426.html. Accessed December 11, 2005.

Lu, Sheldon Hsiao-peng. "Tear Down the City: Reconstructing Urban Space in Contemporary Chinese Popular Cinema and Avant-Garde Art." In Zhang Zhen, ed., *Urban Generation*, 138–60.

Lu, X. B., and E. J. Perry, eds. *Danwei: The Changing Chinese Workplace in Historical and Comparative Perspective*. Armonk, N.Y.: M. E. Sharpe, 1997.

Lü Junhua, Peter G. Rowe, and Zhang Jie, eds. *Modern Urban Housing in China, 1840–2000*. Munich: Prestel, 2001.

Luo Xianming. "Zhiyuan Beijing, you wo yige" [In volunteering for Beijing, count me in]. *Jing bao* [The first], September 26, 2006. www.thefirst.cn/501/2006–11–09/26217.htm. Accessed August 19, 2007.

Lu Wei. "Shuoshuo Zhou Xiaowen" [On Zhou Xiaowen in brief]. In *90 niandai de "diwudai"* ["The Fifth Generation" in the 1990s], ed. Yang Yuanying, Pan Hua, and Zhang Zhuan, 347–58. Beijing: Beijing Guangbo Xueyuan Chubanshe, 2000.

Lü Xingchen. "Nanjing lu shang hao balian" [The good Eighth Company of Nanjing Road]. In *Shanghai jiefang shinian* [Ten years to the liberation of Shanghai], ed.

Shanghai jiefang shinian Zhengwen Bianji Weiyuanhui [The Essay Solicitation and Editorial Committee of Ten Years to the Liberation of Shanghai], 376–87. Shanghai: Shanghai Wenyi Chubanshe, 1960.

———. *Nanjing lu shang hao balian de gushi* [The story of the Good Eighth Company of Nanjing Road]. Illustrated by Mao Zhenhui. Shanghai: Shaonian Ertong Chubanshe, 1961.

Lu Xun et al., eds. *Beijingren, Shanghairen* [Beijingers, Shanghainese]. Hong Kong: Joint Publishing, 2001.

Lü Yuezhu. "Hongtou cangying zhen lafeng" [The red-headed fly truly draws wind]. *Zhongguo shibao* [China times], January 12, 1994.

MacFarquhar, Roderick. *The Origins of the Cultural Revolution*, vol. 3: *The Coming of the Cataclysm, 1961–1966*. New York: Columbia University Press, 1997.

Ma Lin, Da Jiangxia, and Zhu Mei. "*Neighbors*: From the Original Script." Translated by Yomi Braester. *Renditions* 71 (Spring 2009): 65–75.

———. "Zunxun shenghuo de qishi: Guanyu *Linju* de juben chuangzuo" [The revelation of adhering to life: On composing the script for *Neighbors*]. In *"Linju": Cong juben dao yingpian*, 193–204.

Mao Dun. *Ziye* [Midnight]. Hong Kong: Nanguo, 1973.

Mao Tse-Tung [Mao Zedong]. "On the Correct Handling of Contradictions among the People." In *Selected Works of Mao Tse-Tung*, 5:384–421. Peking [Beijing]: Foreign Languages, 1967.

———. "Talks at the Yenan Forum on Literature and Art." In *Selected Works of Mao Tse-Tung*, 3:69–98. Peking [Beijing]: Foreign Languages, 1967.

Ma Qiang, "Weigai haishi qiangqie?" [Housing reform or robbery?]. Essay posted on website of Asia Democracy Foundation: www.asiademo.org/gb/2001/08/20010810c.htm. Accessed December 11, 2005.

"McDonald's in China." Beijing Visitor blog, December 6, 2007. beijingvisitor.blogspot.com. Accessed May 24, 2008.

McGrath, Jason. *Postsocialist Modernity: Chinese Cinema, Literature, and Criticism in the Market Age*. Stanford, Calif.: Stanford University Press, 2008.

Mi Jiashan. "Discussing *The Troubleshooters*." *Chinese Education and Society* 31.1 (Fall 1998): 8–14.

Momphard, David. "The Battle of Treasure Hill." *Taipei Times*, December 21, 2003. www.taipeitimes.com. Accessed June 15, 2007.

Mulvey, Laura. "Visual Pleasure and Narrative Cinema." *Screen* 16.3 (Autumn 1975): 6–18.

Nakamura, Lisa. *Cybertypes: Race, Ethnicity, and Identity on the Internet*. New York: Routledge, 2002.

Nanjing lu shang hao balian [The Good Eighth Company of Nanjing Road]. Beijing: Jiefangjun Wenyishe, 1963.

Nan Shao. "Lishi chelun cao zai shei shou?" [Who holds the wheel of history in his hands?]. *Renmin ribao* [*People's Daily*], January 29. Rpt. in *Zhonggong dianyingjie wenhua dageming ziliao zhuanji, 1964–1971* [Compilation of resources on the

Great Cultural Revolution among film circles in Communist China, 1964–71],
ed. Contemporary China Research Institute, 105–10. Hong Kong: Dangdai
Zhongguo Yanjiusuo, 1972.

Naquin, Susan. *Peking: Temples and City Life, 1400–1900*. Berkeley: University of
California Press, 2000.

Naughton, Barry. "The Third Front: Defence Industrialization in the Chinese Interior." *China Quarterly* 115 (September 1988): 351–86.

"New Coffee Shop Replacing Starbucks in Forbidden City." Official Website of the
Beijing 2008 Olympic Games, September 24, 2007. en.beijing2008.cn. Accessed May 8, 2008.

Nichols, Bill. "Strike and the Question of Class." In *The Hidden Foundation: Cinema
and the Question of Class*, ed. David E. James and Rick Berg, 72–89. Minneapolis:
University of Minnesota Press, 1996.

Nie Wei. "*Nihong deng xia de shaobing*: Zhanzheng yishixingtai longzhao xia de
chengshi gan" [*Sentinels under the Neon Lights*: Urban sensibility under war ideol-
ogy]. Posted on Chinese University of Hong Kong website: www.usc.cuhk
.edu.hk. Accessed April 3, 2007.

Ni Zhen. *Memoirs from the Beijing Film Academy: The Genesis of China's Fifth Generation*. Trans. Chris Berry. Durham, N.C.: Duke University Press, 2002.

——. "Shouwang xinsheng dai" [Expectations for the newborn generation]. *Dianying yishu* 4 (1999): 70–73.

Nora, Pierre. "Between Memory and History: Les Lieux de Mémoire." *Representations* 26 (Spring 1989): 7–25.

"The Organization of Urban Re's." Official site of the NGO OURS: www.ours.org.tw.
Accessed February 23, 2007.

Ou Yangbin. "Tiananmen guangchang bainian libian" [The historical transformation of Tiananmen Square over one hundred years]. Posted on the Phoenix TV
website: www.phoenixtv.com.cn/home/phoenixweekly/146/1501page.html. Accessed March 20, 2007.

Pang, Laikwan. *Building a New China in Cinema: The Chinese Left-Wing Cinema
Movement, 1932–1937*. Lanham, Md.: Rowman and Littlefield, 2002.

——. "Walking Into and Out of the Spectacle: China's Earliest Film Scene." *Screen*
47.1 (Spring 2006): 66–80.

Pan Xulan, ed. *Xin Zhongguo wenxue cidian* [Lexicon of literature in the new China].
Nanjing: Jiangsu Wenyi Chubanshe, 1993.

Peng Yongjie, Zhang Zhiwei, and Han Donghui, eds. *Renwen Aoyun* [Humanistic
Olympics]. Beijing: Dongfang Chubanshe, 2003.

Pickowicz, Paul G. "Social and Political Dynamics of Underground Filmmaking in
China." In *From Underground to Independent*, ed. Pickowicz and Yingjin Zhang,
1–21.

Pickowicz, Paul G., and Yingjin Zhang, eds. *From Underground to Independent: Alternative Film Culture in Contemporary China*. Lanham, Md.: Rowman and Littlefield, 2006.

Po, Lanchih. "Repackaging Globalization: A Case Study of the Advertising Industry in China." *Geoforum* 37 (2006): 752–64.

Presas, L. Melchert Saguas. "Transnational Urban Spaces and Urban Environmental Reforms: Analyzing Beijing's Environmental Restructuring in the Light of Globalization." *Cities* 21.4 (2004): 321–28.

Pu Siwen. "Lao She xiansheng he ta de *Longxugou*" [Mr. Lao She and his *Dragon Whisker Creek*]. In *"Longxugou" de wutai yishu* [The stage art of *Dragon Whisker Creek*], ed. Jiang Rui, 80–86. Beijing: Zhongguo Xiju Chubanshe, 1987.

Qian Chunlei. "Dushi youzou: 'Xin chengshi dianying' " [Urban loitering: "New urban cinema"]. *Shanghai xingqisan* [Shanghai Wednesday], May 30, 2002.

Qiu Haidong. *Chengshi zhanche* [City tank]. Beijing: Zuojia Chubanshe, 1997.

Qi Xiaoping. *Xianghua ducao: Hongse niandai de dianying mingyun* [Fragrant flowers and poisonous weeds: The fate of films in the red years]. Beijing: Dangdai Zhongguo Chubanshe, 2006.

Qu Yuanlin. "Guancha xin Zhongguo de yige shijiao: Shixi Longxugou zhili yu xin Zhongguo xingxiang" [Examining one viewpoint of the new China: An analysis of controlling Dragon Whisker Creek and the image of new China]. *Dangdai Zhongguo shi yanjiu* [Contemporary China history studies] 14.2 (March 2007): 46–51.

"Report and Recommendation of the President to the Board of Directors on a Proposed Loan and Technical Assistance Grant to the People's Republic of China for the Suzhou Creek Rehabilitation Project." Asian Development Bank, internal memo PRC 321 21, May 1999.

Roberts, Kevin. "Brand China, Beijing." An address to the First China International Brand Strategy Conference, Beijing, April 2, 1998. Posted on Kevin Roberts's website: www.saatchikevin.com. Accessed May 10, 2008.

Rosenbaum, Jonathan. *Movie Wars: How Hollywood and the Media Limit What Movies We Can See*. Chicago: A Capella, 2000.

Rosenthal, Elisabeth. "North of Beijing, California Dreams Come True." *New York Times*, February 3, 2003. www.nytimes.com. Accessed May 12, 2008.

Salaff, Janet W. "Urban Communes in Communist China." *China Quarterly* 29 (January–March 1967): 82–110.

Sassen, Saskia. *The Global City: New York, London, Tokyo*. Princeton, N.J.: Princeton University Press, 1991.

———. "Identity in the Global City: Economic and Cultural Encasements." In *The Geography of Identity*, ed. Patricia Yeager, 131–51. Ann Arbor: University of Michigan Press, 1996.

———. "Introduction: Locating Cities in Global Circuits." In *Global Networks, Linked Cities*, ed. Saskia Sassen, 2–37. New York: Routledge, 2002.

Senagala, Mahesh. "Post-spatial Architectures: The Emergence of Time-Like Parametric Worlds." Proceedings of the Seventh Iberoamerican Congress of Digital Graphics, Rosario, Argentina, November 5–7, 2003. cumincades.scix.net. Accessed May 9, 2008.

Shanghai chengshi guihua zhi Bianzuan Weiyuanhui [Editorial Committee for *The Gazetteer of Shanghai's Urban Planning*], ed. *Shanghai chengshi guihua zhi* [Gazetteer of Shanghai's urban planning]. Shanghai: Shanghai Shehui Kexue Yuan Chubanshe, 1999.

Shanghai Dianying Xitong Da Pipan Xiezuo Zu [Writing Group for the Great Criticism of the Shanghai Film System]. "Chedi cuihui zichan jieji de *Bu ye cheng*" [Smash completely the capitalist class's *City without Night*]. *Zhonggong dianyingjie wenhua da geming ziliao zhuanji, 1964–1971* [Special issue of materials on the Great Cultural Revolution from Collected Communist China, 1964–1971], ed. Contemporary China Research Institute, 46–55. Hong Kong: Dangdai Zhongguo Yanjiusuo, 1972.

Shanghai Huangpu Qu Geming Weiyuanhui Xiezuozu [The Writing Team of the Revolutionary Committee of Shanghai's Huangpu District]. *Shanghai waitan Nanjing lu shihua* [A history of the Shanghai bund and Nanjing Road]. Shanghai: Shanghai Renmin Chubanshe, 1976.

"Shanghai renmin yi wubi reqing relie huanying renmin Jiefangjun" [Shanghai's people welcome the People's Liberation Army with unparalleled enthusiasm and warmth]. *Jiefang ribao* [Liberation daily], May 28, 1949.

Shanghai Shi Dang'anguan [Shanghai Municipal Archives], ed. *Shanghai jiefang* [The liberation of Shanghai]. Beijing: Dang'an Chubanshe, 1989.

Shanghai Shi Lishi Bowuguan [Shanghai Municipal Historical Museum], ed. *Zou zai lishi de jiyi li: Nanjing lu 1840's–1950's* [Walking into historical memory: Nanjing Road from the 1840s to the 1950s]. Shanghai: Shanghai Kexue Jishu Chubanshe, 2000.

Shanghai Shi Zonggonghui Xuanchuanbu [Shanghai Municipality Workers' Association Propaganda Team]. "Tongzhi" [Announcement]. Shanghai Municipal Archives. April 19, 1963.

"Shanghai zui zao fanhua de malu" [Shanghai's earliest and most splendid road]. www.archives.sh.cn/docs/200803/d_162516.html. Accessed June 27, 2009.

Shang Jingwen. *Nanjing lu shang hao balian: Jjixu gemingpu xinge* [The Good Eighth Company: A new tune continuing the revolutionary songbook]. Illustrated by Shang Jingwen. Shanghai: Shanghai Renmin Chubanshe, 1971.

"Sharen jihua" [My whispering plan]. Publicity pamphlet, 2002.

Shaviro, Steven. *The Cinematic Body*. Minneapolis: University of Minnesota Press, 1993.

Shen, Ada. "Tom Buys 35% of Huayi Brothers." *Variety*. Posted on website *Danwei: Chinese Media, Advertising, and Urban Life*, December 12, 2004. www.danwei.org. Accessed May 18, 2008.

She Ran. "Siheyuan li de shidai zheguang" [The times reflected in a courtyard]. *Beijing renyi* [Beijing People's Art Theater] 1 (October 1995): 29–30.

Shiel, Mark. "Cinema and the City in History and Theory." In *Cinema and the City: Film and Urban Societies in a Global Context*, ed. Mark Shiel and Tony Fitzmaurice, 1–18. Oxford, U.K.: Blackwell, 2001.

Shi Mingzheng. *Zouxiang jindaihua de Beijingcheng: Chengshi jianshe yu shehui biange* [Modernizing Beijing: Urban development and social change]. Beijing: Beijing Daxue Chubanshe, 1995.

"Shiwei youxing shengkuang" [Spectacular parades]. *Jiefang ribao* [Liberation daily], July 7, 1949.

Shu Ji and Wang Xingzhi. "Lao She juzuo zhuyi mulu" [An index of Lao She's plays and their translations]. In *Lao She lun ju* [Lao She discusses drama], ed. Wang Xingzhi, 294–98. Beijing: Zhongguo Xiju Chubanshe, 1981.

Shu Yi. "Daye? Daye?" *Zhongguo qingnian bao* [China youth daily], July 9, 1995.

Sit, Victor F. S. [Xue Fengxuan]. *Beijing: The Nature and Planning of a Chinese Capital City*. Chichester, U.K.: Wiley, 1995.

Song Zhao. *Mama de yisheng: Wang Ping zhuan* [Mother's life: A biography of Wang Ping]. Beijing: Zhongguo Dianying Chubanshe, 2006.

Stanley, Nick. "Chinese Theme Parks and National Identity." In *Theme Park Landscapes: Antecedents and Variations*, ed. Terence Young and Robert Riley, 269–89. Washington, D.C.: Dumbarton Oaks Research Library and Collection, 2002.

Sun Chen. " 'Xin chengshi dianying' miaozhun dushi qingnianren" ["New Urban Cinema" aims at urban youth]. *Renmin ribao haiwai ban* [*People's Daily* overseas edition], March 9, 2000. web.peopledaily.com.cn/haiwai/200003/09/no_7 .html. Accessed June 30, 2009.

Sun Haoran. "San kan *Shaobing*: Tan *Nihong deng xia de shaobing* de jing" [Watching *Sentinels* three times: On the set of *Sentinels under the Neon Lights*]. Rpt. in *Wutai meishu wenji* [Collected essays on stage art], ed. Zhongguo Yishu Yanjiuyuan Xiqu Yanjiusuo [Graduate Institute of Traditional Drama, Chinese Academy of Arts], 342–47. Beijing: Zhongguo Xiju Chubanshe, 1982.

Sun Keyu, "*Bu ye cheng* waiqu le lishi zhenshi" [*City without Night* has distorted historical truth]. *Dazhong dianying* [Popular cinema], June 1965, 27.

Sun Shaoyi. "Dushi kongjian yu Zhongguo minzu zhuyi: Jiedu sanshi niandai Zhongguo zuoyi dianying" [Urban space and Chinese nationalism: Reading the Chinese left-wing cinema of the thirties]. *Shanghai wenhua* [Shanghai culture] 16 (May 1996): 37–44.

Sun Xiuping. "Beijing chengqu quan xinshi maicang he, hu, gou, keng de fenbu ji qi yanbian" [The distribution and evolution of all rivers, lakes, creeks, and pits buried in recent generations in the municipal area of Beijing]. In *Beijing shiyuan* [Historical records of Beijing], vol. 2, ed. Beijing Academy of Social Science, 222–32. Beijing: Beijing Chubanshe, 1985.

Suosuo. "Xin chengshi dianying de zhu xuanlü" [The main melody of New Urban Cinema]. *Wenyibao* [Literature and arts], October 27, 2001.

Su Shuyang. *"Xizhao jie": Dianying juben* [*Sunset Street*: A film script]. *Su Shuyang juzuo ji* [Collected plays by Su Shuyang], 103–86. Hong Kong: Anding Chubanshe, 1992.

Taibeishi Zhengfu Gongwuju Gongyuan Ludeng Gongcheng Guanlichu [Public Parks—Road and Lamp Section of the Public Works Department of Taipei Municipal Government]. "Taibeishi da'an Qihao gongyuan jianjie" [Brief introduction to Taipei's Da-an Park No. Seven]. Publicity pamphlet. February 1992.

Tang, Xiaobing. *Chinese Modern: The Heroic and the Quotidian*. Durham, N.C.: Duke University Press, 2000.

Taylor, Philip M. *War and the Media*. Manchester, U.K.: Manchester University Press, 1998.

"Tiananmen 35 nian qian ceng mimi chongjian" [Tiananmen was secretly rebuilt thirty-five years ago]. *Renmin ribao haiwai ban* [*People's Daily* overseas edition], April 21, 2005. Posted on the Xinhua News Agency website: news.xinhuanet .com/newscenter/2005–04/21/content_2857146.htm. Accessed September 25, 2008.

"Tizhe naodai paiyan *Nihong deng xia de shaobing*" [Staging *Sentinels under the Neon Lights*, holding one's head high]. *Dongfang dushi bao* [Southern metropolis daily]. Reposted at the Guangzhou Library's website: www.gzlib.gov.cn. Accessed June 27, 2009.

Tong Daoming. "*Beijing daye* xiqi" [The bad habits of a Beijing patriarch]. *Zhongguo xiju* [Chinese drama] 9 (1995): 13.

Tung, Anthony M. *Preserving the World's Great Cities: The Destruction and Renewal of the Historic Metropolis*. New York: Clarkson Potter, 2001.

Tweedie, James, and Yomi Braester. "Introduction: The City's Edge." In *Cinema at the City's Edge: Film and Urban Space in East Asia*, ed. Yomi Braester and James Tweedie. Hong Kong: Hong Kong University Press, forthcoming.

Unger, Jonathan, and Anita Chan. "Memories and the Moral Economy of a State-Owned Enterprise." In *Re-envisioning the Chinese Revolution: The Politics and Poetics of Collective Memories in Reform China*, ed. Ching Kwan Lee and Guobin Yang, 119–40. Washington, D.C.: Woodrow Wilson Center Press, 2007.

United Nations Economic and Social Council. "Implementation of the International Covenant on Economic, Social and Cultural Rights: Initial Reports Submitted by States Parties under Articles 16 and 17 of the Covenant—Addendum: People's Republic of China." March 4, 2004. Available on the United Nations Human Rights website: www.ohchr.org. Accessed August 23, 2009.

Vampley, Wray. *The Turf: A Social and Economic History of Horse Racing*. London: Penguin, 1976.

Vidler, Anthony. *Warped Space: Art, Architecture, and Anxiety in Modern Culture*. Cambridge: MIT Press, 2003.

Virilio, Paul. *War and Cinema: The Logistics of Perception*. London: Verso, 1989.

Visser, Robin. *Cities Surround the Countryside: Urban Aesthetics in Post-socialist China*. Durham, N.C.: Duke University Press, 2010.

Walcott, Susan. "Science Parks as Magnets for Global Capital: Locating High-Tech Growth Engines in Metropolitan Shanghai." In *Globalization, the Third World State and Poverty-Alleviation in the Twenty-First Century*, ed. B. I. Logan, 89–102. Burlington, Vt.: Ashgate, 2002.

Wang, Jing. *Brand New China: Advertising, Media, and Commercial Culture*. Cambridge: Harvard University Press, 2008.

——. " 'Culture' as Leisure and 'Culture' as Capital: The State Question and Chinese Popular Culture." *positions: east asia cultures critique* 9.1 (Spring 2001): 69–70.

Wang, Shujen. "*Big Shot's Funeral*: China, Sony, and the WTO." *Asian Cinema* 14.2 (Fall/Winter 2003): 145–54.

Wang, Yiman. "The Amateur's Lightning Rod: DV Documentary in Postsocialist China." *Film Quarterly* 58.4 (2005): 16–26.

Wang Bo. *FLASH: Jishu haishi yishu* [Flash: Technology or art?]. Beijing: Zhongguo Renmin Daxue Chubanshe, 2005.

Wang Dehua. *Zhongguo chengshi guihua shigang* [An outline of Chinese urban planning]. Nanjing: Dongnan Daxue Chubanshe, 2005.

Wang Dong. "Jinshuiqiao tou de 'paoqun' " [The "artillery battery" at the foot of Jinshuiqiao Bridge]. In *Tiananmen qian* [In front of Tiananmen], ed. *Dazhong dianying* [Popular photography magazine], 66. Beijing: Jiefangjun Wenyi Chubanshe, 1999.

Wang Guangtao. *Beijing lishi wenhua mingcheng de baohu yu fazhan* [Preservation and development of Beijing as a historical city]. Beijing: Xinhua Chubanshe, 2002.

Wang Guohua. *Beijing chengqiang cunfei ji: Yige lao difangzhi gongzuozhe de ziliao jicun* [Records of Beijing's city wall and its disappearance: A compilation of materials by an old gazetteer worker]. Beijing: Beijing Chubanshe, 2007.

Wang Haowei. "Xizhao jie paishe huigu" [Reminiscences from shooting *Sunset Street*]. In *Bu siliang, zi nanwang: Wang Haowei yanjiu wenji* [Immeasurable and unforgettable: Collected research writings on Wang Haowei], ed. Wang Renyin, 57–69. Beijing: Zhongguo Dianying Chubanshe, 2002.

Wang Hongbo. "*Gala'r Hutong* qishilu" [Records of being enlightened by *Forsaken Alley*]. *Zhongguo wenhua bao* [China culture daily], June 8, 1994.

Wang Hongzhi. *Tiananmen guangchang geming jianshi* [A short history of revolutionary events at Tiananmen Square]. Shanghai: Renmin Chubanshe, 1979.

Wang Jinghui, Ruan Yisan, and Wang Lin. *Lishi wenhua mingcheng baohu lilun yu guihua* [Theory and planning of the preservation of historical cultural cities]. Shanghai: Tongji Daxue Chubanshe, 1999.

Wang Jun. "Beijing Jinyuchi baixing yuan le zhufang meng" [The common people of Beijing's Goldfish Ponds have fulfilled their dream of a place to live in]. Xinhua News Agency news release, April 18, 2002. Posted on the Xinhua News Agency website: news.xinhuanet.com/fortune/2002–04/18/content_htm. Accessed December 11, 2005.

——. *Caifangben shang de chengshi* [Cities in a journalist's notebook]. Beijing: Sanlian, 2008.

——. *Cheng ji* [Record of a city]. Beijing: Sanlian Shudian, 2003.

Wang Pei. "Yuan Yifang chuangzao duanxiang: *Linju* paishe zhaji" [Thoughts on creating the character of Yuan Yifang: Notes from shooting *Neighbors*]. In *"Linju": Cong juben dao yingpian*, 257–67.

Wang Shaoqiang, ed. *Zhongguo fangdichan guanggao nianjian, 2003* [Almanac of

China real estate advertisement, 2003). Guangzhou: Lingnan Meishu Chuban-she, 2003.

Wang Shuo. *Ni bushi yige suren* [You're no common person]. In *Wang Shuo wenji* [Collected works of Wang Shuo], vol. 4, 441–504. Beijing: Huayi Chubanshe, 1996.

Wang Wo and Wang Chao. *Renmin wansui* [Long live the people]. Beijing: Duanluo Kongjian, n.d. [ca. 2008].

Wang Xiaoying. "Hongdong Taiwan de *Da cuoche*" [*Moonlight* greatly popular in Tai-wan]. *Anhui ribao* [Anhui daily], November 22, 1984.

Wang Youhai. " 'Nanjing lu shang hao balian' chengming jingguo" [How the Good Eighth Company got its name]. *Wenshi jinghua* 163 (December 2003): 13–18.

Wang Yushi. *Tiananmen*. Beijing: Zhongguo Shudian, 2001.

Wang Zengqi. "Hutong wenhua" [*Hutong* culture]. In Lu Xun et al., *Beijingren, Shanghairen*, 100–103.

Wang Zhi'an. *Jinyuchi* [Goldfish Ponds]. Unpublished manuscript.

Warhol, Andy. *The Philosophy of Andy Warhol: From A to B and Back Again*. New York: Harcourt Brace Jovanovich, 1975.

Wasserstrom, Jeffrey N. *Student Protests in Twentieth-Century China: The View from Shanghai*. Stanford, Calif.: Stanford University Press, 1991.

Wei, Yehua Dennis, Chi Kin Leung, and Jun Luo. "Globalizing Shanghai: Foreign Investment and Urban Restructuring." *Habitat International* 30.2 (2006): 231–44.

Wei Chenglin, ed. *Beijing zhongchouxian chengshi sheji* [Urban design of Beijing's central axis]. Beijing: Jijie Gongye Chubanshe, 2005.

Welland, Sasha Su-Ling. "Ocean Paradise." *Journal of Visual Culture* 6.3 (2007): 419–35.

Wen Fu. *Tiananmen jianzheng lu* [Witness records of Tiananmen]. Beijing: Yanshi Chubanshe, 1998.

Widdis, Emma. *Visions of a New Land: Soviet Film from the Revolution to the Second World War*. New Haven, Conn.: Yale University Press, 2003.

Wide, Stephen. "Baozangyan: Duiyu Marco Taibei you jiceng xilie zuopin zhi yi de tishi" [Treasure Hill: My experience of one of Marco Casagrande's grassroots works in Taipei]. *Egg Magazine*, October 2003, 168–71.

Wu, Fulong. "China's Changing Urban Governance in the Transition Towards a More Market-Oriented Economy." *Urban Studies* 39.7 (2002): 1071–93.

———. "Transplanting Cityscapes: The Use of Imagined Globalization in Housing Commodification in Beijing." *Area* 36.3 (2004): 227–34.

"Wubi baochi jianku fendou de zuofeng" [We must preserve the attitude of arduous struggle]. *Jiefang ribao* [Liberation daily], March 3, 1963. Rpt. in *Nanjing lu shang hao balian*, 9–17.

Wu Hung. *Remaking Beijing: Tiananmen Square and the Creation of a Political Space*. Chicago: University of Chicago Press, 2005.

———. "Tiananmen Square: A Political History of Monuments." *Representations* 35 (Summer 1991): 34–117.

——. *Transience: Chinese Experimental Art at the End of the Twentieth Century.* Chicago: Chicago University Press, 1999.

Wu Liangyong. *Rehabilitating the Old City of Beijing: A Project in the Ju'er Hutong Neighbourhood.* Vancouver: University of British Columbia Press, 1999.

Wu Shibao. "Kaiguo dadian shang de bubing fangdui" [The infantry at the Founding Ceremony]. In *Tiananmen qian* [In front of Tiananmen], ed. *Dazhong dianying* [Popular photography magazine], 13–14. Beijing: Jiefangjun Wenyi Chubanshe, 1999.

Wu Wenguang. "Just on the Road: A Description of the Individual Way of Recording Images in the 1990s." In *Reinterpretation: A Decade of Experimental Chinese Art (1990–2000)—The First Guangzhou Triennial,* ed. Wu Hung, Wang Huangsheng, and Feng Boyi, 132–38. Guangzhou: Guangdong Museum of Art, 2002.

——. "*Xianchang:* He jilu fangshi yuguan de shu" [*Xianchang:* A book concerning methods of documentation]. In *Xianchang,* ed. Wu Wenguang, 274–75. Tianjin: Shehui Kexueyuan Chubanshe, 2000.

Xiao Ji. " 'Xin chengshi dianying' fuchu shuimian" ["New Urban Cinema" has surfaced]. *Dazhong dianying* [Popular cinema], April 2000, 14–15.

Xie Xizhang. "*Beijing daye:* Lishi, wenhua yu ren—*Beijing daye* zuotanhui jiyao" [*Beijing Pretenders:* History, culture, and humanity—Notes from a symposium on *Beijing Pretenders*]. *Beijing wanbao* [Beijing evening news], July 21, 1995.

Xi Longxiang et al. "*Bu ye cheng* mosha jieji douzheng xuanyang touxiang zhuyi" [*City without Night* erases class struggle and promotes capitulationism]. *Dazhong dianying* [Popular cinema], July 1965, 25–26.

Xin Shanghai bianlan [A guide to new Shanghai]. Shanghai: Shanghai Dagongbao, 1951.

Xin Xu. "Modernizing China in the Olympic Spotlight: China's National Identity and the 2008 Beijing Olympiad." *Sociological Review* 54.2 (December 2006): 90–107.

Xu Chengbei. *Jiudu xinxie* [New writings on an old capital]. Xi'an: Shanxi Shifan Daxue Chubanshe, 1998.

Xu Ping and Yu Xiangyang. " 'Nanjing lu shang hao balian' de youlai" [The provenance of the Good Eighth Company]. *Dangshi bolan* [General review of the Communist Party of China], 2001, no. 7.

Xu Renjun. "Qin Hualong mengyuan shimo" [The full story of the injustice done to Qin Hualong]. *Zongheng* [Across time and space] 5 (2002): 56–60.

Xu Yunbin, ed. *Zhanqian guhou: Taibei de jueban, fuke yu xinsheng* [Gazing forward and looking back: Taipei's out-of-print, reprints, and renewed]. Taipei: Taibei Shizhengfu Xinwenchu, 2001.

Yang Chenguang. "Chengshi de 'xuemai' " [The city and the "arteries"]. In *Renwen Aoyun,* ed. Peng Yongjie, Zhang Zhiwei, and Han Donghui, 285–89.

——. "Yangtang zasui yu Man-Han quanxi" [Mutton-broth chop suey and the full Manchu-Han banquet]. In *Renwen Aoyun,* ed. Peng Yongjie, Zhang Zhiwei, and Han Donghui, 277–80.

Yang Dongping. "*Beijing daye*: Zuihou de shouweizhe?" [*Beijing Pretender*: The last guard?]. *Zhongguo wenhua bao* [China culture daily], July 21, 1995.

——. *Chengshi jifeng: Beijing he Shanghai wenhua jingshen* [City monsoon: The spiritual culture of Beijing and Shanghai]. Beijing: Dongfang Chubanshe, 1994.

Yang Jiayou. *Shanghai lao fangzi de gushi* [The story of Shanghai's old buildings]. Shanghai: Shanghai Renmin Chubanshe, 2006.

Yan Zhongxian [Yan Chung-hsien]. *Yizhong jianzhu de shuoshushu, huoshi wu hui chengshi de Aodesai* [An architectural narration, or, five urban Odysseys]. Taipei: Tianyuan Chengshi, 1997.

Yeh, Emilie Yueh-yu, and Darrell William Davis. *Taiwan Film Directors: A Treasure Island*. New York: Columbia University Press, 2005.

Ying Ruocheng and Claire Conceison. *Voices Carry: Behind Bars and Backstage during China's Revolution and Reform*. Lanham, Md.: Rowman and Littlefield, 2009.

"Yongyuan baochi jianku fendou de geming jingshen" [Preserve forever the revolutionary spirit of arduous struggle]. *Renmin ribao* [*People's Daily*], May 28, 1963. Rpt. in *Nanjing lu shang hao balian*, 1–8.

"Youru yitai qinggan zhizaoji *Da cuo che* jixu cuilei" [*Moonlight* continues to tear eyes up like an emotion machine]. *Beijing qingnian bao* [Beijing youth news]. Reposted on Xinhua News Agency website: news.xinhuanet.com. Accessed December 11, 2005.

Yu Huiru. "Tiananmen qian jia 'dapao' " [Installing a 'big cannon' in front of Tiananmen]. In *Tiananmen qian* [In front of Tiananmen], ed. *Dazhong dianying* [Popular photography magazine], 33–34. Beijing: Jiefangjun Wenyi Chubanshe, 1999.

Yu Kanping. Interview with Lin Wenchi, 2007. Unpublished transcript.

Yu Kui. "*Gala'r Hutong* ABC" [*Forsaken Alley* ABC]. *Beijing ribao* [Beijing daily], November 12, 1993.

Yu Qing. "Shei ye dangbuzhu qianjin de chaotou: Huaju *Zuolin youshe* manping" [No one can stop the tide of progress: An idle review of the modern play *Next-Door Neighbors*]. *Jiefangjun bao* [People's Liberation Army daily], November 8, 1980.

Yu Shizhi. "Yanyuan riji zhaichao zhi yi" [Selected diary entries of an actor—1]. In "*Longxugou*" *de wutai yishu* [The stage art of *Dragon Whisker Creek*], ed. Jiang Rui, 174–201. Beijing: Zhongguo Xiju Chubanshe, 1987.

Yusuf, Shahid, and Weiping Wu. *The Dynamics of Urban Growth in Three Chinese Cities*. New York: Oxford University Press, 1997.

——. "Pathways to a World City: Shanghai Rising in an Era of Globalization." *Urban Studies* 39.7 (2002): 1213–40.

Zeng Guangcan. *Lao She yanjiu zonglan, 1929–1986* [A survey of the research on Lao She, 1929–86]. Tianjin: Jiaoyu Chubanshe, 1987.

Zeng Zhizhong and You Deyan, eds. *Zhang Hengshui shuo Beijing* [Zhang Hengshui describes Beijing]. Chengdu: Sichuan Wenyi Chubanshe, 2001.

Zha, Jianying. *China Pop: How Soap Operas, Tabloids, and Bestsellers Are Transforming a Culture*. New York: New Press, 1995.

——. "The Turtles: How an Unlikely Couple Became China's Best-Known Real-Estate Moguls." *New Yorker*, July 11 and 18, 2005.

Zhang, Yingjin. *The City in Modern Chinese Literature and Film: Configurations of Space, Time, and Gender*. Stanford, Calif.: Stanford University Press, 1996.

——. "Rebel without a Cause? China's New Urban Generation and Postsocialist Filmmaking." In Zhang Zhen, ed., *Urban Generation*, 49–80.

Zhang Boqing. " 'Yu lang gongwu,' yingjie tiaozhan: Zhongguo dianying 'rushi' ganyan" ["Dancing with wolves," taking on the challenge: Reflections on Chinese cinema "entering the world"]. In *WTO yu Zhongguo dianying* [WTO and Chinese cinema], ed. Zhang Zhenqian and Yang Yuanying, 217–20. Beijing: Zhongguo Dianying Chubanshe, 2002.

Zhang Chunqiao. "Pandeng xin de shengli gaofeng" [Climbing to a new peak of victory]. In *Shanghai jiefang shinian* [Ten years to the liberation of Shanghai], ed. *Shanghai jiefang shinian* Zhengwen Bianji Weiyuanhui [The Essay Solicitation and Editorial Committee of *Ten Years to the Liberation of Shanghai*], 1–8. Shanghai: Shanghai Wenyi Chubanshe, 1960.

Zhang Donglin and Wang Chao. "Lixing, ganxing, Beijing kuashiji zhuzhai" [Reason, sentiment, and turn-of-the-century residences in Beijing]. *Zhongguo jianshe bao* [Chinese construction news], October 25, 2001. Reposted on the Chungdu investment portal, in the real estate section: fc.cdcss.com. Accessed December 11, 2005.

Zhang Haiping. " 'Changzheng dui' zhanyou" [Comrades-in-arms from the Long March Team]. In *Tiananmen qian* [In front of Tiananmen], ed. *Dazhong dianying* [Popular photography magazine], 78–79. Beijing: Jiefangjun Wenyi Chubanshe, 1999.

Zhang Henshui. *Zhang Henshui shuo Beijing* [Zhang Henshui talks of Beijing]. Ed. Zeng Zhizhong and You Deyan. Chengdu: Sichuan Wenyi Chubanshe, 2001.

Zhang Jinggan. *Beijing guihua jianshe wushi nian* [Fifty years of planning and construction in Beijing]. Beijing: Zhongguo Shudian, 2001.

——. *Beijing guihua jianshe zongheng tan* [On Beijing's urban planning and construction]. Beijing: Beijing Yanshan Chubanshe, 1997.

Zhang Qi. *Beijingren he Shanghairen qutan* [On Beijingers and Shanghainese]. Beijing: Jincheng Chubanshe, 2000.

Zhang Yang. Talk at University of Washington Exploration Seminar. Beijing, August 31, 2005.

Zhang Yuan. Talk at University of Washington Exploration Seminar. Beijing, September 7, 2004.

Zhang Zheming. " 'Nanjing lu shang hao balian' chengming qianhou" [Events surrounding the Good Eighth Company's getting famous]. *Zongheng* [Across time and space] 9 (2002): 19–22.

Zhang Zhen. *An Amorous History of the Silver Screen*. Chicago: Chicago University Press, 2005.

——. "Bearing Witness: Chinese Urban Cinema in the Era of 'Transformation' (*Zhuanxing*)." In Zhang Zhen, ed., *Urban Generation*, 1–45.

——. "Transfiguring the Postsocialist Chinese City: Time and Body in Experimental Image-Making." In *Cinema at the City's Edge: Film and Urban Space in East Asia*, ed. Yomi Braester and James Tweedie. Hong Kong: Hong Kong University Press, forthcoming.

——. "Urban Dreamscape, Phantom Sisters, and the Identity of an Emergent Art Cinema." In Zhang Zhen, ed., *Urban Generation*, 344–88.

——, ed. *The Urban Generation: Chinese Cinema and Society at the Turn of the Twenty-First Century*. Durham, N.C.: Duke University Press, 2007.

Zhang Zhengyu. "Wutai meishu pingdian" [Points of criticism on stage art]. In *Wutai meishu wenji* [Collected essays on stage art], ed. Zhongguo Yishu Yanjiuyuan Xiqu Yanjiusuo [China Art Research Academy, Drama Institute], 336–41. Beijing: Zhongguo Xiju Chubanshe, 1982.

Zhang Zhenqian and Yang Yuanying, eds. *WTO yu Zhongguo dianying* [WTO and Chinese cinema]. Beijing: Zhongguo Dianying Chubanshe, 2002.

Zhang Zuomin. "Gao chang shidai tongxinqu" [Singing aloud the praises of the era in unison]. *Zhongguo wenhua bao* [China culture daily], April 1, 1994.

Zhao Ming. *Ju ying fuchen lu* [Record of a drifting life in theater and cinema]. Beijing: Wenjun Chubanshe, 1991.

Zhao Shuli. "Little Blackey Gets Married" ["Xiaoerhei jiehun"]. In *Zhao Shuli daibiao zuo* [The representative works of Zhao Shuli], 1–16. Zhengzhou: Huanghe Wenyi Chubanshe, 1986.

——. "Li Youcai banhua" [Rhymes of Li Youcai]. In *Zhao Shuli daibiao zuo* [The representative works of Zhao Shuli], 17–60. Zhengzhou: Huanghe Wenyi Chubanshe, 1986.

Zhao Yongge and Wang Ya'nan. *Bainian chengshi bianqian* [Urban change over the last one hundred years]. Beijing: Zhongguo Jingji Chubanshe, 2000.

Zheng Dongtian. "Chengzhang de fannao: Chengshi dianying xinlu saomiao [The sorrows of growing up: A survey of approaches in urban cinema]. *Dangdai dianying yishu* [Contemporary cinema], 1997, 4:67–69.

Zheng Guoen and Qi Hong. "Jiadingxing zhong xunqiu zhenshigan" [Seeking a sense of reality from a false assumption]. In *Zhongguo dianying meixue, 1999* [Chinese film aesthetics, 1999], ed. Hu Ke et al., 77–80. Beijing: Beijing Guangbo Xueyuan Chubanshe, 2000.

Zheng Xin'an. *Jingtou li de shangpin: Zhongguo youxiu guanggao daoyan quan jilu* [Merchandise in the lens: A full record of masterful Chinese advertisement directors]. Beijing: Shijie Zhishi Chubanshe, 2003.

"Zhiyuan Aoyun, you wo yige: Aoyun zhiyuanzhe baoming xuesheng ganbu xuanchuan dongyuan dahui" [In volunteering for the Olympics, count me in: Public relations launch for student and cadre Olympics volunteers]. Posted on the Beijing University of Technology website, at ccyl.bjut.edu.cn/TuanWei/View.aspx?id=2ed4fcb5-e0a8–4c39–8d3f-76d48b977ba7&obj=NewsGQT. Accessed August 19, 2007.

Zhong Dafeng, Zhen Zhang, and Yingjin Zhang. "From *Wenmingxi* (Civilized Play) to *Yingxi* (Shadowplay): The Foundation of Shanghai Film Industry in the 1920s." *Asian Cinema* 9.1 (1997): 46–64.

Zhongguo Caimao Gonghui Shanghaishi Weiyuanhui [Shanghai Commerce Workers' Committee]. "Guanyu Zhongbai si dian, yiyao yi dian, Huamei fuzhuang dian sange danwei xuexi Lei Feng, xuexi Nanjing lu shang hao balian de qingguang huibao" [Report on the situation of studying Lei Feng and the Good Eighth Company of Nanjing Road in the three units of the China Department Store, pharmacies and clothing stores]. Report to the Shanghai Municipal Council, July 3, 1963. Shanghai Municipal Archive.

Zhongguo fangdichan guanggao nianjian [Almanac of real estate advertisement in China]. Guangzhou: Lingnan Meishu Chubanshe, 2003.

"Zhongguo meiti beiling tingzhi baodao chaoqian wenti" [Chinese media ordered to stop reporting on the problem of demolition-and-relocation]. September 26, 2003. Posted on the Boxun News website: www.peacehall.com. Accessed March 28, 2007.

Zhongguo Renmin Geming Junshi Bowuguan [Chinese People's Revolutionary Military Museum], ed. "Nanjing lu shang hao balian shiji guatu" [Posters on the deeds of the Good Eighth Company of Nanjing Road]. Shanghai: Shanghai Renmin Meishu Chubanshe, n.d [ca. 1964].

"Zhongguo renmin Jiefangjun zong zhenzhibu guanyu 'Nanjing lu shang hao balian' zhengzhi sixiang gongzuo jingyan de jieshao" [The PLA political commissar on introducing the political thought and work experience of the Good Eighth Company of Nanjing Road] (1963). Rpt. in *Nanjing lu shang hao balian*, 85–126.

Zhong Jieying. "Juben gousi xunji" [Tracing the conception of a play script]. *Beijing renyi* [Beijing People's Art Theater] 1 (October 1995): 24–26.

——. "Zhi yuan shen zai ci shan zhong" [You can't see the mountain when you're in the hills]. *Beijing ribao* [Beijing daily], 1995 (n.d.; clipping from the Beijing People's Art Theater archive).

Zhou Siyuan. "Xijian Beijingren chongshen ziji" [I am glad to see Beijingers reassess themselves]. *Wenyibao* [Literature and arts], September 8, 1995.

"Zhou Xingchi + Feng Xiaogang = daxia + dian xiaoer?!" ["Stephen Chow plus Feng Xiaogang equals martial arts master and inn attendant?!"]. Posted on the website of Tianjin Enorth Netnews: ent.enorth.com.cn. Accessed October 17, 2004.

Zhou Xuelin. *Young Rebels in Contemporary Chinese Cinema*. Hong Kong: Hong Kong University Press, 2007.

Zhou Yang. "Cong *Longxugou* xuexi shenme?" [What do we learn from *Dragon Whisker Creek*?]. *Renmin ribao* [*People's Daily*], March 4, 1951.

Zhu, Jieming. *The Transition of China's Urban Development: From Plan-Controlled to Market-Led*. Westport, Conn.: Praeger, 1999.

Zhu, Ying. *Chinese Cinema during the Era of Reform: The Ingenuity of the System*. Westport, Conn.: Praeger, 2003.

Zi Zhongyun. "The Clash of Ideas: Ideology and Sino-U.S. Relations." In *Chinese Foreign Policy: Pragmatism and Strategic Behavior*, ed. Suisheng Zhao, 224–242. Armonk, N.Y.: M. E. Sharpe, 2003.

Avant-garde art, 182, 242, 266, 270, 290, 291

Baiwan xiongshi xia Jiangnan (A Million Heroes Descend on Jiangnan), 57, 60, 63, 70
Bakhtin, Mikhail, 18
Baober in Love (Li Shaohong), 22, 266, 308–9
Baozangyan (Treasure Hill, Taipei), 17, 211–20, 222
Battle for Shanghai, The (Wang Bing), 57, 69–72, 73, 84
Baudrillard, Jean, 14, 304
Bawang bie ji (Farewell My Concubine), 22, 228, 245, 249–56, 257
Bazin, André, 14, 226
Beautiful New World (Shi Runjiu), 270
Beijing: acts and ordinances, 127–28, 130, 132, 286; alleys (*hutong*), 19, 46, 47, 49, 96, 116, 120, 145, 152, 229, 231, 237, 278, 249, 251, 252, 255–58, 261, 262, 267, 298; central axis, 156; city plans, 49, 157, 236, 264, 270, 276; city walls, 18, 30, 32, 113, 157, 238, 258; as cultural center, 236; demolition of landmarks in, 99, 106, 108, 123, 147, 189, 224; in early film, 45; as "event-city," 308; as garden city, 133; as global city, 283, 300, 301; growth of, 31, 177, 257; as "historic city," 236; image overhaul of, 1, 29, 48, 51–52, 133, 147, 224, 281–83, 298, 299, 309; industrialization of, 3, 53–54, 73, 317n99; as "international city," 286, 299; liberation of, 27, 31, 34, 35, 43, 48, 50, 100, 155, 240; in literature, 44, 48, 65; local flavor, 48, 103, 105, 115, 116, 146, 147, 238, 251, 262, 277, 281, 286, 298; master plan (1993), 224, 286–87, 337n7; modernization of, 50, 51, 96, 106, 119, 120, 121, 130, 138, 237, 239; municipal government of, 3, 4, 21, 29, 30, 35, 42, 49, 52; Municipal Planning Institute, 112; as national capital, 28, 30, 31, 34, 49, 112, 117, 152, 155, 156, 185, 250, 270, 283, 286, 287; "new Beijing," 28, 53, 73, 95, 97, 128, 133, 136, 278, 298, 309; nostalgia for old Beijing, 102, 105, 116, 138, 145, 146, 228, 239, 250, 253–57; representation through iconic landmarks of, 36, 48, 51–53, 108, 112, 128, 134, 168, 176, 224, 236, 247, 252, 253, 283, 290, 298, 299; Public Works Bureau, 3, 33, 36, 39; Quake III as allegory for, 306; smokestacks in, 53–54, 136; toilets in, 103–4, 127, 135, 143, 243, 298; topography of, 31. *See also* Courtyard houses; Courtyard plays; Olympic games
Beijing Bastards (Zhang Yuan), 180, 242
Beijing Bicycle (Wang Xiaoshuai), 239, 288
Beijing CCTV Tower, 149, 299
Beijing Cultural Relics Bureau, 296
Beijing daye (*Beijing Pretenders*), 97, 105–11, 113–18, 121, 127, 144, 150, 238
Beijing de feng hen da (There Is a Strong Wind in Beijing), 184–85, 276
Beijing Film Academy, 172
Beijing Flavor (Chen Jiangong), 262
Beijing Pretenders (Zhong Jieying), 97, 105–11, 113–18, 121, 127, 144, 150, 238
Beijingren (Peking Man), 45, 96
Beijing Sixth Development and Construction Company, 130
Beijing's New Architecture (Zhang and Li), 161
Beijing Urban Planning Exhibition Hall, 149
Beijing Workers' Cultural Palace, 295–96
Beijing World Park, 299–303
Beijing xin jianzhu (Beijing's New Architecture), 161

Courtyard houses (*cont.*)
128; working class associated with, 4,
19, 28, 37, 43, 100
Courtyard plays, 19–20, 44–47, 95–
150, 240–41
Courtyard with a Backyard, A (Zheng
Xiaonong), 123
Crows and Sparrows (Zheng Junli), 45,
65, 91
Cultural brokers (*dawan'r*), 282, 284,
288–98, 338*n*17
"Cultural economy," 117, 120, 138, 288,
295
Cultural heritage: architecture as, 23,
99–100, 105, 108, 113, 119, 194, 212,
253, 269, 281, 292, 295, 303, 304;
commercialization as threat to, 23,
111, 118–21, 287, 289, 295, 297, 303,
304; as cultural capital, 117, 136, 138,
292; globalization as threat to, 287;
preservation of, 19, 106, 112, 113–14,
127, 146, 152, 212, 225, 236, 253, 255,
269, 281
Cultural Revolution: demolition attributed to, 99–100, 127, 229, 230,
232; films and stage plays during, 89,
98, 240, 253; GEC campaign during,
93; in later narratives, 96; prefigur-
ing in GEC campaign of, 80, 91; rehabilitation after, 98–101, 103, 106,
118, 229, 240, 255, 322*n*11; rethinking
symbols of, 169–70, 176; Tiananmen
during, 161, 167–68, 183; urbanization after, 177
Culture: commodified, 116, 293; commodity culture, 10; "culture fever," 177;
of leisure, 18, 48, 49, 61, 62, 104, 114,
153, 177, 183, 224, 302; urban, 10–11
Cyberspace, 303, 306–7

Da-an Forest Park (Taipei), 198, 209–
10, 211, 221
Da cuo che (Yu Kanping), 21, 192, 193,

195–200, 208, 209, 211, 220, 329*n*11;
PRC productions inspired by, 198
Dai houyuan de siheyuan'r (A Courtyard
with a Backyard), 123
Dai Jinhua, 260
Da jinzhan (The Great Combat), 93
Dancing with Migrant Workers (Wen Hui
and Wu Wenguang,), 291
Da saba'r (After Separation), 178–79
Dashalan'r (Beijing), 106, 279, 307
Da tuanyuan (The Reunion), 45
Davis, Darrell, 193, 199, 203
Dawan'r (Big Shot's Funeral), 23, 25,
284–85, 289, 291–98, 303, 304
Dawan'r (cultural brokers), 282, 284,
288–98, 338*n*17
Daybreak (Sun Yu), 91
Daye, 109, 114–15
Days, The (Wang Xiaoshuai), 272
Da yuebing (The Big Parade), 154, 169–
72, 173, 175, 178, 252
de Certeau, Michel, 13, 49
Deleuze, Gilles, 25
Demolition: city made unrecognizable
by, 224; compensation for, 102, 124,
131, 132, 237; during Cultural Revolution, 99–100; demolition-and-
relocation, 7, 19–23, 31, 33, 37, 40,
96, 97–98, 102, 110, 113, 119, 120–
50, 190, 192, 197, 199, 203, 208–23,
226, 230, 236–38, 252, 255–80, 298,
299, 304; facilitation by urban planning of, 7, 112, 157, 189, 225; images
of, 22, 116, 151, 173, 187–88, 195, 204,
207, 227, 239, 240, 250, 259–63,
266–67, 275, 276–77, 280, 304; in
name of modernization, 97, 100, 105,
106, 108–11, 113, 114, 116, 207, 249,
259; poetics of, 192. *See also* Documentary impulse; Residents: discontent with housing among
Demolition and Relocation (Zhang Yuan),
226, 267–68, 272

Deng Xiaoping: Four Modernizations initiated by, 232, 234; Ladder-Step Doctrine of, 101; reforms initiated by, 16, 92–93, 99–102, 108, 111, 112, 116, 164, 167, 169, 224, 228, 229, 232, 235, 242, 299, 302; return to power of, 169–70; *Sentinels* endorsed by, 82

Dialects and accents: Beijing, 45, 47, 316*n*73; Northern, 89; rural, 185, 208; Shandong, 66, 89; Shanghai, 88–90; Sichuan, 89; Suzhou, 89; Taiwan, 196, 197, 199, 208; Tianjin, 273

Digital media: animation 256, 302, 308, 309; blue screen technology, 302; camcorders, 22, 273, 275–79, 306; film manipulation, 151, 174, 266, 303; DV, 247, 273–74, 278–80, 291, 302, 303; Internet, 203, 270, 275, 284, 285, 302–7, 336*n*112; VCD and DVD, 93, 97, 131, 140, 141, 147, 290, 292; video art, 151, 172–75, 214, 266, 273, 285, 304–8; video games, 173, 283, 285, 304–7

Dingzi hu (Demolition and Relocation), 226, 267–68, 272

Dingzi hu (stuck-nail tenant), 124, 128, 131–32, 240, 261, 267–68, 272, 279, 301

Dirt (Guan Hu), 242, 266

Docudrama, 154, 160, 162, 167

Documentary film and TV, 27, 57, 60, 61, 68, 70, 74, 140, 153–56, 158, 160, 161, 169, 172, 176–85, 202, 203, 212, 240, 267–68, 273, 276, 279–80, 292, 301, 307, 326*n*19; integration into fiction films of, 41, 45, 63, 64, 90, 162–65, 167, 171, 173, 313*n*1, 327*n*30; New Documentary movement, 179, 226–27, 291

Documentary impulse, 22–23, 226–28, 233, 241–42, 246, 261, 278–80, 306

"Documentary realism" (*jishi zhuyi*), 226–27, 233, 332*n*7

Document 19 (Management of Accelerated Reconstruction of Hazardous and Old Houses in Beijing Act, 2000), 127–28, 130, 132

Dong, Madeleine Yue, 30, 43, 47, 49

Dong'an Market (Beijing), 51, 106, 168

Dongchun de rizi (The Days), 272

Dongfang hong (The East Is Red): film, 161–62; tune, 109, 123, 164, 170

DPP (Democratic Progressive Party; Minjindang), 191, 202, 210

Dragon Whisker Creek (Beijing) 18–19, 25, 27–54, 95, 129, 133, 138, 140; anthropomorphized, 39; Beijing landmarks named after, 31; preliberation conditions at, 37, 43, 315*n*31. *See also* Jinyuchi

Dragon Whisker Creek (film, Xian Qun), 18, 25, 27, 38, 48–49, 53, 136, 140

Dragon Whisker Creek (stage play, Lao She), 27, 29–54; Beijing's spaces redefined by, 4, 18, 58, 69, 97, 147–48, 309; as contribution to urban discourse, 19; as documentation of everyday life, 64, 114, 160, 233, 303, 316*n*68; endorsement by leaders of, 16, 35; Jinyuchi influenced by, 131, 146; Jiao Juyin's stage version of, 50–51, 145; Lao She's death and, 311*n*4; performances of, 35, 48, 314*n*27, 316*n*68; as precedent for later plays, 8, 19, 28, 40, 44–45, 47, 95, 98, 100, 106, 107, 122, 123, 125, 129, 133, 138–39, 142, 232, 240, 322*n*11; sculptures of scenes from, 139; *Shower* influenced by, 278; writing of, 3–4, 5, 29, 313*n*3, 313*n*4, 317*n*93; Zhao Shuli and, 315*n*45, 317*n*95

Dream Factory (Feng Xiaogang), 284–85, 287, 294, 298

Drum Tower (Beijing), 51, 229, 255

Duan Jinchuan, 328*n*58; *The Square*, 21, 155, 179–84, 210, 267, 276

Duan Muqi, 146
Dushi fengguang (Cityscape), 64
DV (digital video), 247, 273–74, 278–80, 291, 302, 303

"East Is Red, The," 109, 123, 164, 170
East Is Red, The (Wang Ping), 161–62
Economic reforms, 16, 92–93, 99–102, 108, 111, 112, 116, 164, 167, 169, 224, 228, 229, 232, 235, 242, 299, 302
"Economic rent," 101–2, 106
Eiffel Tower, 47, 285, 299
Eisenstein, Sergei, 14
Electricity, 29, 33, 46, 53, 127, 130, 141
Ellul, Jacques, 14
Environmental design, 22, 31, 98, 112, 113, 130, 133, 136, 147–48, 257, 189, 192, 203, 210, 212, 214, 225, 238, 246, 278, 281, 333n29. *See also* Public works; Sewage system; Urban preservation
Erbaiwu xiaozhuan (Opera Heroes), 45, 254–55
Ershisi chengshi (24 City), 266
Erzi (Sons), 243
Espionage, 57, 81, 92; counterespionage films, 84–85
Everyday life: Benjaminians' fetishizing of, 10; demolished sites and, 96, 187, 252, 264, 269; documented, 229, 233; proletariat identified with, 44, 49, 51–52, 98; as staged spectacle, 47–49 state control vs., 8, 55, 103–4, 151, 153–54, 175–77, 179, 181–86; stereotypes upheld by, 115; as theatrical realism, 46–47, 123, 145, 229, 239, 240. *See also* Courtyard plays

Family Love (Wu Xuan), 194
Fang Ke, 128, 268
Fang Zhenzhu (Lao She/Xu Changlin), 34, 38, 48
Farewell My Concubine (Chen Kaige), 22, 228, 245, 249–56, 257

Fashion shows, 290, 293
Fate in Tears and Laughter (Zhang Shichuan), 45, 254
Feichang xiari (A Lingering Face), 243
Feixia Ada (The Red Lotus Society), 201, 206, 207, 217
Feng Jicai, 113, 120, 269, 271
Fengkuang de daijia (Obsession), 242
Feng Mengbo, 285, 304–8
Feng Xiaogang, 178, 179, 271, 288, 290; *Big Shot's Funeral*, 23, 25, 284–85, 289, 291–98, 303, 304; *Dream Factory*, 284–85, 287, 294, 298
Fengyun ernü (Children of Troubled Times), 156
Fifth-Generation directors: Maoist aesthetics and, 9, 172, 243; New Taiwan Cinema vs., 200; Sixth-Generation concerns and, 255, 261
Film: art film, 270, 334n47; as bodily experience, 11; at "city's edge," 24; celluloid, 306; commercial, 18, 270, 271, 287, 289, 294; as continuation of city by other means, 13; decadent, 65; as documentation, 1, 22, 41, 225–26, 229, 239, 241–42, 246, 250, 254, 259, 261–65, 267–68, 275–80, 284, 304, 305; as event, 5, 13–14, 308; as ideological apparatus, 5; manipulation of historical time in, 2; modernity and, 11, 242; New Year's movies, 273, 287, 294; planning of subject matter (*ticai guihua*), 16; reception of, 2, 4, 12; set design in, 233, 254; stage plays adapted as, 3, 20, 53, 69–70, 83, 90, 98, 162, 167; as subjective experience, 5, 11–12; theater's influence on, 240, 277; as tool of social criticism, 7, 8, 15, 17, 18, 22, 23, 192, 202–4, 215, 225–28, 235–36, 240, 243, 249, 259, 260, 268, 272, 279, 301; "underground," 227
Film industry, 24, 59, 182, 294, 337n5;

Mulvey, Laura, 11

Music: jazz, 58, 59, 61, 66, 86, 91, 92; popular, 85, 300; rock 'n' roll, 151, 173, 242, 292, 293; techno, 174. *See also* Film scores

My Memories of Old Beijing (Wu Yigong), 228, 255

Myriad Lights, A (Li Longyun), 95–98, 141–48

My Whispering Plan (Qu Youning), 21, 193, 211, 214–20, 274

Nadar, Félix, 10

Nakamura, Lisa, 302

Naked City, The (Dassin), 240

Nanchizi (Beijing), 100

Nanjing lu shang hao balian (The Good Eighth Company of Nanjing Road), 74

Nanjing Road (Shanghai), 19, 57–62, 65, 68, 73–76, 78, 81–88, 111; "Nanjing Road studies," 59; repairing of, 56, 94

National allegory, 202, 250, 329n10

National Opera House (Beijing), 149

National Theater Company of China, 144

Neighborhood committees (*juweihui*), 8, 69, 102, 237, 264

Neighbors (Zheng and Xu), 17, 22, 226, 228–34, 238, 242

Neon signs, 64, 66, 68, 86, 87, 91, 245, 321n95

New Documentary movement, 179, 226–27, 291

News media, 6, 113, 202, 203, 269; CNN, 178, 305–6, 339n58

New Taiwan Cinema, 8, 17, 194, 198, 204, 329n9; as "cinema of authorship," 203; Fifth-Generation films vs., 200; as new Taipei cinema, 200, 207, 220; as reaction to "healthy realism," 193

New Urban Cinema, 18, 22, 270–71, 275, 288, 298

New Woman (Cai Chusheng), 91

New Year's movies, 273, 287, 294

Next-Door Neighbors (Su Shuyang), 97, 98–102, 121, 123, 147, 239

NGOS (non-governmental organizations), 6, 191; OURS, 202, 203, 211–12; Snail without Shell, 210

Nianqing de yidai (The Young Generation), 85

Niaoren (Bird Men), 103–4, 144, 254

Nichols, Bill, 226

Nihongdeng xia de shaobing. See Sentinels under the Neon Lights (film, Wang Ping); Sentinels under the Neon Lights (stage play, Shen, Mo, and Lü)

Ni neibian jidian (What Time Is It There), 188

Ningjing hai (The Silent Lake), 194, 329n9

Ning Ying, 22, 226, 249–50, 258, 268, 269, 278, 290; *For Fun*, 224, 228, 262–63, 276; *I Love Beijing*, 224, 262–63, 265, 270; *On the Beat*, 239, 242, 262–64; *Perpetual Motion*, 264

Niqiu yeshi yu (Loach Is a Fish Too), 266

Ni Zhen, 261, 270

Noise (Wang Wo), 185–86

Nora, Pierre, 222

No Regret about Youth (Zhou Xiaowen), 22, 228, 249, 255, 257–62

Nostalgia: for demolished houses, 102, 145, 208, 213, 235, 238, 256, 269, 273–78; documentary impulse and, 22, 189, 220, 278; for future, 44; as impetus for preservation, 43; for old Beijing, 102, 105, 116, 138, 145, 146, 228, 239, 250, 253–57; redevelopment vs., 96, 145–47, 226, 239

Nostalgia (Shu Haolun), 278–79

Obsession (Zhou Xiaowen), 242

Ocean Paradise (Beijing), 291

Propaganda: aesthetics and rhetoric of, 29, 38–40, 143, 145, 174, 180, 183; CCP image bolstered by, 4, 33, 34, 57, 125, 143–44, 167, 232–33; challenges to, 151, 154, 166, 172, 174, 181, 251, 284–85; experimental aesthetics' influence on, 8; film as tool of, 159; genre likened to, 15; parades as, 71; policy changes and, 66, 68; scholarly approaches to, 13–15; theater as tool of, 16, 34, 43, 96–97, 101, 103, 104, 122–23, 124, 125, 127, 129, 131, 133, 141, 143–45, 149, 226, 314n20. *See also* Campaigns; Main melody productions

Propaganda units, 83, 122, 131, 143, 146, 147, 162, 147, 158, 162; Central Committee of the CCP, 20; Propaganda Bureau, 16; Youth League, 76

Public art, 131, 134, 139–40, 146

Public debate, 8, 17, 109, 111–17, 191, 193, 209, 212, 226, 267–69

Public sphere, 11–12

Public works, 27, 29–33, 38–40, 42–43, 95, 133

Pu Cunxin, 141, 144, 275, 278, 275, 278

Pudong (Shanghai), 74, 93–94

"Purloined Letter, The" (Poe), 219

Pu Siwen, 35

Q3 (Feng Mengbo), 285, 304–8

Qianmen Gate (Beijing), 106, 134, 323n30, 326n4

Qianru routi de chengshi (The Concrete Revolution), 301

Qingchun de jiaobu (The Footsteps of Youth), 16–17

Qingchun wuhui (No Regret about Youth), 22, 228, 249, 255, 257–62

Qingmei zhuma (Taipei Story), 207

Qingshaonian Nazha (Rebels of the Neon God), 207

Quan shi Beijingren (We're All Beijingers), 97, 117–21, 138

Quitting (Zhang Yang), 243

Qu Youning (Arthur Chu), 215; *My Whispering Plan*, 21, 193, 211, 214–20, 274

Real estate development: through demolition-and-relocation, 19, 23, 105–17, 124, 127–31, 134, 190, 210, 246, 252, 258; developers and investors, 5, 107–11, 193, 204, 208, 220–22, 237, 265, 267–68, 272, 283, 287–88, 290, 291; globalization's boost to, 23, 110, 224, 283, 286–87, 289, 300; sites' cultural value used by, 131, 135, 139, 146, 149–50, 286, 288–91, 295–97, 303; in virtual space, 204–5, 307–8

Realism: Chekhovian, 99; "documentary," 226–27, 233, 332n7; documentarylike, 247, 255; "healthy," 193; hyper-, 304; neo-, 264; "revolutionary," 101, 233; "slice-of-life," 243; Stanislavskian, 46, 229, 316n68; theatrical, 46–47, 123, 145, 229, 239, 240

Rebels of the Neon God (Tsai Ming-liang), 207

Red Beads (He Jianjun), 243

Red Lantern, The (Cheng Yin), 101, 171, 204–7

Red Lotus Society, The (Lai Shengchuan), 201, 206, 207, 217

Renao (Noise), 185–86

Rendao (Humanity), 91

Ren Ming, 127, 144

Requiem (Xu Dawei), 273

Residents: anxiety about urban development among, 4, 33, 40, 50–51, 55, 215; discontent with housing among, 8, 37, 131, 123–25, 132, 133, 141–43, 147, 189, 202, 231–32, 234–37, 258–59, 267–69, 272–73, 279–80, 337n2, 337n7; in urban contract, 3, 5, 6, 7. *See also* Housing

Shiel, Mark, 12–13

Shi Hui, 45, 48, 49

Shijie (The World), 23, 285, 298–303

Shiqi sui de danche (Beijing Bicycle), 239, 288

Shopping malls, 96, 146, 147, 157, 257, 260, 263, 281, 300

Shopwindows, 61, 86

Shouji (Cell Phone), 271

Shower (Zhang Yang), 22, 228, 239, 275, 278

Shu Yi, 35, 113–16, 258, 260, 268

Siheyuan'r. See Courtyard houses

Silent Lake, The (Lin Fudi), 194, 329n9

Simulacrum, 14, 304

Singsong, 34, 38, 47, 48, 52, 133

Sixth-generation filmmakers, 8, 18, 180, 242, 245, 255, 270, 334n63

Skywalk Is Gone, The (Tsai Ming-liang), 187–88, 207

Slums, 21, 28, 31, 48, 58, 95, 138, 193, 199, 200, 244, 330n19. *See also* Veterans' villages

Small Well Lane (Li Longyun), 97, 98–104, 110, 122, 123, 129, 138, 141, 144, 145, 238, 239, 322n11

Socialist utopia, 41, 44, 138

soho China, 287, 289–90, 307

Song Dandan, 141, 144

Sons (Zhang Yuan), 243

Space: abstracted, 90, 145; any-space-whatsoever, 25; the cinematic defined by, 13; commercialized, 296; consumerist, 105, 204; economy of, 61, 207; extraurban, 153; haunted, 212, 218, 220; interior, 1, 45, 280; lived, 1, 55, 184, 213, 264; material, 8, 172, 235, 285, 303, 307; monumental, 21, 28, 44, 152–53, 175, 178, 184, 307; national, 153, 154; "no space," 295; open, 28, 48–52, 54, 55, 130, 177; perception of, 8; postspatial, 284, 285, 303–4, 306–9; private, 249; privat-

ized, 125; productive, 100; public, 1, 16, 19, 20, 21, 50, 186, 208, 210, 231, 245, 253, 295; rational, 49; recreational, 224; regulated, 55, 181, 213; representational, 159; residential, 28, 45, 50, 54, 153, 225; social, 13, 235; spatial practices, 6, 21, 153, 193, 295; "spatial turn," 4; symbolic, 296; transnational, 300; urban, 8, 46; virtual, 23, 204, 284, 285, 295, 299, 303, 306

Spectacle: cinema as, 5; city as, 10, 44, 47–54, 51–52, 53, 55, 72, 133, 136; everyday life as, 47–49, 184; Olympic games ceremony as, 282; street spectacles, 52–53, 59–61, 62–64, 70, 100, 153; urban attractions, 60–61. *See also* Parades

Spectators, 2, 5, 12–14

Spectatorship theory, 9, 11–14, 308

Spicy Love Soup (Zhang Yang), 270

Spielberg, Steven, 282

Spoken drama (*huaju*), 44, 48, 97, 98

Spring Subway (Zhang Yibai), 270

Square, The (Duan and Zhang), 21, 155, 179–84, 210, 267, 276

Stage design, 46–47, 55, 87, 90, 96, 97, 103, 104, 123, 125, 135–36, 147

Stage Sisters (Xie Jin), 254

Stanley, Nick, 301

Stand Up, Don't Stoop (Huang Jianxin), 274, 276–77

Stanislavsky, Konstantin, 46, 229, 316n68

Starbucks, 297

State Administration of Radio, Film, and Television (SARFT), 16, 20, 265.

Steadycam shots, 244, 245, 251

Still Life (Jia Zhangke), 198, 266, 308

Strangers in Beijing (film, He Qun), 22, 228, 234–36, 301

Strangers in Beijing (novel, Hei Ma), 236

Street Angel (Yuan Muzhi), 64

Urban policy: ban on raising animals, 264; "cities of emphasis," 56; Management of Accelerated Reconstruction of Hazardous and Old Houses in Beijing Act (2000; Document 19), 127–28, 130, 132; Management of Demolition-and-Relocation in Beijing Act (1998), 127; PRC vs. Taiwan, 21–22, 24; urban contract and, 3, 6; Urban Housing Demolition Ordinance (1991/2001), 128; Urban Planning Act (1991), 112; Urban Real Estate Management Act (1994), 110. *See also* Laws; Weigai

Urban preservation: city-scale, 236; cultural value of, 43, 212, 236; debates over, 105–16, 249, 268–69, 299, 334*n*57; demolition integrated with, 97, 258; economically motivated, 281, 286, 291, 295; film as, 1, 22, 224–80, 268, 273, 284; of historic landmarks, 7, 152, 157, 254; as isolated museumization, 202, 264; Lao She's endorsement of, 46; limited to "cultural landmarks," 19, 225, 236; limited to valuable assets, 121, 126–27; to maintain community, 46, 213; Maoist iconology upheld by, 173; official discourse and policy of, 149, 192, 213, 226, 242, 246, 253–54, 258, 268, 270; "preservationists" vs. "developmentalists," 113–14, 120, 226, 268; of trees, 113, 125–26, 255–56, 272. *See also* Documentary impulse

Veterans' villages (*juancun*), 21, 189–92, 195–97, 201–20, 330*n*19; Chenggong Xincun, 221, 223; Forty-Four South Village, 20; Jianhua Xincun, 198, 199, 200, 208, 209, 222

Video art, 151, 172–75, 214, 266, 273, 285, 304–8

Video games, 173, 283, 285, 304–7

Vidler, Anthony, 303–4

Virilio, Paul, 206

Virtual reality, 23, 306–7

Visser, Robin, 8, 224, 248

Vive l'amour (Tsai Ming-liang), 21, 192, 201, 208, 210, 211, 219

Visual practices. *See* Advertising; Architecture and visual practices; Cultural heritage; Film; Photography; Spectacle; Stage design

Waimian (Outside), 183

Wang, Jing, 288

Wang Bo, 302

Wangfujing (Beijing), 51, 106, 146, 273, 297

Wang Guangtao, 130, 149

Wang Haowei, 238–40

Wang Jun, 268, 317*n*99

Wang Ping, 90, 91–92; *The East Is Red*, 161–62; *The Undying Transmission*, 83

Wanglu shidai de aiqing (Love in the Internet Age), 22, 270, 275, 277

Wanjia denghuo (A Myriad Lights), 95–98, 141–48

Wang Shuo, 179, 243, 249, 258, 287, 293

Wang Wo, 183, 185–86

Wang Xiaoshuai, 270; *Beijing Bicycle*, 239, 288; *The Days*, 272; *Frozen*, 242, 243

Wang Zengqi, 116

Wang Zhi'an, 144

Wanxiang gengxin (Cosmic Renewal), 161

Wanzhu (The Troubleshooters), 243, 293–94, 298

Wanzi qianhong zongshi chun (Women of the Great Leap Forward), 57, 69

Warhol, Andy, 297

Wayward Cloud, The (Tsai Ming-liang), 188

Weekend Lover (Lou Ye), 22, 242, 244, 248

YOMI BRAESTER is a professor of comparative literature and cinema studies at
the University of Washington. He is the author of *Witness against History: Literature, Film, and Public Discourse in Twentieth-Century China* (2003).

Library of Congress Cataloging-in-Publication Data

Braester, Yomi.
Painting the city red : Chinese cinema and the urban contract / Yomi Braester.
p. cm. — (Asia-Pacific: culture, politics, and society)
Includes bibliographical references and index.
ISBN 978-0-8223-4706-4 (cloth : alk. paper)
ISBN 978-0-8223-4723-1 (pbk. : alk. paper)
1. Motion pictures—China.
2. Cities and towns in motion pictures.
3. City and town life in motion pictures.
4. Theater—China.
I. Title.
II. Series: Asia-Pacific.
PN1993.5.C4B73 2010
791.430951—dc22
2009047583